FIELDBOOK

FIELDBOOK

THIRD EDITION

Boy Scouts of America
Irving, Texas

Boy Scouts of America
Irving, Texas 75038-3096
Copyright 1967, 1984 by the Boy Scouts of America. All rights reserved.
First edition published in 1944. Third edition 1984.
Printed in the United States of America

Library of Congress Catalog Number: 84-072053
ISBN 0-8395-3200-8
No. 33200
1994 Printing

*Dedicated to American youth and adults
who seek challenging high-adventure
opportunities in the great outdoors*

IN APPRECIATION

The *Fieldbook* is based on the outdoor experiences of the Boy Scouts of America in the United States.

Norman R. Augustine, *President*
Jere B. Ratcliffe, *Chief Scout Executive*

Harry E. Bovay, Jr., Joseph S. Coco, Frank H. Collins, M. Gene Cruse, Julian L. Dyke, Roy W. Hawkinson, Ralph W. Jordan, Donald P. Olson, and Lawrence R. Thibault

Special thanks to the following individuals for their research and assistance:
Jeff Birkby, Robert C. Birkby, Dugald Bremner, Linda W. Callaghan, Rosalie Cutrer, Scott Fischer, William Forgey, Marne Freize, Wallace H. Jeffrey, H. H. Kincey, Jr., James C. Langridge, Norman Lawson, Neeljean McConeghey, John C. Page, Dave Parsons, Adolph Peschke, Rod Replogle, Paul Rice, Douglas Robinson, and Walter J. Wenzel

NATIONAL STAFF SUPPORT

Project director: David R. Bates
Managing editor: John J. Breitling
Rewrite editor: Robert Birkby
Comprehensive design and layout editor: John C. Page
Art director: Mary H. Hager
Copy chief: Jimmye Anderson
Copy editor: Debbie Sizemore
Proofreaders: Raymond Sleater and L. M. Ray
Resource information: Ann McVicar
Production: Al Wheelhouse, Jr., Brenda Benavides, and Dominick Spilatro
Printing coordinators: William C. Bacic and James R. "Bob" Anderson

Cover illustration by Jeff Segler

Table of Contents

III. APPRECIATING OUR ENVIRONMENT

- **Treks in remote wilderness areas**
- **High-adventure treks (involving strenuous activity and or specialized knowledge and skills)**
- **Treks in frequently used areas**
- **Primitive camping**
- **Summer camp**

Outdoor program has many levels representing increasingly more challenging activities and culminating with treks into remote rugged terrain. Each outdoor experience should be matched to the capability of the group.

Foreword

Have you ever longed to climb a mountain, shoot the rapids, explore subterranean passageways, or photograph a herd of elk? Have you ever dreamed of backpacking the Appalachian Trail, packing horses over the Continental Divide, cross-country skiing through the Sierras, or bicycling along the Gulf Coast? Ever wished you possessed the skill and wisdom of a tracker, an explorer, a voyageur, or a mountaineer? Then the *Fieldbook* is for you.

This book highlights the finest outdoor adventures. It is written for all youth and adults who seek to enjoy the outdoors. Drawing upon the combined experience of millions of Scouts, the Boy Scouts of America's national high-adventure programs and dozens of leading authorities, the *Fieldbook* has essential information for every outdoor enthusiast.

Captured in these pages is the romance of the outdoors. Color photographs and quotes from famous Americans introduce each chapter. These people knew how to live in the outdoors and relished opportunities for new adventures. Theirs is a heritage we share.

Today, Scouts cherish the backcountry and delight in opportunities to enjoy it safely without leaving a trace. They've developed great respect for other people, for the land and its resources.

As you read the *Fieldbook*, let it spark your imagination. Then sharpen your skills, plan outings, and follow your dreams. Explore parks and woodlands near your home. Hike those historic trails you've always heard about. Expand your camping seasons to include winter. Master the arts of snowshoeing, using map and compass, making equipment, cooking, swimming, and astronomy. You'll soon discover what outdoor leaders have always enjoyed—the challenge, the ecstacy, and the fun of outdoor adventures are fresh and alive.

I.
PREPARING FOR OUTINGS

"I have climbed its mountains, roamed its forests, sailed its waters, crossed its deserts, felt the sting of its frosts, the oppression of its heats, the drench of its rains, the fury of its winds, and always have beauty and joy waited upon my goings and comings."

John Burroughs, 1837-1921

"We should all realize that every right implies a responsibility, every opportunity an obligation, every position a duty, and that the most effective sermon is expressed in deeds instead of words."
(See biographical sketches, pages 607-620)

Waite Phillips, 1883-1964

Chapter 1

Reducing Our Impact

Paul Petzoldt
Renowned Outdoorsman; Executive
Director, Wilderness Education
Association; Author of *The New
Wilderness Handbook*

J. W. Shiner, Ph.D.
Chairman, Department of Parks and
Recreation, Slippery Rock University

There was a time not long ago when the whole of North America was a wilderness. Virgin forests extended from the coastlines far into matchless mountain ranges. The prairies of the heartland were rich with wildlife, flowers, and grasses. Rivers and lakes teemed with fish, and the air above was as clear as the rushing waters.

Native Americans were the first to experience and appreciate this great wilderness. Abundant resources provided them with food, clothing, and shelter. Out of necessity and practicality they chose ways of living that caused little harm to their surroundings. Out of awe and fear they based many of their religious beliefs on natural occurrences as spectacular as volcanic eruptions and solar eclipses, and as subtle as the gradual changing of the seasons. Out of this awareness, the earliest Americans developed a close bond between the natural environment and their own needs.

Much has changed since those simple days. As immigrants flocked to the new land, a prevailing philosophy of young America was to tame the wilderness and expand a new society across the continent. The remarkable westward migration of trappers, pioneers, settlers, cowboys, shopkeepers, hunters, ranchers, and men and women of a thousand other trades transformed great tracts of wilderness into farms, ranches, and towns. Trappers explored new regions and blazed trails. Farmers broke open the prairies and covered them with fields of corn and wheat. Lumberjacks felled great forests for the building of ships and cities. Miners burrowed into the mountains to bring forth ore and coal to feed factories that could provide thousands of jobs. With hard work, ingenuity, and the wealth of the land, Americans created transportation systems and communications networks that today allow us opportunities of travel and information unimaginable even a few decades ago. Our country's ability to produce an abundance of food, to strike down disease, and to provide homes, educations, and jobs for millions of people has helped lay the foundations of the most remarkable nation the world has ever known.

In the course of all this development, our relationship with the land has changed. Rather than dipping buckets into streams, we usually draw our drinking water from faucets.  Rather than planting seeds and harvesting crops, we find our food packaged on the shelves of grocery stores. Minerals and metals appear in the shapes of finished consumer goods that look nothing like the hillsides from which they were dug. Enclosed in comfortable homes, surrounded by the concrete and asphalt of cities, and entertained by television and radio, it is easy for us to lose sight of the importance of open land.

Although we have become removed from the natural world, an awareness of our reliance on the land is more vital now than at any time in the past. There are more of us on the globe, each requiring food, shelter, and the space in which to thrive. There are more demands from industries, each needing sufficient raw materials to create its products. And there are more people eager to relish the beauty of wild country and to discover their collective pasts in historic and prehistoric sites.

With the freedom to use the land comes the responsibility to use it wisely. For our country to flourish, we must draw on the natural resources that are America's strength, and we also must balance the use of those resources against the impact on the land. Financial gain alone is not sufficient reason to change the integrity of the backcountry. As with past Native American cultures, we must have the good judgment and courage to take from the land only what we need, waste nothing, and protect what is left.

◀ **Grave Lake**

YOUR ROLE

Rugged, wild, and magnificent, the undeveloped territory of the continent symbolizes much that is good about the American spirit. Caring for such an important resource begins with the way in which you conduct your everyday life, even if you live miles from the nearest undeveloped land. You can conserve. You can recycle. You can learn where things come from and discover which practices are good for the environment and which are not. In short, you can develop a positive land use ethic that protects and enhances our natural resources.

The chapters in this *Fieldbook* describe a broad variety of backcountry adventures. Yet for all its variety, the basic message of the *Fieldbook* is simple—enjoy the backcountry, thrive on its wildness and the challenge it offers, but conduct yourself in a way that assures your own safety and *leaves no sign of your passing.*

CHERISHING THE BACKCOUNTRY

Some call it *low-impact use* or *the minimum-impact method.* Others refer to it as *wilderness manners* or *no-trace camping.* Whatever you call it, the practice of outdoor ethics is essential in the backcountry. It's a state of mind rather than a list of approved methods. It relies on clear judgment rather than inflexible rules. And not only does common sense protect the backcountry, it also can enhance your outdoor adventures.

Consider the experience of modern rock climbers. For many years climbers protected themselves against falls by hammering iron pins called *pitons* into cracks in the cliffs they ascended. By attaching their climbing ropes to the pitons, they could anchor themselves to the rock. Unfortunately, the pitons chipped and shattered the rock, especially on popular routes where climbers pounded them into the same cracks time and time again.

Then an interesting thing happened. A few climbers began using *chocks* rather than pitons. Chocks are small, oddly-shaped pieces of metal that can be wedged into cracks in the rock without causing damage. A rope clipped into the wire loop on each chock secures climbers as well as pitons do. In order to use chocks well, however, climbers discovered they had to become very sensitive to the shape and feel of the rock. That sensitivity ensured their safety as it made them feel more closely involved with the rock they'd come to enjoy. In switching from pitons to chocks climbers not only protected the rock, they also lifted their art to a new aesthetic height. Today, almost all climbers rely on chocks, and since chocks leave the rock unscarred, climbers refer to their use as *climbing clean.*

Another example of a growing awareness of our impact on the land is the changing attitude of mountaineers scaling the great mountains of the world. Years ago, expeditions assaulted the summits with armies of climbers and porters, and thousands of pounds of equipment and supplies. Today, mountaineers are much more likely to travel lightly in small teams. They carry their own gear, and at the end of their trips they haul out all their trash.

Of course, you don't have to be a rock climber or a Himalayan mountaineer to develop a deep respect for the land. Wherever you travel in the backcountry, you'll find opportunities to simplify your life and to weave yourself deeply into the cadence and flow of the wilderness. Climbers "climb clean." You can just as easily "hike clean," and discover in the simplicity of no-trace adventures a new awareness of the lands you have come to enjoy.

SCOUTING'S CHANGING ATTITUDES

There have been many developments in the ways Scouts hike and camp, but perhaps the greatest change is a growing awareness of our impact on the land. The Scout handbooks and fieldbooks of the past have always emphasized the careful use of the backcountry and urged readers to utilize the best hiking and camping techniques known at the time. The 1911 *Handbook for Boys* suggested that no camp was complete without a big, roaring fire at its center. The 1944 edition of the *Fieldbook* explained how to build lean-tos in the wilderness, and advised Scouts to line their beds with fresh green boughs. The *Fieldbook* of 1967 made no mention of backpacking stoves. And yet each volume was right for the year in which it was written.

Today we know that open fires are not always desirable, and that pioneering projects are better left for council camps rather than undeveloped territories. Scouts would no more consider cutting live trees to cushion their beds than they would think of digging ditches around their tents.

Of course, innovations in backpacking equipment have helped change many of our camping habits. Efficient backpacking stoves allow wilderness travelers to cook without campfires in areas where open flames might damage the environment. Secure tents with waterproof floors make lean-tos unnecessary and allow hikers to camp where they will not harm vegetation. Lightweight cooking gear and crew equipment allow backpackers to travel in small groups more compatible with a wilderness experience than a large crowd.

"Afoot and light-hearted I take to the open road,
Healthy, free, the world before me,
The long brown path before leading wherever
    I choose."

Walt Whitman, 1819-1892
"Song of the Open Road"

However, the largest change has occurred in the hearts of Scouts. As they discover the pleasures of backcountry adventures, they're also realizing the demands placed on the wilderness. They are cherishing the backcountry, and by caring for it, they are helping assure its future.

▲ Resting by a waterfall

◄ Checking out the trail ahead

Enjoying the scenery ▶

Taking time to see the flowers ▼

Chapter 2

Hiking

David L. Caffey, Ed.D.
Chief Ranger, Philmont Scout Ranch,
1974–77; Author, *Head for the High
Country;* Director, Harwood
Foundation, Taos, New Mexico

Have you ever climbed a rugged mountain trail and discovered in the slow unfolding of peaks and valleys the awesome beauty of the backcountry? Have you ever left home at dawn to walk through rolling farmland during planting season when the air is rich with the fragrance of freshly turned soil? Ever packed a lunch, laced up your boots, and spent a day exploring on foot the parks and historical monuments scattered about a great city?

In the mountains, the plains, and the cities, Scouts just like you are traveling on foot, getting to know their world a little better by examining it one step at a time. Along the way, they're finding that the leisurely pace of walking gives them opportunities to think, to enjoy the company of companions, and to feel good about themselves and their surroundings. They are hiking, and there is no better adventure in all of Scouting.

Hiking provides plenty of opportunities for you to practice the skills of a backcountry traveler. You can learn about gearing up, wilderness navigation, backcountry weather, safety precautions, and wildlife observation, and before long you'll have the knowledge and confidence to meet the challenge of outdoor adventures.

So how do you begin? What must you know in order to become a good hiker? Ask yourself the following questions before you set out on a trail. Your answers should provide all the information you'll need.

WHERE DO I WANT TO HIKE?

The most obvious areas for hiking are parks and forests, but you needn't limit yourself. Beaches, pastures, and woodlands close to home invite hours of easy rambling, and the sidewalks of cities are like concrete trails through skyscraper canyons. See if you can include scenic overlooks and natural or historical landmarks in your hike plan, and try to plot a loop route so that you won't need to retrace your steps. If your trip will take you onto private lands, contact the owners ahead of time and obtain permission to cross. When you need transportation to and from the beginning and ending points of your walk, have a responsible adult drive you or use public transportation, but don't hitchhike. Thumbing a ride can be dangerous, and it spoils the spirit of hiking.

(For more information, see "Where to Go" and "Planning.")

HOW FAR CAN I GO?

Hiking is one of the best all-around exercises. It will strengthen your heart and lungs, and toughen your thighs and calves. Experienced walkers in peak condition can cover extraordinary distances, though they may become so interested in what they see that they're satisfied to amble just a couple of easy miles.

The distance you can cover depends on the terrain, your physical condition, and your reasons for hiking. Is the country rugged? Are you lean and strong, or a little out of shape? Do you walk with a fast, steady stride, or at a leisurely pace with frequent pauses to study flowers, watch wildlife, and take photographs? As a general rule, an average hiker can walk about 1½ to 2 miles an hour on level trails. Steep ascents require considerably greater time allowances; add 1 hour for every 1000 feet of elevation gain.

On your first hike, walk about 5 miles in all and see how you feel. If you come home weary and sore try a shorter distance next time, but if you're fit and rested you'll know you can add a few miles to your outings. However, the total distance is not nearly as important as what you experience along the way. A hike should be a pleasure, not a race against time.

(For ways to get in shape for hiking, see "Becoming Fit.")

WHO WILL COME ALONG?

One of the best parts of hiking is sharing the adventure with others. Through the eyes, ears, and observations of a few good friends and Scout leaders, you'll be made aware of much you might otherwise have missed. Include at least four people in your crew. That way you'll be able to help each other if you run into difficulties.

Traveling in a group puts certain responsibilities upon all the members. Each must do everything possible to help the others have a safe, enjoyable walk. No one should be left behind or made to feel unwanted. When you are in the lead, set a smooth, even pace that everyone can maintain, and stop occasionally so hikers can adjust their clothing and gear, have a bite to eat, and take in the scenery.

You can also be an effective leader by setting a good example. Enjoy the beauty of wild, open country and the tremendous variety of crowded city streets, but do nothing to disturb the areas through which you pass. Be courteous to those you meet along the way, respect their desire for privacy, and be ready to help them if they are in trouble. Finally, keep your spirits high even when the rains fall, your legs ache, and you have miles left to go. Cheerfulness is infectious, and if you help your buddies overcome the adversities of the trail you can transform miserable conditions into an adventure you'll remember for a long time to come.

(For guidelines on choosing companions and limiting group size, see "Planning" and "Reducing Our Impact.")

**Making way for ▶
downhill traffic.**

WHAT SHOULD I WEAR?

Footwear

The most important part of your hiking outfit is what you put on your feet. Sturdy running shoes are fine for hiking without a heavy pack on smooth ground, but you'll want the protection and support of good boots to negotiate rugged trails and for cross-country travel. Be sure the boots you choose fit well, and break them in on short walks before wearing them on longer hikes.

Guard your feet against blisters, and watch for early signs of athlete's foot, ingrown toenails, corns, and bunions. Footwear that is too tightly laced is a frequent cause of blisters. By keeping your feet clean and dry, trimming your toenails straight across, and wearing properly fitted shoes, you can keep your feet healthy and yourself on the trail.

(For pointers on selecting boots and socks, see "Gearing Up." For information on preventing and treating blisters, see "Outdoor First Aid.")

Clothing

You may set out from home on a cool, misty morning, find yourself pounded by a broiling sun at noon, and be in a drenching rainstorm later in the day. In addition to weather, you'll also be at the mercy of insects, brambles, and brush. Prepare for any contingencies by dressing in clothing that is comfortable, functional, and versatile.

Functional clothing satisfies specific hiking needs. For instance, shirts and pants with roomy pockets give you quick access to your compass, pocketknife, and matches. Clothes made of tough fabrics protect you from thorns and heavy foliage. A long-sleeve shirt with snug cuffs wards off mosquitoes and black flies. If you hike at night, clothing light in color makes you more visible to others in your group.

Be ready for the worst extremes of weather you expect to encounter by layering on lightweight shirts, sweaters, and jackets rather than donning one heavy, "all or nothing" coat. With layers, you can put on or peel off just enough clothing to keep yourself warm and dry at any given moment.

(For details on using the layering system, see "Gearing Up.")

WHAT SHOULD I TAKE?

On most hikes you'll want a small pack in which to carry your food and gear. If you don't already have one, see "Making Equipment" for an easy way to transform a pair of pants into a day pack.

The equipment and provisions you put into your pockets and pack will vary depending on backcountry conditions. However, the following items are so useful you'll probably want to consider them essentials for every backcountry adventure:

_____Full canteen or plastic water bottle

_____Rain gear

_____Map

_____Extra clothing (depending on conditions)

_____Compass

_____Watch

_____Pocketknife

_____Coins for emergency phone calls

_____First aid kit

_____Food

_____Flashlight

_____Cup and spoon

_____Matches in a waterproof case

_____Sunglasses (essential for travel in snow and at high altitudes)

_____Optional gear—insect repellent, sunscreen, toilet paper, camera and film, binoculars, nature books, etc.

(For a discussion of each item, see "Gearing Up.")

Food

On the day of a hike, your most important meal will be the one you eat before you hit the trail—breakfast. Lay a solid nutritional base for the day with a real "stick to the ribs" feast such as hot cereal, cocoa, and fruit, or pancakes, eggs, and sausage. A substantial breakfast will get you up even the steepest trails well through the morning.

Carry a good lunch, too. Sandwiches, fruit, crackers, jelly, peanut butter, sardines, cheese—take whatever you like as long as it won't spoil or be crushed in your pack. Some hikers enjoy an extended lunch break by a stream or in a cool, shaded glen, while others would rather nibble a bit of lunch every hour or two. Try each way and see how your body responds, and don't forget to take along a handful of hard candy, dried fruit (fruit "leather"), or a trail mix made of raisins, candy-coated chocolate bits, and nuts. It will give you a quick burst of energy whenever your feet begin to drag.

(For more on food selection and preparation, see "Trail Menus and Cooking.")

Drink

The amount of water you'll carry on a hike depends on the season, the terrain, and the weather. Where fresh, purified water is readily available you may need to carry nothing more than a cup, while in dry, hot territory a couple of canteens full of water may not be enough. As with food, take a little more water than you think you'll need and you'll never find yourself unable to slake your thirst late in the day.

Sip a little water each hour during a hike, especially in the winter when you may not feel thirsty even though you are sweating away body moisture. You may want to carry packets of beverage mix to stir into water in your cup for a lunchtime treat. It's best not to pour the powder directly into a canteen. Some mixes will corrode metal, while others leave a long-lasting taste in plastic water bottles.

(For information on purifying backcountry water, see "Outdoor Safety." For suggestions on finding water in cold weather, see "Winter Camping.")

WHAT ABOUT SAFETY?

Hiker safety is a matter of foresight and good judgment. When you've planned your trip well, included responsible people in your group, and left a trip plan with someone, you can embark on an adventure confident you are prepared to handle any situation.

If an emergency does arise—a hiker is injured, for instance, or becomes ill—calmly consider all courses of action, then make sound decisions. It may be necessary to go for help, but always use your brain before you use your legs. Think first, then act.

(For information on the importance of trip plans, see "Planning." For more on safe hiking, see "Outdoor Safety," "Outdoor First Aid," and "Survival Preparedness.")

Traffic

Chart a hike route that avoids busy highways. When you must walk along a road, travel in single file on the shoulder facing oncoming traffic, and be alert to the actions of drivers. Wear light-colored clothing if you

Face oncoming traffic ▶

hike at night, and devise a makeshift reflector by tying a white handkerchief around your leg or arm. Better yet, pull on a reflective orange vest like those worn by hunters and highway construction workers.

Lightning

Keep an eye on the clouds and you'll know when a thunderstorm is rolling in. When lightning crackles overhead, seek shelter indoors or in a low area away from solitary trees, rock formations, high ridges, wire fences, telephone and electric lines, large open fields, and lakes.

Hypothermia

In damp, cool, and windy weather, a hiker may become so chilled that his body can no longer warm itself. This condition is known as hypothermia, and it may result in incoherence, unconsciousness, and even death. Yet hypothermia is easy to prevent. Stay dry and warm and eat plenty of high energy foods. If a companion begins shivering or acting strangely, warm him quickly. When you aren't equipped for the weather, stay home.

(For more on predicting conditions, see "Weather." For information on hypothermia and on dealing with adverse weather, see "Outdoor Safety," "Outdoor First Aid," "Survival Preparedness," and "Winter Camping.")

Getting Lost

Should you become confused about where you are, don't panic. Look around for landmarks that will indicate your location. Check your maps. In your mind, retrace your steps. Discuss the situation with your companions. If you still can't make sense out of the surrounding terrain, follow a road to help or, in the wilderness, make a brief, controlled check of the immediate area. If that doesn't give you any clues, stay where you are, make yourself comfortable, and remain calm. Searchers will find you in time.

(For more on staying found, see "Backcountry Navigation." For a course of action to follow if you do become lost, see "Survival Preparedness." For suggestions on finding lost or injured hikers, see "Wilderness Search and Rescue.")

CROSS-COUNTRY HIKING

Most of your backcountry hikes will be along trails, and where vegetation could be damaged by the pressure of your footsteps you'll want to be sure to stay on existing paths. However, when the conditions are right, cross-country travel can be an extremely satisfying and enlightening form of wilderness travel. Since you'll have no trails to guide you, you'll need to be especially aware of where you are and where you're headed. You'll want to watch where you put your feet, and carefully consider the route over rough terrain.

An effective way to travel quickly and safely across trailless territory is by dividing the responsibilities of such a trek among the members of your group. There are four basic duties—those of the *scout*, the *smoother-upper*, the *leader*, and the *sweep*.

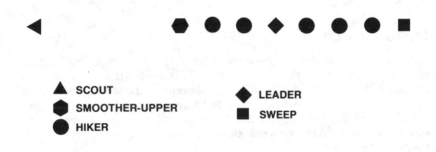

Scout

With map and compass in hand, the scout strikes out a little ahead of the rest of the group in search of a route everyone can follow. Careful to maintain a course that leads toward the crew's destination, the scout stays within earshot of the group leader.

Smoother-Upper

The smoother-upper takes a position in front of the group and "smooths up" the route established by the scout to assure the other hikers the easiest walking possible. For instance, the scout might climb up and over a steep knob or plunge through a dense thicket. The smoother-upper may decide instead to lead the group around the obstacle and rejoin the scout on the other side. The smoother-upper also sets the pace for the entire crew.

Leader

The leader comes along midway in line in order to monitor the progress of all the hikers. Leaving the determination of route and pace up to the scout and smoother-upper, the leader decides when to take a rest stop, where to eat lunch, when to seek shelter from inclement weather, and whether to stop or turn back. When a decision is made a message is passed up the line to the smoother-upper and the scout.

Sweep

Bringing up the rear is the sweep, who carries the first aid kit and is responsible for seeing that all the other hikers are accounted for and are staying on course. If someone in the group needs to stop, the sweep calls a halt by passing the message up the line.

If there are more than four hikers in the crew, those without a specific duty hike near the group leader who, at regular intervals, will rotate the responsibilities of scout, smoother-upper, and sweep so that everyone will have a chance to master the skills required of each task.

To reduce their impact on the land, cross-country travelers should take care not to walk directly in one another's footsteps. Those at the rear of the group should seek alternate routes through fallen timber and rocks to avoid beating a path.

(For more on backcountry vegetation, see "Plants." For more on cross-country hiking, see "Mountain Hiking and Climbing.")

RULES OF THE TRAIL

As with any public thoroughfare, a trail has certain rules its users must obey. There aren't many of them, but they are important matters of common sense.

- If there is a registration box at the trailhead, sign in. Officials of the agency in charge of the area will know where you've gone, and they can use your registration information to better determine the needs of future hikers.

- Use switchbacks properly. Switchbacks zigzagging a trail up a mountainside help prevent erosion by easing the steepness of the grade. When hikers cut across switchbacks rather than staying on the pathway, their boots can loosen the earth, disturb vegetation, and make it easier for rain and melting snow to wash away the soil.

  (For more on switchbacks, see "Trail Building and Maintenance.")

- Be kind to the countryside. Meadows and alpine tundra are fragile. Protect them by staying in the center of main trails, and by taking rest breaks and camping in the trees rather than on the clearings themselves.

- Treat other hikers courteously. Many people enjoy hiking, and in your travels you will meet some of them. Most are friendly and in an emergency you can count on them for help, but be polite. Step aside to let them pass. Respect their privacy and, if you camp, find a site hidden away from other tents. As a hiker you represent Scouts everywhere. Leave a good impression.

- Give livestock the right-of-way. Horses and pack animals are sometimes nervous around strangers. When you meet riders on the trail, step at least 10 feet off the path on the downhill side and stand quietly while they pass. If the trail is too narrow for that, ask the lead rider for instructions.

- Leave gates the way you found them—open or closed. Ranchers and farmers grazing animals on the lands through which you hike will appreciate your thoughtfulness.

- Pick up litter. Unfortunately, there will always be a few careless users of the backcountry who drop candy wrappers on the trail and leave food packets around campsites. Do the land a favor and set a good example by packing out any trash you find and by asking hikers you meet if they have litter you can carry to the trailhead for them.

"Jim Bridger's habit of keen observation and the knowledge it brought subsequently served him well when guiding expeditions through the pathless western wilds. He noticed every feature of the country, especially its configuration, and possessing as he did a retentive memory, he could invariably recall all landmarks with unerring accuracy, even though he had not seen them for years."

Capt. J. Lee Humfreville, 1864

Chapter 3

Backcountry Navigation

Finn Blom Christensen
International Orienteering
Instructor, Veteran Mountain
Climber and Cross-Country Skier

Nature has provided many of its creatures with keen senses of direction. Homing pigeons can travel long distances over unfamiliar territory to reach their roosts. Certain species of birds migrate thousands of miles between warm southern climes and northern breeding grounds. Some butterflies also are migratory, and animals as diverse as honeybees, bats, whales, and reindeer seem to move with an unerring certainty of where they are.

Humans, however, do not have that gift. Left in an empty field on an overcast, windless day, or adrift at sea with no points of reference, we can only guess which direction might lead us to our destination. Instead of the instincts of migratory animals, we must rely on the reasoning ability of our minds and supplement that ability with navigational instruments.

Before the development of compasses, explorers had to look to the North Star, the prevailing winds, and the movements of ocean currents for guidance. Overland travelers could follow sketchy maps and the reports of other wanderers, but early mariners were careful to keep their ships near the coastlines, fearing that to sail out of sight of land would leave them unable to find their way home.

Then came the compass. At first it was nothing more than a magnetized iron needle stuck through a straw floating in a bowl of water. By Columbus's time, it had evolved into an instrument sufficiently reliable to guide the explorer's three ships across the Atlantic.

Guided by the silent swing of a compass needle and the simple lines of a map, you, too, can find your way deep into territory you've never seen before, and then get home again. In addition, you'll be able to plot the easiest, safest, most scenic routes to your destinations, and you'll share one of humankind's oldest dreams—the ability to know at all times exactly where you are.

MAPS

One of the first impulses of early explorers probing the vast North American continent was to make maps. Maps could be taken back to the cities and shared with others. They could be used to point out the best areas for farming and hunting, good sites for villages, and potential routes of travel. They filled people with hopes and plans, and gave them the information they needed to find their ways west in search of adventure, good land, and new lives.

As the territories of the United States became more settled, the government put a high priority on having lands accurately mapped. This desire stemmed in part from a need to establish clear legal boundaries, and to give settlers the guidelines they needed to mark the limits of their property, but the motivation came also from a basic human curiosity to know what's out there.

Today, map makers (known as *cartographers*) have produced detailed maps of nearly all of North America, and those once-numerous blank expanses simply marked "UNEXPLORED TERRITORY" are fewer and fewer in number. Nonetheless, you can still experience the mystery and grandeur of discovering territory that you've personally never seen close up, and good maps will enhance the joy and safety of your treks into even the most familiar lands.

TOPOGRAPHICAL MAPS

Topo means "place," *graphia* "to write." Topographical maps are written records of places. Showing natural and man-made features as well as giving a three-dimensional picture of the shape of the terrain, they provide a wealth of information for wilderness travelers.

How to Order Maps

Topographical maps are prepared primarily by the U.S. Geological Survey, a part of the Department of the Interior. You may be able to purchase the maps you want at local camping and travel stores. If not, write to USGS Map Sales, Box 25286, Denver, CO 80225 and ask for an index of maps for your area, a price list, and an order form.

An index is a map of a state divided into sections called "quadrangles." Each quadrangle map has a name by which it can be ordered from USGS Map Sales. If you need further assistance in finding the maps you need, call the U.S. Geological Survey at 1-800-USA-MAPS.

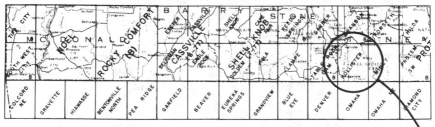

Southwest corner of Missouri index map.

Map Margins

Obviously it's impractical to put a full-size image of the backcountry on paper, since such a map would itself be as large as the area it represented. Instead, cartographers have devised symbols for important features, and scales to help users orient their maps and determine distances. Much of the information you'll need to use a map is printed in its margin.

Look in the margin of almost any map and you'll find the date it was prepared and when it was last revised. Like a photograph, a map records things as they are at a particular instant in time. The newer a map, the more accurately it will portray the current appearance of an area. The margin also may have a location identifier, often in the form of a small outline of a state. A tiny blackened square within that outline will show the general location of the territory represented by the map.

Next, look for the indication of *scale.* If you've ever built a model airplane from a kit, you may have noticed that it was advertised as being a certain size—say, $\frac{1}{25}$ as large as a real airplane. Known as the *scale* of the model, the size ratio could have been written 1:25, meaning that one inch on the model equaled 25 inches on the original.

MISSOURI

QUADRANGLE LOCATION

COMPARING MAPS OF DIFFERENT SCALE			
Scale	Minutes	Approximate Inches/Mile	Advantages/ Disadvantages
1/24,000	7½	2½"	Detailed, but may require many maps.
1/62,500	15	1"	Compromise—shows less detail
1/250,000	60	¼"	Useful for planning treks, covers large area

A map is essentially a flat scale model of an expanse of land, but the scale will be much different from that of a toy airplane. A common scale for topographical maps is 1:24,000, which means that an inch on the map equals 24,000 inches, or 2,000 feet, on the ground. Near the scale notation, you'll find several bars called *distance rulers* that will help you visualize what that scale means. Usually one bar is divided into scale miles, another into scale feet, and a third into scale kilometers.

Finally, locate in the margin the *contour interval* of the contour lines on the map. Contour intervals may be anywhere from 10 to 200 feet or meters. To understand how they work, look at the map itself.

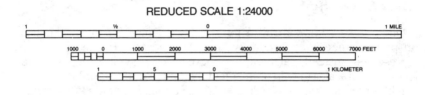

REDUCED SCALE 1:24000

CONTOUR INTERVAL 20 FEET
DATUM IS MEAN SEA LEVEL

Contour Lines

Imagine the backcountry as a giant, multilayered birthday cake. All the layers are the same thickness say, 40 feet and a little brown frosting has oozed out where the layers are fitted together. Now imagine flying over that backcountry cake and looking straight down on it. Where the terrain is steepest, the frosting lines will appear to be close together; where the slopes are more gentle, the lines will seem farther apart.

The lines of frosting marking the edges of the layers are exactly the same as the brown contour lines drawn on a map to indicate variations in elevation. In addition, some contour lines are darker than others, and are marked somewhere along their lengths with their exact elevation in feet or meters above sea level. For instance, on a map with 40-foot contour intervals, every point along a dark line marked *200* will be 200 feet above sea level. Any point on the next brown line above the 200-foot contour will be 220 feet above sea level, while any point on the line below it will be 180 feet above sea level.

CHAPTER 3

Note that every contour line eventually connects with itself. Those near the tops of hills and mountains are very small circles, while lines that wander through valleys or across rolling prairie may go on for miles and cross several maps before they complete their large, irregular loops.

As you examine the contour lines on a map, try to visualize the layers of land they represent, and create in your mind a picture of the actual terrain. With a little practice, you'll be able to turn the information on a flat map into a three-dimensional mental image of the backcountry.

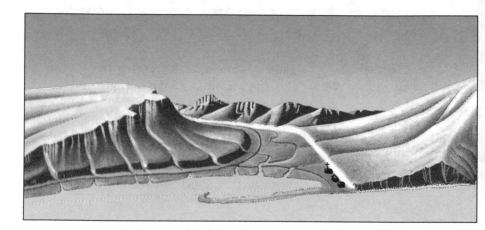

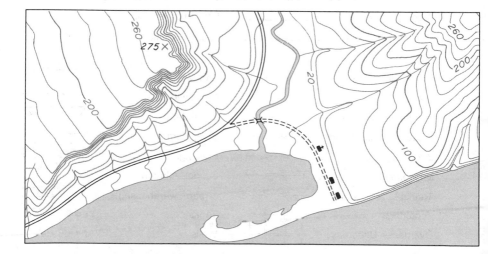

Symbols

Most topographical maps are multicolored, and each color has a special meaning. In general, black is used to show man-made features: railroads, buildings, trails, boundaries, location names. Blue indicates water: streams, marshes, lakes. Green areas are covered with forests or shrubs, while white stands for the open country of meadows, talus slopes, beaches, and alpine tundra. Red is reserved for improved roads and for grid lines and numbers that, when used with a compass, can improve the accuracy of your navigating.

MEANING OF MAP COLORS

Green	Major vegetation (forest, brush, orchard)
Blue	Water (lake, stream, spring, marsh, water tank)
Red	Highways or boundaries
Black	Man-made structures and place names (buildings, roads, trails, bridges, railroads)
White	Absence of major vegetation, (prairie, meadow, tundra—above timberline)
Brown	Contour lines and standard elevations

TOPOGRAPHIC MAP SYMBOLS

Primary highway

Secondary highway

Light-duty road

Unimproved road

Trail

Railroad: single track

Railroad: multiple track

Bridge

Drawbridge

Tunnel

Footbridge

Overpass—Underpass

Power transmission line

Landmark line .... Telephone

Dam with lock

Canal with lock

Large dam

Small dam

Buildings

School—church

(barn, warehouse,)

Tanks .... Water Tank

Wells .... o Oil .... o Gas

U.S. mineral prospect .... ▲ x

Quarry—Gravel pit .... ⊗ .... ⋈

Mine shaft .... ◪ .... Y

Campsite—Picnic area ...... ⚑ .... ⋊

Landmark—Windmill .... ○ .... ⚒

Exposed wreck ....

Rock or coral reef ....

Foreshore flat ....

Rock: bare or awash ....

Horizontal control station .... △

Vertical control station ...... ×671 ^BM ×672

Road fork .... ⟍429 + 58

Checked spot elevation .... × 5970

Unchecked spot elevation .... × 5970

Index contour ....

Supplementary cont.

Cut—Fill ....

Mine dump ....

Dune area ....

Sand area ....

Tailings ....

Intermediate contour ...

Depression contours ...

Levee ....

Large wash ....

Tailings pond ....

Distorted surface ....

Gravel beach ....

Glacier ....

Perennial streams ....

Water well—Spring .....

Rapids ....

Channel ....

Sounding—Depth curve ...

Dry lake bed ....

Intermittent streams ....

Aqueduct tunnel ....

Falls ....

Intermittent lake ....

Small wash ....

Marsh (swamp) ....

Land subject to
controlled inundation

Woodland ....

Submerged marsh ....

Orchard ....

Vineyard ....

Mangrove ....

Scrub ....

Wooded marsh ....

Bldg. omission area ..

COMPASSES

When a topographical map is right side up, you can be pretty certain that the top of it is north and the bottom is south. However, when you're in the backcountry you may not know which direction is which. That's where a compass comes in handy.

An ordinary orienteering compass is ideal for most wilderness travel. Wonderful in its simplicity, it consists of a magnetized needle floating inside a circular, rotating housing that's mounted atop a flat, rectangular baseplate. The plate is etched with a direction of travel arrow. The floor of the compass housing is engraved with a compass housing arrow that helps simplify compass use.

The circumference of the housing is divided into directions—north, south, east, and west—and further divided into degrees—360 of them in all, just as in any circle. 0° coincides with north, 90° with east, 180° with south, 270° with west, and 360° is again north (0° and 360° overlap, completing the circle).

Any direction can be indicated in degrees. For example, 95° is a little south of straight east, while 315° is halfway between west and north.

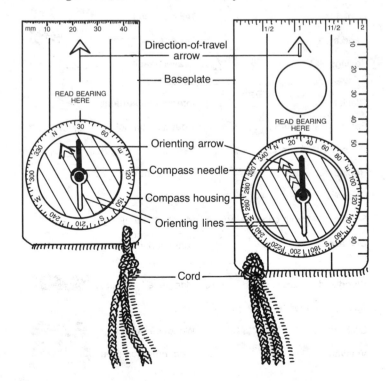

Magnetic North and Declination

Somewhere north of Canada's Hudson Bay lies the center of a natural magnetic field strong enough to pull the tip of a compass needle toward itself. More than a thousand miles away from the North Pole, this area is called *magnetic north,* and it is toward magnetic north that all compass needles point. Most maps, however, are made with the symbols oriented toward the North Pole, which is true north. In the Midwestern States, that difference doesn't cause much difficulty, since a fairly straight line can be drawn from the North Pole through magnetic north and south to Chicago and Atlanta. In other words, a compass in Madison, Wisconsin, or Montgomery, Alabama, points at magnetic north, which, by chance, is lined up with true north.

However, if you were to move that same compass west or east it would continue to point at magnetic north, but a line connecting the two norths with the compass would no longer be straight. At Philmont Scout Ranch in New Mexico, the compass needle points about 11 degrees to the right of true north, while in Seattle it points 20½ degrees to the right. Moving east from Chicago, the opposite occurs. In New York City a compass needle pointing to magnetic north swings 12½ degrees to the left of true north, and at Maine National Adventure Area it points 19½ degrees to the left.

This difference in degrees between true north and magnetic north is called *declination.* The margin of a topographical map usually contains two arrows, one pointing toward true north, the other toward magnetic north. The angle between those arrows is the map's declination, and you should find it recorded in degrees near the arrows.

1984 MAGNETIC DECLINATION MAP OF THE U.S.A.

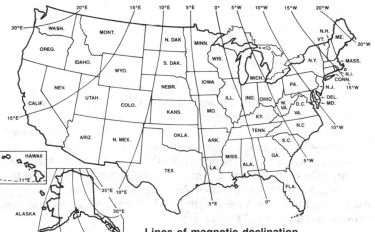

**Lines of magnetic declination
are gradually shifting westward.**

29

Preparing a Map

Before you carry a map into the field, take a few minutes to prepare it for easy use. You'll need a sharp pencil and a good yardstick with a very smooth, straight edge. Spread the map on a table and, if necessary, weight the corners to keep it flat. Place the yardstick alongside the magnetic-north arrow in the bottom margin so that the stick lines up with it perfectly. Keeping the yardstick still, draw a magnetic-north line along its edge all the way up the map. Check the line for accuracy; you want the magnetic-north arrow to extend across the entire map.

When you're satisfied the first line is properly drawn, lay the yardstick along it again and draw a parallel magnetic-north line along the opposite edge. Move the first edge of the yardstick to the new line and again draw a line along the opposite edge. Continue moving the stick and drawing lines until there are parallel magnetic-north lines spaced evenly across the map.

Magnetic-north lines allow you to *orient* a map so that its top points directly north, and the symbols on the map are aligned with the actual landmarks they represent. You also can use magnetic-north lines to identify landmarks, find your own location, and follow compass bearings without orienting the map, and that can save you lots of time and trouble.

Orienting a Map

Rotate the compass housing on your compass until the compass-housing arrow lines up with the direction of travel arrow on the baseplate. Notice the setting, or *compass bearing*, can be read as *North* or as *0°*. Next, place the long edge of the compass baseplate alongside any one of the magnetic-north lines you drew on the map, or next to the magnetic-north arrow in the bottom margin. Turn the compass and the map as a unit until the compass needle is aligned with the compass-housing arrow. When that happens, the map is oriented, which means that the features on the map are aligned with the actual features of the landscape.

Identifying Landmarks

Have you ever seen a distant ridge of mountains and wondered what each summit was called? With a good compass and a sharp eye, you can identify any landmark prominent enough to appear on your map. Here's how.

Holding the compass in the palm of your hand, point the direction-of-travel arrow on the baseplate at the landmark in question, and turn the housing until the needle is aligned with the compass-housing arrow. Place the compass on your map with the long edge of the baseplate touching the spot that represents your present location. If magnetic lines have been drawn on the map, it need not be oriented. Ignoring the needle, rotate the entire compass around your location spot until the compass-housing arrow parallels the magnetic-north lines. Finally, beginning from the symbol for your location, draw an actual or imaginary line *away from yourself* along the edge of the baseplate. The line should intersect the point on the map representing the landmark.

Pinpointing Your Location

If you're not sure where you are but you can see on the land a couple of features indicated on the map, it's easy to pinpoint your location. First, point the baseplate direction-of-travel arrow on your compass at one of the landmarks—a mountaintop, the outlet of a lake, a building, etc. Holding the baseplate still, turn the compass housing until the needle aligns with the compass-housing arrow. You've just taken a bearing on the landmark.

Next, place the compass on the map with the edge of the baseplate touching the symbol representing the landmark. The map need not be oriented. Ignoring the needle, rotate the entire compass around that

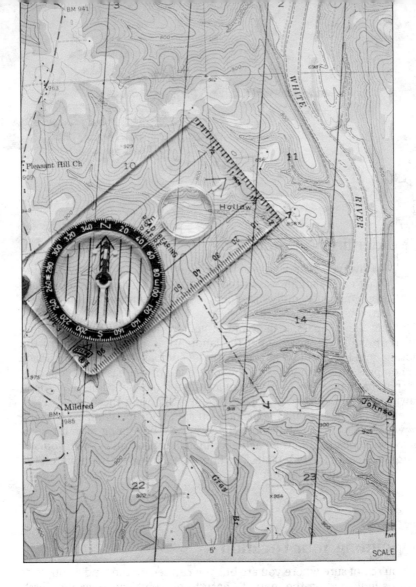

symbol until the compass-housing arrow parallels the magnetic-north lines. Lightly pencil a line along the baseplate edge from the landmark symbol *toward* yourself.

Find a second landmark, and repeat the process of taking a bearing, placing the compass on the map, and drawing a line toward yourself. The point at which the two lines intersect indicates where you are. To confirm your location, repeat the procedure with one or two more landmarks.

Following a Compass Bearing

Assume that you know where you are in the backcountry, and that on the map you see a lake you'd like to reach by the most direct route. Place the long edge of your compass baseplate on a real or imaginary line connecting the map points representing your present location and that of the lake. If magnetic lines have been drawn on the map, it need not be oriented. Turn the compass housing until the compass-housing arrow parallels the magnetic-north lines.

Now lift the compass off the map and hold it at waist level, the direction-of-travel arrow on the baseplate pointing away from you. Without adjusting your compass setting, turn your entire body until the compass needle aligns itself with the compass-housing arrow—the tip of the needle will point to 0 degrees. The direction-of-travel arrow will be aiming at the lake.

Look up along the direction of travel, and if you can see the lake, you need make no further use of the compass. If the lake is out of sight, however, locate an intermediate landmark—a tree, boulder, or other feature—toward which the direction-of-travel arrow is pointing, and walk to it. Again, hold the compass in your palm and turn your body until the compass needle aligns with the compass-housing arrow. Look ahead for the next landmark along your direction of travel, and go to it. Continue until you've reached your destination.

Determining Distance

Think again of that wilderness lake. A compass bearing can point you in the right direction, but it can't tell you how far along that line of travel you'll have to go to reach the water. For that, you'll need to refer to the distance rulers in the map's margin.

The edges of most compass baseplates are marked off in millimeters and fractions of inches. Use an edge as a ruler to measure the distance on your map between the spot where you're standing and the spot marking your destination. Now measure that same distance on the distance rulers. Say you discover that the distance to the lake is 1000 meters; a hiker of average height can cover 100 meters of open forest in about 125 steps, so 1000 meters would take approximately 1250 steps. If you follow your compass bearings for 1300 steps and haven't come upon the lake, you may have taken an inaccurate bearing.

To improve your distance judging skills, mark out a 100-meter course on flat, open ground and walk it, counting your steps. Simplify the process by counting only when your right foot strikes the ground, and figure on half as many numbered paces to reach your destination. In the field, heavy underbrush, changes in elevation, and other backcountry obstacles may cause your stride to vary.

Offset Technique

Experienced backcountry travelers know that even a slight error in taking and following compass bearings can throw them quite a distance off their intended courses. One way to be sure you'll reach your destination is to aim intentionally for a point to the left or the right of it, and then follow natural features known as *backstops* to it.

For instance, assume the lake you want to reach is very small, but on the map you notice that a creek flows from it to the left, perpendicular to your line of travel. Rather than take a bearing on the lake itself and risk missing it altogether by passing too far to the right, aim for a point on the creek a few hundred yards below the lake. When you reach the creek anywhere along its length, all you need to do is follow it upstream until you reach the lake. Streams, power lines, fences, drainage ditches, trails and ridges all make good backstops and guidelines.

ROUTE FINDING

A most important part of backcountry navigation is finding and then sticking to a good route. If there are trails leading to your destinations, it's usually best to follow them, both for ease of passage and to avoid damaging the land. However, there will be times when no trails lead to the places you want to go.

Route finding should begin at home as you plan a trek. Studying topographical maps and using all you know about an area, try to determine whether the destination you want to reach is within the abilities of everyone in your crew. In many regions of the country, the main routes up prominent mountains are detailed in guidebooks that also may describe local historical, botanical, and biological features. Add to that the advice you can glean from hikers who have visited the territories that interest you, and information from officials of the agencies overseeing those lands, and you should have a fairly good idea of what to expect.

The best route between two backcountry points is seldom a straight line. Take into consideration gains and losses of elevation; if you hike around the end of a ridge, you may walk more miles but save the energy you would have expended going over the top. Examine the map for indications of marshes, bogs, wide stream crossings, and long rocky slopes; detouring around obvious obstacles can save you many hours of travel.

Even if you think you'll have no trouble with a route, it's a good idea to chart an alternative course that bypasses any terrain that could prove too difficult. You may, for instance, have in mind a trek that will go over a certain high pass. While the route may seem quite manageable from the vantage point of your living room, looking up at it in bad weather or with a tired crew growing uncertain of its climbing abilities may make it obvious that you should not push on. If you've plotted a lower, less exposed route, you can abandon your original plan and still have a safe, satisfying adventure.

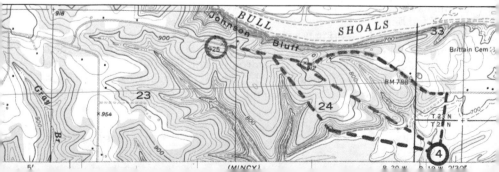

ORIENTEERING

A map and compass are tools essential for the sometimes serious business of wilderness navigation, but with them you also can enjoy the exciting sport of *orienteering*. Often sponsored by orienteering clubs, Boy Scout troops, Varsity Scout teams, and Explorer posts, orienteering meets can put your map reading and route finding skills to a real test.

Before a contest begins, meet organizers will lay out a course. Ideally it will cover an area of varying ground cover and interesting terrain, and will be matched to the abilities of the competitors. Along its length— anywhere from a hundred yards to many miles—red and white flags mark the control points that are key to the game.

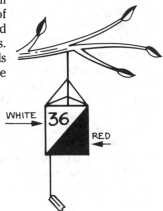

WHITE → 36
RED ←

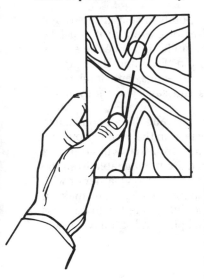

Dressed for cross-country travel and equipped with a compass, each orienteer is given a map of the area. While topographical maps can be used, special orienteering maps are more frequently employed. Larger in scale than standard topographical maps, they show the landscape in great detail, including prominent boulders, depressions, ditches, and knolls.

As competitors begin the race, they are given maps marked with the locations of the flags. Quickly scanning the map, each orienteer determines the quickest route by which to reach all the flags. That done, the real fun begins.

Although orienteering is a race against time, it is not a game of physical fitness alone. Contestants must use their minds in order to read their maps, take compass bearings, plan routes, and find the flags. They have to weigh the advantages of taking shortcuts, using backstops, and circumventing obstacles, and often it is the smartest orienteer who prevails rather than the fittest.

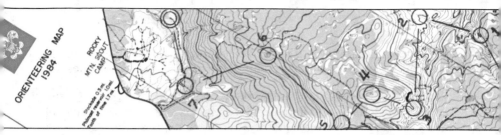

ORIENTEERING MAP 1984

As they reach each flag, orienteers use special paper punches hanging nearby to make uniquely shaped holes in control cards, which must be presented at the finish line to prove they have covered the entire course. In cross-country orienteering, the person who locates all the flags and completes the course in the shortest time is the winner, but there really are no losers. The chance to be in the backcountry traveling under one's own steam and guided by one's own wits is victory enough for almost everyone.

Map Making

An interesting way to learn some of the map maker's techniques is to make a map of your own. Of course, it's easy to do a rough sketch of an area, and anytime you draw a map in the dust with a stick you're practicing the cartographer's art. To get a real feel for the demands of map making, though, try your hand at precision mapping. All you'll need are your compass, a pencil, and plenty of paper.

First, determine what you want to map. Start with a fairly small, uncluttered area and make a list of all the features you want to have on your map. In the case of a campsite, for instance, your list might include a fire ring, an oak tree, a space for a tent, and the beginning of a trail.

Starting with any of the features, take a compass bearing on any of the others, and then walk to it, counting your paces. Write down the number of steps from the first point to the second, and also the degree reading on your compass. For example, from the fire ring to the oak tree you may have taken 52 paces at 90°.

From the second feature, take a compass bearing and walk to the third, and from the third to the fourth, and so on, always writing down the degree reading and number of paces between each pair of features.

Now you're ready to start drawing. Using a ruler or the end of your compass, begin by lightly drawing parallel lines about 3 centimeters apart straight down the page. Since the top of your map points due north, these reference lines run north and south, from 0° to 180°.

Next, decide what feature will be shown in the middle of the map—the firelay, for example—and in the center of the page draw a small symbol for it. Now decide on a scale that will allow you to put all the features on one sheet of paper. For instance, 1 centimeter on the map could correspond to 10 paces on the ground. That done, refer to your notes for the compass reading and number of paces from the first feature (the firelay) to the second feature (the oak tree). Rotate the compass housing until the bearing you recorded on the oak tree (90°) lines up with the direction-of-travel arrow. Place the compass on your map so that the compass-housing arrow on the floor of the compass housing is parallel to the north-south lines drawn on the map. The long edge of the baseplate should just touch the symbol for the firelay. Since the scale of your map is 1 centimeter for every 10 paces, and since you took 52 paces between the firelay and the oak tree, measure 5.2 centimeters along the edge of the baseplate and draw a symbol for an oak tree.

Repeat the process between the second feature (the oak tree) and the third (the tent site), then between the third and the fourth (the trail head), and so on until you've sketched all the features on the paper. When you're done, you'll have an accurate map drawn to scale.

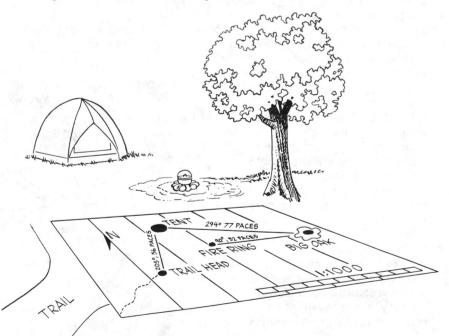

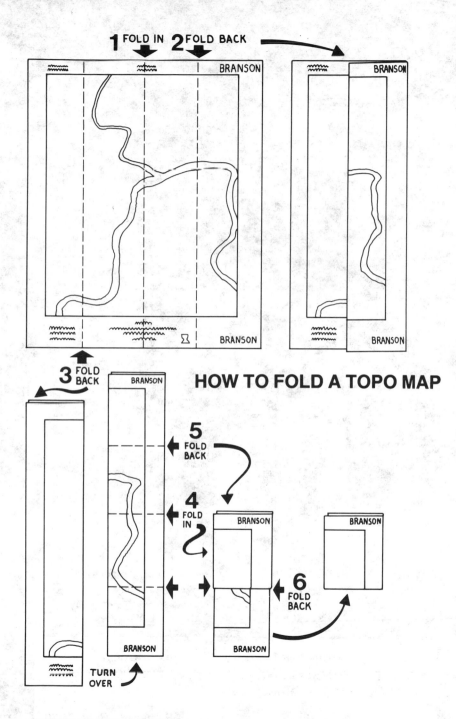

HOW TO FOLD A TOPO MAP

"Camping equipment must be strong enough to withstand the hardest kind of handling, and yet light enough not to be cumbersome."

Richard E. Byrd, 1930

Chapter
4

Gearing Up

Clyde S. "Sandy" Bridges
Director of the Northern Tier
National High Adventure Programs
and Founder of the Okpik Winter
Camping Program

A s a boy wandering the Cascade Mountains of Washington State, future Supreme Court Justice William O. Douglas rolled his provisions inside a blanket, tied his frying pan and hatchet outside the blanket, and traveled with the bundle draped over his shoulder.

Famed naturalist John Muir sometimes hiked into the mountains carrying nothing but a blanket, some bread, and a bag of tea.

The English poet William Wordsworth, who often walked 20 miles a day, occasionally tied up his belongings in a bandana and balanced the bundle atop his head.

Author Henry David Thoreau used a 10-foot square of white cloth for a tent, sipped his drinks from a tin dipper, and whittled spoons from alder branches.

When the first Scouts hit the trail in the early years of this century they pinned together the edges of blankets to make bed rolls, got along with heavy woolen clothing and rain slickers, wore work boots, and made do with Army surplus equipment.

The basic needs of a backcountry traveler are still the same—clothing, shelter, and food. Add to that the equipment needed for safety, cleanliness, comfort, and enjoyment, and you'll be prepared for any trek.

The gear you take on an adventure usually rides on your shoulders, in the bottom of a canoe or raft, or in panniers hung across the back of a pack animal or bicycle. The lighter the load, the easier it will be to carry. As you become proficient at wilderness travel, you'll be amazed at how many things you can leave at home. John Muir's blanket, tea bag, and crust of bread may be too Spartan for most of us today, but he had the right idea—keep it light and simple, but include all the essentials.

CLOTHING

In the outdoors, clothing is your first line of defense. It keeps you warm in the winter, cool in the summer, dry in storms, and shielded from insects, sun, and wind. To help decide what you need, learn about the materials from which clothing is made.

Wool

The long, red underwear of miners and settlers was made of wool, and for good reason. Wool is durable and water resistant, and even when soaked it can keep you warm.

Wool clothing is ideal in cold weather, and a wool shirt or sweater will ward off the chill of summer evenings, too. Wool makes excellent blankets, hiking socks, hats, and mittens. If wool irritates your skin, you may be able to wear wool blends or substitutes such as polypropylene.

Cotton

Cotton is cool, comfortable, and sturdy, but unlike wool it will not keep you warm when it is wet. Of course, in hot weather that may be an advantage. Underwear and liner socks often are made of cotton, as are caps, shirts, and bandanas.

Synthetics

Manufactured fabrics such as nylon, orlon, and polypropylene have plenty of outdoor uses. Many are waterproof, and some are good insulation. Strong, lightweight, and easy to clean, they are used in rain gear, windbreakers, tents, packs, parkas, and sleeping bags.

Blends

Blended fabrics combine the advantages of several materials in a single piece of cloth. For example, a blend of synthetics and cotton makes shirts and shorts that are neat in appearance, yet tough enough for any wilderness adventure. A mixture of synthetics and wool goes into long-wearing socks, shrink-resistant shirts, and warm jackets.

LAYERING SYSTEM

For the most comfort in the outdoors use the layering system. Choose loose-fitting clothing that will meet the most extreme weather you expect to encounter, and be sure you can put it on and take it off a layer at a time. For example, on a chilly autumn day you might leave home wearing a long-sleeve Scout shirt, long pants, a wool shirt, a sweater, mittens, and a stocking hat. As you hike, exercise will cause your body to generate more heat than it needs. Peel off the sweater and stuff it into your pack. If you're still too warm, unbutton the wool shirt or slip off the mittens and hat.

When you reach your campsite and are no longer exerting yourself, stay warm by reversing the procedure, pulling on just enough layers of clothing to stay comfortable. After the sun goes down, you may want to add an insulated parka and wool trousers or long underwear.

You can also use the layering system to keep cool in the summer by stripping down to hiking shorts, a T-shirt, and a brimmed cap. Despite the heat, always carry long pants and a long-sleeve shirt for protection against sunburn, bugs, and brush.

Versatility in your clothing is the key to a successful layering system. Several shirts, a sweater, and a jacket will allow you to adjust your garb in many more ways than will a single heavy coat.

Woolen gloves with water repellent overmitts are ideal for cold weather.

Wear two pairs of socks.

Start with underwear and two pairs of socks...

next a wool shirt, wool trousers and heavy boots...

then a wool turtleneck sweater.

In colder weather, add a light jacket, wool cap and shoepacks.

In very severe cold put a water repellent jacket over other clothes and add mukluks.

Rain Gear

No matter how clear the skies as you pack for a trek, prepare for nasty weather. That means always taking along a poncho or raincoat, a pack cover, and perhaps rain pants and gaiters. Choose rainwear that fits loosely enough to give you freedom of movement and to allow perspiration to evaporate without condensing on the inside of the fabric.

Long a favorite of adventurers, ponchos provide wet-weather security for both hikers and their gear. In emergencies, ponchos can serve as temporary shelters. They can, however, blow around in a strong wind, and thus may not give full protection in severe storms.

Backpacker rainsuits are almost invincible. Many feature hoods and large cargo pockets. Rain pants and rain chaps will protect your legs from wind, rain, and heavy dew, while gaiters will keep pebbles, water, mud, and snow out of your boots and away from your socks.

(For more on using gaiters, see "Winter Camping.")

Although most packs can repel rain for a time, make sure your gear stays dry by taking along a pack cover. You can make a simple one by cutting a slit in a plastic garbage bag and tucking the loose ends around your pack frame, or you can buy or sew a cover especially contoured to fit your pack.

(For information on making rain gear and pack covers, see "Making Equipment.")

Warm-Weather Clothing List

_____Long-sleeve shirt

_____T-shirts

_____Long pants

_____Hiking shorts

_____Sweater or warm jacket

_____Underwear

_____Socks

_____Moccasins or running shoes (for wear around camp)

_____Visored cap

_____Bandanas

_____Rain gear

Cold-Weather Clothing List

_____Long-sleeve shirt

_____Wool Shirt

_____Long pants (wool military surplus pants are fine)

_____Wool sweater

_____Long underwear preferably polyester or polypropylene)

_____Socks (preferably wool)

_____Insulated parka or coat with hood

_____Wool stocking cap

_____Mittens

_____Insulated booties or mukluks

_____Bandanas
(For more on winter clothing, see "Winter Camping.")

FOOTWEAR

Many backcountry treks involve miles of trail hiking. Others, such as kayaking, rafting, mountain climbing, and cross-country skiing, require specialized shoes or boots, but even then you may find that you need to walk some distance to reach a river, a mountain, or a snowfield. No matter how you spend your time in the outdoors, you'll probably want to have a pair of good, durable hiking boots.

Leather Boots

When you're hiking, your feet and ankles take a tremendous pounding. Quality hiking boots will give them the support and protection they need to withstand the jarring of each step. The best leather boots are made of top-grain leather, which breathes, allowing moisture from your feet to escape. A minimum of seams keeps wetness from penetrating. Lug soles provide the most traction, though smoother soles are usually adequate, frequently lighter, and often less damaging to trails. Since a pound of weight on your feet is equal to 5 pounds on your back, stick with boots that weigh no more than 3 to 5 pounds a pair for trail wear. Mountaineering boots are heavier and more rigid, and appropriate only for the specialized needs of climbers.

Ultralight Trail Boots

Made with the same synthetic materials and high performance designs as running shoes, ultralight trail boots weigh just a few pounds a pair, need little breaking in, dry quickly, and are fine for walking well-maintained trails. They may not be sufficiently waterproof for wet, muddy trails or sturdy enough for rugged backcountry use, especially if you are carrying a heavy pack.

Selecting Footwear

When you go into a store to try on boots, wear the socks in which you plan to hike. Unlace a boot, slip in your foot, and kick your toes forward. If the boot is the right length, you should be able to slide two fingers between your heel and the back of the boot.

Next, kick your heel back into the heel pocket, and with the boot snugly laced, walk around the shop, go up and down some stairs, and do a few deep knee bends. You want to be sure your heel isn't sliding up and down inside the boot, and that the widest part of your foot isn't swimming around or being squeezed. After you've tried out one pair, run the same tests on several other models, taking plenty of time to get a real feel for the fit. Inspect each boot for quality workmanship, and get the opinions of experienced hikers. Before you buy, make sure the store will allow you to bring the boots back, undamaged, if they don't fit. That way you can take them home and wear them for several days inside the house. If they still feel good, you've probably got a pair that's right for you.

Sturdy hiking boots ▼

Lightweight hiking boots ▶

Basic Maine hunting boots ▶

Breaking in Leather Boots

Like new baseball gloves, new leather boots usually are stiff. They must be broken in before you wear them on an extended trek or you're in for a crop of blisters.

First, treat your boots with the dressing recommended by the manufacturer. Rub it thoroughly into the leather with a rag or your hand. This will protect the boots and help them repel water. You may also want to guard the boot seams against moisture and abrasion by applying a commercial seam sealer.

Wear the boots around the house and on short hikes until they have loosened. Gradually extend the length of the walks on which you wear them, and soon they'll feel like a natural part of your feet.

Caring for Boots

No matter what kind of boots you have, clean them after every outing. When boots are muddy, use a stiff brush to remove the mud, then apply more dressing to the leather. If they become wet, dry them at room temperature. Never expose them to more heat than you can tolerate on the back of your hand. Synthetics may melt, and leather can become hardened and cracked. Take care of your boots and they'll give you years of good service.

Running Shoes, Moccasins, Mukluks, and Booties

When you reach camp after a long hike, it's sheer heaven to get your feet out of the boots that encased them all day and slip into moccasins or running shoes. On the trail, you can also change into running shoes if you need to wade a stream. You'll have the foot protection you need, and your boots will stay dry. In the winter, mukluks and insulated booties with nonskid soles are great for wearing around camp and in your tent.

Mukluks ▶

GROUP GEAR/PERSONAL GEAR

In addition to safety, one of the greatest advantages of traveling in a group is that your pack will be lighter than if you were alone. Of course, each person must tote personal gear—clothing, eating utensils, etc. But tents, cook kits, stoves, and the like, the food, and stove fuel can be divided among all the team members. In fact, in order to fairly distribute group gear, cook kits can be separated into individual pots and pans, and rain flies and poles carried separately from their tents.

The equipment you can consider to be group gear will depend on the kind of adventure for which you're preparing, and the size and interests of your crew. As you gear up, set aside those items that will be used by more than one person, and then divvy them up in such a way that everyone has a pack that is light enough to be carried comfortably. To avoid confusion in camp, keep a complete list of your crew's group gear and note the pack in which each item is being carried.

(For more on loading packs, see "Backpacking.")

SHELTER

Desert campers need open, airy shelters that shade them from the sun. Long-distance hikers want tents that are light in weight yet appropriate for many variations in weather. The safety of mountaineers and winter campers depends on tight, strong tents able to withstand the force of wind-driven snow and sleet. Fortunately, there are shelters that will satisfy every outdoor traveler. Among the most common are tarps, bivouac bags, A-frames, domes, and hybrids.

Tarp

The simplest of all tents, a nylon tarp weighs just a few pounds and can be set up in dozens of ways. You can use it as your primary shelter, or as a dining fly protecting your group's cooking area from the elements. A tarp has no floor, which can pose problems in soggy country, nor does it have mosquito netting. Still, for lightweight shelter in mild climates, it is hard to beat.

(For information on turning a sheet of plastic into a tarp, see "Making Equipment.")

Bivouac Bag

First developed as an emergency shelter for mountain climbers forced to spend nights on cliffs far from camp, the bivouac bag is a waterproof envelope that slips over a sleeping bag and protects a camper from wind and rain. Some are made of fabrics that shed rain, yet allow body moisture to pass through into the night air. Others, held open with fiberglass wands and equipped with zippered doors, mesh windows, and detachable rain flies, are almost tiny one-person tents. At 1 to 3 pounds total weight, bivouac bags are the lightest of shelters. They are also small and confining, factors you'll want to consider if you intend to travel where you may need to stay inside for a day or two waiting out a storm.

A-frame Tent

Essentially a pup tent made light and strong with modern materials and engineering, the A-frame is roomy and usually has a water-proof floor and mosquito netting. Breathable fabric allows moisture to escape from inside the shelter, while a waterproof rainfly protects the tent from exterior moisture. Weighing 4 to 8 pounds, an A-frame tent will keep several hikers and their gear warm and dry.

Dome

Contemporary designs and fabrics have made possible a variety of dome-shaped tents. Their configurations help them stand up to wind,

rain, and snow, and the spaciousness of their interiors makes them great for two to four campers. A dome tent can be flipped upside down in the morning to dry the bottom of the tent floor quickly.

Hybrids

Bend the poles of an A-frame tent, and its shape becomes that of a tube. Combine the curves of a dome tent with the length of an A-frame, and you have a wedge-shaped tent with a narrow width and a high ceiling. Add a rear door. Attach a vestibule in which to stow packs and equipment. Lower the center. Raise the sides. Put a window in the roof. Remove the stakes and guy ropes. Sew the rain fly to the inner tent, or do away with the fly altogether.

Tent makers, like automobile manufacturers, are constantly trying to improve their designs. Sometimes the results are silly, but occasionally there are real advances that make tents lighter, roomier, stronger, and more functional. With so many tents on the market, you'll have to decide what your needs are, and then shop around until you find the shelter that is exactly right for you. Talk to veteran campers about the tents they find reliable. If you can, borrow or rent different tents and use them on overnight treks to see what they are like. In equipment stores, have sales people help you set up tents in the showroom, then crawl inside and check them for size, comfort, and quality construction.

Finally, pick a color that will blend with the hues of the wilderness. Greens, browns, and rusts are perfect. A few too-bright tents can make an area seem crowded.

While a new tent doesn't need to be broken in like a pair of hiking boots, take the time to practice setting it up at home. It's better to learn the quirks of your shelter in your own backyard than on a high mountain with a storm crashing around your ears.

(For more on tents, see "Camping Know-How.")

Ground Cloth

A sheet of plastic under your tent will protect the floor from rocks and twigs, and keep moisture from seeping through. Prevent rain from running between the tent floor and the ground cloth by placing the cloth so it doesn't extend beyond the area covered by the tent. Carry the ground cloth near the top of your pack and use it in sudden showers to cover your gear.

Tent Stakes

Don't expect to whittle stakes at each campsite. There may be no wood available, and if a storm is brewing, you won't have time. A set of plastic or metal pegs weighs only ounces and lasts for years.

BEDROLL

In a way, your bed is an extension of your shelter, keeping you warm while you sleep. The chapter titled "Camping Know-How" explains how to make a ground bed that begins with a ground cloth or tent floor and a foam pad or air mattress. The bedroll that goes on top may be a couple of wool blankets folded over and held at the edges with large safety pins, or, more likely, a sleeping bag.

A sleeping bag keeps you warm by trapping the heat your body generates. The bag's thickness, known as its loft, determines how much heat the bag will retain. Usually the more loft a bag has, the warmer you will be.

The fabric shell of a sleeping bag often is made of nylon. Loft is created by filling the shell with natural or synthetic materials, and partitions sewn inside the shell hold the fill material in place.

In less expensive bags, partition stitching may go through the shell, resulting in cold spots where the loft is thin. In better bags, mesh or nylon walls called *baffles* divide the interior of the shell into compartments that keep the fill evenly distributed without lessening its loft, thus preventing cold spots. The best bags also have tubes of fill material backing the zippers to keep warm air from escaping, and they may be equipped with insulated hoods that can be drawn about a sleeper's face.

Sleeping bag construction. Sections through wall of bag illustrate how filling is kept in place

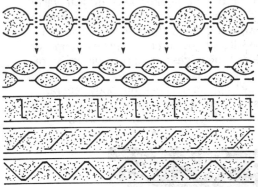

Simple quilting. Loses heat where the stitching passes through the fabric.

Double quilting. Two quilts fastened together in an off-set way to eliminate cold spots. Material tends to be heavy.

Box wall. Prevents the filling from moving about.

Slant wall. Prevents down from moving about and gives it room to expand.

Overlapping tube or V-baffle. Very efficient, but because it uses a lot of material it tends to be heavy.

Goose down and synthetic fibers are the most frequently used fill materials. Both also insulate parkas, vests, booties, caps, and mittens. In making your equipment choices, weigh the advantages and disadvantages of each.

Goose Down

Down refers to the delicate feathers geese grow next to their skins. Ounce for ounce, it insulates better than any other fill material, and it lasts for years. It is also expensive. Down requires careful laundering, and when it becomes wet it loses its loft and cannot keep you warm.

Synthetic Fibers

Synthetic fibers are made from petroleum products. To match the warmth of down, a fiber-filled bag must be a bit heavier and bulkier, but it will retain some of its insulating value even when it is damp. Fiber-filled bags are easy to clean and often quite economically priced.

(For information on putting together a foam sleeping bag, see "Making Equipment.")

Caring for Sleeping Gear

On the trail, carry your bag and blankets tightly rolled, or in a stuff sack strapped low on the pack frame or tied to the top of the pack itself. Some packs, especially those without frames, have special zippered sleeping bag storage compartments.

If you expect wet weather or stream crossings, place your bedroll in a plastic garbage bag before you stow it in a stuff bag. Twist the end of the garbage bag to form a gooseneck that can be securely tied.

(For more on waterproof packing, see "Canoeing.")

After a trek, unroll your bag, let it air thoroughly, then hang it in a closet or store it in a large cloth sack such as a laundry bag. Prolong the life of your bag by cleaning it when it becomes soiled, but only according to the manufacturer's instructions.

COOKING GEAR AND FOOD

For a full discussion of backcountry food preparation and cooking gear, see "Trail Menus and Cooking." You'll see how to use the following equipment and provisions.

Canteen or Plastic Water Bottle

A 1-quart container is sufficient if water sources are abundant. For easy access, stow it in an outside pocket of your pack. Where water is scarce, and for convenience in camp, take along a collapsible water bag.

Backpacking Stove

For information on choosing and safely operating a portable stove, see "Stoves and Fires."

4⅝"

6½"

This model weighs 2 pounds 10 ounces empty.

Fuel capacity: 10 ounces

Personal Eating Gear

_____Cup

_____Spoon

_____Deep dish plate (an empty margarine tub is fine)

Group Cooking Gear

_____Pots and utensils
(For information on making your own pots, see "Making Equipment.")

_____Hot pot tongs (get a pair that can firmly grip your pots)

_____Can opener (use the one on your knife, or carry a small army surplus opener)

_____Litter bag

_____Trail foods (nutritionally balanced and nonperishable)

PACKS

A pack serves as your backcountry storeroom, attic, garage, and basement. A good one will ride lightly on your shoulders, protect your equipment from the elements, give you easy access to things you need along the way, and leave your hands free. To choose the pack that's right for you, you'll need to know the advantages and disadvantages of soft packs, internal frame packs, and packs with external frames.

Soft Packs

Known as a rucksack, haversack, or Duluth pack, the large soft pack is basically a cloth bag with shoulder straps attached. The cloth may be canvas or a tough synthetic, and the bag may have exterior pockets and accessory straps, zippered flap compartments, and a shape that conforms to a hiker's back. The advantages are that a soft pack will hold plenty of gear and can be stowed in tight places, making it ideal for day hikes, short portages, and light loads. However, a loaded soft pack places most of its weight on a hiker's shoulders, and that can be uncomfortable.

Internal Frame Packs

Built much like a soft pack, a pack with an internal frame has several metal stays sewn into it that form a frame directing the weight of the load into a hip belt attached to the base of the bag. You can swing the pack onto your back, tighten the padded belt around your waist, then adjust the shoulder straps so most of the weight rides on your hips. The weight is supported by your bone structure and the strong muscles of your legs so that a full load can be

carried with relative ease. The compact shape and snug fit of internal frame packs are suitable for travel in heavy brush and on cross-country skis, as well as on open trails.

External Frame Packs

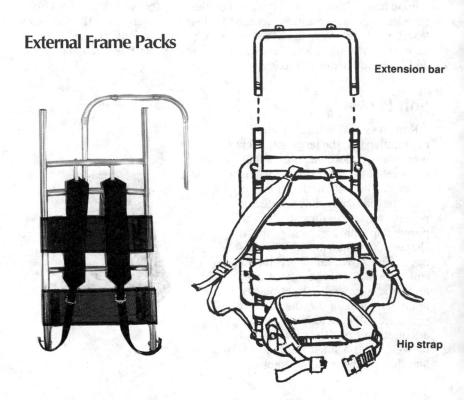

Extension bar

Hip strap

The weight distribution principles of an exterior frame pack are essentially the same as for a pack with an interior frame, but since the frame is outside the bag it can be larger and more rigid, and thus can more efficiently transfer the weight from the shoulder straps to the hip belt. Most frames also provide room for you to lash on a sleeping bag or tent, and with the pack bag removed, you can use the frame to haul anything from firewood to a chain saw.

When shopping for a new backpack, look for one that matches the kinds of adventures you'll use it for most. It may be a little large for your overnight campouts, but just right for 2- and 3-day treks. Insist on strong materials that have been securely sewn, and notice how pack bags are attached to external frames. Sturdy clevis pins secured with split rings will keep them from coming apart.

CHAPTER 4

When you try on a pack, put some weight in it, then wear it around the store and see how it feels. Will it ride close to your back? Does the weight rest on your hips rather than your shoulders? Could you carry it all day on a trail?

(For information on loading, hoisting, and carrying a pack, see "Backpacking.")

Fanny pack

Day Packs

Day packs are small soft packs just large enough to hold the lunch, clothing, rain gear, and first aid kit you need for a single day's hike. On extended adventure treks, you may want to carry a day pack in your backpack, and use it for excursions you make from your camp.

(For instructions on turning a pair of pants into a day pack, see "Making Equipment.")

Panniers, Haul Bags, and Saddlebags

Certain outdoor activities require special packs for transporting food and equipment. Bicyclers and horse packers may need panniers or saddlebags to hold their supplies, while climbers, cross-country skiers, and snowshoers may choose to drag their gear behind them in tough, protective haul bags. In any case, choose panniers and bags that are as well made as any pack you would put on your shoulders. Halfway through a trek is no time to discover your gear isn't up to the challenge of the backcountry.

THE REST OF YOUR GEAR

You'll probably spend plenty of time selecting your clothing, boots, bedroll, and shelter. Use the same care assembling the rest of your gear, and the result will be a light, efficient load containing everything you need in the wilderness—and not an ounce more.

TOOLS

Pocketknife

A sharp pocketknife with a can opener on it is an invaluable backcountry tool. Keep it clean, sharp, and handy. Avoid large sheath knives. They are heavy and awkward to carry, and unnecessary for most camp chores except for cleaning fish.

Matches

Take along wooden kitchen matches for lighting stoves and fires. Store them in a matchsafe or a small plastic container with a tight lid. To be safe, carry some matches in your pocket and some in a plastic bag with your firestarters. You might also want to carry an inexpensive butane lighter, but don't depend on it exclusively.

Fire Starters

When you need to build an open fire in the backwoods, a firestarter will make it easier for you to kindle a blaze.

(For information on making and using firestarters and guidelines on the use of camp fires, see "Stoves and Fires.")

Flashlight

A reliable light is important, especially if you must go for help after dark. Carry a small, strong flashlight with fresh batteries and a good bulb. Even better is a battery-powered headlamp that leaves your hands free to tend to camp tasks and nighttime first aid emergencies. During the day, reverse the batteries or put a strip of tape over the switch to prevent the light from clicking on in your pack.

Watch

Many people go to the hills eager to escape the tyranny of the clock, though a watch is useful for computing how far you've traveled, how much daylight is left, and when you should arrive at your destination.

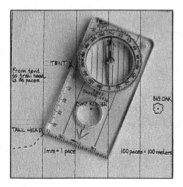

Compass and Map

Keep your compass handy by looping the lanyard through a buttonhole on the pocket flap of your shirt. Protect your map from the elements with a clear plastic bag.

(For information on the use of map and compass, see "Backcountry Navigation.")

Repair Kit

Include thread, needles, rubber bands, safety pins, tape, wire, and a couple of buttons along with any spare parts for your stove, pack, and specialized equipment. Scissors go in the first aid kit.

rd

In addition to the rope you use to hang your bear bag, a few shorter lengths of cord may come in handy when you pitch your tent, replace a shoelace, hang out wet clothing, or lash together a broken pack frame.

Pencil and Paper

Be prepared to write down emergency information as well as notes on the highlights of your adventures.

Hiking Stick

A hiking stick will help you keep your balance as you wade across streams. It is also good for use as a tent pole for a trail tarp or dining fly. During rest breaks, you can prop your pack against the stick to form a convenient backrest.

A hiking stick doesn't have to be fancy; a piece of dead wood you pick up along the path is all you need. However, you may want to whittle a special stick out of oak or ash, and carry it on all your hikes. Decorate the staff with carvings, and keep track of your mileage by cutting a small notch in it every 10 miles.

GEAR FOR HEALTH AND SAFETY

First Aid Kit

Put a few adhesive bandages in your pocket to protect minor scrapes and abrasions, and be sure that someone in your group has a well-stocked first aid kit stowed where everyone can get to it quickly. Know how to use it.

(For more on first aid and the contents of a kit, see "Outdoor First Aid.")

Emergency Coins

Carry enough change for several calls from pay telephones.

Whistle

Three short blasts signal that you are in need of aid. Keep a plastic whistle in your pocket and use it only in emergencies.

Mirror

A small mirror is handy if you have something in your eye, want to check a tooth, or need to flash a distress signal.

(For more on attracting attention with a whistle or mirror, see "Survival Preparedness.")

Sunglasses

Wearing sunglasses is a good idea in any bright, open country. When you travel in snow, they are essential for protecting your eyes from the glare that can cause headaches and even temporary blindness.

(For more on eye protection, see "Mountain Hiking and Climbing.")

Sunscreen or Sunblock

It doesn't take long for the sun to burn bare skin, even on overcast days. At high altitudes, on snowfields, and on open water, the danger increases. Before the symptoms of sunburn appear, apply plenty of sunscreen with a protection rating of at least SPF-15, especially to your face, ears, neck, and exposed portions of arms and legs.

Lip Balm

Lips, too, can become burned and chapped by sun and wind. Have a tube of lip balm in your pocket and use it regularly.

Insect Repellent

Nothing makes a trek more miserable than a black cloud of blood-thirsty insects swarming endlessly around your head. In bug country, your comfort will depend on your ability to ward off mosquitoes, flies, and "no-see-ums", so take along an effective repellent. Those containing a large percentage of the chemical N,N-Diethyl-meta-toluamide are very effective.

However, no repellent is perfect. When bugs are especially bad, a mesh head net will keep them away from your face. Button your sleeves and pant legs to prevent the tiny beasts from crawling under your clothing. A tent with a floor and mosquito netting may be necessary if you are to have a night of unmolested sleep.

,othbrush

An everyday toothbrush is fine, handle and all. Between uses, slip it in a plastic bag to keep it clean.

Toothpaste

Small sample or trial-size tubes and almost-empty tubes contain as much toothpaste as you're likely to need.

Soap

Biodegradable camping soap comes in solid and liquid forms. Use it sparingly for washing your dishes, your clothing, and yourself, and keep it out of rivers, lakes, streams, and springs. It too will pollute.

(For more on washing up, see "Camping Know-How" and "Trail Menus and Cooking.")

Towel

If you carry a towel, it should be small. Some campers stitch together two edges of a thin towel and use it as a pillow at night by stuffing it with a sweater or jacket. You can also use it to sop up the moisture from your tent. As with wet socks, you can hang a damp towel on the outside of your pack and let it dry as you walk.

Water Filters Purification Tablets

For information on purifying water, see "Outdoor Safety."

Garbage Bags

Need a temporary raincoat? A waterproof cover for your gear? A place to stow your trash? A bear bag for your food? Heavy-duty garbage bags can serve a multitude of purposes.

(For information on hanging a bear bag, see "Camping Know-How.")

NONESSENTIAL GEAR FOR LEARNING AND FUN

Books and Guides

Bird and plant identification guides, books on weather, geology, and the history of the region through which you are traveling can enhance your enjoyment of any trek. If you're storm-bound in a tent for a day or two, a good book will help pass the time.

Camera

Snapshots and slides will help keep alive the memory of an adventure long after it's over.

(For information on using and protecting a camera, see "Outdoor and Nature Photography.")

Binoculars

Extend your range of vision with binoculars. Small pairs are made especially for outdoor use. A 7×35 binocular will have magnification and light-gathering powers suitable for most backcountry needs.

Fishing Gear

You'll never know when you might come upon a perfect stream or lake teeming with hungry fish. Compact, collapsible fishing tackle won't take much room in your pack. Get a license and you'll be ready to go after the big ones.

(For more on selecting and using tackle, see "Fishing.")

"Smith (Jedidiah—early trapper and explorer) had made bullboats before. He knew how to cut limber willow shoots nearly as thick as his wrist... how to bend them over and lash them into a rounded framework, how to weave and lash smaller branches across this sturdy frame into a basket.

"Finally, Smith had a leather tub big enough to float him and his packs, light enough to be carried on his back, and small enough to be easily concealed..."

Stanley Vestal, 1937

Chapter 5

Making Equipment

James Gilbert Phillips
Snow Camping Instructor, University
of New Mexico, Widely Recognized
Authority on Snow Camping

Clyde S. "Sandy" Bridges
Director of the Northern Tier
National High Adventure Programs
and Founder of the Okpik Winter
Camping Program

Have you ever wanted to take a day hike from a base camp and discovered you had nothing in which to carry your lunch? Ever needed a pair of rain chaps, but didn't have the funds to buy a ready-made pair? How would you like to have some nylon stuff sacks to hold the loose items you need on a trek? Do you need a compact first aid kit you can carry anywhere? Would you like to have all sorts of terrific and inexpensive winter camping equipment?

You can have all of these and many more by making your own gear. Not only will you save money, you also can take pride in having constructed your equipment with your own hands. Each item can be customized to fit your needs exactly, and you can even design special gear that will make your outings safer, easier, and more enjoyable.

In this chapter, some of the basic ideas behind making equipment are discussed. Also included are specific instructions for some projects, suggestions for others, and sources of information you may find helpful as you work on your own gear. Making equipment will at times mean nothing more than pulling a piece of plastic out of your pack and shaping it to meet the needs of the moment. For other projects, however, you'll need a sewing machine and perhaps some help from someone with a knack for cutting and stitching cloth. In any case, the idea is to have as much fun as you can as you learn the ins and outs of making gear.

RAW MATERIALS

The materials you need for homemade equipment are as varied as the projects themselves. A pair of pants can become a day pack. A few tin cans can be transformed into a cook kit, and a garbage bag into a rain cover. It's often a matter of using everyday articles in new ways.

For lots of backcountry equipment, though, you'll buy fabric by the yard, and fill material by the ounce. They're available at many camping stores, and by special order from the catalogs of larger outfitters. Below are some of the items you probably will use.

Nylon pack cloth. A heavy, tough material that resists abrasion, nylon pack cloth is treated with a coating that keeps water out. Use it for making packs, panniers, saddlebags, and haul bags, and for reinforcing the seats and knees of wool pants.

Nylon taffeta. Much lighter than pack cloth, coated nylon taffeta makes a good outer shell for windbreakers and wet-weather clothing, as well as stuff bags. It has an abrasion-resistant surface.

Nylon tricot. Strong, lightweight nylon material with an open pattern that makes it highly breathable, nylon tricot is excellent for making liners for sleeping bags, mukluks, mittens, and parkas.

Ripstop nylon. Ripstop nylon is crisscrossed with hundreds of strong threads that will stop a tear in the fabric (thus the name "ripstop"). Light and strong, uncoated "breathable" ripstop makes up the bodies of many tents and the shells of sleeping bags, while waterproof coated ripstop is used for tarps and rain flies.

CHAPTER 5

Gore-Tex. Sandwiched between layers of nylon, Gore-Tex will allow the moisture of perspiration and respiration to pass through from one side, but won't allow rain to enter from the other. Used in foul weather clothing, Gore-Tex lets a wilderness traveler ward off downpours without suffering the clammy internal dampness of nonbreathable garments. Used in bivouac bags and tents, it creates dry shelters for sleepers at a minimum of weight and bulk. Gore-Tex, however, is expensive and it loses its unique properties when it becomes excessively soiled.

Mosquito netting. Head nets and tent doors are the obvious uses of mosquito netting, but it also can be used to make see-through stuff bags and compartments on first aid kits.

Polyester/cotton cloth. A blend of synthetic and natural fibers can combine the advantages of both in a light, strong material useful for both inner and outer clothing.

Batting and goose down. Several of the best synthetic-fill materials can be purchased by the yard and used to insulate clothing and sleeping bags. Goose down is sold by the ounce, or as part of a ready-to-assemble kit.

Foam. With the lightweight (about 1 pound per cubic foot), low-density, inexpensive foam sold by furniture stores, you can make a complete winter wardrobe and a sleeping bag that will keep you warm and dry. To insulate properly and allow moisture to escape, the foam must be low-density polyurethane. Items made of foam are easy to clean; put them in a tub of warm water with a little soap, squeeze the water through, then rinse thoroughly with clear water. Hang the items outdoors in the sun to dry.

Accessories. Stores that carry material for outdoor gear will stock other supplies you will need to complete your projects—nylon thread, grommets, hook and pile closures, toggles, webbing, zippers, snap fasteners, liquid waterproofing.

PROJECTS

The following plans and patterns will show you ways to construct some terrific outdoor gear, and also give you an idea of how to think about equipment in terms of making it. The resources at the end of the book contain patterns for many other projects.

Day Pack

Have you ever been on a wilderness trek and wished you had a small pack in which to carry your lunch and extra clothing during a day hike away from camp? Here's how to make one out of a pair of long pants.

Lay the pants flat on the ground with the zipper and snap closed. Tie a 1-foot length of cord around the cuff of the right pant leg. Fold the leg in half at the knee, then run an end of the cord through the belt loop just to the right of the zipper. Tie the cord tightly. Using a second length of cord, repeat the procedure with the left leg, tying the cuff to the belt loop just to the left of the zipper. Take a third piece of cord, about 3 feet long, and run it through all the belt loops to form a drawstring. Fill the pants-pack with your supplies, loading soft items such as rain gear and clothing near the front where the pack will press against your shoulders. Maps and snacks can go in the pockets. Pull the drawstring tight, tie the ends, and you're ready to swing the pack onto your back.

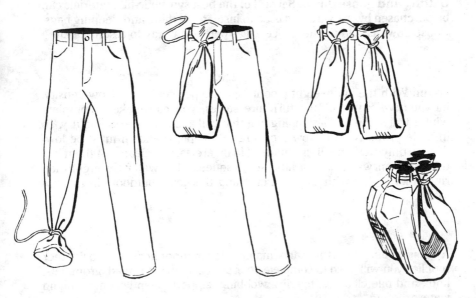

Cook Kit

Inexpensive aluminum or stainless steel pans from department stores and garage sales are just right for outdoor cooking, but the handles make them awkward to carry. You can solve that problem and transform a few pans into a compact cook kit by making the handles removable.

Two to four campers will need a saucepan with about a 6-cup capacity, another that will hold around 8 cups, and a 7-inch frying pan. Choose saucepans with lids. Using a hack saw, cut off the handles ¾ inch from the lips of the pans. Smooth the edges of the handles and the stubs with a file. Next, clamp each handle onto its stub and drill a ³⁄₁₆-inch hole through both. Insert ¾-inch-long round-headed aluminum screws and secure them with wing nuts. Remove the handles for packing and place the screws in the handle holes so you won't lose them. Nest together the pans and their lids. Stow the unit in a stuff bag, and it's ready to go.

Large tin cans can be used as pots. Make bails by punching two holes under the top edge of each can and inserting and twisting the ends of a piece of heavy gauge wire. Fashion lids from aluminum foil.

Plastic Tarp Tent

The polyethylene plastic sheeting used by carpenters and painters can be turned into an inexpensive, ultralight tarp tent. Available at building materials stores in various widths, polyethylene sheeting comes in thicknesses measured in mils. For a tent, 4- to 6-mil plastic is your best choice, and the sheet should be 12 feet wide and 12 feet long.

Before you take the tarp on the trail, reinforce it with ½-inch filament tape applied to the underside of the sheet according to the diagram below.

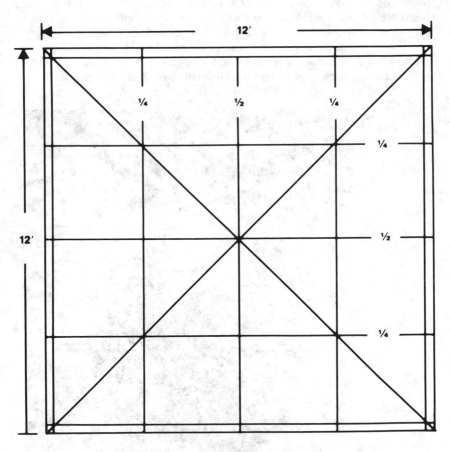

Taping diagram

To make the job easier, apply tape to all four sides about 5 inches from the edges. Fold the sheet in half so that a crease shows down the middle and tape the crease line. Then fold the sheet in other ways to form the creases you need to guide the rest of your taping.

To pitch your tent, you'll need to tuck a smooth stone under the edge. Loop a nylon cord around the stone and the plastic, and secure it with a clove hitch or double half hitch. Do this at each of the corners and at several intermittent places. The more tie-downs you have, the less likely the tent is to flap in the wind.

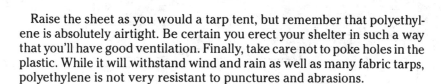

Raise the sheet as you would a tarp tent, but remember that polyethylene is absolutely airtight. Be certain you erect your shelter in such a way that you'll have good ventilation. Finally, take care not to poke holes in the plastic. While it will withstand wind and rain as well as many fabric tarps, polyethylene is not very resistant to punctures and abrasions.

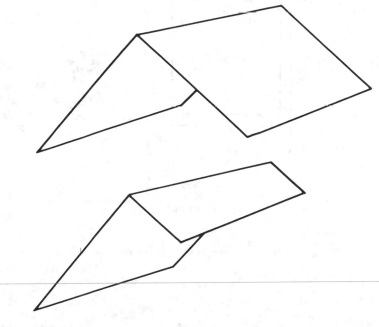

Stuff Bags

With stuff bags in different shapes and sizes, you can organize your backcountry gear. Use a large sack made of pack cloth to hold your sleeping bag, medium sized bags constructed of thin nylon or cotton for cooking gear and clothing, and small nylon or mosquito net bags for all the small items you'll need on a trek.

Stuff bags are not difficult to make, and if you're interested in learning how to sew they're an easy project for beginners. Decide how deep and wide you'd like the finished bag to be, add 2 inches to the length to allow for a drawstring and 1 inch to the width for seams, and cut a piece of fabric that's double the finished length. Turn down the ends 1 inch and sew them to form a drawstring channel. Fold the fabric in half with the drawstring seams together facing out, and stitch the sides of the bag. Turn the bag right side out so all the seams are inside, run a nylon cord through the drawstring channel, and you're done.

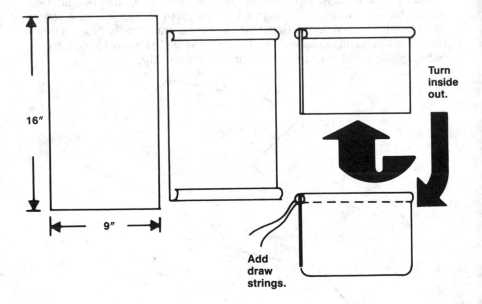

16"

9"

Turn inside out.

Add draw strings.

First Aid Kit

Need a convenient way to carry your first aid supplies? This kit can be rolled to fit in a side pocket of your pack, and unrolled beside an injury victim, putting everything you need right at your fingertips.

Begin with a brightly colored piece of nylon 18 inches wide and 36 inches long. (It may be a little longer or a little shorter, depending on the fabric available.) Next, cut two strips of mosquito netting, each 9 inches wide and as long as the nylon cloth.

Stitch a ½-inch hem down one side of each strip, then pin each to the nylon, aligning the unsewn edges with the outside edges of the cloth. Fold over the edges ½ inch and sew a seam completely around the nylon, fastening down the mosquito netting in the process. Finally, sew some seams across the width of the kit, forming pockets in which you can stow your first aid gear. It's a good idea to lay out the contents of your kit before you sew the pockets, and make each pocket just wide enough to hold a particular item.

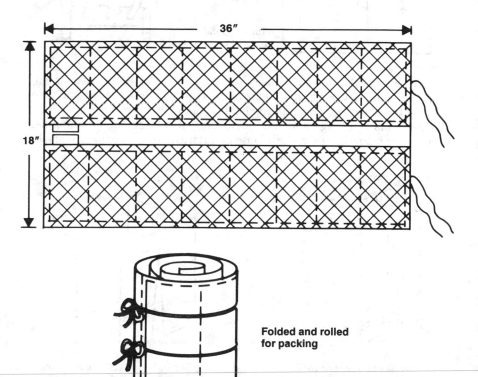

Folded and rolled for packing

Pack Cover

A plastic garbage bag liner makes a good temporary rain cover for your pack. Simply slit it two-thirds the way up the front, then cut a few inches across the top of the slit to form a T-shaped opening. Slip the bag over your pack and tuck the loose ends of the plastic around the straps or under the bars of your pack frame.

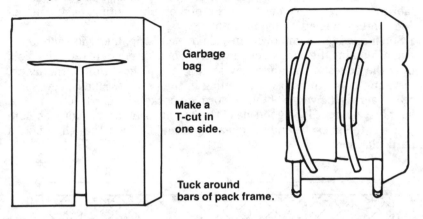

Garbage bag

Make a T-cut in one side.

Tuck around bars of pack frame.

For a more durable cover, use coated nylon fabric. Begin by wrapping sheets of newspaper around your pack, taping them together, and trimming them with scissors until you have a paper version of a pack cover. Be sure to make it long enough to cover the entire pack and anything tied above or below it. Also make it loose enough to fit over your pack when it's

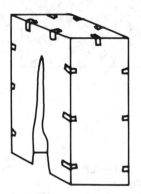

Drape newspaper over pack and tape mockup.

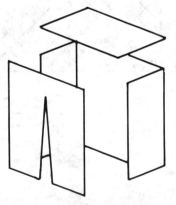

Separate parts. Cut out nylon, adding enough fabric for seams.

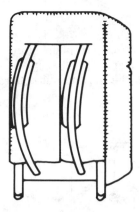

bulging with gear. Remove the paper mock-up and carefully cut it until it will lie flat on the floor (it may be in several pieces). Pin each piece to the nylon and cut around it, allowing an extra ½ inch for seams. Stitch the pieces together, reinforce the edges with seam binding, and sew on a few fabric ties 6 inches long and 1 inch wide

Rain Chaps

Rain chaps will keep your legs dry in a downpour and protect them from mountain winds. They're easy to make and easy to wear. Start with a piece of coated nylon (ripstop or taffeta) or Gore-Tex. On it, lay out the pattern below, sizing the pattern to your leg length. Cut the cloth to fit the pattern, hem edges A and B, and stitch together edges C and D to form the chap. A couple of 6-inch long shoestrings sewn to the chap at E can be tied to a belt loop of your pants to hold up each chap. Reverse the pattern for the other chap.

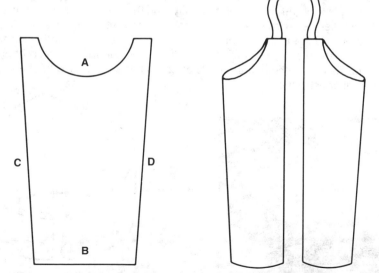

For rain pants, you can use the pattern for a pair of pajama bottoms, and put a two-way zipper up the outside seam of each leg.

Foam Hat

Using 1-inch-thick low-density polyethylene foam from a furniture store, you can make light, comfortable winter camping gear that will keep you warm in even the most severe conditions. One of the most useful is the foam hat.

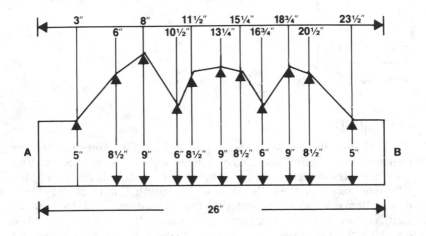

Start with a piece of foam 26 inches long and 8 inches wide. Draw the pattern on a piece of stiff paper, cut it out, lay it on the foam, and outline it with a felt-tip marker. Use scissors or a very sharp knife to cut the foam according to the pattern. Bend the foam around until edges A and B meet, and glue them together with an adhesive such as 3-M Spray Cement. Known as "butt-glueing," this method of cementing two flat edges together is used in almost all foam gear construction.

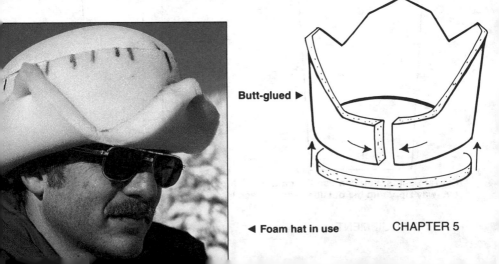

Butt-glued ▶

◀ **Foam hat in use**   CHAPTER 5

Foam Sleeping Bag

For a wilderness bed that will keep you cozy wet or dry, construct your own foam bag. Begin with a piece of 1¼-inch foam 92 inches long and 64 inches wide. As with the foam hat, draw a full-size pattern of the sleeping bag on paper. Cut it out, then transfer the pattern to the foam. Cut the foam along the lines and use 3-M Spray Cement to butt-glue edges A to B, C to D, and E to F. Cut out the two wedges at the top of the bag, and glue edges G to H, and I to J.

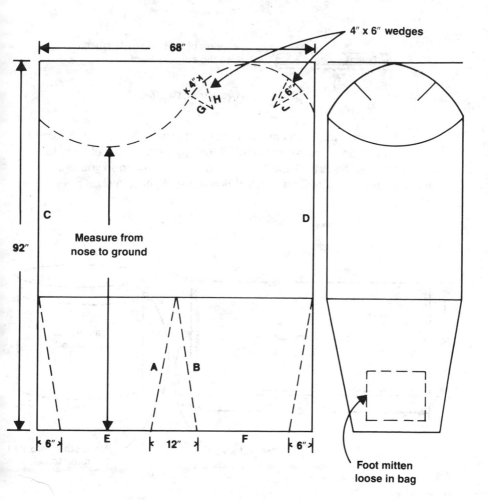

Complete the bag by making an inner liner of light nylon chiffon, tricot, or uncoated ripstop nylon, and an outer cover of lightweight uncoated ripstop nylon. Add 2 inches all around the sleeping bag pattern for the inner liner, and 6 inches all around for the outer cover. Sew liner edges A to B, C to D, and E to F, then do the same with the edges of the outer cover. Slip the liner into the foam bag, and put the bag into the outer cover. Stitch the liner seams and cover seams together around the head-hole of the bag.

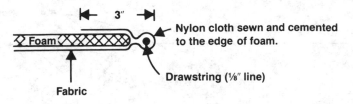

For a little extra insulation around your feet as you sleep, make a foam foot mitten. Begin with a 1- by 14- by 30-inch piece of foam. Fold it in half and butt-glue edges A to B and C to D. Leave the top open so you can slip your feet into the mitten, and tuck it down inside your finished sleeping bag.

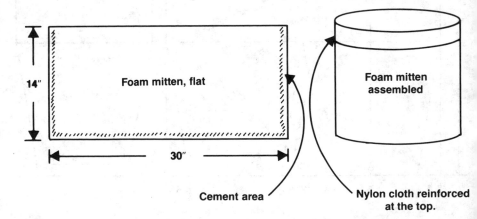

MUKLUKS

Over the centuries, Eskimos have developed very effective ways of staying warm. Key to their clothing system are mukluks large enough to hold their feet and plenty of effective insulation. The soles are waterproof while the uppers are breathable to allow moisture to escape, keeping their feet dry and warm. The fur ruff around the top prevents the entry of snow. By combining the ages-old principles of the Eskimo with modern materials, you can make cold weather footwear that will keep your feet comfortable at temperatures far below zero.

Mukluk soles. The Eskimos use the tough hides of animals for mukluk bottoms; you can use the soles of large overshoes, shoepack boots, insulated "moon boots," or Army surplus winter footgear. Since they must be big enough to hold your feet and the bulk of foam socks (see below), start with soles several sizes larger than your regular shoe size; a size 12 sole will make a mukluk that will fit feet sizes 7–10. Cut the tops from the soles, leaving a 4-inch collar around each heel and 1 to 1½ inches up each side.

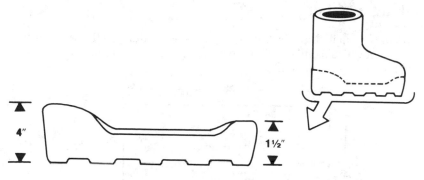

Mukluk upper shell. To make the upper shells of a pair of mukluks, Eskimos use soft leather or canvas. You'll need a 38- by 50-inch piece of heavy, *breathable* cloth that will not absorb moisture. It must not be waterproof. Nylon parapack cloth, heavy dacron, or breathable pack cloth work well and are available at fabric stores and backpacking equipment shops.

In addition, you'll need the following:
- 40 inches of flat ¾-inch nylon webbing cut into 4-inch lengths for lacing cord loops. (Check fabric and upholstery shops, sporting goods stores.)

- 34 feet of woven nylon cord, ⅛ inch in diameter. (Hardware stores.)
- Heavy nylon or acrylic carpet, 4 to 6 pieces, 5 inches by 14 inches, to line the bottom of the sole and serve as removable padding and insulation. Do not use shag carpet. Trim each piece to fit inside the sole. (Furniture stores.)
- 16 brass grommets, size ⅜ inch.
- Grommet setter, for installing grommets.
- Sewing awl and heavy waxed, nylon stitching cord. (Tent and awning stores, hobby shops, BSA Supply Division catalogs.)
- Imitation fur, two pieces, each 6 inches by 24 inches. (Fabric stores.)
- Foam, two pieces each about 2 inches by 22 inches by ½ inch. (Use scraps left from making foam socks).
- 12 cord toggles. Use plastic machine nuts or quarter-size leather disks with a hole punched in the center of each. (Hardware and electrical supply stores.)

Making a Mukluk

1. Using a pencil, draw the mukluk upper shell pattern on the fabric and cut it out. You'll end up with two pieces of cloth, each shaped to serve as the upper of one mukluk.

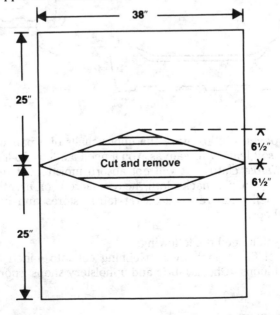

2. Sew a ½-inch hem across the top of each shell.

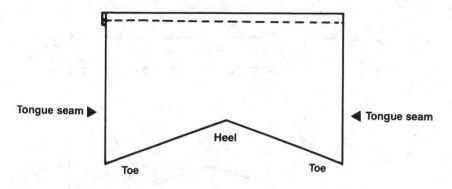

3. Draw the fold lines onto the fabric.

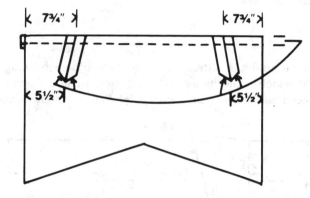

4. Fold the top 1½ inch of the shell fabric away from you and sew it down to form the draw-cord tunnel.

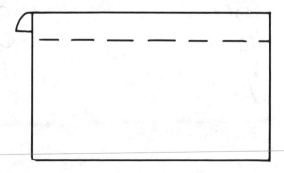

5. Fold and sew the lacing cord eyelet folds.

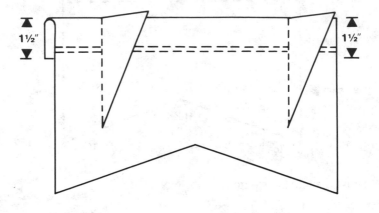

6. With a grommet setter, place a grommet in each lacing cord eyelet fold ¾ inch below the seam of the draw cord tunnel. Space three more grommets below it in each eyelet fold at about 3-inch intervals.

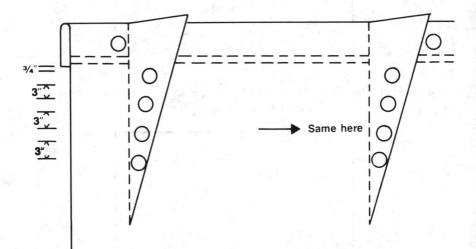

Same here

7. Sew tongue center seam.

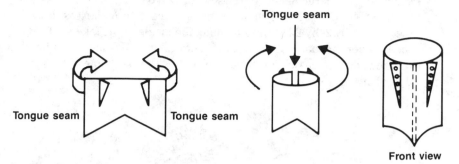

Tongue seam

Tongue seam   Tongue seam

Front view

8. Use the sewing awl to securely stitch five lacing loops to each mukluk sole in the pattern shown below.

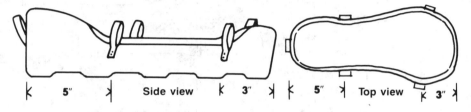

5″   Side view   3″   5″   Top view   3″

9. Stitch the mukluk upper shell to the mukluk sole with the sewing awl, folding the fabric over the edge of the sole as shown below.

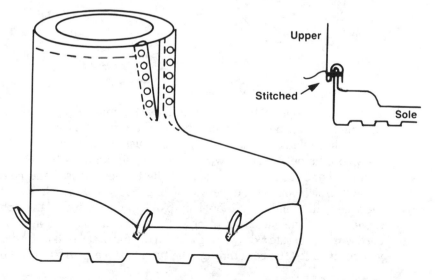

Upper

Stitched

Sole

10. Center and fold a strip of imitation fur over the top of the mukluk shell and use a large needle or the sewing awl to stitch the inside edge to the shell below the stitching of the draw cord tunnel. Next, lay a piece of ½- by 2- by 22-inch foam along the inside of the fake fur. Fold the fur over the foam and over the top of the mukluk shell, and stitch the free edge to the outside of the shell below the stitch line of the top draw cord tunnel.

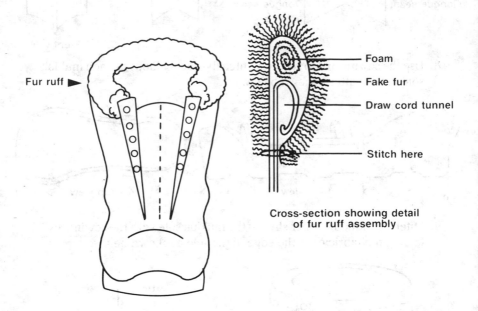

Cross-section showing detail
of fur ruff assembly

11. Take a 3-foot length of flexible wire and twist a small loop in one end. On the inside of the mukluk just ahead of the fake fur, snip a small hole in the mukluk shell fabric so you can push the wire loop into the draw cord tunnel. Work the wire all the way through the tunnel and snip a second hole in the far side of the tunnel opposite the hole through which you pushed the wire. Work the loop of the wire out of the second hole and run a 2-foot length of ⅛-inch nylon cord through the loop. Pull the wire back through the tunnel so that it draws the cord with it to create a drawstring around the top of the mukluk. After you've threaded the cord through the tunnel, slip a cord toggle onto

each end of the cord, then knot the cord to keep the toggles in place and to prevent the cord from being pulled out of the tunnel.

12. Tying up the lacing loops attached to the mukluk sole requires two cords, each 8 feet in length. Tie the end of one cord to lacing loop #1 with a bowline. Run the other end through loop #2, eyelets #3 and #4, through loop #1 again, over the toe, and through loop #5. Attach a cord toggle.

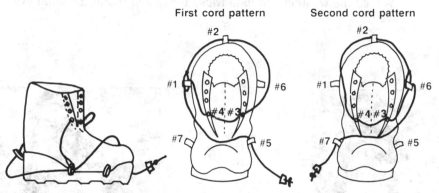

First cord pattern   Second cord pattern

Take the second 8 foot cord and tie it to lacing loop #6. Thread the free end through loop #2, eyelets #4 and #3, loop #6 again, over the toe, and through loop #7. Attach a cord toggle.

13. Finally, take a 7-foot length of cord and lace it through the eight grommets in the eyelet fold. Attach cord toggles to the ends, slip a couple of pieces of carpet into each mukluk to serve as an insole, and you've got a finished mukluk.

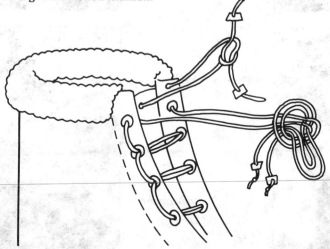

Foam Socks

To insulate your foot inside a mukluk, use a circular piece of 1-inch-thick low-density polyurethane foam 30 inches in diameter. Fold it in half twice, then pull back the top layer. Wearing heavy wool hiking socks or no socks at all, put your foot in place and wrap the foam around it as shown in the accompanying illustrations. Insert your bundled foot into a mukluk, tighten and tie all the lacing cords, and your foot will stay warm no matter how cold the weather. On long trips, unfold and rotate the foam every three days.

◀ 1. Sock flat

2. Folded in half ▶

◀ 3. And in quarters

4. Sock open ▶

◀ 5. Mukluk open

6. Foot and sock
in mukluk ▶

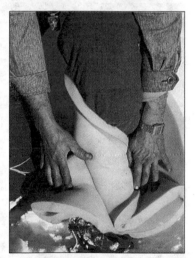

◀ 7. Wrap layer
left against
leg.

8. Next, wrap right ▶

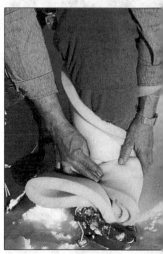

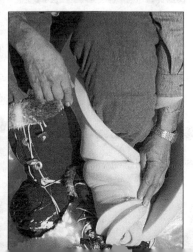

◀ 9. Then left

10. And right ▶

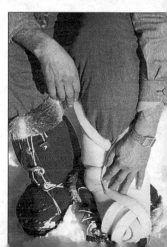

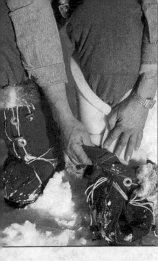

◀11. Pull up mukluk
top.

12. Lace ▶

◀13. Pull tight; tie.

14. Warm from
head to toe ▶

CHAPTER 5

"Camp is usually located in some spot sheltered by hills or rocks for the double purpose of securing the full warmth of the sun's rays, and screening it from the notice of strolling Indians that may happen in its vicinity. Within a convenient proximity to it stands a grove, from which an abundance of dry fuel is procurable when needed, and equally close the ripplings of a watercourse salute the ear with their music."

Rufus Sage, 1846

Chapter

6

Camping Know-How

Joyce Schroeder
Chief Ranger, Philmont
Scout Ranch,
1981–83

Perhaps you've seen a group of experienced backcountry travelers making camp. They chose an ideal site, and with smooth efficiency pitched their tents, prepared a cooking area, stowed their equipment and food, and took care of sanitation needs. Before long, they probably had their supper cooked and their ground beds made. If a storm blew in, they were prepared for it, but they were just as ready to enjoy the blaze of stars in a clear night sky. The next morning they broke camp. After they had left, it was so clean, a clue that they'd ever been there couldn't be found. They made the whole process look easy, but only because they'd taken the time to learn the know-how of camping.

Camping with skill, grace, and ease is one of the most satisfying of outdoor adventures. Lord Baden-Powell realized that, and when he founded the Scouting movement in the early 1900s, he made camping its primary activity. He encouraged everyone to master the art of living outdoors, for he believed that a person able to spend days and nights in the forest would naturally have the confidence to meet the other challenges of life. He was right.

Camping without leaving a trace will draw upon many of your outdoor skills, as well as your knowledge of ecology, weather, and animal behavior. Most of all, you'll need to use common sense as you make decisions in the backcountry. The first of these will be selecting a place to camp.

CHOOSING A CAMPSITE

The right camp location is important not only for your safety and comfort, but also for the protection of the land. In fact, choosing a campsite may have as much to do with the success of a night in the backcountry as anything else you do. While it isn't difficult, site selection does take a keen eye and an understanding of low-impact camping techniques.

In most cases, it's better to use established sites. There's no reason to scar the land with a new campsite if one already exists. Even so, don't assume any site is acceptable until you consider it in light of the following guidelines.

General Location

A campsite facing the south will get more sunlight and generally will be drier than one on the north side of a hill or in the shade of mountains or cliffs. Cold, damp air tends to settle, causing the bottoms of valleys to be cooler and more moist than locations a little higher. On the other hand, hilltops and sharp ridges can be very windy, and may become the targets of lightning strikes.

Size and Shape

A good campsite has plenty of space for your tents and enough room to conduct your activities. It should be usable as it is, so you won't need to do any digging or major rock removal to reshape the area. The less rearranging you do, the easier it will be to leave the site exactly as you found it.

Protection

Consider the direction of the wind and the direction from which storms may come. Is your campsite in the open or is it protected by a hill or a stand of trees? Is there a solitary tree nearby that may attract lightning? Don't camp under dead trees or trees with dead branches that could be blown down in a storm. In the mountains, avoid avalanche chutes.

Access to Water

You can't camp long without water. In some cases, that means hauling all you'll need from home. In the winter, you may be able to melt snow to replenish your water supply, but in other seasons you'll want to make your camp within walking distance of a stream, lake, or river. However, pitch your tents at least 200 feet from the edge of the water and out of the path of runoff. That way there is little chance you'll pollute the fresh water as you cook and wash, you'll be less likely to trample fragile shorelines and stream banks, and you're not apt to be caught by a rising flood.

Insects and Animals

Insects and other animals all have their favorite habitats. The best way to avoid mosquitoes and biting flies is to camp away from marshes, bogs, and pools of stagnant water. Breezes also discourage insects, so you might look for an elevated, open campsite. Don't forget to check around for beehives, hornet nests, and ant mounds. Their inhabitants usually won't bother you as long as you leave them alone, but give them plenty of room. The same goes for most animals. Make your camps away from lairs, dens, and obvious feeding grounds. In grizzly bear country, give a wide berth to areas with signs that bears are frequent visitors, and pitch your tent near plenty of climbable trees.

(For more on dealing with wild animals, see "Outdoor Safety.")

Ground Cover

Any vegetation covering a campsite will receive a lot of wear and tear. Tents will smother it, sleepers will pack it down, and walkers will bruise it with the soles of their shoes. Some ground cover is tough enough to absorb the abuse, but much of it is not. Whenever you can, make your camp on naturally bare earth, gravelly soil, sand, or on ground covered with pine needles or leaves. While grassy meadows may seem inviting locations for camps, set up your tents in the trees at the edges of clearings rather than in the open. You'll have shade and protection from the wind, and meadow vegetation won't be harmed.

Alpine ground cover demands even more consideration. Because of harsh climatic conditions, plants at high altitude often require years to grow even a few inches, and the pressure of boots and tents may cause irreparable damage. Use established sites if you can, or search for a bit of bare soil on which to make your camp.

Drainage

While you'll want a campsite that is relatively flat, it should slope enough to allow rainwater to run off. On the other hand, you don't want to be in the path of natural drainage. Check above the site and be sure you're not in a dry stream bed that could fill during a storm. With a proper location, you'll never have to ditch a tent.

Privacy

One of the pleasures of the backcountry is being away from crowds. Select campsites that are out of sight and sound of trails and other tents. That way you'll have your privacy while you respect the peace and quiet of other campers.

Beauty

The beauty of a spot often is what first attracts visitors to it. Being able to look out from a tent and see towering mountains, glistening lakes, or miles of canyon land or rolling prairie is part of what camping is all about. Find a campsite that gives you spectacular scenery, but use it only if it is appropriate for every other reason, too.

MAKING CAMP

Once you've picked a good site, you're ready to make camp. That usually means establishing places for cooking, sleeping, storing food and gear, and disposing of waste. A good way to start is by erecting your shelter.

Dining Fly

If your group is carrying a dining fly, put it up first. The fly will serve as your kitchen, help determine the layout of the camp, and give you a place to stow the rest of your gear while you pitch your tents.

A dining fly is a tarp that can be erected in a number of ways. One of the easiest is to string it between two trees with rope tied through two grommets. Stake down the back of the fly, then raise the front and tie the corners to other trees, hiking sticks, or to collapsible tent poles you've brought from home. Face the fly away from the wind. If weather conditions change, you can lower a corner or shift a stake to provide

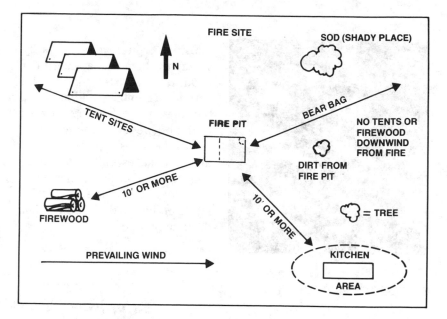

maximum deflection of wind, rain, and snow. When you use a firelay, place it 10 feet in front of the fly—far enough away that sparks won't harm the fabric, yet close enough that cooks can step underneath during a downpour.

(For more on firelays, see "Stoves and Fires." For more on organizing a camp kitchen, see "Trail Menus and Cooking.")

The dining area of a camp may be centrally located, but in bear country it's better to do your cooking and eating 30 or 40 yards downwind from the tents in which you'll sleep. Bears attracted by the odors of food may limit their curiosity to the dining area and leave the tents alone.

Tents

Select a tent site upwind from any firelays and clear it of stones and sticks that could poke through the floor. Don't disturb layers of leaves, pine needles, and humus; they'll improve drainage, soften your bed, and cushion the ground from the impact of your camp.

A tent usually is most stable when its back is aimed into the wind, but there may be reasons to situate it differently. Is there a scenic vista nearby? You might want the door of the tent to open in that direction. Will the first rays of the rising sun reach your camp? There's no better way to wake up than with the warmth of early morning light on your face. The sun also will quickly dry your tent and gear.

You can pitch most tents by spreading them over a waterproof ground cloth, staking out the corners, assembling and inserting the poles, then pulling the guy lines taut and pegging them down. Adjust the ropes and, if necessary, move the stakes until the tent floor and walls are free of wrinkles. Since rain can cause some shrinkage of fabric and cord, don't draw a tent drum-tight.

Bowline

Tautline Hitch

Bowline and Tautline Hitch

Two knots useful for pitching tents are the bowline and tautline hitch. Use the bowline to attach cords and guy lines to the grommets of tents and dining flies, and the tautline to tie lines to stakes. The bowline will never slip, yet it is easy to untie. The tautline is adjustable, allowing you to tighten or loosen the tension on the tent.

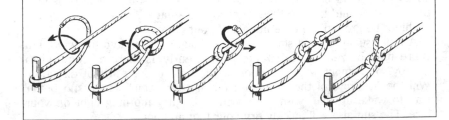

CHAPTER 6

Ground Bed

The sounder you sleep at night in the backcountry, the better you'll feel during the day. For the best possible rest, make a comfortable ground bed.

Experienced campers know that what is underneath them at night is more important in keeping them warm and dry than what's on top. Start with a plastic groundsheet or a tent floor to protect your bed from moisture. Next, put down a layer of insulation. A foam pad is best for year-round use. You can also use layers of newspaper, clean straw, dry grass, or extra clothing. Air mattresses, which won't do much to keep you warm, are all right in the summer, but never cut boughs or strip tree branches to make a bed; there are plenty of better, less harmful alternatives.

Bedroll Layer System

Just as you wear layers of clothing that can be adjusted to meet changing weather conditions, you can set up your bedroll to match night temperatures any time of the year. Start with a good general-use sleeping bag designed to be effective at temperatures of 20°F to 30°F. On warm evenings you can leave the zipper open. If the night is cold, zip the bag to your chin, and if you need more warmth pull on your long underwear and a stocking hat, wool socks, and mittens. Further increase the insulation by lining the inside of your bag with a blanket or two, and on extremely cold nights you can wear insulated booties and put on a parka, or wrap your coat around your hips and thighs.

Sleeping Bag Hints

On dry days, unroll your sleeping bag early so it can fluff up as much as possible. In rainy weather, however, leave the bag in its stuff sack until bedtime so it won't absorb moisture from the air and become damp and clammy. When you're ready to turn in for the night, you can make a pillow by putting some extra clothing in a stuff bag or inside a sweater with the sleeves tied together. To keep your bag clean and yourself comfortable, don't sleep in the clothes you wore all day. Pajamas in the summer and long underwear or a sweatsuit in the winter make good night wear, and a fresh pair of socks will keep your feet warm. If the night is cold, pull a stocking hat down over your ears.

On treks lasting several nights, air your bedding every day the weather is fair. Shake out your bag and blankets and hang them awhile in the sun. Rainstorms have a way of sneaking up on empty campsites, so if you'll be away from your tent during the day put away your bedroll before you leave.

(For more on selecting a sleeping bag, see "Gearing Up.")

Food Storage

Wherever you camp, it's a wise practice between meals to gather your food into a bag and hang it from a tree. Although there may not be a bear within a thousand miles, ground squirrels, mice, raccoons, and dogs can create havoc with unprotected provisions, and if there are bears around, it's extremely important that you get all the "smellables" out of your tent and pack before you bed down for the night.

While there is still plenty of daylight, find a tree with a sturdy horizontal branch about 20 feet above the ground. Tie one end of a 50-foot bear bag line around a rock and toss it over the branch, taking care not to let the stone strike anyone on its way down. Stash your provisions in a sturdy plastic trash bag, or in a burlap or mesh sack lined with plastic, twist it closed and tie it to one end of the line with a clove hitch. Pull the other end to raise the bag until it is beyond the reach of bears that might stand beneath it—at least 12 feet—or that may crawl up the tree trunk and out onto the branch, and secure the cord to a tree.

A second bear-bag technique requires two lines. Toss the end of one over a high branch and tie it to a tree trunk, then toss the other end over a branch of equal height on a tree some distance away. Pull the cord tight and tie that end, too. Next, tie one end of the second line to the food bag, and throw the free end over the center of the line between the trees. Pull the bag into the air and secure the line to the tree, suspending your bear bag far from the reach of prowling animals. Campers who frequently use

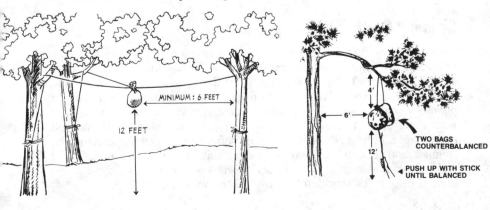

98

this method find that it's easier to pull the bag aloft if they run the bear bag cord through a small pulley attached to the center of the cord strung between the trees.

Bears accustomed to raiding campsites may be smart enough to drop food bags by clawing cords tied to trees. To prevent that from happening divide your provisions equally into two bags. Using a bear rope tossed over a branch, raise one bag in the usual way, then tie the free end of the cord to the second bag. Lift it overhead and use a stick or hiking staff to shove it out of reach. The bags will counterbalance one another, and your food will be safe. To retrieve the bags, use the stick to push one bag even higher, causing the other to come down within your grasp.

Clove Hitch

One of the most widely used knots, a clove hitch is ideal for tying a cord to a bear bag or to a post. Because it passes around an object in only one direction, the hitch puts little strain on rope fibers.

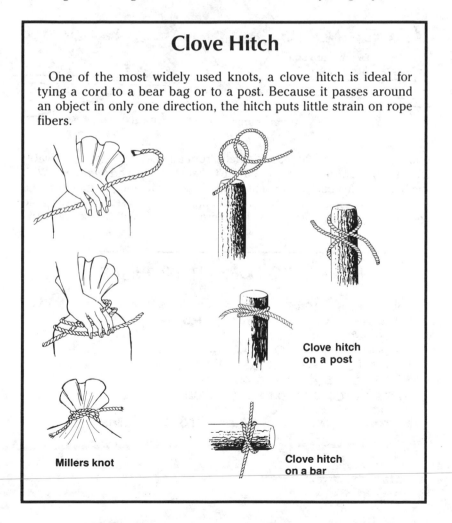

Millers knot

Clove hitch on a post

Clove hitch on a bar

Personal Sanitation

Complete your campsite preparations by making arrangements for waste disposal. If your group is small (no more than five or six) and staying only a night or two at a site, you can each use a cathole to get rid of human waste. A cathole is efficient because the top layer of soil in most areas is full of microorganisms that decompose the remains of plants and animals.

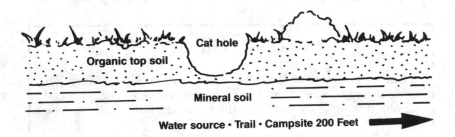

Make each cathole at least 200 feet from any campsite, trail, or water source, and choose a location that isn't likely to be visited by others. With the heel of your boot or a small trowel, dig a hole about 6 inches deep, but no deeper than the rich, organic topsoil. After use, cover the hole completely, and in a few days the microorganisms will break down the waste.

HOW LONG DOES LITTER LAST?

- Aluminum cans — 80 to 100 years
- Vibram soles — 50 to 80 years
- Leather — up to 50 years
- Nylon fabric — 30 to 40 years
- Plastic film — 20 to 30 years
- Plastic bags — 10 to 20 years
- Plastic coated paper containers — 5 years
- Wool socks — 1 to 5 years
- Orange peel — 2 weeks to 5 months

When a larger group goes camping and there are no established toilet facilities, dig a trench latrine. Find a secluded site at least 200 feet from water, trails, and campsites, and dig the pit several feet long, 6 inches wide, and about 6 inches deep. Leave the shovel nearby for each person using the latrine to sprinkle a little soil into the trench to prevent flies from infesting the waste. Should you need a larger trench, dig your pit longer, not deeper. The bacteria essential for decay are only in the top layer of earth.

Bury nothing in a latrine or cathole except human waste. Animals will dig up buried garbage and scatter it around the forest, and materials such as plastic, glass, metal, and cardboard take years to decompose. Take all your trash home with you. If you packed it in, you can pack it out.

Personal Cleanliness

Backcountry cleanliness is important for your health and happiness. While you probably won't wash as frequently as you do at home, you can take a good bath with just a couple of pots of water. Carry them at least 200 feet from springs, lakes, or streams, and give yourself a thorough scrubbing with a washcloth, biodegradable soap, and the water in one pot. Use water from the second pot for rinsing by dipping it out with a cup. In the summer, you can let the water warm in the sun before you use it, while chilly weather may call for heating it over a stove or campfire.

Drinking Water

Purify all water you get in the wild, no matter how clean it appears to be. Some bacteria thrive in remote mountain lakes, and there is no way of knowing what might have fallen into the water upstream.

(For complete instructions on purifying water, see "Outdoor Safety.")

Taking a
bucket bath ▶

BREAKING CAMP

When it's time to go home, there's only one rule governing your departure from a campsite: *Leave no sign you were ever there.*

Break camp by reversing the order of the tasks with which you made it. If you built an open fire, be sure it is cold-out, dismantle the firelay, properly dispose of ashes and mineral soil, and scatter any extra firewood. If you dug a latrine, fill it completely, and neatly replace any sod you removed.

(For more on erasing all traces of a fire, see "Stoves and Fires.")

Next, pack your personal and group gear and, if the weather is bad, stow your pack under the dining fly or in the shelter of a large tree. Brush debris out of your tent, then take it down, roll it tightly, and strap it to your pack. Be sure you've got all the stakes and pole sections. Finally, strike the dining fly and spend a few minutes inspecting the area, picking up every bit of litter. Don't leave until the site is as clean and natural as it was when you arrived.

When You Get Home

After a trek is over, there are still a few things to do. Before you get on with other activities, take time to unpack and put away your gear. Air out your sleeping bag, pad, and blankets. Wash your eating kit and store any unspoiled, leftover food. Clean your share of the group equipment, and return it to storage. If your tent and dining fly are wet, hang them in a basement, a garage, or on a clothesline in the sun until they are dry before you roll and store them. Never put away gear that is wet; mildew can rot and ruin even the finest fabrics.

KEEP A LOGBOOK

As Lewis and Clark explored the vast wilderness that would one day become the western United States, they wrote in their journals the locations of all their encampments, the number of miles they had traveled, and the things they had seen and done. Their logbooks became an invaluable record of their explorations.

You'll want to keep a record of your adventures, too. A wirebound notebook makes a fine log, and so do hardbound blank journals. Within a day or two of every trip, while the memory of the outing is still fresh in your mind, write down the dates of the trek, the names of the participants, where you went, and a summary of the highlights. Soon you'll have a logbook as important to you as Lewis and Clark's was to them.

```
┌──────────────────────────────────────────────────────┐
│                                                        │
│         SAMPLE  LOGBOOK  PAGE                           │
│   Date: _____ Time:_____                     │
│   Companions: _____              │
│   _____               │
│   Weather conditions:_____              │
│   _____               │
│   What we did today:_____              │
│   _____               │
│   _____               │
│   _____               │
│   Personal thoughts:_____              │
│   _____               │
│   _____               │
│   What I will do next time: _____              │
│   _____               │
│   Equipment and supplies to replace or add: ___        │
│   _____               │
│                                                        │
└──────────────────────────────────────────────────────┘
```

FOLLOW UP

Even the best campers can improve their skills. After each adventure, get together with your buddies and discuss what was good about the trip and what could have been better. Were the meals as easy to prepare and as tasty as you had hoped? Did everyone stay dry? Did you take the right equipment and supplies? Was the campsite a good one, and were you able to leave it unmarred? Learn from the successes of each trek as well as the mistakes, and before long you will have mastered the know-how of camping.

"Cold night weighs down the forest bough,
Strange shapes go flitting through the gloom.
But see—a spark, a flame, and now
The wilderness is home!"

Edwin L. Sabin, 1870-1952

Chapter 7

Stoves and Fires

J. W. Shiner, Ph.D.
Chairman, Department of Parks and
Recreation, Slippery Rock University

There was a time when backcountry travelers could build fires wherever they wished. The skill with which they could kindle a blaze was a mark of their woodland expertise, and the fires they created became the centers of their camp activities. They cooked over them, dried wet clothing next to them, warmed themselves near them, and gazed into them long into the night. Few could imagine an evening without a fire, and even so thoughtful a wilderness advocate as Henry David Thoreau saw little wrong with building a bonfire in the Maine woods and leaving the embers glowing as he traveled on.

We live in an age different from Thoreau's. In his day, most of America was wild; today, the opposite is true. Intelligent campers realize that much of the remaining backcountry cannot withstand the impact of unwise camping practices. Of course, there are times when a fire is fine and even desirable, but if it is misused, a campfire can be the most damaging of intrusions on unspoiled land. Fortunately, lightweight stoves provide an ecologically sound alternative to open fires, and the mark of experienced campers has become not just the ability to build wood fires, but also the wisdom to know when not to light one. By considering the advantages and disadvantages of campfires and stoves and then using the heat source most appropriate for a given situation, you'll find that your own outings will be enhanced rather than inhibited.

(For more on protecting the environment, see "Reducing Our Impact.")

CAMPING STOVE

Advantages

- A stove will not scar the earth.
- It burns nothing native to the backcountry.
- It operates reliably under adverse conditions.
- It creates steady heat that won't blacken rocks or cooking gear.
- It is quick and convenient enough to heat a cup of soup at midday.
- It makes travelers self-sufficient, able to camp high on a rocky mountain, deep in a treeless desert, or in the drifts of a snowy forest.

Disadvantages

- A stove requires the handling of flammable liquid or gaseous fuels.
- It must be carried and kept in good working condition.

CHOOSING A STOVE

Of the many stoves on the market, those burning the following fuels are most appropriate for backcountry use.

Kerosene

A hot-burning, nonexplosive fuel, kerosene is available almost everywhere, and it's relatively safe to use. Before it can be lit, a kerosene stove must be pre-heated, usually by squeezing a dab of flammable paste into a depression at the base of the burner stem. As the paste burns, the heat increases the pressure inside the fuel tank, forcing vaporized kerosene up the stem and into the burner where it can be ignited with a match. Once the burner is roaring, it will keep the fuel tank hot enough to maintain a steady supply of vaporized fuel.

Optimus OO ▶
35.9 oz. with fuel

◀ Mountain Safety
Research MSR
Model G/K
39.8 oz. with fuel

The simplicity and reliability of kerosene stoves makes them the choice of many extended mountaineering expeditions. Large kerosene stoves are available for use by groups of more than two or three campers.

White Gas

White gas is a highly distilled fuel used in the majority of North American backpacking stoves. Before being lit, some white gas stoves must be pre-heated. Others are equipped with pumps to pressurize their fuel tanks, a real advantage in cold weather. Keep any open fuel containers far away from open flames, and always let stoves cool completely before bringing white gas near them.

◄Coleman
Peak 1
36.2 oz. with fuel

Svea▶
123R
19.1 oz. with fuel

Butane/Propane

Simplicity, safety, and convenience are advantages of butane and propane cartridge stoves. Employing gaseous fuels stored under pressure in metal containers, cartridge stoves need no preheating; simply attach a cartridge, turn the control knob, and light the burner. Cartridge stoves work well in warm weather and at high altitudes, but they lose efficiency as the temperature drops, especially at lower elevations. Protect spare cannisters from puncturing and heat, and carry empty ones out of the backcountry for proper disposal.

Bleuet stove with fuel cartridge▶
12 oz. without cartridge

Other Fuels

Chemical pellets seldom produce enough sustained heat for real cooking, but they do make good fire starters and can be used to heat small amounts of water for hot drinks.

PACKING AND USING
STOVES AND FUEL

On any but the shortest trips, you'll need more fuel than your stove will hold. Check the manufacturer's guidelines to determine how much fuel you should carry. In cold weather, take half again as much as in warm conditions, and even more if you intend to melt snow for water.

Propane and butane cartridges are ready to go just as they are, while liquid fuels must be stored in special fuel bottles. Use high-quality metal bottles made especially for carrying petroleum fuels, and see that they have tight-fitting lids with gaskets that will prevent leakage. Choose red bottles, or mark them with several strips of bright red embossed plastic tape to prevent any possibility of confusing them with water bottles in either daylight or darkness. Keep fumes from spoiling your provisions by stowing fuel containers and stoves in plastic bags, then storing them in the outside pockets of your pack. You can protect a stove further by rolling it in a piece of foam and securing the bundle with rubber bands.

When you're ready to use your stove, place it on a flat, stable surface that will not be harmed by heat. A smooth rock or a patch of bare ground is all you need. While the stove is still cold, attach a cylinder or fill the tank with fuel. Pouring liquid fuels is easy if you use a small plastic funnel or a special fuel bottle cap with a spout built into it. Store extra fuel far away from the cooking area, then follow the manufacturer's stove lighting

◄ **Pouring liquid fuel into an aluminum funnel**

CHAPTER 7

directions exactly. For quick reference, you may want to protect the instruction sheet with a plastic bag or a clear laminate and keep it with the stove. For winter camping, carry along a 6-inch square of plywood. You'll have a good platform for your stove that will prevent snow and cold ground from drawing heat away from the pressurized fuel tank.

Practice using your stove before you leave home. Every stove exhibits its own peculiar traits, and you don't want to be surprised by the strange habits of your stove when it is dark and sleeting and all you really want is a cup of hot cocoa. Furthermore, if you're well acquainted with your stove, you'll know what spare parts to include in your repair kit and how to use them should the stove break down.

Finally, remember that a stove is a remarkable tool, but one whose temper flares if it is mishandled. Never take a stove for granted; it demands all the respect you can give it. In addition to the guidelines discussed above, keep the following safety rules in mind.

STOVE SAFETY RULES

1. Never use a stove inside or near a tent.

2. Do not open the fuel cap of a hot stove.

3. Never attempt to refuel a hot stove.

4. Let a stove cool completely before you put it away.

5. Even if they are empty, keep fuel bottles and cannisters away from sources of heat.

6. Use chemical stoves only with knowledgeable adult supervision.

OPEN FIRES

Advantages

- An open fire creates heat suitable for cooking food, drying gear, and warming chilly campers.
- It requires no special equipment.
- It allows a cook to bake in dutch ovens and reflector ovens, and to broil foods on grills.
- It provides a psychological lift on cold, stormy days, and it serves as the focus of fellowship and contemplation.

Disadvantages

- A firelay is unsightly and stains rocks with soot.
- Fire poses a potential hazard to the surrounding forest.
- It requires an adequate supply of firewood or charcoal.
- It can be difficult to start and maintain in foul weather.
- In any weather, it takes time to build and feed.
- It blackens pots and pans.
- It is illegal in many parks, forests, and wilderness areas and may be allowed only by permit, especially during periods of drought.

▼ Using a backpacking stove.

CAMPFIRES

Under the right conditions, there is nothing as pleasant as a campfire. Fire comforts us. It draws us toward its warmth and light. It makes us feel more secure. Perhaps there is something basic in our fascination with flames, a flashback to a time when a fire could mean the difference between life and death.

While the ability to kindle a blaze may in rare instances save a life even today, campfires usually are built by choice rather than out of necessity. If the ground cover is fragile, if the forest is dry, if the wind is strong, if wood is scarce, or if there is a chance of creating a new scar on the land, responsible campers will forego open fires and use stoves. However, when the conditions are right and the proper permits have been obtained, they can make a fire just big enough for their needs and then dismantle it so well there won't be the least clue it ever existed.

FIRELAY

Heat can scorch the earth beneath a fire, leaving it barren. A firelay creates an insulating cushion to protect the soil, and helps contain the fire so it will not spread.

The best firelays are permanent ones found in established campsites. These may be stone fireplaces, metal fire rings, or raised grills. If your campsite has such a firelay, use it. There is no need to make a new scar on the land by burning firewood elsewhere.

When you camp away from developed sites, you'll need to build your own firelay. Essential to the process is a good supply of **mineral soil**—silt, clay, and sand that does not contain organic matter that can be harmed by heat. You'll find mineral soil along stream beds and gulleys, on beaches, and in the bottoms of latrine holes.

Choose a site for your firelay that is in the open, away from overhanging tree branches that could ignite and boulders that could be stained with soot. Clear a 10-foot circle of any burnable material, setting aside twigs, pine needles, and dry grass so you can put them back in place when you have finished with your fire; then build a firelay appropriate to the nature of the ground cover.

Pit Firelay

One way to reduce the impact of a campfire is to use a pit firelay. With a shovel or backpacker's trowel, cut a square of sod approximately 1 foot wide and 2 feet long. Work the tool beneath the sod and carefully remove it in several large pieces. Lay the pieces aside and, if the weather is dry, sprinkle them with water to refresh the plant life. Next, remove earth from the pit until you reach mineral soil, piling the extra dirt where it will not be trampled. Build your fire in the lower end of the pit and, when you are done with it, crush the remaining ashes and mix in the soil from the pit's edge. Then replace the sod, mounding it slightly so that over time it will settle into its original position.

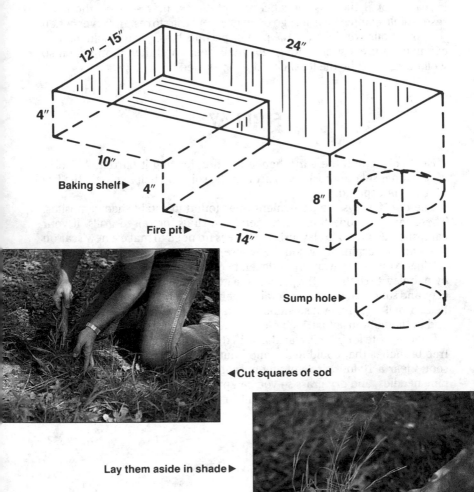

12" – 15"

24"

4"

10"

Baking shelf ▶ 4"

8"

Fire pit ▶ 14"

Sump hole ▶

◀ Cut squares of sod

Lay them aside in shade ▶

Dig the fire pit, sump hole, and baking shelf. ▶

◀ Remove loose mineral soil and square corners.

Build fire for bed of coals. ▶

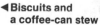

◀ Biscuits and a coffee-can stew

◀ Douse fire, stir, and douse until coals are cold. Return everything to where it was.

Bare Ground Firelay

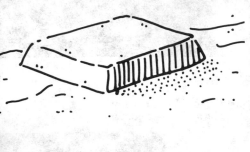

When the ground is bare, haul enough mineral soil to the center of the cleared circle to make an earthen pad about 2 feet long, 2 feet wide, and 3 inches thick. Kindle the fire on top of the pad, and the mineral soil will protect the ground from the heat. After you have properly extinguished the blaze and disposed of unburned wood, crush the remaining ashes, mix them with the mineral soil, and return it to the sites from which you borrowed it.

Flat Rock Firelay

It may seem odd to think that rocks can be damaged by fire, but heat and smoke can discolor rocks, leaving a permanent sign of your passing. If you intend to build a fire on a slab of rock, treat the stone as if it were bare ground. Lay down an insulating pad of mineral soil and keep your fire small. After you remove the firelay, wash the rock with plenty of water to rinse away every trace of soot and ash.

Winter Firelay

Winter conditions present special difficulties for fire builders. Snow and ice can melt under a fire and extinguish it. Frozen ground can thaw and be damaged by heat. Stoves may be the best answer, but if you do need an open fire, build it on a firelay made of sticks 2 or more inches in diameter and several feet long laid side by side on packed snow. When you are done, put out the fire, dismantle the firelay, and scatter charred wood over a wide area.

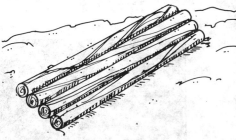

114

◀ Pitch Pine

GATHERING FUEL

Once the firelay is in place, gather a sufficient quantity of wood. You'll need three types.

Tinder

Weed stalks and tops

Tinder is fine, dry material that will burst into flame at the touch of a match. Pine needles, the inner bark of dead branches, weed fluff, dry grasses, abandoned rodent nests, and shavings whittled from a stick all are good sources of tinder. Gather a double handful. Store another double handful in a plastic bag to keep in your pack for an emergency supply. Carefully shave a few pieces of pitch that has oozed from the bark of a conifer. The pitch will flare instantly at the touch of a flame and help ignite your tinder.

(For information on homemade and commercial firestarters, see "Survival Preparedness.")

Kindling

Kindling is material that will burn with a little encouragement. Twigs are the easiest to find. In damp weather you can often find dead twigs that are dry. You can also split open wet logs and cut off pencil-thick lengths of the dry inner wood. You'll need a small armload.

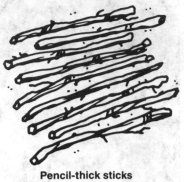

Pencil-thick sticks

Fuel

Fuel is the firewood you'll use to keep your blaze burning. Since you'll want to keep the fire small, you can usually gather all you need without having to use axes and saws. Dry branches lying on the ground are a fine source of fuel. Stack your firewood neatly near the firelay and, if bad weather threatens, protect it with a sheet of plastic or a dining fly.

Every camper has favorites when it comes to kinds of firewood. Hardwoods such as oak, maple, hickory, ash, and apple will burn a long time and make a hot, even bed of coals. Pine, spruce, fir, and other softwoods burn quickly, produce lots of fast heat, and throw off a good deal of smoke and sparks. As a general rule, the heavier a piece of wood, the longer it will burn and the more coals it will produce.

Occasionally, you may find it necessary to fuel your fire with charcoal you've carried to the site. Handle it the same as wood: prepare a firelay, use tinder and kindling to ignite the charcoal, and properly dispose of ashes and unburned briquettes.

CHAPTER 7

Light face from windward side.

Add fuel one piece at a time.

STARTING A FIRE

Loosely arrange your tinder and a handful of kindling in the center of your firelay. Light the tinder and, as it begins to burn, add kindling one piece at a time, taking care not to smother the flames. When the kindling is burning brightly, add larger pieces of fuel wood. Keep an eye on the fire as long as it is burning; never leave it unattended. That's really all there is to starting a fire, though there are dozens of ways to add tinder, kindling, and fuel. Here are two.

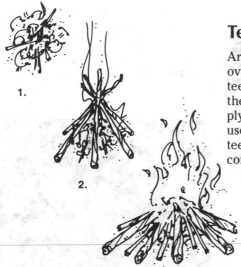

1.

2.

3.

Teepee

Arrange several pieces of kindling over the tinder in the shape of a teepee. Add larger pieces of fuel as the flames rise. When a good supply of glowing coals can be seen, use a stick to collapse the burning teepee and push the embers into a compact bed.

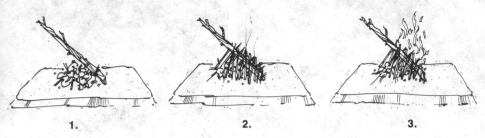

1.   2.   3.

Lean-to

Push a small stick at a 45° angle into the firelay, the upper end of the stick pointing into the wind. Place tinder beneath the stick, light it, and lean kindling against both sides of the stick. When the kindling is burning well, lean sticks of fuel against it. Air blowing into the lean-to will keep the flames growing.

EXTINGUISHING FIRES

The most important part of tending a campfire is what happens to it when you've finished using it. If you properly extinguish the flames and dispose of the ashes and firelay, you can leave the area certain you've done nothing to harm the land.

Put out a fire by sprinkling it with plenty of water, stirring the embers to moisten them thoroughly. Don't stop until the remains of your fire pass the cold-out test, which means you can safely run your hand through the extinguished coals and ashes.

◀Sprinkle with water.

Stir the fire embers. ▶

▲ Sprinkle/stir again and again . . .   until it is cold out. ▲

After the fire is dead out, crush the ashes, mix them with the mineral soil of the firelay, and return the soil to the pit from which it was borrowed. In established, frequently used campsites, you can leave a neat pile of firewood for the next campers to use, but everywhere else you'll want to scatter your extra firewood over a wide area to help remove every sign of your camp.

Finally, replace any ground cover you disturbed, and do whatever else you can to return the fire site to the condition in which you found it.

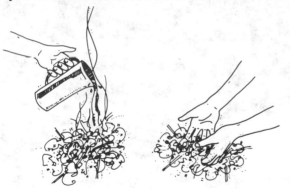

Run your hands through the coals.

Keep working until it feels cold.

A FINAL WORD

The ability to generate heat can enrich your outings, but with fire comes the responsibility to use it wisely. Do your part by carrying a camping stove on all your camping trips and using it whenever an open fire might harm the environment. You'll have the convenience of a stove when you need it, the pleasure of an open fire when you want it, and the satisfaction of always camping cleanly, responsibly, and well.

"We carried coffee, sugar, pork, and beef from home, and ate potatoes three times a day. We had a delightful time, and came home fattened up somewhat; but I will admit that I did not call for potatoes when I got back to my father's table, for some days."

John M. Gould, in his 1877 book,
How to Camp Out

Chapter

8

Trail Menus and Cooking

Donald R. Wilson
Professional Scouter, Los Angeles
Area Council; Former Marketing
Director, National Trail Food
Company; Former Trail Food Buyer,
Philmont Scout Ranch

Donna Cunningham
National Exploring Committee and
Health Food Store Employee

A camp cook stirs a pot of stew bubbling over the flame of a backpacking stove. Climbers hanging on a mountain cliff reach into their pockets for handfuls of fruit, jerky, and trail mix. Horse packers bake biscuits and cobblers in a Dutch oven, and cross-country skiers dig into a tasty, nourishing meal that will help them stay warm through the night.

Anyone who has spent much time in the outdoors knows that eating is one of adventuring's greatest pleasures. Rugged activities whet your appetite, the clean air sharpens your senses of smell and taste, and there's nothing better than chowing down a terrific camp feast. When the going gets tough, a nutritious, stick-to-the-ribs meal will always lift your spirits. Best of all, as you learn to whip up everything from a trailside snack to a four-course backpacker's banquet, you'll discover that preparing food can be almost as much fun as eating it.

PLANNING MENUS

Working out the menus for a backcountry adventure may appear to be a huge effort, but it's really not difficult if you do it one step at a time. First, think through your nutritional needs, the demands of the activities you've planned, the size of your group, and the amount of time you want to spend cooking. Make some notes and you'll see that you've broken the big job of menu planning into a number of small, manageable tasks.

Nutrition

While you'll need to eat more food for some activities and conditions than for others, your basic nutritional needs will always be met if you prepare meals that include a good mix of protein, carbohydrates, fruits and vegetables, dairy products, fats, and water.

Protein. Protein is one of your body's primary building blocks, essential for developing muscles and repairing injuries. Beef, poultry, fish, and eggs are all good sources of protein. If you would rather not eat animal protein, various combinations of grains and legumes or grains and dairy products provide the complete proteins necessary for healthy growth. (Corn and beans are a good example, as are whole-wheat bread and peanut butter, macaroni and cheese, and oatmeal with milk.)

Dairy products are a source of protein. Milk and dairy products supply essential calcium and many important vitamins. Powdered milk is easy to carry, and in addition to drinking it you can add it to puddings, omelets, cereals, biscuit mixes, and soups. Hot cocoa is a winter favorite, morning, noon, and night, and hard cheeses will stay fresh for several days of campout lunches.

Carbohydrates. Whole-grain bread, cereals, rice, and pastas such as noodles, macaroni, and spaghetti provide lots of energy and help fill the empty corners of your stomach. Bake biscuits, muffins, pancakes, and dumplings in camp, or bring crackers and breads from home. (To save space, you can open a bread wrapper and carefully squeeze the air out of the loaf as if it were an accordion. The slices will be thin, but the taste and food value will be unchanged.) Whenever possible, choose products made of unprocessed grains as close as possible to their original forms. The heavy processing necessary to make flour white also removes many important nutrients and much of the roughage essential for good health.

Sugar also is a carbohydrate, one that creates quick rather than lasting energy. Don't rely on sugar for much of your diet, especially in the winter when your body needs plenty of slow-burning fuel.

Vegetables and fruits are complex carbohydrates. Full of vitamins and minerals, vegetables and fruits are essential menu components. Make supper special by wrapping potatoes or apples in foil and baking them in the coals. Dried fruits taste great alone or in pudding and cereal. Many vegetables are dried or canned for convenient transport and storage.

Fats. While many people concerned with controlling their weight may think of them as taboo, fats are an important part of outdoor menus.

Fatty foods such as butter, margarine, nuts, cheese, salami, and bacon slowly release their energy over a long period of time, keeping you warm and energized for hours. You'll want to include more fats in your winter menus than those you use in the summer. Eating a chunk of cheese before you go to bed or drinking a cup of cocoa in which you've melted a pat of butter or margarine will help keep you warm throughout the night.

Water. Water is as essential for good health as any of the food groups. Before you leave your home, find out if there will be abundant sources of water near your camps or if you'll need to carry your water with you. Purify water collected in the backcountry by boiling it, filtering it, or treating it with water purification tablets.

(For more on safe water, see "Outdoor Safety." For more on the importance of water in cold weather, see "Winter Camping.")

Activities

Going backpacking in rugged territory? Get ready to burn lots of calories. Planning to sit on a river bank and fish all day? That bass about to take your lure may more than satisfy your hunger. Crawling into your bag for a cold night at timberline? A big, warm supper in your belly may do more to keep you cozy than any number of extra blankets. Photographing wildlife in the desert? The heat can sap your appetite so much you'll want nothing but a little lunch and plenty of water.

Nutritious food is fuel for the body. The harder your body works, the more fuel it uses and the more food you'll need to eat. Since you probably have a good idea where you'll go on an outing and what you'll do, you can adjust the amounts and kinds of provisions you take so that they meet all your energy needs. Hot weather and easy days mean light meals and little or no cooking, while in the dead of winter, extra fats and carbohydrates will keep you warm. The strenuous efforts of climbing, boating, caving, and skiing demand a steady reserve of carbohydrates and protein augmented by spurts of power from foods full of quick energy. On long treks such as an Appalachian Trail hike lasting several weeks or months, you may need to fortify your diet with special meals to be sure you're getting enough vitamins and minerals.

TRAIL MENUS AND COOKING

Group Size

Most backcountry trips are best undertaken by small groups, so you'll often need only a camp stove, a few utensils, and a couple of pots to prepare meals plentiful enough to satisfy everyone. Groups with more than four or five members may want to split into small cooking teams, each with its own stove, cook kit, and provisions.

FOOD PREPARATION TIME

When you plan to be busy most of the day, you'll want meals that are fast and easy to prepare. In fact, you don't really have to cook at all, for while the warmth of main courses may enhance your eating pleasure, cold food is just as nourishing. Some backpackers occasionally even leave their stoves and cook kits at home and rely completely on foods that can be eaten as they are, and it's always a good idea to carry ready-to-eat foods in case you don't have time to light your stove or build a cook fire. On the other hand, it's great fun to spend a whole afternoon preparing a savory, gourmet feast that will be the highlight of a trek. For long trips, plan some quick menus, and also some that are more involved. You'll have the variety you need to keep eating interesting, and the flexibility to match your meals with your activities.

The elevation and temperature of your camp may also influence cooking times. If it takes 5 minutes to cook an item at sea level, you'll need at least twice as long to cook it at timberline in the Rockies because of the lower boiling temperature of water. Likewise, the colder the weather, the more time you'll spend completing every camp task, including cooking.

Forms of Backcountry Food

A century ago, adventurers had a limited choice of provisions that were compact enough to carry and stable enough to last until they were needed. For the most part, wilderness travelers relied on flour, beans, and jerky or pemmican. Hikers today still carry some dried foods, but modern processing methods have filled the shelves of stores with a vast array of food preserved in an other forms, too.

Fresh. Fresh foods are tasty and nutritious. Many won't keep long without refrigeration, but if you don't mind carrying the weight you can include fresh fruits, vegetables, and some meats in your meals during the first days of a trek. In the winter, fresh stews, soups, and chili will hit the spot. Prepare them at home, freeze them in plastic containers, and carry them to your campsite where they can be stored in a snowbank until you're ready to empty them into pots and slowly thaw them over a stove.

Canned. So many foods are canned that you can build almost any menu around them. The disadvantage is the weight of not only the can and the

Dehydrating Your Own Foods

Commercial processors market hundreds of dehydrated and freeze-dried foods, though you can dehydrate your own meat, fruits, and vegetables in an oven at home. Here's how.

To make beef jerky, slice a pound of lean beef into strips about ¼-inch wide, cutting with the grain. Season the strips with a little salt and pepper, then drape them over the bars of a rack in the oven. Place a cookie sheet underneath to catch any drippings, and leave the oven door open just a crack to let moisture escape. Turn the oven's temperature control to its lowest setting—around 120°—and let the meat dry for about 8 hours until it is shriveled, chewy, and delicious. Seal the jerky in plastic bags and you've got a great addition to your backcountry larder.

You can dehydrate vegetables and fruit in much the same way. Begin with fresh, ripe produce. Wash it well, remove cores and stems, and slice it thinly. Next, break down natural enzymes that could speed deterioration by briefly steaming the fruits and vegetables in a collander or vegetable steamer placed in a large pot containing ½ inch of water. Cover the pot, put it on a burner, and bring the water to a boil. In a few minutes the produce should be limp and ready for oven drying.

To prevent slices of fruits and vegetables from falling through an oven rack, tightly stretch cheesecloth or a tea towel over the rack and secure it with safety pins. Spread the slices on the cloth, then set the oven at its lowest temperature and leave the door ajar, just as you did for making jerky. In 8 hours, sample a few slices. When they are dry but not brittle, pack them in plastic bags. During a trek you can eat them as they are, add them to dishes you are cooking, or soak them a few hours in water to restore their original sizes and shapes.

food it contains, but also the water in which the food is packed. You'll probably want to keep the number of canned foods you use to a minimum, and always take empty cans home for proper disposal.

Dehydrated/freeze-dried. Each of these processes accomplishes the same end—the removal of some or all of the moisture from a food. The result is a product that weighs only a few ounces, won't take up much room in your pack, and won't deteriorate before you're ready to use it. Trail preparation varies from letting dehydrated ham cubes soak overnight to simply adding boiling water to freeze-dried main dishes. The disadvantages of commercially prepared dehydrated and freeze-dried foods are high cost and an occasional loss of nutritional value.

Dry foods. Pastas, flour, beans, popcorn, rice, seeds and other naturally dry foods can be a major part of your camp diet, and so can dried dairy products and meats.

Convenience foods. Every supermarket has dozens of convenience foods that are quick to prepare. Intended primarily for home use, many are also ideal for camp meals. Instant rice, gravy mixes, granola bars, pancake mix, and entrees in flexible metal retort pouches are just a few you may want to use. However, be sure to consider their nutritional values. While many convenience foods are high in nutrients, others are loaded with sugar and salt or so heavily processed they've lost much of their goodness.

Sample Menus

There is no single right way to plan backcountry meals. As long as the food you prepare and eat is nutritionally balanced and there is plenty of it, menus can take any form you like. One good plan looks like this.

Breakfast. Breakfast may be the most important meal of the day. It lays down an energy base to power you along until lunchtime. Skip breakfast, and by mid-morning you'll find you're slowing down.

Every breakfast should contain some fruit, a drink, and a main course. The fruit can be fresh or dried, in juice form, or chopped up and mixed into the main course. On chilly mornings, nothing beats a steaming hot cup of cocoa, though a glass of juice or milk might be more pleasurable in the summer.

The dish you use for a main course depends on how much time you've got to prepare it. If you're eager to get out of camp, a bowl of nutritious homemade granola with nuts and grain will do the job. Cold breakfasts can be convenient, but they must provide enough good food to satisfy the energy needs of hungry campers.

You may want to crank up your stove and cook a pot of hot cereal, or prepare pancakes, hash browns, bacon and eggs, or French toast. During berry season, stir wild fruit into muffin and pancake batters. Scramble fresh, powdered, or freeze-dried eggs, or turn them into omelets full of cheese, onions, and bits of jerky or sausage.

Lunch. As the breakfast calories burn away, recharge yourself with a good lunch. Some adventurers like to sit down at noon and have a meal, while others would rather nibble a few bites of food at each rest break during the activities of morning and afternoon. Try each way and see how your system responds.

If you'll be away from camp, plan foods that need no cooking, though a cup of soup or cocoa tastes great when the wind is cold and sharp. Fill up on whole-grain crackers or bread covered with peanut butter and jelly, cheese, sausage, sardines, or freeze-dried chicken salad, egg salad, or ham salad. Add a little fresh or dried fruit, and you'll be ready for the afternoon.

Dinner. At the end of the day you'll have time to relax and enjoy a good meal. Dinner will give you a chance to catch up on any nutrients your other meals may have lacked, and you'll have the fuel you need to keep you warm during the night.

To begin with, you might want to sip a cup of soup while the main course simmers. There are hundreds of entrees, and thousands of ways to prepare them. Add variety to your dinners by trying various ethnic foods—a Mexican dinner one night, for instance, and an Asian meal the next. Include a vegetable in the main dish or serve it separately, drink plenty of cocoa, milk, juice, or fresh water, and end the meal with a satisfying pudding, cobbler, or other dessert.

Trail snacks. When you are active, you're bound to feel an occasional energy lag between meals. Keep going with a trail snack that's high in

MEAL PLAN	FRESH	CONVENIENCE	CANNED	DRIED	DEHYDRATED FREEZE-DRIED
BREAKFAST Fruit or fruit drink	Fresh fruit	Tang		Dried Fruit	Orange juice crystals
Main course	Fresh Eggs	Oatmeal Wheat Hearts 7-grain cereal Instant Ralston Instant Cereal Instant Breakfast Grapenuts Granola Dry cereal Powdered milk Pancake mix Syrup Brown sugar Margarine			Ham Syrup Bacon bars Sausage patties Hash browns Scrambled eggs Omelets
Hot drink		Cocoa Coffee, instant Tea Hot apple cider			Coffee
LUNCH Crackers	Bread Muffins Bagels	Saltines Wheat Thins Triscuits Wheatsworth Pilot biscuits Rye Krisp, etc.		Trail mix	
Protein spread	Sausage Cheese Monterey jack Cheddar Swiss Edam	Peanut butter Jelly Squeeze cheese Sardines	Deviled meats Corned beef Sardines Sandwich spread	Jerky	Peanut butter Dried jelly Powdered cheese Dehydrated tuna salad, egg salad, or ham salad

energy, easy to carry, and a pleasure to eat. You'll feel better and have more endurance if you avoid excessive amounts of refined sugar. Instead of candy bars, try a trail mix made by combining mixed nuts, unsweetened coconut, and raisins. Eat some fresh or dried fruit. Have a handful of granola, or some honey-sweetened cookies you made at home.

The chart shows a sampling of the foods you can use to fill each of your menu needs, and the forms in which they are available.

MEAL PLAN	FRESH	CONVENIENCE	CANNED	DRIED	DEHYDRATED FREEZE-DRIED
LUNCH Fruit drink Candy and energy foods	Fresh fruit Peanuts Other nuts	Beverage mix Candy bars Caramels M&M's Granola bars Fruit "leather"		Apple Slices Peaches Apricots Banana chips Raisins Dates Pears Figs	Fruit cocktail Peaches Apricots Strawberries Ice cream Apple chips Banana chips Pineapple
DINNER Main course		Quick-cook noodles (Ramen noodles) Minute Rice	Tuna Shrimp Chicken	Beans Lentils etc.	Entrees (as listed in text) Chili Macaroni and cheese Beef Stroganoff Turkey tetrazzini Spaghetti and meatballs Assorted casseroles
Hot drinks		Bouillon Soups, assorted Cocoa Hot tea Coffee Hot apple cider			
Desserts		Custard Instant and cooked puddings Cheesecake mix Cookies Fig Newtons/Oreos		Dried fruit	
Evening Treats	Fruit	Popcorn			

Meal Plans

Here are suggestions for meals that are easy to fix and for meals requiring more involved preparations.

Quick Breakfast: cocoa; dried fruit or juice made from fruit crystals; cold granola cereal with reconstituted powdered milk.

Quick Lunch: fruit drink; crackers; cheese; sardines; dried fruit; nuts.

Quick Dinner: tuna/rice casserole (powdered gravy mix, instant rice, dried peas, canned fish); bread or crackers; instant pudding; cocoa or milk.

Full Breakfast: cocoa; fruit or fruit juice; freeze-dried scrambled eggs with cheese, onion, and summer sausage; hash browns.

Full Lunch: soup; bread; peanut butter; jelly; fresh fruit; nuts.

Full Dinner: beef stew with vegetables (use fresh and/or dehydrated and freeze-dried ingredients); biscuits; peach cobbler; cocoa or milk.

Spices

The tastier your food, the happier you'll be. Enhance the flavor of your meals with spices. Empty 35-millimeter film cannisters make good spice containers, as do empty plastic pill bottles. Label them with masking tape so you'll know what spices are inside, and carry them in a plastic bag. For starters, include salt and pepper, cinnamon, and garlic powder. Use each spice sparingly; if you need more, it's easy to add, but if you put in too much it can't be removed.

PURCHASING FOODS

After you've decided what you would like to eat, studied the recipes, and listed how much of each ingredient you'll need to feed your companions and yourself, you'll be ready to buy provisions. The best place to start is your neighborhood grocery store. There you'll find fresh fruits, vegetables, and meats, and plenty of canned, dried, and convenience foods. Food co-ops, particularly those specializing in health foods, often have extensive offerings of nuts, grains, and honey, while ethnic shops can supply the more exotic ingredients for your special recipes. Back-packing stores and sporting goods outlets usually stock dehydrated and freeze-dried meals packaged especially for hikers and campers, and while the selections can be expensive, they may sometimes be just what you need.

Repackaging Food

Most grocery store food comes sealed in an abundance of cardboard, metal, paper, plastic, and glass. All that packaging is cumbersome, and useless in the backcountry. Eliminate it, and you'll get rid of excess weight as you organize your food for easy transport and preparation. Here's how it's done.

Divide your food supplies into piles, one for each meal you'll prepare during a trek. Next, gather several dozen clear plastic bags of various sizes. Use empty bread wrappers and fruit sacks, freezer and sandwich bags, or storage bags with self-locking closures. You'll also need a few refillable plastic squeeze tubes or a couple of plastic jars with screw-on lids.

Beginning with the first meal of the trip, read every recipe aloud, and as you do so, measure the exact amount of each ingredient that recipe calls for and put it into a plastic bag. For example, you may be planning a quick dinner of tuna/rice casserole, crackers, instant pudding, and cocoa. To feed yourself and three companions, you need 4 cups of instant rice, four 3-oz. packets of gravy mix, and four 6 oz. cans of tuna. Measure the rice into a bag and stow it along with the gravy packets and cans of tuna in a second bag. Write the cooking instructions on a slip of paper:

1. Pour gravy mix into 4 cups cold water.
2. Heat to boiling, stirring frequently.
3. Add tuna and instant rice. Stir.
4. Simmer 3 minutes, seasoning with a little salt and pepper.

Put the instructions into the second bag, and seal it. On masking tape attached to the outside, write DINNER 1—TUNA/RICE CASSEROLE.

For dessert you'll need two 3 oz. packages of instant pudding mix. Open them and pour the contents into a plastic bag. Because most mixes require the addition of milk, pour into the same bag the appropriate quantity of powdered milk (usually about ¼ cup of milk powder per package of pudding). Write the instructions on a slip of paper, and insert it into the bag:

1. Slowly add 4 cups cold water to contents, stirring briskly to break up lumps.
2. Let stand, covered, for an hour.

Seal the bag and label it with masking tape: DINNER 1—PUDDING.

Count out four individual serving packets of cocoa and place them in a bag, then put all the food bags and a box of crackers into a large plastic bag and label it DINNER 1. You'll have the entire meal packaged as a single unit and when you are ready for dinner on the first day in camp, all you need to do is open the large bag and follow the instructions you've enclosed.

Use the same technique to repackage the rest of your provisions, and soon you'll have a neat, easy-to-pack row of bags, each containing all the ingredients for a single meal.

(For information on reprovisioning long treks, see "Backpacking.")

Pots and Pans

As you repackage each meal for a trek, it's a good idea to make a list of all the gear you'll need to prepare the food. Cooking equipment can add a lot of weight to your load, so if you need to travel lightly, select menus that are easy to prepare. Pots and pans that nest together can save space, and so will those that have a number of uses. The items listed here will give you an idea of the variety of equipment from which you can choose.

Natural containers. Did you ever cook an egg in the emptied half of an orange peel, or bake fish and whole potatoes by coating them with mud and burying them in hot coals? You also can bake bread on a split stick, turn a chicken on a spit, and steam shellfish in wet seaweed.

Tin cans. Cans are light, functional, and free. In them, you can boil water, simmer stew, cool pudding, and complete any of a hundred other kitchen tasks. They'll be easier to handle if you attach a wire bail to holes punched through the rim of each can and use hot pot tongs to lift cans onto and off of stoves.

Backpacking cook kit. Many backpacking stoves have cook kits designed especially for them. Sufficiently large for the needs of up to four hungry diners, the pots of each kit nest together for compact carrying. A kit may also contain a windscreen to shield the flame of a stove and to provide a stable base upon which to rest the pots. Some kits contain a donut-hole baking pan.

Camp cook kit. A large crew cooking as a unit may need the capacity of 8-quart pots and large frying pans such as those in cook kits available from Scouting equipment distributors.

(For information on devising your own cooking gear, see "Making Equipment.")

Dutch oven. A cast iron Dutch oven is too heavy to carry on many treks, but in a base camp you can use one to turn out pies, cakes, bread, donuts, cobblers, stews, and chowders. Flip the lid upside down and use it alone as a griddle for hotcakes. In fact, almost anything you can prepare in an oven at home can be prepared in a Dutch oven on the trail.

Iron is a porous metal that needs to be "seasoned" before it's used for cooking. To season a Dutch oven, warm it over a flame, then melt a dab of grease in the bottom and use a clean cloth to spread it over the oven's hot interior. Warm and treat the lid too, and finish the job by wiping off excess grease. The metal will be protected from rusting, and the foods you prepare will cook and taste better. Since soap can strip away grease, reseason any iron pot, pan, or griddle that's been washed with detergent.

Reflector oven. Bake mouth-watering biscuits in a reflector oven. When you have finished, fold the oven flat for easy transport.

Utensils. With the spoon in your mess kit and the knife in your pocket you can complete most kitchen jobs. Mark increments on your drinking cup to show ¼, ⅓, and ½ cup amounts, and use it for measuring liquids, grains, and powders. Depending on the recipes you intend to prepare, you may also need to carry a spatula, ladle, fork, and can opener.

Cooking Routine

When it's time to fix a meal, organize your cooking routine so that everything is done neatly and efficiently. Members of small groups may pitch in and help with every aspect of meal preparation and cleanup while larger groups can divide the responsibilities and, on long treks, rotate the duties daily so everyone has a chance to try each task. In either case, someone must light the stove or fire, get water, do the cooking, and clean up.

Fuel and water crew. Maintains water supply; gets stoves ready for use, or builds a firelay and gathers tinder, kindling, and firewood or charcoal; lights stoves or fires in time for cooks to have meals ready on schedule.

Cook crew. Assembles provisions and follows recipes exactly to serve meals on time; stores food, puts cook pots to soak, and has cleanup water heating before sitting down to eat.

Cleanup crew. Sets up wash and rinse water, cleans cooking pots and utensils; extinguishes stoves and fires and stores equipment; disposes of garbage and trash, then polices kitchen and dining areas.

"God has entrusted us with a beautifully complicated material mechanism known as the human body. This gift carries with it the assumption that we have pride enough in the possession to take care of it and treat it with respect and dignity. Take care of your body by deep breathing, proper food, exercise and positive thinking. There is nothing better in this life than to keep it in good repair and condition through vigorous walking and distance running for the body is the temple of the spirit."

Rudy Fahl, manager of the Pikes Peak Marathon and 80-year-old marathon runner, 1968

Chapter
9

Becoming Fit

William H. King, M.D.
Retired Colonel, United States Air
Force; Staff, Dallas Aerobics
Center, Cooper Clinic

Matt Guidry, Ph.D.
Director, Community Services for the
President's Council on Youth Fitness

W e all know that physical and mental fitness is important for health. Nutritious food, regular exercise, adequate sleep, and the avoidance of tobacco, alcohol, and drugs all contribute to the making of strong bodies and minds. In the backcountry, fitness is especially important. When you're in good shape, you're better able to enjoy wilderness activities. Should an emergency arise, you'll have plenty of reserves of energy from which to draw, and the clear thinking that may mean the difference between success and failure.

No doubt you already spend a good deal of time planning your outdoor activities, readying your gear, and learning Scouting skills. Devote the same energy to preparing your mind and body, and you can develop the physical and mental toughness to see you through most wilderness situations.

PHYSICAL FITNESS

Endurance, strength, and mental alertness are signs of physical well-being, and so is the ability to sleep well, fight off disease, shed stress, and control body weight. However, being fit doesn't mean you must have bulging muscles. A slender cross-country runner may be healthier than a football player twice as large.

Age and genetic makeup contribute a great deal to the general shape and size of your body. Beyond that, however, the way you treat it and the exercise you give it will determine how well your body will work, and for how long. Before beginning any exercise routine, it's a good idea to get a thorough physical exam. Your doctor will give you the green light to undertake reasonable activities, or explain any limitations you must place on yourself. A physician can also help you plan a program for getting into shape.

There are many ways to exercise, and you'll want to find an activity sufficiently appealing for you to stick with it. Regularity is essential to effective exercise. It doesn't really matter how fast or how far you push your body; the important thing is that you do it for 30 to 60 minutes three to five times a week, and that you gradually increase the duration, number of repetitions, and intensity of your exercises. Some people set aside an hour after school for exercising, or get up at the crack of dawn for a morning run. Others fit a workout into their noon hours, or during school physical education periods.

Avoid exercising right after a meal or just before bedtime. Outdoor exercise is best done during daylight hours so you'll be able to see what you're doing. Air temperature is important too; a range of 30°F to 80°F is best for avoiding the problems of excessive cold and heat.

As you develop a routine, include exercises that will improve the ability of your heart, lungs, and circulatory system to supply your cells with oxygen, and exercises that will tone and strengthen the rest of your muscles. One way to do that is by combining aerobic and anaerobic activities.

Aerobic Exercise

Aerobic means "with air," and aerobic exercises are those that require lots of oxygen. Brisk walking, jogging, running, jumping rope, swimming, cycling, and cross-country skiing can be aerobic exercises if you do them for prolonged periods (usually at least 20 minutes or more). They will require your heart to pump great quantities of oxygenated blood to your muscles, and the heart will react to the demands placed upon it by becoming stronger and more efficient. By gradually increasing the intensity and duration of aerobic exercises, you'll cause your circulatory system to continually improve itself. This will improve your cardiovascular (heart and blood vessels) fitness, which is essential to enjoying rugged outdoor activities that require plenty of endurance.

Anaerobic Exercise

Exercises that do not cause the body to burn large amounts of oxygen are called *anaerobic*, which means "without air." These exercises are of brief duration, such as a short dash, pullups, and lifting weights. Well

planned anaerobic exercises can force muscles to work beyond their usual capacity, and they'll respond by becoming stronger. Pullups, situps, leg raises, jumping jacks, and toe raises are good muscle developers, as is participation in many individual and team sports. The key is to engage in strenuous activities on a regular basis at least three times a week. If you exercise less frequently than that, you aren't likely to realize much improvement.

METHODS

Starting out

Trying to do too much in the beginning can cause strained muscles and pulled ligaments, and you don't want that. If you can, have a school physical education teacher or coach help you prepare an exercise program that takes into consideration the current condition of your body. Plan to work out slowly at first so your muscles can adjust to new activities and you can get a feel for how far, fast, and hard you can exercise without hurting yourself. Increase the duration and intensity of your routine gradually, and if you intend to do much running, wear shoes that give your feet adequate cushioning and support.

Warming up

Warming up at the beginning of an exercise session stretches and loosens your muscles and prepares them for action, and gradually raises your heart rate and temperature. The more strenuous the exercise will be, the longer and more vigorous a warmup period you'll need. Sudden, quick bursts of activity such as sprinting and cold weather sports such as hockey require extended warmups.

Many athletes spend 15 minutes or more going through stretching routines. Others don't get much out of stretching, and instead begin a session with slow, easy exercises or a short game of catch. Runners may start by jogging very slowly for a few hundred yards, and gradually increase their speed as they feel their muscles loosening.

As with most routines, the best way to discover whether stretching is right for you is to give it a try. Carefully assume each stretch position and hold it for about 30 seconds. Stretch after you exercise, too, and you may find it increases your flexibility and helps prevent muscle soreness.

Thigh Stretcher

Standing an arm's length from a wall, place your left hand on it for support. Grasp your right ankle with your right hand and pull your foot back until the heel touches your buttocks. Lean forward from your waist as you lift. Hold your foot in position for 30 seconds and repeat stretch with the other hand and foot.

Achilles Tendon and Calf Stretches

Standing about 3 feet from a wall, lean forward placing the palms of your hands flat against it. Keeping your back straight and your heels firmly on the floor, slowly bend your elbows. Hold this position for 30 seconds.

Back Stretcher

Lie on your back with your legs straight and your arms at your sides with palms down. Slowly lift your legs, hips, and lower back and try to touch your toes to the floor behind your head. Keeping your legs straight, hold this position for 30 seconds.

Leg Stretcher

Resting your left hand on your left thigh, grasp the inside of your right foot with your right hand. Keeping your back and legs straight, slowly raise your right leg to a 45° angle from the floor. Hold position for 30 seconds.

Hurdler's Stretch

Sit on the floor with your left leg straight ahead. Bend your right knee so that the sole of your right foot touches the left thigh, forming a triangle. Extend your hands along the straight leg and hold for 30 seconds. Repeat with the other leg.

Straddle Stretch

Sit on the floor and spread your legs about twice shoulder width. Slowly lean forward from your waist, sliding your hands along the floor as far forward as you can. Hold position for 30 seconds.

Return to the starting position. Slowly stretch over your right leg, sliding both hands to your right ankle. Try to keep your knee straight and touch your chin to your right knee cap. Hold position for 30 seconds and repeat stretch with left leg.

Cooling down

At the end of your exercise, keep moving at a slower pace for at least 5 minutes to allow your heart rate and body temperature to decline gradually. Breathe deeply and evenly and let your muscles slowly relax. As with warmups, the more strenuous the exercise, the longer you'll need to cool down.

Exercising

Even after you've warmed up, begin every exercise activity slowly to give your body the time it needs to shift into gear. Drink fluids if you feel thirsty, and don't overextend yourself. Remember, the idea is to get plenty of safe exercise on a regular basis.

Exercises for General Conditioning

Squat thrusts

Flying pushups

Jumping jacks

Body stretches

Aerobic Exercises for Endurance

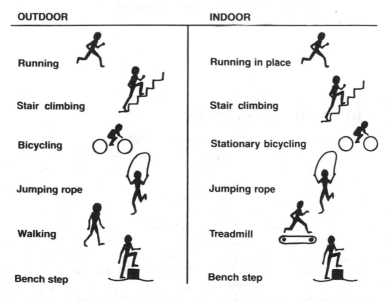

OUTDOOR	INDOOR
Running	Running in place
Stair climbing	Stair climbing
Bicycling	Stationary bicycling
Jumping rope	Jumping rope
Walking	Treadmill
Bench step	Bench step

(Bench step—Step up onto 1-foot-high platform and step down. Repeat.)

Sports for Aerobic Exercise

Cross-country skiing

Swimming

Running

Bicycling

Gymnastics

Aerobic dancing

Walking

Exercises to Improve Physical Skills, Coordination, Balance, and Agility

• Jumping straight ahead, up, down, and with twists
• Rolls and somersaults
• Balance beam maneuvers
• Manipulating a soccer ball with the feet

Exercises to Promote Strength

• Nonresistance exercise—muscles work only against gravity
• Resistance exercise—muscles work against a load
• Isometric exercise—muscles work against immovable objects, such as walls or door frames

Exercises to Prepare for Specific Outdoor Activities

In addition to a general exercise regime that keeps you strong and healthy, you can devise a few special exercises to ready yourself for specific backcountry activities. If you're going on an extended backpacking trip in a month, for example, you may want to swing a loaded pack onto your back and carry it a few miles each day. Wear your boots to school and around home to toughen your feet. Strengthen your hands for rock climbing by squeezing a rubber ball. Take a number of short rides before a wilderness horseback trek to get your legs in shape for long hours in the saddle. Prepare your palms for paddling kayaks and canoes by twisting a dowel rod in your hands. And while you may have to put away your skis and snowshoes for the summer, lots of running, roller skating, and swimming will keep your body ready for action when the first snows fall.

Record Your Workouts

Keep track of when and how you exercise. By writing down the routines you use and the number of repetitions of each exercise, you'll have a record of your physical progress that will give you a sense of accomplishment as it reminds you when to exercise next. Calendars or small notebooks make good record keepers. Write your entries immediately after you exercise.

MENTAL FITNESS

Physical and mental fitness are tightly intertwined. By keeping your body well conditioned, you have done much to assure your ability to think clearly and to concentrate for long periods of time. While we don't often think of exercising our minds in the same rigorous way we do our bodies, there are ways to increase your ability to think clearly under pressure, to develop leadership qualities, and to more fully enjoy the experience of being in the wild. The time may come when alertness, resourcefulness, and mental toughness will get you through a tight spot, but you must prepare for that possibility now, long before the difficult situation arises. Of course, mental fitness is important not just on the trail, but in your everyday life as well. Practice the points discussed below in everything you do—your schoolwork, your jobs, your relationships with others—and you'll find that you're developing a positive attitude, a belief in yourself, and the confidence to overcome hardships.

Be Thorough

When you begin a task, stick with it until it's done and done right. Perseverance is just as essential in finishing a homework assignment as it is for finding shelter in a bad storm, or keeping an accident victim safe and warm until help arrives.

Be Confident

Confidence comes through training and experience. Learn what to expect in the out-of-doors by reading, asking questions, and watching others, then practice your backcountry skills until they become instinctive.

Be Assertive

Wisely take advantage of new experiences. It's important to push yourself beyond what you've done before, but only in reasonable, safe ways. Be assertive around others, too, by taking the lead to get things accomplished. If you see camp tasks that need doing, take the initiative to complete them. If you aren't sure where you are, pull out your map and compass and pinpoint your location. If you believe a river is too swift to cross or a snowfield is too steep to traverse, be assertive enough to turn back and take a safer route.

Be Willing to Learn
From Successes and Failures

Campers with many years of experience in the woods are not necessarily good campers if they've made the same mistakes over and over again. When things go well during a trek, figure out why and try to repeat them. When things go badly, determine what you did wrong in the planning or execution of the trip, and do things differently next time. Every time you go to the woods you can learn something new about living comfortably and safely in the wild outdoors.

Be Conscientious

There aren't many people in the backcountry, and often no one to watch what you are doing. Because of that, your wilderness activities must be guided by your own standards. Camp and hike without leaving a trace, and be ready at all times to help other travelers. Your peace of mind will be your greatest reward.

(For more on mental attitudes on the trail, see "Reducing Our Impact.")

"Be prepared to do that thing the moment the accident does occur. I will explain to you what ought to be done in the different kinds of accidents, and you must practice them as far as possible. But the great thing for you Scouts to bear in mind is that wherever you are, and whatever you are doing, you should think to yourself, 'What accident is likely to occur here?' and, 'What is my duty if it occurs?'"

Baden-Powell, 1908

Chapter 10

Outdoor Safety

Frank S. Lisella, Ph.D., M.P.H.
Chief, Program Development Branch,
Environmental Health Services
Division; Center for Environmental
Health, Atlanta, Georgia

Stan G. Bush
Silver Beaver Scouter; Director of
Emergency Planning Department,
Littleton, Colorado

Paul Petzholdt
Renowned Outdoorsman; Executive
Director, Wilderness Education
Association; Author of *The New
Wilderness Handbook*

A n injury that doesn't happen needs no treatment. An emergency that doesn't occur requires no response. An illness that doesn't develop demands no remedy. Obviously, the best way to stay safe in the outdoors is not to get into trouble in the first place. That requires planning, leadership, and good judgment. As long as you keep your wits about you and clearly consider the consequences of your actions, you'll be able to enjoy even the most remote wilderness areas safely.

Veteran mountain climbers have a saying: "Mountains don't care." What they mean is that the mountains won't look after the safety of those who climb their flanks. But mountains aren't hostile, either. Like rivers, lakes, prairies, beaches, deserts, and your own front yard, they are simply masses of rock, soil, water, and vegetation acted upon by the forces of gravity, precipitation, and weather. They don't willingly cause accidents to happen any more than a roller skate on a step willingly causes someone to fall. The responsibility for your safety, whether you are at home or in the backcountry, rests squarely on your shoulders.

And yet, while concern about safety is important, it needn't become such a worry that it detracts from your enjoyment of a trek. Just as you automatically step around the roller skate on the stairs and then move it out of the way so no one else will fall, you can make outdoor safety awareness a habit.

Preparation

The preparations you make before a trek can do a lot to ensure your safety in the backcountry. Thorough planning means you'll have all the clothing, camping equipment, provisions, and survival gear you'll need. You will have thought through the route you intend to follow, checked weather forecasts, practiced any special skills the outing will demand, and left a complete trip plan with responsible people who will search for you if you are overdue in returning home. Since your chances of getting into difficulties are greatly reduced when you travel with others, you will have at least four people in your group. In short, you'll have done everything you can to foresee and avoid problems before they can occur.

(Many chapters in this book provide important information about getting ready for back-country adventures. For specific discussions on trip preparations, see "Planning," "Gearing Up," and "Where To Go.")

GENERAL SAFETY CONSIDERATIONS

On the Trail

Much of the backcountry is accessible only by trails, and even activities like boating, mountaineering, and caving may require that you spend part of your time portaging or hiking. Accidents are more likely to occur when you are weary, so set a pace that everyone in your group can manage, and plan your itinerary so you won't have to travel after dark. Keeping the group together will make it easier for you to share the pleasures of the trip, and to warn one another of holes in the trail, loose rocks, and low-hanging branches. Use the buddy system while on the trail.

In Camp

You can avoid most camp dangers by choosing your sites carefully. An area with good natural drainage, away from the targets of lightning or the paths of flash floods, sheltered from the wind, and free of dead trees or snags that could fall during a storm is ideal.

(For more on selecting a campsite, see "Camping Know-How.")

CHAPTER 10

The activities you've planned for a trek should make you pleasantly tired by the time you get to camp, though you may want to designate areas away from the campsite for games. That way you'll have a good place to let off excess energy without the danger of tripping over guy lines, firewood, and equipment. Keep the camp tidy and use good sense in handling axes, saws, and knives, and in lighting and maintaining stoves and open fires. Proper storage of food will protect your provisions from insects and animals, and in bear country it will let you get an uninterrupted night's sleep.

(For details on hanging bear bags, see "Camping Know-How.")

SPECIAL SAFETY CONSIDERATIONS

Backcountry conditions pose challenges you'll need to be prepared to meet. While some are present at any time of the year, most can be divided into categories determined by the kind of weather during which they most often occur.

COLD-WEATHER SAFETY

Winter adventures can be exciting, and as long as you are prepared to keep yourself warm, you'll be fine. Layers of wool and insulated clothing, snug shelters, and plenty of high energy food will help you generate and conserve body heat and fight off the major dangers of cold weather—hypothermia and frostbite.

(For more on layering clothing, see "Gearing Up.")

Hypothermia

When a person's body temperature drops too low, the body will no longer be able to warm itself. In effect, the body's furnace has gone out. Conditions need not be extreme for hypothermia to develop. Any combination of cool weather, damp clothing, and wind can bring it on. In fact, most cases occur when air temperature is well above freezing. In wet, cool weather, do all you can to keep yourself and your clothing dry, and prevent the loss of heat through your head by pulling on a warm cap. Keep an eye on your companions and watch for any sign they are becoming too chilly. Shivering, poor coordination, a slow pace, irritability, slurred speech, fatigue, and questionable judgment are all signs of the onset of hypothermia, which, if untreated, can lead to stupor, collapse, and even death. If symptoms do appear, get yourselves warm, dry, and fed as soon as you can.

(For information on treating hypothermia, see "Outdoor First Aid.")

Frostbite

Flesh exposed to low temperatures is in danger of freezing, and the longer the exposure the more damaging the injury. Since they are far from the body's core, toes and fingers are especially susceptible to frost nip, and so are noses, ears, and cheeks. Prevent frost nip and frostbite in cold weather by keeping your skin covered. Mittens will insulate your hands better than gloves. Your boots and the straps of snow shoes and crampons should not bind so tightly that they slow the circulation of blood in your feet. Use a scarf and a warm knit or insulated hat or hood to shield your head and face. As with hypothermia prevention, watch your companions. Warn them if you think they're not taking enough care to protect themselves, and be alert for the first signs of frostbite: stiffness and numbness in a part of the body, and the appearance of a greyish or whitish color on the skin.

(For treatment of frostbite, see "Outdoor First Aid.")

WIND CHILL CHART

Actual Thermometer Reading	Estimated Wind Speed MPH								Danger From Freezing of Exposed Flesh
	5	10	15	20	25	30	35	40	
35°	32°	22°	15°	11°	7°	5°	3°	2°	Some danger
30°	27°	16°	9°	4°	0°	-2°	-4°	-6°	to exposed
25°	21°	10°	2°	-3°	-7°	-10°	-12°	-14°	flesh
20°	16°	4°	-5°	-10°	-15°	-18°	-20°	-21°	
15°	11°	-2°	-11°	-17°	-22°	-25°	-27°	-29°	
10°	6°	-9°	-18°	-25°	-29°	-33°	-35°	-37°	
5°	0°	-15°	-27°	-32°	-36°	-40°	-42°	-45°	Increasing
0°	-5°	-21°	-36°	-39°	-44°	-48°	-49°	-53°	danger to
-5°	-10°	-27°	-40°	-46°	-51°	-55°	-58°	-61°	exposed flesh
-10°	-15°	-33°	-45°	-53°	-59°	-63°	-67°	-69°	
-15°	-20°	-39°	-52°	-60°	-66°	-71°	-74°	-77°	Great danger
-20°	-26°	-46°	-58°	-67°	-74°	-79°	-82°	-85°	to exposed
-25°	-31°	-52°	-65°	-75°	-81°	-87°	-90°	-93°	flesh
-30°	-36°	-58°	-72°	-82°	-88°	-94°	-98°	-100°	

WIND SCALE

**WIND SPEED
MILES PER HOUR**

SMOKE RISES UP   **0**

SMOKE DRIFTS   **1-3**

**LEAVES RUSTLE
FLAGS STIR**   **4-7**

**LEAVES AND
TWIGS MOVE**   **8-12**

**BRANCHES MOVE
FLAGS FLAP**   **13-18**

**SMALL TREES SWAY
FLAGS RIPPLE**   **19-24**

**LARGE BRANCHES
MOVE, FLAGS BEAT**   **25-31**

**WHOLE TREES MOVE
FLAGS EXTEND**   **32-38**

Thin Ice

When the ice on a lake or stream is thick, you can use it as a pathway to territory you can't reach in the summer, and as a playground for skating, skiing, and sledding. However, you'll want to be sure it's safe before you venture onto it, and this old chant about the thickness of ice is a good general guide:

1 inch	No way
2 inches	One may
3 inches	Small groups
4 inches	OK!

The thickness of ice can vary from one part of a body of water to another. It's usually thickest near the shore and thinnest where the water underneath is moving, especially close to springs and the inlets and outlets of lakes. When you have any doubts about the safety of ice, stay on shore. If you feel the ice underneath you giving way, try to get to safety before it breaks. Should someone fall through, throw a rope, reach with a pole, a ski, a branch, or the sleeve of a jacket; or, as a last resort, form a human chain by grasping the wrist of the person ahead of and behind you and then, lying on the ice to distribute your weight, ease out toward your struggling companion. Once ashore, immediately treat the victim for hypothermia.

Carbon Monoxide Poisoning

Odorless and colorless, carbon monoxide is produced during the incomplete burning of wood, coal, charcoal, stove gases, or any other fuel containing carbon. In the open, there is sufficient ventilation to disperse the carbon monoxide produced by a flame before it can create a danger, but a person exposed to carbon monoxide in the confines of a shelter such as a tent, cabin, snow cave, or vehicle may suffer headaches, dizziness, and drowsiness. Extended exposure to the gas can bring on nausea, vomiting, and heart irregularities. Unconsciousness and death may follow.

Preventing carbon monoxide poisoning is simple—keep fires and glowing coals out of enclosed spaces. Do your cooking in the open, and no matter how cold the weather outside, avoid the temptation to bring a fire or heater into your shelter.

HOT-WEATHER SAFETY

When the weather is hot, your body will do all it can to keep itself cool, but if it overheats you can suffer from a number of illnesses including heat exhaustion, sunstroke, dehydration, and sunburn. Avoid these difficulties by preparing yourself for hot weather just as carefully as you do for cold conditions. Regularly drink plenty of liquids to replenish moisture lost through sweat and respiration. Reduce your activities during the heat of the day, staying in the shade and taking it easy, and limiting strenuous events to the cool of the evening and early morning. Wear loose, light-colored clothing that protects your skin from sunburn, and use sunglasses to shield your eyes. Heavy perspiring can deplete your body's minerals, and you may find you feel better if you increase the amount of salt you normally use on your food. However, it's better not to take salt tablets, which may upset your stomach.

WET-WEATHER SAFETY

Staying dry and cheerful during a stretch of rain is a challenge for anyone, yet wet weather brings a strange, misty beauty to the backcountry, and the drum of rain on a tent at night is one of the nicest sounds in camping. However, wet conditions also bring with them a few hazards, and you'll want to be ready to meet them.

Lightning

You won't soon forget the sight of a lightning bolt splitting the mountain sky, or the sound of thunder bouncing off canyon walls. Lightning is as dangerous as it is spectacular, but you can keep yourself safe by knowing when and where it is most likely to strike.

Any time a backcountry storm moves toward you, think about lightning. You may see the clouds coming, you may feel a sudden rush of cold air as the leading edge of a storm front passes overhead, or you may smell ozone in the air as the atmosphere becomes electrically charged. What-

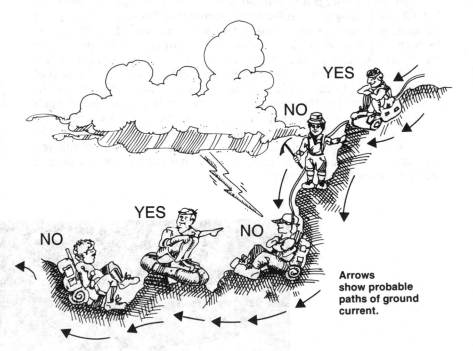

Arrows show probable paths of ground current.

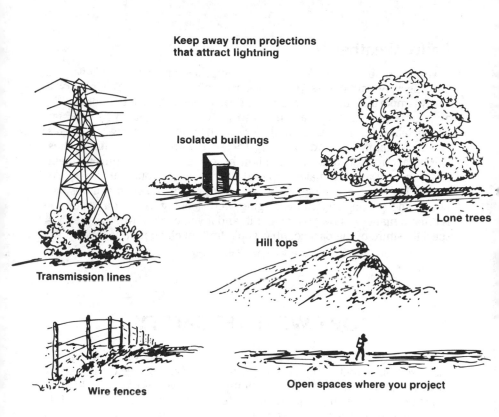

Keep away from projections that attract lightning

Isolated buildings

Lone trees

Transmission lines

Hill tops

Wire fences

Open spaces where you project

ever the signals, take shelter immediately. Lightning tends to hit the highest point in an area, though ground currents may run through fissures in rocks, down wet ropes and damp cracks, and along the surface of the earth. Descend from mountain summits and ridges on the leeward side, get off open water, and stay away from pinnacles and solitary trees. You'll be relatively safe among the shorter trees of a forest, but if a storm moves in too quickly for you to find shelter, drop your pack, remove metal objects from your pockets and belt, and crouch between two boulders or in a dry depression. Insulate yourself from the ground by kneeling on your rolled sleeping bag, a foam pad, or a coiled rope.

Flooding

Choose your campsite carefully so rainwater will drain away from your tents rather than running under them. A dry gully may channel a flash flood several miles—a good reason never to camp in one.

(For more on lightning and flooding, see "Weather." For information on the treatment of a lightning victim, see "Outdoor First Aid.")

Rainy Weather

Wet conditions can make trails and campsites slippery, so you'll want to be especially cautious as you move from place to place. Staying dry is always important, but with good rain gear to wear, a tight tent for shelter, and some plastic trash can liners to protect your gear, you can stay comfortable. Secure your camp before a storm hits, checking tent stakes, stowing equipment, and lowering the windward sides of dining flies. During a long, stormy siege you might have to spend lots of time in a tent, and you may need to make a special effort to keep your spirits high. An interesting book, a small chess board, or a journal can keep you busy for hours, and so can storytelling, singing, and sleeping. Having a good time is often a matter of how you look at it, and if you can see wet weather as a special feature of the backcountry, you'll find much about it to enjoy.

(For tips on taking great wet-weather photographs, see "Outdoor and Nature Photography.")

DRY WEATHER SAFETY

Extremely dry weather presents two dangers—dehydration and the increased likelihood of forest and grass fires. You can avoid the first by drinking plenty of water and reducing your level of exertion to slow moisture loss through perspiration. Protect your lips with a coating of lip balm, moisturize your skin with lotion, and if the weather is hot, be alert for the symptoms of heatstroke and heat exhaustion. You can lessen the danger of wild fires by planning meals that need no cooking, or by cooking over a backcountry stove. Don't light an open fire if there is any chance the sparks will ignite nearby brush, trees, or ground cover.

SAFE WATER

The safest water to use on an outing is that which you carry from home. Always start out with a full water bottle, and when you can replenish your supply from tested public systems, do so.

On adventures of long duration, streams, lakes, springs, and snowfields all are potential sources of water, but be sure to purify all water you get in the wild, no matter how clean it appears to be. Bacteria can thrive in untreated water, and the parasite *Giardia lamblia,* which can cause diarrhea, nausea, and vomiting, thrives in many wilderness lakes and streams.

The surest method of making your water safe is to bring it to a boil, then let it cool. At higher elevations, boil it for several minutes to kill micro organisms because the boiling temperature of water will be lower. If the water is muddy, allow it to stand awhile in a cook pot and the silt will settle to the bottom. Dip the clear water off the top and purify it by boiling. Organic debris can be removed by straining water through a clean bandana.

Available at drug stores and camping supply outlets, water purification tablets will kill most waterborne bacteria. The tablets contain iodine, halazone, or chlorine. Over time they gradually lose their potency, so keep your supply fresh. You also may want to investigate the compact filtering devices now available for backcountry use.

SAFETY AROUND ANIMALS

Animals often will be an exciting part of your adventures. Seeing them in their natural habitats is almost always a pleasure, but it's wise to remember that they are the permanent residents of the backcountry while you are a visitor. Treat them with dignity, give them enough space so they'll not feel threatened by your presence, and they'll seldom present a threat to your safety. However, when an animal feels frightened, threatened, or trapped, it may fight for its life by squirming, biting, and scratching. In the event you are injured by a warm-blooded animal, seek treatment quickly, for a doctor must determine whether rabies treatments will be necessary.

(For information on treating animal bites and scratches, see "Outdoor First Aid.")

Snakes are beneficial members of the animal community, and they normally shun humans. Even in areas with a large snake population, a hiker may walk for days without seeing one. Still, a snake will bite if it is

startled or cornered, so take precautions to prevent that from happening. As you hike and camp, watch where you put your feet and hands. Avoid thick brush, and when you're climbing, don't reach blindly over a ledge.

(For information on treating snakebites, see "Outdoor First Aid.")

When you camp in bear country, protect your camp by keeping your cooking area clean, hanging all your food and "smellables" in a bear bag, and properly disposing of garbage. Fresh bear droppings on a trail should cause you to be alert for the bears themselves. Like other animals, they usually will avoid humans whenever they can, though a bear that is startled or has cubs can be quite dangerous. Whistle, sing, shake a few pebbles in a can, or hang a bell from your pack as you walk through territory inhabited by bears, and they'll give you plenty of leeway.

Include a good insect repellent in your camping and hiking gear to ward off the attacks of mosquitoes, black flies, and "no-see-um's." Repellents containing the chemical N,N-Diethyl-meta-toluamide (also known as DEET) are especially effective. In many parts of the country, you'll want to check your body, hair, and clothing daily for ticks. Wherever bugs are a nuisance you can keep them at bay by tucking the cuffs of your pants into your socks, buttoning your sleeves and collar, and keeping your shirttail tucked in. Adding a mesh head net and canvas or cotton gloves will give you almost total protection. However, if you know you may have a severe allergic reaction to insect stings, be sure you consult your doctor to learn what to do if you are stung. You may need to carry an emergency treatment kit. Let your companions know what to do should you need their help.

(For information on treating animal bites and scratches, see "Outdoor First Aid." For tips on bear-proofing a campsite, see "Camping Know-How." For more on wildlife, see "Wildlife.")

CHAPTER 10

SAFETY AROUND PLANTS

Like animals, vegetation greatly enriches outdoor experiences. Hazardous plants will seldom cause concern for most backcountry travelers, though you will want to be able to recognize irritants such as poison ivy, poison oak, poison sumac, and nettles. When you are with experienced campers who know which plants can spice up a stew and which will make a tasty salad, you can learn plenty about safely selecting and preparing

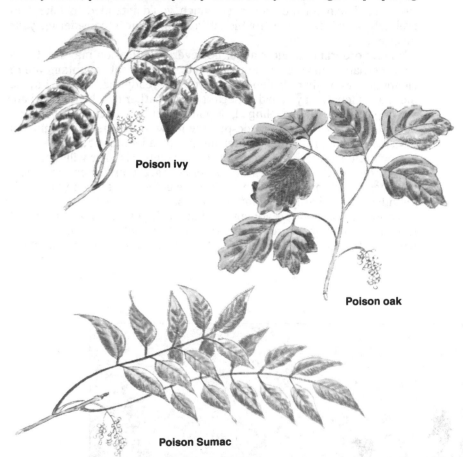

Poison ivy

Poison oak

Poison Sumac

edible vegetation. However, do not eat any wild plants, including mushrooms, unless you are *positive* you know what they are and that they are safe for human consumption.

(For more on vegetation, see "Plants.")

WHEN TO STOP OR TURN BACK

When lightning crackles across the sky, the rocks around you begin to buzz with electricity, and the smell of ozone is heavy in the air, you don't need to be told it's time to abandon your immediate plans to reach a mountain's peak. When you discover that the bridge your trail should have crossed was washed away by a raging torrent, or that a bear has eaten all the food you'd intended to eat for the next 4 days, or that 3 feet of snow has fallen on the pass over which you'd intended to hike, you probably won't have any trouble sitting down and reconsidering your itinerary.

When borderline dangers arise, however, the decision may not be so easy. Perhaps you've become exhausted. Maybe that mountain you're climbing is a tougher challenge than you are ready for. A river may be more turbulent than you had expected. The weather may be turning bad. A companion might be feeling ill, or you may simply be having a miserable time. Should you push on despite the growing adversity? Should you devise a new plan? Should you terminate the adventure altogether and just go home? A mark of wise wilderness travelers is their willingness to stop or turn back if an adventure becomes hazardous, since they know that such a decision can spell the difference between a safe and satisfying outing and a foolhardy flirtation with disaster.

As you're planning an adventure, talk with your companions about situations that might cause you to change or terminate your trip, and don't head for the hills until you agree that you all are willing to stop anytime

backcountry hazards develop, and you will not to be afraid of deciding to alter your activities for the sake of everyone's safety and happiness.

Dangerous situations can develop slowly or quickly, and from just about any source. The fact that they often are unexpected is part of what makes them dangerous. Among the most common are these.

Bad Weather

Weather is the outdoor condition that can vary the most, and thus it can have great effects on your safety. Wind can shred a dining fly, whip waves over a canoe, or make bicycle riding all but impossible. Lightning can drive you off lakes and rivers, and down from mountains. Rain and chilly temperatures bring with them the potential for hypothermia. If you can't keep your clothing and equipment dry and yourself warm and safe, it's time to retreat to an area where you can.

Difficult Terrain

As you plan a trip, you'll find out all you can about the terrain you expect to encounter, but what you see on a map at home and what you see when you're on the trail may differ considerably. The climbs may be steeper and longer than you had anticipated. The trail tread may be rocky or overgrown with brush. You may be tempted to push on, hoping the terrain will ease before long, but to do so invites exhaustion. Don't look on the bright side, look on the realistic side. If the terrain is rugged, shorten the distance you intend to cover each day, choose an alternate trail, or turn back.

Fatigue

Outdoor activities often require quick coordination and sharp thinking. You have neither when you are overly tired, and that increases your susceptibility to injury and illness. Stop when you become weary and refresh yourself with food, relaxation, and sleep.

Darkness

Late afternoon is a time you'll want to be particularly alert to the dangers of overextending your energies. You and your companions probably will be tired from the day's exertions, and if your intended campsite is still several miles away, you may be tempted to rush to reach it before dark. A kayaker might want to try squeezing in one more set of rapids before dusk, while a climber might like to ascend a last pitch or two before going home. Before you press on, though, determine whether you have plenty of time before sunset to complete the activity you're planning, and also to take care of tasks such as making camp and cooking supper, getting ashore and portaging to a road, or rappelling down to the base of a cliff. If not, stop now. The distant camp, the river rapids, and the unclimbed pitch will still be there in the morning.

Rough Water

A boater drifting into water too rough to handle is in trouble. A hiker trying to wade a stream that is too swift and deep may be in for a quick, cold dunking. Use good sense around water, especially cold water, traveling on it or crossing it only when you are sure you can do it safely.

Insufficient Time

An ideal trip plan will include plenty of time for every activity, plus a few hours of leeway in case a crew falls behind schedule or finds additional things to see and do along the way. However, once you've filed a trip plan and noted when you expect to come home, allow ample time to return on schedule. If that means omitting some of your planned activities, then do it. Allow time to meet your deadline without taking risks or becoming exhausted.

Inadequate Food

A group enjoying an outdoor adventure will burn up lots of calories, and they'll need plenty of food to replenish their energies. Going without food is not only uncomfortable, it also can impair a crew's ability to hike, make camp, and keep warm. If your provisions run low, it's time to go home.

Low Morale

When trip goals are not accomplished, when poor judgment of distances and time leads to exhaustion, and when clothing and equipment do not keep a crew warm and dry, morale can collapse. The outdoors is for enjoyment, not for suffering and unhappiness. Rectify the situation if you can, but if not, consider abandoning the trek and trying again after conditions improve.

"Doctor Whitman extracted an iron arrow, three inches long, from the back of Captain (James) Bridger, which was received in a skirmish three years before with the Blackfeet Indians. It was a difficult operation because the arrow was hooked at the point by striking a large bone and a cartilaginous substance had grown around it. The doctor pursued the operation with great self-possession and perseverance; and his patient manifested equal firmness."

Doctor Parker, 1835

Outdoor First Aid

Stan G. Bush
Silver Beaver Scouter, Director,
Emergency Planning Department,
Littleton, Colorado

The rugged nature of outdoor activities makes it likely that you'll suffer a minor scrape or bruise now and then, or pick up a blister or a mild case of sunburn. Most injuries in the backcountry are not very troublesome, and soap, water, and a bandage or two will take care of most medical problems you'll encounter. However, the complications posed by more serious injuries are magnified by the distance from professional medical help. Miles up a trail or down a river, high on a mountain or deep in a cave, you must rely on yourself and your companions for emergency first aid.

PREVENTION AND PLANNING

Carefully plan and conduct your treks, and you can avoid most hazards. Still, unexpected circumstances may arise that cause injury or illness. Prepare for them by learning first aid techniques before you need them. Study first aid textbooks and pamphlets. Sign up for emergency medical courses offered by the Boy Scouts of America, the Red Cross, and other trained groups, and practice first aid methods with your friends, parents, and members of your Boy Scout troop, Varsity Scout team, or Explorer post.

(For more on preventing injuries, see "Planning" and "Outdoor Safety.")

First Aid Resources

During a backcountry emergency, your first aid training will be your most valuable tool, but your resources are seldom limited to only the knowledge in your head. You can use your tent, ground cloth, hiking stick, pocketknife, clothing, and anything else within reach. You can fashion a splint out of a tree branch or a piece of cardboard, and rip up a shirt to make bandages. You can draw on your camping experience to improvise a shelter, kindle a fire, purify water, and prepare hot meals. Keep your wits about you, and you can figure out ways to surmount almost any backcountry problems.

(For more on improvising in the backcountry, see "Survival Preparedness.")

A sure way to supplement your emergency training is to carry a first aid kit on all your adventures. A good, basic kit should contain the following items.

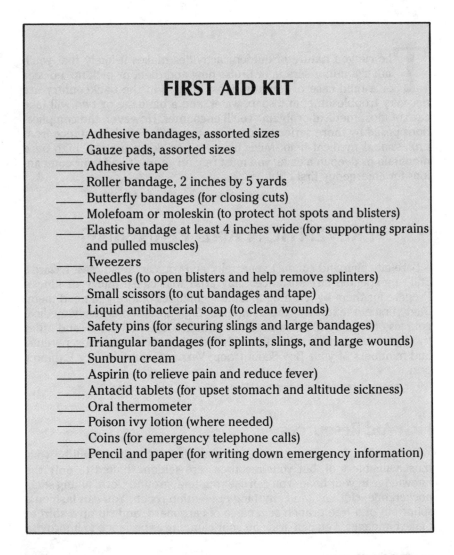

FIRST AID KIT

____ Adhesive bandages, assorted sizes
____ Gauze pads, assorted sizes
____ Adhesive tape
____ Roller bandage, 2 inches by 5 yards
____ Butterfly bandages (for closing cuts)
____ Molefoam or moleskin (to protect hot spots and blisters)
____ Elastic bandage at least 4 inches wide (for supporting sprains and pulled muscles)
____ Tweezers
____ Needles (to open blisters and help remove splinters)
____ Small scissors (to cut bandages and tape)
____ Liquid antibacterial soap (to clean wounds)
____ Safety pins (for securing slings and large bandages)
____ Triangular bandages (for splints, slings, and large wounds)
____ Sunburn cream
____ Aspirin (to relieve pain and reduce fever)
____ Antacid tablets (for upset stomach and altitude sickness)
____ Oral thermometer
____ Poison ivy lotion (where needed)
____ Coins (for emergency telephone calls)
____ Pencil and paper (for writing down emergency information)

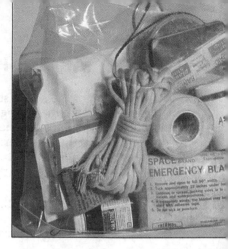

Pack your medical supplies in a small metal or plastic box with a snug lid, or in the compartments of a nylon kit that can be rolled into a bundle. Stow the first aid kit in an outside pocket of your pack, and be sure everyone in your crew knows where to find it.

(For instructions on making a nylon first aid kit, see "Making Equipment.")

Although your travels may take you far from roads, there is still a large network of people ready to assist you during an emergency if you can alert them to your needs. As you plan a trek, take time to identify and learn how to contact search and rescue teams and medical personnel, as well as public officials or private landowners whose knowledge of the area into which you are traveling could prove useful should you run into trouble. Pinpoint the locations of the nearest roads and telephones, and think through a course of action you would take to get help.

Handling Backcountry First Aid Emergencies

When someone is injured or ill, you'll naturally want to assure that person's safety and ease discomfort by using proper first aid methods. However, do only those things you have been trained to do. Well-intentioned but faulty handling of injury victims may do them more harm than good, which is all the more reason to get plenty of training and practice before you need it.

Despite the chaos that can exist during a medical emergency, there is a tried and true sequence of actions to take that will give a victim every possible chance to survive the ordeal and recover from an injury. This section describes that sequence. Later in the chapter, you'll find more detailed information on specific first aid techniques.

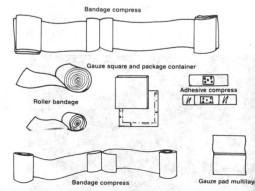

Bandage compress

Gauze square and package container

Roller bandage

Adhesive compress

Bandage compress

Gauze pad multilayer

C.A.U.S.E. P.ATIENT C.ARE

The key letters of the seven steps for handling backcountry first aid emergencies make up the saying, "CAUSE Patient Care." Memorize the steps, practice them until they become automatic, and in an emergency follow them in exactly this order:

C—Take charge

A—Approach safely

U—Urgent treatment

S—Shock treatment

E—Examine thoroughly

P—Plan a course of action

C—Carry out your plan

C—Take Charge

The scene of even a minor accident often is confusing, and when serious injuries occur the confusion may be compounded many times. The hazard that caused the accident may still pose a threat. The sight of blood, broken bones, and vomit can sicken rescuers. The number and extent of injuries may seem overwhelming, and rescuers as well as victims are likely to experience panic, revulsion, and fear. What every accident scene needs are calm and rational decisions on the part of those able to help victims. That means someone must take charge.

At the beginning of a trek, many crews appoint a first aid leader trained in emergency procedures and respected by the others in the group. Should an accident occur, the leader can evaluate the situation, determine what needs to be done, and direct the rescue efforts of the crew. When you are alone or in a group without an assigned leader, take command with quiet confidence. A calm, authoritative voice and a clear plan of action

◄ Taking charge

BACKCOUNTRY INJURY OR ILLNESS REPORT FORM

Full name of injured person _____
   Address _____
   Phone _____
Age _____ Sex _____ Height _____ Weight _____
Emergency contact
   Name _____
   Address _____
   Phone _____
Exact location of injured person marked on a map and a
description of how to get there: _____
_____
_____

Detailed description of symptoms or injury:
   What are the patient's complaints? Describe as to
   severity, location, duration, and previous occurrence.
_____
_____
_____
_____

Pulse _____ Temperature _____
Respiration rate _____

Describe cuts and burns as to extent and severity. Is the patient
   conscious, unconscious; hot, cold; breathing quickly, slowly,
   shallowly, deeply? Is the patient pale, flushed, sweating,
   clammy? Has any bleeding been stopped?
_____
_____
_____
_____
_____

Describe treatment given:
_____
_____
_____
_____

NOTE: Give this report to medical and/or rescue personnel.
      Also record subsequent treatment given to patient.

will do much to reassure your companions and raise the spirits of those injured. When other crew members also have a good grounding in first aid methods, you can assign each a specific rescue task, but hold yourself in reserve if you can, watching the big picture and making sure everything is done properly.

A—Approach Safely

Nothing complicates a backcountry emergency more than having rescuers also become injured. While your initial instinct upon seeing an accident may be to rush to the victim's side, your first duty after taking charge of the situation is to study the location of, and quickly determine how best to reach, the injured person. Perhaps a hiker has slipped off a trail and tumbled partway down a mountainside. Will you also be in danger of falling if you hurry directly down the slope? Coming from above, could you dislodge rocks that might roll onto the victim? Should you set up a rappel rope? Would it be better to descend by a safe route and approach the accident scene from below? Consider your own safety as well as that of the victim, and don't aggravate the situation by being injured yourself.

If a victim's location threatens his safety—he's fallen into a stream or is at the foot of an unstable boulder field or ice fall—it may be necessary to move him to a safer location before first-aid treatment can begin. A group of rescuers can gather around the victim, lift him in the same position in which they found him, carry him to safety, and gently put him down. Take special care to prevent the victim's neck from moving by holding his head before, during, and after an emergency move.

U—Urgent Treatment

Breathing, Beating, Bleeding—those are your primary concerns as soon as you reach a victim. If the person is not breathing, the heart is not beating, or there's severe bleeding, death may be only a few minutes away unless you administer treatment. Determine what aid is necessary by making a rapid, hands-on survey of the victim. As you feel for the pulse in the neck, place your ear next to the mouth and nose to listen for the rush of air, your head turned so you can watch for the chest's rise and fall. That done, run your hands over the body from head to toe in search of severe bleeding and serious injuries. With practice, you can conduct this initial survey very quickly.

If the victim is not breathing, administer mouth-to-mouth artificial respiration, and if the heart also has stopped, use cardiopulmonary resuscitation (CPR). Stop serious bleeding with pressure on pressure points and on the wounds themselves. Since you cannot yet know the extent of any neck or spinal injuries, don't move the victim unless the body position makes it

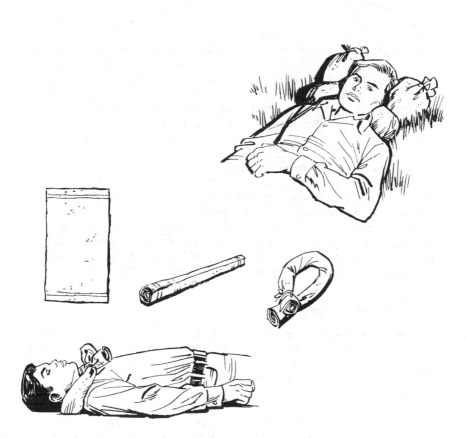

impossible to perform urgent first aid. Even then, keep movement to an absolute minimum.

Urgent treatment also includes immobilizing the neck and head to prevent fractured vertebrae from damaging the spinal cord. One member of a rescue party can hold the victim's head and provide just enough traction to keep the neck in proper alignment. As soon as other urgent treatment has been completed, stabilize the victim's head and neck with a collar made of a towel, sleeping pad, or articles of clothing, or with padded objects placed on either side of the head.

S—Shock

Once life-threatening dangers have passed, treat EVERY accident victim for shock. Make the person as comfortable as possible, warm, safe, and calm. It is natural for an injured person to be frightened, panicky, delirious, or despairing, so keep someone with the casualty at all times to monitor physical and emotional condition, hold a hand, converse, and give reassurance. Curiously enough, someone who appears to be unconscious may be able to hear and understand nearby conversations, and will respond positively to tender loving care. NEVER leave a victim alone. The condition of someone with serious injuries can change quickly. Even when an accident victim is mobile and seems to be fine, shock may set in later. The person may be dazed enough to wander away. Rescuers discussing the seriousness of an injury should do so only out of the victim's earshot.

An accident victim's physical condition can be affected by fear and isolation. Talk to the victim all the time, even if he is unconscious. Let him know that he is going to be all right. If your rescue team is large enough, assign one person to provide constant reassurance to the victim.

Crew members not involved in administering first aid can help greatly by setting up tents, preparing hot drinks and meals, and establishing a comfortable camp. As a first aid leader, you'll need to keep an eye on the rescuers as well as the rescued and see that they stay safe, warm, and dry.

E—Examine Thoroughly

After you've dealt with urgent conditions and treated for shock, the victim should be stabilized enough for you to conduct a thorough hands-on examination. The object is to learn everything you can about the person's physical condition and determine the appropriate treatment for the injuries you find. Completing a thorough exam may take 30 minutes or more, but it can be time well spent.

Begin the exam at the head, slowly running your fingertips over the skull in search of anything that feels unusual. Look in the ears for signs of blood or spinal fluid, and check the eyes for dilated or unmatched pupils. Without allowing the head to move, feel the vertebrae of the neck and note any jagged edges or sense of grating in the bones—signs of a possible broken neck.

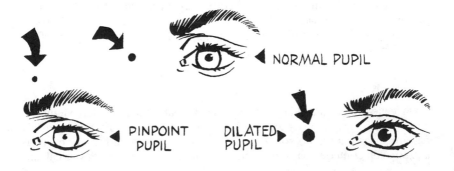

NORMAL PUPIL

PINPOINT PUPIL

DILATED PUPIL

CHAPTER 11

The head and neck done, slide your hands down the torso and arms, always squeezing firmly so you can feel broken bones. A groan from the victim will alert you to possible injuries. Be sure to get your hands under clothing and make your examination at skin level; you'll be more likely to feel closed fractures, and you won't be fooled by synthetic clothing that can trap and hide blood flowing from lacerations.

With patience and care, work your hand under the victim and feel all the vertebrae of the spine for anything out of the ordinary. If the person is conscious, push against each of the hands and feet, asking for resistance to the pressure. If the victim can do that and if there was nothing in your examination of the spine or in the nature of the accident to suggest a fracture, you can feel fairly confident about allowing the injured person to move or be transported without damaging the spinal cord.

Continue your examination by pressing on the abdomen in search of swelling or irregularities that could indicate internal bleeding. Check the buttocks, then test for fractures by firmly pushing together the sides of the pelvis, and then squeezing along the length of each leg with enough pressure to feel through heavy thigh and calf muscles. Finally, slip off each boot and inspect the ankles and feet for fractures or cuts.

P—Plan a Course of Action

After the complete examination, you'll be able to treat any remaining injuries and determine what you should do next. In many cases, you'll need to send for help. Carrying someone down a trail is difficult, exhausting work, and trained rescuers will want to have from 18 to 24 litter bearers on hand to transport each victim.

Your plan of action may require you to care for the victim of a backcountry accident for an hour, a day, or perhaps even overnight. If the victim is conscious, keep him well hydrated with sips of water. Provide shelter for someone who cannot be easily moved by cutting a slit in the floor of a tent and setting it up over the victim.

(For more on transporting injured persons, see "Wilderness Search and Rescue.")

C—Carry Out Your Plan

When you must summon aid, assess your options and carefully decide how it should be done and who should go. Perhaps it is late evening, the victim is resting comfortably and is out of danger; there's no reason for crew members to rush off into the darkness. On the other hand, if the person's condition is deteriorating, or there are injuries beyond your ability to manage, a life may depend on getting help quickly.

Ideally, at least two crew members will go for help. Before they leave, have them write down all relevant information, using as a guide the letters L-I-F-E.

> **L**—Location of the victim, which should be pinpointed on a map if possible
> **I** —Injury or illness suffered
> **F**—First aid you have given and what still needs to be done
> **E**—Equipment needed for rescue and equipment you have at the accident site

The messengers must know where they are going, how to contact help, and where to lead rescuers. They may want to mark the way with pieces of foil, brightly colored surveying ribbon, or strips of clothing.

TREATING OUTDOOR INJURIES

In addition to a thorough grounding in basic first aid techniques, you'll want to know how to handle the emergencies you're most likely to face while in the backcountry.

Stopped Breathing

Near-drowning, lightning strikes, blows to the head, falls, the smoke of a forest fire—there are many outdoor hazards that can cause a person to stop breathing. Except for rare cases of people immersed in very cold water, no one can live more than a few minutes without oxygen. You'll need to breathe for an accident victim until the person is able to breathe normally or until trained medics arrive.

If the victim is lying face up, place your thumbs beneath the chin and lift, tilting the head back so that the jaw drops. If the injured person is lying in some other position, you may still be able to administer mouth-to-

TONGUE BLOCKING
AIR PASSAGE

HEAD TILTED
BACK TO CLEAR
AIR PASSAGE

Blow in and the chest rises.   **Turn head and listen for escaping air.**

mouth resuscitation, but if not, you may have to risk complicating a spinal injury and alter the body position just enough to perform artificial respiration.

Clear the mouth of any foreign material, then pinch the nostrils closed. Using a mouth-barrier device to prevent direct contact with body fluids, seal your mouth tightly over the victim's, and blow until the chest rises. Turn your head to one side and listen for an exhaled breath. Breathe again into the victim's mouth, repeating the procedure a dozen times a minute. DON'T GIVE UP! You may be able to keep a person alive for a long time this way.

If the chest does not rise as you breathe into the mouth, check the air passages, reposition the head, and try again. If you still have no luck, apply four glancing blows to the back with the heel of your hand. Should that fail, use four abdominal thrusts. Sweep deep into the mouth and throat with two fingers, dislodging any obstructions.

When the victim revives, treat for shock and stay close in case breathing stops again.

Cardiopulmonary Resuscitation

In severe accidents and heart attacks, the heart may stop along with the ability to breathe. You'll need to circulate the blood as well as do the breathing.

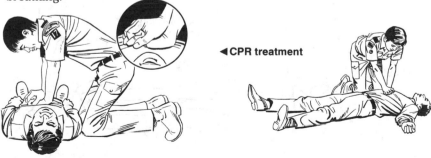

◀CPR treatment

Cardiopulmonary resuscitation, or CPR, is a rescue procedure every person should master, whether a backcountry traveler or not. Reading about it is not enough; you need to learn and practice CPR under the guidance of trained instructors, and take occasional refresher courses to keep your rescue reflexes sharp. In a CPR course, you'll discover how to combine artificial respiration with chest compressions in a ratio that may keep someone alive until medical help arrives. You'll practice CPR on special lifelike mannequins so that when an emergency does arise, you will know exactly what to do. However, as with most first aid techniques, you must learn CPR *before* you need to use it.

Bleeding

Heavy bleeding can kill in a short time, making this an urgent emergency. Stop the flow of profuse bleeding by firmly pressing a large bandage, handkerchief, shirt, or other padding directly over the wound. You can further slow the rush of blood by elevating bleeding limbs, and by using the flat parts of your fingers or the heel of your palm to press on the pressure points in the victim's groin, armpits, or neck. Hold bandages in place with strips torn from a shirt or with other wide bands of cloth tied snugly but not so tightly that they impede circulation.

Tourniquets should be used only when a limb is severed or so badly mangled you cannot stop profuse bleeding any other way. Make a tourniquet out of a wide strip of cloth, never cord, wire, or any other thin material. Tie the strip with an overhand knot above the wound; place a stick, tent peg, or whatever else you can grab on the knot, and tie it down with a square knot. Twist it just until the bleeding stops, then secure the stick so the tourniquet won't come loose. Write the time on the victim's forehead, and do not adjust or remove the tourniquet unless a physician authorizes it.

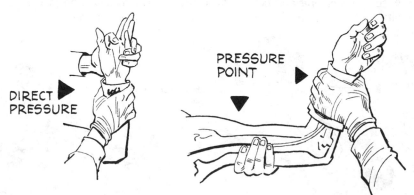

DIRECT PRESSURE

PRESSURE POINT

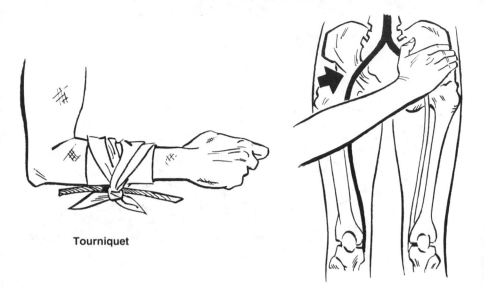

Tourniquet

Poisoning

The chances of being poisoned while on an outing are probably not as great as they are at home, since there are simply fewer poisonous substances to ingest. However, poisonings do occur. An unwise hiker may eat toxic berries or mushrooms, or confuse fuel and water bottles and swallow a mouthful of stove gas. Whatever the case, treatment must be swift and accurate. Find out what was swallowed by asking or, if the victim can't speak, by looking for evidence such as a medicine bottle, nearby vegetation, or an open fuel container. If there is a telephone nearby, immediately call a hospital, physician, or poison control center. Describe the symptoms and the suspected poison, and then follow instructions exactly. When you are far from help, you may need to act on your own to treat the victim for poisoning, and stand by to give mouth-to-mouth resuscitation should breathing stop.

Petroleum products and corrosive substances. When the poison is gasoline, kerosene, lighter fluid, or an acid or strong lye, do not induce vomiting. Instead, dilute the poison with plenty of milk or water.

Noncorrosive substances. When the poison is one that won't burn delicate tissues—wild mushrooms, for instance—give the victim several cups of salty water and induce vomiting by touching a spoon to the back of the throat. Have the person bend over far enough to prevent any vomit from getting into the lungs, and save some of the vomitus to help the doctor with a diagnosis. Give the victim more water and induce vomiting again.

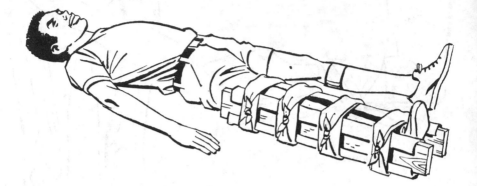

Broken Bones

The basic first aid for broken bones is to immobilize fractures until they can be treated by medical professionals. A person with a simple fracture that has been splinted may be able to travel out of the backcountry under his own power. When injuries involve the bones of the back, neck, or head, those areas should be immobilized to avoid further damage to the spinal cord or brain, and the victim should be kept still until trained medical help arrives.

How to identify a fracture. Broken bones usually are quite painful. During your hands-on examination, a victim will probably groan and flinch when you apply pressure near a fracture. The flesh around the fracture may be swollen and discolored, and the victim may have difficulty moving the affected area.

How to treat a fracture. Begin by determining whether the fracture is closed (the skin is not broken) or open (the skin is broken). Stop severe bleeding from an open fracture and bandage the wound. Next, position the injured area so the victim suffers as little discomfort as possible. Apply splints to prevent the fractured bones from moving. Use sticks, folded cardboard, hiking staffs, tent poles, or any other long, sturdy materials to fashion the splints you need. Secure them with wide strips of cloth tied so that they do not impede circulation. Treat for shock and keep the victim comfortable until help arrives.

Shock

When a person is injured or under great stress, the cardiovascular system may not be able to circulate enough blood to maintain normal bodily functions. The condition is called shock, and it can strike the victim of any accident or emotional trauma. Shock may develop soon after the injury has occurred, or it may not appear until minutes or even hours later. Sometimes shock is more dangerous than the injuries that brought it on, and in severe cases it can cause death.

How to spot it. A person suffering from shock may be cold, may shiver, and may have cold, clammy skin pale in color. Breathing could be shallow, and there may be vomiting. On the other hand, there may be few obvious signs that shock is setting in.

How to treat it. Treat every accident victim for shock, even if there are no definite symptoms. Since shock is sometimes a delayed reaction to an accident, prompt treatment may prevent it from occurring at all. Be especially alert when rescuers arrive, since the relief a victim feels may give shock a chance to take hold.

Keep the person lying down. Unless there are head injuries, elevate the legs slightly to increase the flow of blood to the head. Put an insulated pad underneath, and wrap the person in a sleeping bag, jackets, or rescue blanket for warmth. Be sure you have correctly treated any wounds. If the victim is about to vomit, roll him on his side to prevent choking, and keep his air passages open. Obtain a physician's care as soon as possible.

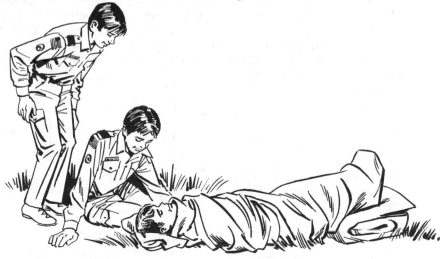

Lacerations

Direct pressure on a wound will stop most bleeding. However, dirt and debris can enter any break in the skin and cause infection that may become a more serious threat than the original injury. By thoroughly cleansing a laceration (physicians call this "debriding a wound") you can greatly enhance its chances of healing well. This is especially important if circumstances prevent quick access to a physician.

First, be sure you've treated for shock and the victim has become stable and calm. Explain what you intend to do and the reasons for it so your actions will not come as a surprise.

Wash your hands, then get some sterile gauze or a few clean scraps of wool, and plenty of clear water. Of course, sterile water would be ideal, but you're not likely to find that at an accident scene. Just use the cleanest you have. For best results, put the water into a container from which you can squirt a steady stream—a bota bag works well. In a pinch you can modify a plastic bag from your food supplies by pricking a small hole in one corner, filling the bag with water, twisting the top closed, and then applying enough pressure to force a jet of water from the hole.

Gently pull the sides of the wound apart and quickly clean away debris and dead tissue by flushing the area with a stream of water and swabbing it with gauze or wool. Use plenty of water—"the solution to pollution is dilution"—and in just a few moments you'll have a relatively clean wound. The process of debridement can restart the bleeding, but it shouldn't be difficult to stop by placing a sterile gauze pad over the cut and applying direct pressure.

Physicians use stitches to hold together the edges of a wound and assure prompt healing. In the backcountry you can close wounds with tape rather than needle and thread. Simply draw the sides of the cut together and secure them with tape—butterfly bandages, sterile wound-closure strips, or regular adhesive tape. If the injury is on a flexible part of the body—an elbow or a knee, for instance—apply a splint to immobilize the joint and prevent the wound from coming open. Cover the laceration with a clean bandage and monitor the progress of the healing. Even very severe wounds will heal nicely in a few weeks.

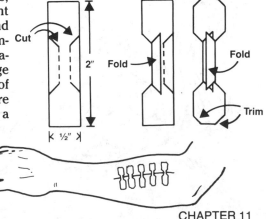

AILMENTS CAUSED BY COLD

Hypothermia

Hypo means "a lack of." Thermia means "heat." Hypothermia occurs when a person's body core temperature drops so low that it is no longer possible to keep warm. In effect, the body's furnace goes out. Conditions need not be extreme for hypothermia to develop. Any combination of cool weather and damp clothing, wind, exhaustion, or hunger can bring it on. In fact, most cases occur when air temperature is well above freezing.

How to spot it. In order to function well, the brain must stay warm. As the body begins to cool, the victim will shiver in an attempt to create heat. Other symptoms may include irritability and, as the temperature of the brain begins to drop, disorientation, sleepiness, and incoherence. The ability to make clear judgments will be impaired, perhaps causing a victim to push on long after conditions dictate turning back. As the person becomes even colder, shivering will stop, followed by a slip into unconsciousness, and perhaps death.

Since it first affects the ability to think clearly, hypothermia is as sneaky as it is dangerous. Someone beginning to suffer from its effects may have no idea there is any danger, and, in growing confusion, may reject any suggestions to stop and get warm. When you are outdoors in cool, damp, or cold weather, use the *hypothermia challenge* to determine if you or others in your crew are in danger. Here's how it works.

If you suspect that another member of your group is acting strangely, you can challenge your companion to walk a 30-foot line scratched on the ground. It's a test similar to that used by police officers to check the sobriety of suspected drunken drivers. If a hiker can walk heel-to-toe the length of the line without difficulty, hypothermia is still not a problem. However, if there is unsteadiness, loss of balance, or other signs of disorientation, see that your companion gets warm and dry even if the person protests. Everyone in the crew must pass the hypothermia challenge before you travel on.

How to treat it. Rewarming and preventing further heat loss is the answer. In mild cases you can move the victim into the shelter of a building or tent, remove wet clothing, and zip the person into a sleeping bag until body temperature warms to normal. Make sure the head is covered with a warm hat or the sleeping bag hood. Give hot drinks and soup, if possible.

In more severe cases, you'll have to take more active steps to warm the victim's body. Get the person into a shelter and into a sleeping bag, ideally a dou-

183

ble-size bag made by zipping together two single bags. Crawl into the bag with your companion, and then strip the clothing from both of you. The effort of removing damp clothes will help you generate body heat, and the bag will protect you both from the cold outside. If the bag is large enough, have a third person crawl inside and strip down, too. Skin against skin, the heat of your bodies can rewarm the victim and perhaps save a life.

Frostbite

Flesh exposed to low temperatures is in danger of freezing, and the longer the exposure the more damaging the injury. Far from the body's core, toes and fingers are especially susceptible to frostbite, and so are noses, ears, and cheeks.

How to spot it. As flesh freezes, it may become painful and then numb, though sometimes the victim is not aware the injury is occurring. If the freezing continues, the area will stiffen and become grayish or whitish in color.

How to treat it. Get the affected area warm and keep it warm. In the field, thaw fingers by holding them beneath your clothes and under your armpits. Press a bare palm over a frosted nose, ears, or cheeks. If you can get to shelter, place cold feet on a companion's bare belly, or immerse frozen areas in lukewarm water. DO NOT use hot water or hold the injury close to a hot stove or open fire. DO NOT rub it with snow. Excessive heat and abrasion can seriously damage tissues already made tender by the cold.

A mountaineer or hiker whose feet have become badly frozen miles from help may need to delay thawing the injury. In desperate survival situations it's possible to walk on frozen feet; once they've been warmed, however, further travel will be impossible.

**Backcountry weather ▶
can be frigid.**

Snow Blindness

How to spot it. Eyes exposed to the bright glare of sunlight on snow-fields and glaciers can become red and sore. The victim may suffer headaches, and eyes can swell and feel as if they are full of sand.

How to treat it. Darkness is the antidote for snow blindness. Keep the victim in a dark shelter and lay cool, damp cloths over the eyes. In severe cases, recovery may take several days.

INJURIES CAUSED BY HEAT

Hyper means "excessive," and thermia means "heat". Hyperthermia occurs when the body becomes overheated. It can take a variety of forms, including heat exhaustion and heatstroke.

Heat Exhaustion

How to spot it. Heat exhaustion occurs when the body's cooling mechanisms have failed; a type of shock occurs. The core temperature may rise a few degrees Fahrenheit and the victim's skin will be moist, but it may be either warm or cool. The patient may act strangely and feel faint and/or nauseous.

How to treat it. Have the victim lie down and slightly elevate his feet. Move the person to the shade, cool by fanning, and let him rehydrate by sipping water to which a pinch of salt has been added. Recovery is usually rapid; though, if conditions persist, consult a physician.

Heat Stroke

Less common than heat exhaustion, heat stroke is much more serious. The body's cooling mechanisms become so overworked they simply stop functioning. As a result, the victim's temperature soars, becoming life-threatening.

How to spot it. The skin will be hot, red, and dry, and disorientation may become apparent. Breathing is labored and noisy, and the pulse weak and rapid.

How to treat it. You must cool the victim immediately, perhaps with a dip in a lake or stream. If there is none nearby, lay the person in the shade, soak clothing with water, and drape bare skin with wet cloths. When your companion is able to drink, give all the water wanted. Treat for shock and obtain the care of a physician.

Burns

Burns are not unusual backcountry mishaps, but fortunately they are most often minor—a spark from a campfire landing on the skin, for instance. However, the possibility of severe burns does exist. A pot of boiling macaroni may spill on a cook's foot, a stove might flare, the sun can fry unprotected skin.

How to spot them. Mild burns cause a painful reddening of the skin. More serious burns raise blisters. The most severe burns char layers of skin and flesh.

How to treat them. First, here's what NOT to do: don't treat any burns with jellies, creams, greases, or sprays. In many cases they impede healing, and once applied, they are very difficult to remove. (An exception is mild sunburn, which may respond well to specially formulated lotions.)

Relieve the pain of mild burns without broken skin by applying ice packs or damp, cold cloths, or dipping them in cool water. Do not break any blisters. Let the affected area air dry, then cover it with a loose bandage.

Protect a serious burn by draping it with a clean, damp cloth. Treat for shock, and if the victim is able to drink, give lots of milk or water. Obtain medical attention as soon as possible.

OTHER OUTDOOR EMERGENCIES

Altitude Sickness

Some people find that exertion in the thin air of high mountains upsets their systems. Fortunately, the sickness usually is more miserable than dangerous, and it seldom develops below 8,000 feet. However, if you or a companion begins coughing, breathing becomes labored and noisy, and pulse quickens, get down the mountain quickly.

How to spot it. The victim may have a headache, feel a lack of energy, or loss of appetite, and become nauseous.

How to treat it. The only practical remedy is a descent to a lower elevation. The symptoms should soon disappear.

Blisters

Blisters develop when skin is irritated, usually by friction or heat. For outdoor travelers, blisters on the feet are the most common and troublesome. You can help prevent blisters from forming by keeping your feet dry and clean, using foot powder, wearing properly fitted boots, and frequently changing your socks.

(For tips on choosing appropriate footwear, see "Gearing Up.")

How to treat them. A "hot spot" on your foot signals the beginning of a blister. Stop immediately and reinforce the tender area by cutting a hole the size of the hot spot in a piece of moleskin or molefoam and using it to encircle the potential blister. Use the same procedure to take the pressure off blisters that do form, building up several layers of moleskin or molefoam if necessary.

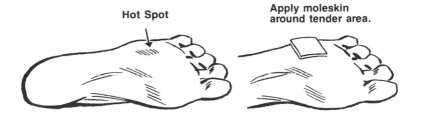

Hot Spot

Apply moleskin around tender area.

You may find that you'll be able to hike more comfortably if you drain a blister. Thoroughly wash your foot with soap and water, then prick the edge of the blister with a needle you've sterilized in a flame and press out the fluid. Protect the wound as you would a hot spot, taking care not to stick adhesive bandages directly to the injury.

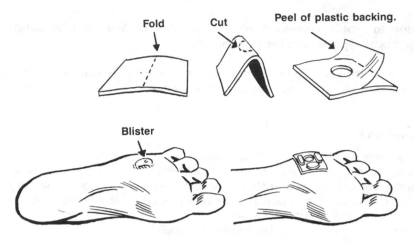

Fold   Cut   Peel of plastic backing.

Blister

Add strips of moleskin to
raise level of padding
around blister.

Sprained Ankle

Twist your ankle and you're likely to strain ligaments and injure muscles, especially if you are carrying a heavy pack. Slight sprains cause only mild discomfort, but in serious cases you could be temporarily disabled. Prevent sprains by wearing good boots and by watching where you step, especially as you cross boulder fields, logs, and streams.

How to treat. If you suffer a sprain, don't take off your boot. Swelling around the ankle may make it impossible for you to put your boot back on once you've removed it. Reinforce your ankle by wrapping it, boot and all, with a bandanna, elastic bandage, or Scout neckerchief, and you may be able to hike back to camp or to a road.

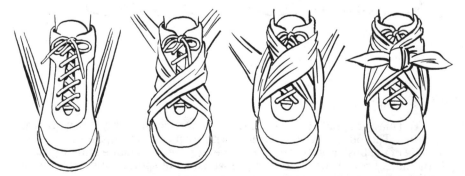

Mammal Bites and Scratches

Injuries inflicted by mammals should be washed thoroughly with soap and water, treated for bleeding, and protected with a bandage. Then you MUST see a physician, who can decide whether to administer rabies shots.

Insect Bites and Stings

The bites of mosquitoes, chiggers, and no-see-ums are irritating but not usually dangerous. Potentially more troublesome are ticks, which bury their heads beneath the skin. If a tick gets a good hold on you, coat its body with grease or oil to close its breathing pores. In half an hour you should be able to ease it loose with tweezers. Wash the area well.

More painful and sometimes dangerous are the stings of bees, wasps, hornets, and some ants. Remove a stinger by scraping it out with a knife blade; squeezing it with tweezers or fingernails will force more poison into the skin. Some people suffer severe adverse reactions to insect stings, and should carry special treatment kits prescribed by a physician. They should explain to others in the crew the nature of the allergy, how it is to be treated, and where to find the kit in an emergency.

Bites of black widow spiders and brown recluse spiders and stings of scorpions are rare but serious. Get the victim to a doctor.

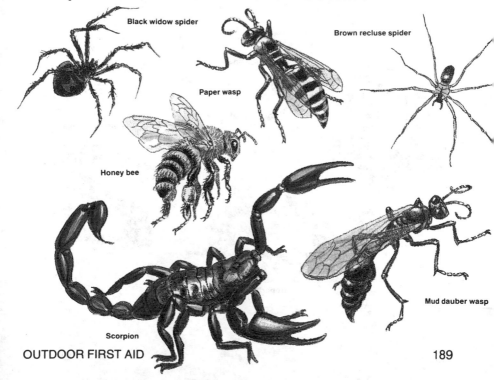

Black widow spider

Brown recluse spider

Paper wasp

Honey bee

Mud dauber wasp

Scorpion

Snakebite

Snakes prefer to avoid contact with humans. They will seldom strike at a person unless they feel threatened. Only about one- fifth of all snakebites in the United States are caused by poisonous snakes, and of those, the snakes do not always inject venom into their victims.

Leave snakes alone, and you aren't likely to be bitten. Don't reach over blind ledges, and avoid the temptation to poke your hands or feet into hollow logs, old woodpiles, and crevices in rocks.

The most common North American poisonous snakes are pit vipers (rattlesnakes, copperheads, water moccasins, and cottonmouths). Recognizable by distinctive pits in front of their eyes, pit vipers use long, curved fangs to inject venom. Coral snakes have black noses and body markings consisting of red and yellow bands side by side, separated by bands of black. They inject a venom that suppresses the nervous systems of their victims, while the toxin in pit viper venom disrupts circulatory systems.

Reactions to snake venom vary greatly, depending on a person's size, the location of the bite, the kind of snake, and the amount of venom injected. Pain, swelling, skin discoloration, nausea, shallow breathing, blurred vision, and shock are all possible, though not necessarily probable.

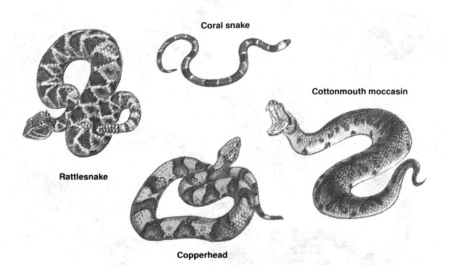

Coral snake

Cottonmouth moccasin

Rattlesnake

Copperhead

CHAPTER 11

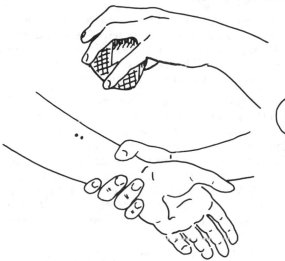
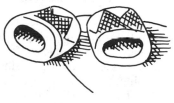

Snakebite cannot be treated in the field. Get the victim to a medical facility as soon as possible so that physicians can administer snake antivenom and monitor the victim's condition. A snakebite victim may be able to walk to a trailhead where transportation is available. If the bite may result in swelling of the hand or arm, remove rings and wristwatches.

First-aid manuals long described making cuts over the fang marks and then sucking blood and venom from the wounds. Current research has shown that cutting is of little value. The danger of severing blood vessels, nerves, and tendons outweighs almost any beneficial effects of making incisions. An instrument called the Sawyer Extractor, which applies suction without the need of cuts, can remove a significant amount of venom if it is used within 3–5 minutes of the snakebite.

Poisonous Plants

Poison ivy, poison oak, poison sumac, and stinging nettles can make a backcountry traveler miserable. If you come in contact with irritating plants, wash the affected skin with soap and water and, if you have it, sponge the area with denatured alcohol. Clothing that has touched poisonous plants can irritate your skin, so remove it carefully.

Emergency Evacuation Litter

Since carrying an injured person can be a difficult and exhausting task, search and rescue litter teams normally are composed of several dozen members. However, an emergency evacuation litter may allow a small crew to carry a stabilized victim out of the backcountry.

(For a full discussion of search and rescue evacuations, see "Wilderness Search and Rescue.")

Begin making the litter by laying down two 16-foot poles, each 3 to 5 inches in diameter, parallel to one another. Lash a couple of pack frames between the poles to form the litter platform, and pad it with foam pads and a sleeping bag. Position the first frame about 3 feet from the end of the litter poles. Lash a third frame perpendicular to the poles 1 or 2 feet from what will be the front of the litter, and a fourth frame perpendicular to the poles 1 or 2 feet from the back. This will leave 4 to 5 feet between the back frame and the platform so the rear litter bearer will be able to see obstacles in the path. The shoulder straps of the frames must face forward, and the lashings must be secure.

Gently lay the victim, zipped in a sleeping bag, on the litter platform. If you have them, use wide strips of webbing or torn cloth to tie the victim to the litter.

Pack Frame Litter

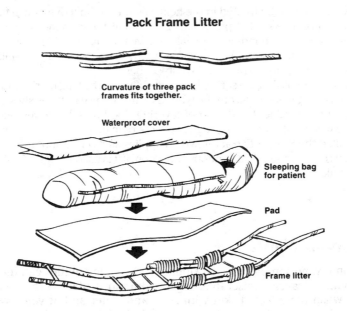

Curvature of three pack frames fits together.

Waterproof cover

Sleeping bag for patient

Pad

Frame litter

Pole and Frame Litter

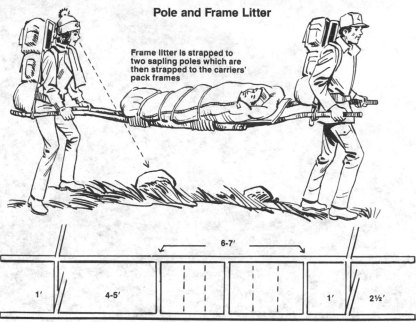

Frame litter is strapped to two sapling poles which are then strapped to the carriers' pack frames

6-7'

1' 4-5' 1' 2½'

16' pole 3-5" in diameter

The first two litter bearers position themselves and, with the help of all the members of the crew, lift the litter high enough off the ground for them to slip their arms through the shoulder straps of the upright frames. The bearers should be able to carry the litter without too much strain.

Since the litter is narrow, it is ideal for use on hiking trails. Furthermore, the length of the poles provides places for group members other than the bearers to grab on and help carry the weight during stream crossings, up steep embankments, and over rough terrain. To prevent anyone from becoming overly tired, switch bearers frequently. Constantly monitor the victim, and stop the evacuation if changes in the injured person's condition warrant it.

"The worst thing you can do is to get frightened. The truly dangerous enemy is not the cold or the hunger, so much as the fear. It robs the wanderer of his judgment and of his limb power; it is fear that turns the passing experience into a final tragedy . . . Keep cool and all will be well . . . Use what you have, where you are, right now."

Ernest Thompson Seton, 1906

Chapter 12

Survival Preparedness

Robert Brown
Executive Director, American Outdoor
Safety League

Every day of our lives, we are engaged in surviving. Continually, we need air to breathe, food and water to nourish ourselves, and protection from the elements. As a society, we've created intricate networks of food production, distribution, and storage that can put fresh fruits on our tables in the dead of winter and make eating ice cream an everyday occurrence, even where there are no cows and no ice. Our water comes from public systems that are so convenient we seldom think about the wonder of having fresh, pure water piped into our homes. Our homes are sturdy and secure, insulated against heat and cold and kept comfortable by furnaces and air conditioners that may rely on energy sources hundreds of miles away.

Most of the time we survive without much effort, but when we travel in the backcountry, down wild rivers and across rugged terrain, we remove ourselves from the familiar networks of society. For a while we are on our own, fully responsible for our comfort and safety. That responsibility means we must do all we can to be prepared to survive.

Survival preparedness is being able to cope in situations where your safety is not automatically assured by the resources to which you are accustomed. Suppose a ski breaks, stranding you miles from the nearest road or a vehicle in which you're traveling breaks down far from help. You become injured or ill. On a hiking or boating trip, you are separated from your companions and become confused about your location. Bad weather disrupts your travel plans. To deal with unexpected circumstances, you'll need to understand the nature of the danger and know how to stay alive until you can get to safety.

(For more on preparing for outings see "Planning.")

In other chapters of the *Fieldbook,* you've discovered the importance of learning about the territory into which you intend to travel, and about the conditions of weather and terrain you're likely to encounter. You know you should equip yourself properly and carry plenty of provisions, but good judgment, resourcefulness, and mental toughness can see you through even without gear. You won't embark on an adventure without several companions who can share the pleasures and responsibilities of the trek, and you're wise enough to leave a detailed trip plan with a responsible adult.

In addition to carrying a first aid kit, you can further prepare yourself by taking a lightweight survival kit on all of your outings. Put the following items in a small plastic container, tape it shut, write the date on it, and open it only to replace perishable items or for a real emergency.

(For a listing of the contents of a first aid kit, see "Outdoor First Aid.")

Survival Kit

Rescue blanket
50 feet of nylon cord
Hard candy, chocolate, meat bar
Matches/metal match and
    0000 steel wool
Candle/fire starters
Plastic whistle

Small glass signal mirror
Pen light with spare batteries
Small, sharp pocketknife
Metal cup or plastic water bottle
Water purification tablets
Clear plastic sheet or an
    emergency shelter

A survival kit provides a few familiar resources to use in case of an emergency. The most important survival tool, however, isn't one that fits inside a kit, or something you can ever forget to carry. It is your mind. Here's how to use it.

Suppose you become lost in a wilderness. You have no idea where you or your companions are, and you have only the gear and provisions in your pockets and packs. As you realize the gravity of your situation, you'll probably feel a wave of panic sweeping over you. You'll be understandably frightened and perhaps a little disoriented, and questions will come fast: What will I do? Where should I go? How can I get help? The way to find these answers is to Stay, Think, Observe, and Plan—STOP!

Stay
Think
Observe
Plan

▶ **Stop!**

Stay!

At the first sign of trouble, STOP! The urge to walk faster or run blindly to escape your predicament will be difficult to resist, but rushing about will only confuse you more. Stopping helps you fight panic, and it greatly improves your chances for survival. If you're in a boat, get ashore. If you're on foot, slip off your pack, sit down, and relax. If anyone is injured, administer first aid, and then rest. Fifteen or 20 minutes may pass before the panic subsides, so be patient. Remember, you probably got into this situation by yourself; you can get out the same way.

Think!

As you relax, think. If you're lost, study a map and look for recognizable landmarks. How long ago did you know where you were? Are there footprints in snow or soft ground that will guide you home? Can you hear traffic on a distant highway? Does the motion of a river current or the wind on a lake suggest the direction in which you should steer your boat in order to reach your destination?

Take time to think, and you'll almost always figure out where you are and how to get back on course. Don't make hasty judgments. If you have any doubt about where you are, stay put and observe.

Observe!

When you are late returning home, searchers will come looking for you, so your task is simple—keep safe and visible until rescuers arrive. Look around carefully and size up your situation. Determine the extent of any injuries. Look for hazards that may pose threats to your security. Note how many hours of light you'll have before the sun sets, and check the resources in your pack and your pockets. Is there firewood nearby? A clearing visible from the air? A lookout from which you can observe the surrounding countryside? Sources of water and shelter? Mentally list everything, then plan.

Plan!

After considering all sides of your predicament, decide how best to utilize your resources and your energies. Be deliberate and practical in your planning. Jumping from one course of action to another can lead to inefficiency and exhaustion. What should you plan? Your plan should be a blueprint of how you intend to stay sufficiently supplied with each of the following survival essentials, listed in order of importance.

1. **The will to live.** You cannot survive long without it.

2. **Oxygen.** If you are deprived of air, you can live just a few minutes.

3. **Shelter/clothing.** In extreme conditions, you'll last only about 3 hours without them.

4. **Fire.** The more adequate your shelter and clothing, the less your need for a fire, but it can give heat, light, and a lift to your morale.

5. **Rest.** Conserving energy will extend your survival time and keep you mentally alert.

6. **Signals.** These attract the attention of rescuers.

7. **Water.** Without water, you can live about 3 days.

8. **Food.** Because you can live 3 weeks or more without food, it is the lowest survival priority.

The Will To Live

History is filled with accounts of ordinary people who, when threatened by extraordinary circumstances, were able to walk hundreds of miles, endure intense heat and cold, and overcome great hunger, thirst, pain, and loneliness. With the right frame of mind, a person can survive for a long time without shelter, clothing, nourishment, and rest. No one can survive without hope.

How can you develop a positive mental attitude? Some people seem to have a natural ability to remain optimistic in the face of adversity, and everyone can practice the mental toughness survival situations demand. If you enjoy athletics or you're trying to master an academic subject or artistic skill, you know it's not easy to work hard at it every day, and yet by doing so you not only come closer to achieving your goal, you also discipline your mind. For example, you may go on an outing and, after an exhausting hike, want nothing more than to sit against a tree and let someone else make camp. If you fight off that yearning and pitch the tent, get supper cooking, and secure your gear for the night, you'll probably discover you had a reserve of energy just waiting to be tapped. Push yourself now and then when conditions are right so that you realize you have those energy reserves and mental toughness, and in a real emergency they may tip the balance in your favor.

Oxygen

On land, breathing usually is not a problem, but if you've capsized a boat or if smoke or chemical fumes are billowing around you, breathing becomes more difficult. You may have only a few moments to get to open air. Even as your body fights for oxygen, try to keep panic under control. To escape an overturned boat or turbulent surface waters, you may have to descend before you can surface. In heavy smoke, you might need to crawl to safety, or to work your way upwind. In an avalanche, you'll have to create an air pocket by pushing settling snow from your face. Stop, think, observe, and plan, even if you must do all four in a split second.

Clothing/Shelter

Once immediate life-threatening situations have passed, you can turn your attention to life-extending matters. Chief among these is protection from the elements. In cold weather, you'll need to keep warm to ward off hypothermia; in hot conditions, you'll need to stay cool. Do it by using your clothing and preparing a good shelter.

It is difficult to improvise clothing in the wilderness, so probably all you can count on is what you brought with you. Keep your clothes as dry as you can, especially in cold weather. Wear just enough layers to keep yourself comfortable. In the hot sun, prevent sunburn and dehydration by wearing a loose, long-sleeve shirt, long pants, a brimmed hat, and sunglasses.

(For more on clothing, see "Hiking" and "Gearing Up." For more on the adverse health effects of hot and cold weather, see "Outdoor First Aid.")

A shelter will act as an extension of your clothing, blocking the wind, creating shade, and keeping your body's temperature at a reasonable level. Tents, caves, overhangs, canoes, tarps, and the undersides of large fallen trees are excellent ready-made shelters. A vehicle such as an automobile or a downed aircraft is often easily sighted by search teams, and in extreme temperature conditions it can be a haven. However, if the interior is extremely hot or cold, you'll probably be safer if you camp under or near the vehicle rather than inside.

When you must build a shelter, the type you construct will depend on the materials you can find and the adverse conditions you expect—heat, cold, rain, and wind. A hot-weather shelter should shield you from fierce ultraviolet light and keep you cool. Make your shelter in the shade and keep it loose so air can circulate freely. Stifling heat stays close to the ground, so a knoll or hilltop may be cooler than lowlands. Blazing daytime temperatures in desert regions may drop dramatically at night. Dig a shallow trench during the day and the sun will warm it. When you become chilled, you can lie in it and cover yourself with warm sand.

In cold weather you'll find that the smaller the shelter, the easier it is to build and the warmer it will be. A shelter 7 feet long, 3 feet wide, and 3 feet high usually is big enough for one person. Simplest of all is improving natural shelters. For instance, using a boulder, a fallen tree, or tangled roots as a base, you can prop branches 1-3 inches in diameter against the side away from the wind, angling them sharply so they will shed rain. Weave smaller branches among the large ones, then thatch the framework with sticks and foliage and cover it all with boughs stripped from evergreen trees. The shelter will be snug, warm, and dry.

(Note: On first reading, you may question the propriety of stripping green boughs from living trees. In a real survival emergency you must use every resource at your disposal to ensure your safety, even if that means cutting live trees and destroying ground cover. Your life far outweighs any damage you may cause. However, if you are practicing survival techniques when no emergency exists, follow low-impact camping ethics and leave the area unmarred by your presence.)

Another way to make a shelter is by tying together the tops of bushes and small trees, and then weaving brush and boughs among their branches. You might even start a shelter by bending down the top of a sapling and tying it to a rock or log, or lashing two upright, 4-foot-long poles to a ridge pole about 8 feet long. Prop branches on either side of the resulting frame, weave in plenty of branches, cover them with conifer boughs, and you'll have a shelter that can weather quite a blow.

Shelters like those described above are easy to make, but if the ground is covered with snow, the materials you need may not be available. Still, keep in mind the basic shelter principles—construct the simplest structure that will meet your needs, and keep it small. In snowy conditions, that probably means building a tree pit, snow pit, snow trench, snow cave, snow dome, or igloo.

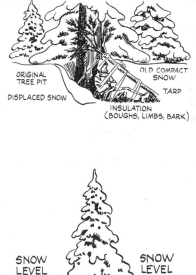

ORIGINAL TREE PIT

DISPLACED SNOW

OLD COMPACT SNOW

TARP

INSULATION (BOUGHS, LIMBS, BARK)

SNOW LEVEL

SNOW LEVEL

Tree pit. The area beneath the branches of an evergreen tree often is nearly free of snow. Crawl underneath, snap off branches that are in the way, and form a place to sit or recline. Bare earth radiates some heat, so remove the snow underneath you if you can. Insulate the bottom with a foam pad or 10 inches or more of evergreen boughs, and you'll be ready to move in. A tree pit gets you quickly out of the wind and cold. Construction time for one person is 15 minutes.

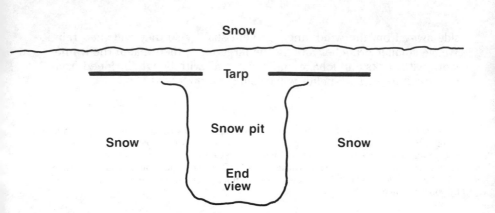

Snow pit. If you can't find a tree pit, you can dig a long, narrow pit in the snow. Insulate the bottom, then stretch a tarp or ground cloth over the top of the trench, weigh down the edges with branches or snow, and cover the material with a thin layer of snow. Tunnel into one end of the pit and, once you are inside, fill the entry with snow to keep out the cold. Poke a few ventilation holes and check them occasionally to keep them clear. Construction time for one person is 30 minutes.

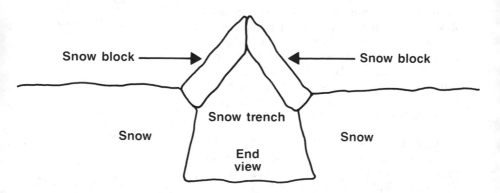

Snow trench. When snow is firm, cut it into blocks to form a trench in which you can recline. Place the blocks on edge along the sides of the excavation, then lean them against one another to form a roof. Construction time for one person: 2 to 4 hours.

Any of these shelters will protect you from winter storms and arctic cold, and you won't waste much energy getting them ready. If you must stay a long time in a snowy environment, you may want to construct a snow cave, a snow dome, or an igloo, especially if there are several people in your party and you've already assured your immediate safety with quick and simple shelters. Igloos, domes, and caves take time, effort, and expertise to build, so be sure you have the physical resources to expend before you begin.

(For instructions on building snow caves, domes, and igloos, see "Winter Camping.")

Fire

The tighter and smaller your shelter the less need you'll have for a fire, though a flame can do much besides warm you. It can provide light, boost your morale, attract the attention of rescuers, purify your water, and heat your food. Still, you must weigh the advantages you can gain from a fire against the energy you must expend to build and maintain it. You may enhance your immediate chances of survival by spending time improving your shelter rather than gathering firewood.

(For information on kindling a fire, see "Stoves and Fires.")

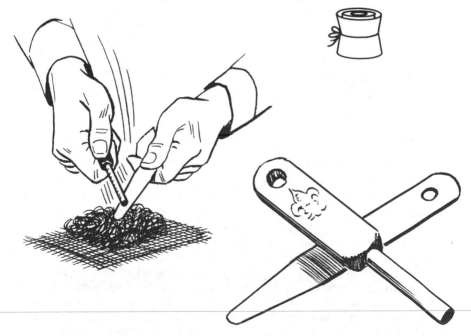

If you don't have a match to light your fire, you may be able to use a convex lens from your eyeglasses, camera, or binoculars to focus a hot pinpoint of sunlight on the tinder. With luck, you can strike sparks from a piece of flint with the steel edge of a closed pocketknife and catch them in charred cloth, the fine fluff of weeds, the dry inner bark of some trees, or 0000 steel wool. A metal match works in much the same way. Increase your chances of kindling a blaze by using a fire starter from your survival kit. Commercial fire starters include heat tabs and flammable pastes. Prepare your own fire starters at home by rolling 1-inch-wide strips of newspaper until they are about an inch thick, then tie them with string and dip each into melted paraffin. In place of a fire starter, put a candle stub under your tinder and light the wick. It should burn long enough to ignite a blaze.

Rest

Survival emergencies often occur after backcountry travelers have been pushing hard for hours or even days, and their energy levels are low. Exhaustion makes them less able to keep warm, build a shelter, and clearly think through their situation.

When you first realize you are in trouble, stop and rest. While resting, you'll have an opportunity to think, look, listen, and plan future activities. Elderly, injured, or very young members of a party will need extra rest. In extremely hot climates, you can conserve body water by resting in the shade during the day, and becoming active only after the sun has set. Rescuers normally search during the daytime, so your chances of missing a rescue by sleeping at night are minimal.

Signals

To attract the attention of rescuers, use signals that make you louder, larger, or more colorful than usual. Motion and colors that contrast sharply with their background are especially effective in attracting attention.

Audible signals. When you first become separated from your group, you might be able to attract their attention by blowing a whistle. Later, searchers may be close to you but unable to see you. Blow on a whistle occasionally in groups of three blasts to signal your location.

Passive visible signals. Many searches are conducted from aircraft, so large, angular ground signals that contrast in color with natural hues may catch the eye of an airborne rescuer. You can make the most common ground-to-air signal—a large X—by laying out brightly colored tents, tarps, or rescue blankets; by stamping down sand or snow with

**REQUIRE
ASSISTANCE**

your boots; by pulling out clumps of turf; or by lining up branches and stones. A great advantage of ground signals is that they need no further effort once you've completed them, though as with other visual signals they are effective only when the sky is clear and light. Be sure to dismantle your ground signals after you've been rescued.

**YES OR
AFFIRMATIVE**

**PROCEEDING IN
THIS DIRECTION**

**REQUIRE
MEDICAL ASSISTANCE**

**NO OR
NEGATIVE**

Active visible signals. Active visible signals don't work by themselves. They include mirrors, fires, and flares.

On a sunny day, the flash of a mirror can be seen by aircraft many miles away. If the mirror in your survival kit has an aiming device, use it. If not, hold the mirror in one hand near your face, extend the other hand in front of you, and tilt the mirror until you can fill your empty palm with reflected light. Make a V with your illuminated fingers, then sight across the top of the mirror and through the V toward an aircraft and drop your

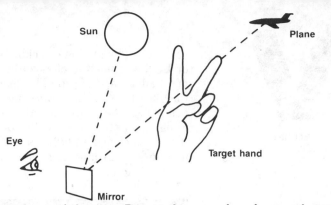

empty hand out of the way. Repeat the procedure frequently to adjust your aim, and be especially certain to signal as a plane is flying toward you. A glass mirror reflects light better than one made of metal, but if you have no mirror, try using the lid of a tin can, a piece of foil, or any other shiny object.

Smoke and flame are also good signals. Lay green leaves and evergreen boughs on a fire to create dense smoke that may attract the attention of pilots and fire wardens. Better yet, prepare second and third fires about 50 yards from the one that is burning, locating them so the three are the points of a large triangle. Keep a torch of easily flammable material near the blazing fire, and as soon as you hear an approaching aircraft, quickly ignite the additional fires. (A combination of any three signals is a universal sign of distress.)

Flares and smoke devices are useful for signaling; but since each can be used just once, activate them only when you've sighted a rescue craft. Follow the directions carefully.

Water

Two-thirds of the human body is water. Because we lose water constantly through perspiration, respiration, digestion, and waste disposal, our body fluids must be replenished regularly. Without sufficient water, sweating ceases, blood circulation slows, and tasks become arduous. Even in temperate weather, people can survive only a relatively short time without water. In hot deserts, they'll need a gallon or more a day each.

Even though your water supply may be limited, drink enough to keep your body healthy, then do all you can to prevent the loss of moisture through perspiration. In hot weather, limit your activities to the cool hours of the evening and early morning. Keep your clothing loose and stay in the shade. If you can get a few feet above the ground, even by sitting on a brush pile, you'll find the temperature is a good deal cooler than it is on the desert floor. In cold weather, force yourself to drink now and then, even if you don't feel particularly thirsty. The low humidity of winter can steadily drain the moisture from your body.

Your sources of emergency water are groundwater, rain, snow, ice, dew, succulent plants, and the clear sap of trees, vines, and fruit. Where water is scarce, look for green vegetation in the bottoms of ravines and gullies, and dig where the soil is damp. When clouds form, get ready to catch rain in plastic ponchos and ground cloths, and cook pots. Pockets in boulders may contain water, and early in the morning you can use a handkerchief to mop dew from leaves and rocks. Melt snow and ice in a pot over a fire. In hot weather, a solar still can provide some of your water needs. Standing water and water from streams and lakes should be purified with tablets or by boiling.

HOW TO MAKE A SOLAR STILL

When the sun is beating down, you can get a pint or two of pure water a day from a solar still. Here's how.

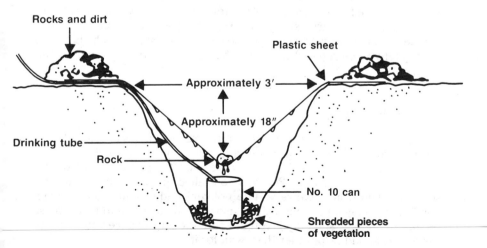

Rocks and dirt

Plastic sheet

Approximately 3'

Approximately 18"

Drinking tube

Rock

No. 10 can

Shredded pieces of vegetation

Line a cone-shaped hole with slices of succulent plants. Place a cup in the bottom of the hole, and run a 6-foot length of rubber tubing from the bottom of the cup over the edge of the hole. Cover the hole with a sheet of transparent plastic, seal its edges with stones and dirt, and place a small stone in the center of the plastic so the depression it makes is just above the cup. As the sun warms the still, plant moisture will rise, condense on the plastic, and drop into the cup. You can sip the water through the tubing without dismantling the still.

Food

Surprisingly, food is a relatively unimportant survival consideration. A healthy person can live 3 weeks or more without eating, and since most lost persons are found within 2 or 3 days there is little danger of starvation. However, in extremely cold conditions, when the body is burning lots of calories to keep itself warm, food becomes much more vital. If you are familiar with edible plants or if you are knowledgeable in the ways of wilderness fishing and trapping, you can forage for food if you desire, but don't waste energy you can't replenish. It may be better to wait quietly to be rescued than to exhaust yourself trying to eat off the land.

Going For Help

In most instances, a lost person's best course of action is to stay put until rescuers come. However, there are a few circumstances where you may need to move to a safer location, or even attempt to get out of the backcountry on your own. Perhaps you failed to leave a trip plan with someone who would realize you've not returned on time. One of your companions may be seriously ill or injured. The decision to travel must be made carefully, and only if you are sure the only chance you have for survival is to find help rather than wait for it.

CHAPTER

Should you decide to leave, mark the direction of your travel well, with a large ground-to-air arrow. In a plastic bag leave a note describing your condition, the time and date of your departure, and your intended route and destination. Use brush, rocks, or deep footprints to make a large arrow pointing in the direction you will travel. Also, at regular intervals, leave bits of cloth or paper, break branches, make blaze marks on trees, and do whatever else you can to give searchers a trail that's easy to follow should they reach the area after you've left. Wherever it's possible, make your trail signs at eye level, each mark in sight of the one before it.

PRACTICING SURVIVAL SKILLS

You can practice using emergency survival skills by playing a mental game whenever you are in the field. Ask yourself questions that force you to think in terms of survival. What would I do if my partner fell right now and broke a leg? If I needed shelter right away, where could I find it? What course of action would I follow if I became lost here? If my canoe overturned and I lost my pack, how could I build a fire to dry my clothes?

If you don't know how to respond to a question, ask experienced backcountry travelers for advice and read all the books you can about survival. In time, the answers will come quickly, and should a real emergency arise you'll be able to respond at once. The mind is, after all, your most powerful survival tool. Remain calm, have faith in your ability to deal with any situation you may face, and you're certain to find ways to ensure the safety of yourself and your companions.

''Oh! The old swimmin'-hole! whar the crick so still
 and deep
Looked like a baby-river that was laying half asleep,
And the gurgle of the worter round the drift jest below
Sounded like the laugh of something we onc't ust
 to know.''

James Whitcomb Riley, 1938

Chapter 13

Swimming and Lifesaving

Albert E. Cahill

Silver Beaver and Silver Antelope
Scouter; Vice-chairman, National
Health and Safety Committee;
Recognized Authority on Aquatics
Programs and Water Safety

T he backcountry is full of water. Quiet ponds and lakes glisten under wide-open skies. Mountain streams crash over cliffs and boil through rugged gorges. Wide rivers roll along with slow, relentless power. Beautiful and inviting, thunderous and awesome, water is at the heart of many adventures. Fisherman wet their lines in it. Canoers, kayakers, and rafters glide over its surface. Backpackers splash through it and campers search it out to refill their canteens. Water makes life in the outdoors possible, and it can provide you with plenty of fun, beauty, and excitement.

If you've ever been in a swimming pool, you probably already have a healthy respect for water. You're aware of the precautions taken by pool directors to assure your safety. The water is clear and free of obstructions. The depths are marked. Swimmers are grouped according to ability, and trained lifeguards keep a watchful eye on everything that happens. Novices are encouraged to improve their skills by enrolling in swimming and lifesaving courses.

When you head for the backcountry, you leave behind the familiar security of the neighborhood pool. River currents are unpredictable. Lake depths can be deceptive. The chill of open water creates a danger of hypothermia. It's up to you to choose aquatics activities that are within your abilities, and then to do your floating, fishing, and swimming only under safe, properly supervised conditions.

Equally important is knowing what to do when something goes wrong and an accident occurs. A kayaker may strike his head on a rock. A hiker might slip off a log and fall into a rushing stream. A fisherman's boat could capsize. If you're prepared to act, the event probably will result in nothing more than wet clothes and a bad scare, but you must learn all you can about aquatic safety ahead of time. In the confusion of an emergency, you'll have to rely completely on what you already know. Most important of all is knowing how to swim.

BECOMING A SWIMMER

To consider yourself a swimmer, you should be able to swim at least 100 meters/yards, covering the first 75 meters/yards with a strong, steady sidestroke, breaststroke, crawl, or trudgen, or a combination of strokes. Swim the last 25 meters/yards with an easy, resting backstroke, and include in the total distance at least one sharp turn. Finally, demonstrate your ability to rest in the water by floating with a minimum of motion.

A good way to learn how to swim is to enroll in a course at a pool or lake near your home. The Boy Scouts of America, Red Cross, YMCA, and other organizations offer expert instruction at little or no cost. Each of the strokes you'll learn has its use in the backcountry.

Crawl

Combining continuous arm motion with a strong flutter kick, the crawl is the fastest of the basic swimming strokes. It also is the most tiring. The

1

2

3 **Breathe**

4

5

6

crawl will get you quickly away from danger, pull you to a nearby shore, or help you win a race, but if you have far to swim or must be in the water a long time, choose a stroke that will not so easily exhaust you.

Breaststroke

The breaststroke is an easy, energy-conserving way to swim. You extend your arms in front of you, sweep them out until they are almost even with your shoulders, return them to the starting point, glide a moment, then repeat the motion. Meanwhile, use your legs to push yourself along with a whip kick or breaststroke kick. To rest as you use the breaststroke, you can swim with your face in the water, raising it to catch a breath of air each time you sweep with your arms. In rescue situations, you can use the breaststroke to keep your head high and see what you are doing as you approach a struggling swimmer.

Elementary Backstroke

Similar to a breaststroke done on your back, the elementary backstroke allows you to rest as you glide. You'll be able to cover long distances without expending too much energy, making this one of the most important survival strokes. Take a breath of air as you end each stroke so that you'll have full lungs to make you more buoyant while you glide, but don't glide too long. Start your next stroke before you stop moving from the force of the last one.

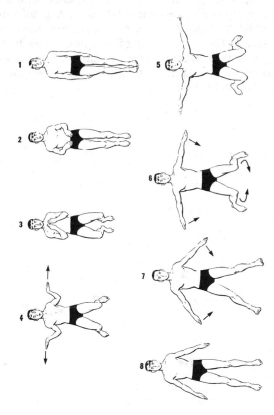

Sidestroke

The sidestroke depends for propulsion on a scissors kick that uses the power of leg muscles conditioned by walking and running. Paired with a smooth arm motion, the kick gives you a long glide between strokes, and the position of your head makes breathing easy. Like the elementary backstroke, it is good for long survival swims.

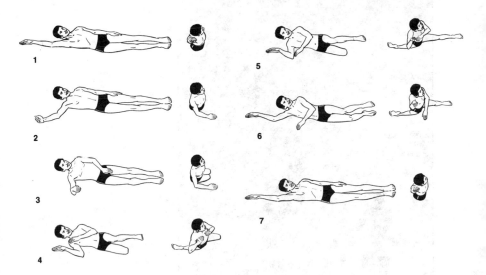

Trudgen

The trudgen is a combination stroke that employs the arm motion of the crawl and the scissors kick of the sidestroke. It's fast and efficient over short distances and for lifesaving in rough water.

SWIMMING SAFELY

Mastering the strokes is only part of enjoying backcountry swimming. Where, when, and how you swim also have a lot to do with your safety. First, never swim alone. Use the buddy system, and keep an eye on your partner while he watches out for you. Swim only in areas that are free of underwater obstructions, strong currents, and other dangers, and then only when trained lifeguards have been posted along the shore.

Unfortunately, even the most careful preparations cannot prevent every outdoor mishap. The time may come when through no fault of your own you find yourself dumped into a lake or a river, or you come upon someone struggling in deep water far from shore. While you may not be able to prevent such an accident, you can keep it from becoming tragic if you know how to save yourself and how to rescue others.

(For more on preventing backcountry accidents, see "Outdoor Safety and Precautions.")

CHAPTER 13

SAVING YOURSELF

Personal rescue skills are as important as swimming strokes. In an emergency they can keep you alive as you make your way to shore, or until help arrives. As with all swimming and lifesaving skills, learn these in shallow water first, and then practice them in deeper water until they become almost instinctive. Learn them now, before your life depends on them.

Floating

Almost all of us can float, even if we may not do it with much style. Start learning by standing in chest-deep water. Take a deep breath, arch your back, and lean back until you become buoyant and your feet lift toward the surface. You may not float level, but that's all right as long as your mouth and nose stay above the water and you can breathe. If you're having difficulty getting the hang of floating, grasp a canoe paddle, a kickboard, or any other flotation device. It will give you added lift.

Motionless floating

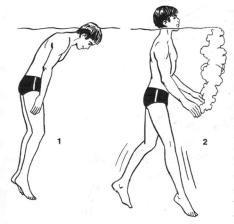

Survival Floating

Floating on your back will keep you safe when the water is calm, but what if you've been washed out to sea by a strong current, or capsized a boat in a dark, choppy lake and have no idea which way to swim to reach the shore? You may need to stay afloat for many minutes or even hours waiting to be rescued. Treading water is out of the question, since it takes even more energy than a slow breaststroke. In water above 70°F, the answer is survival floating.

The next time you're chin-deep in a swimming pool, fill your lungs with air, then relax completely and float, face down, arms dangling like a jellyfish. The back of your neck will probably just break the surface of the water. After holding your breath for a few seconds, slowly spread your legs and lift your arms. As you exhale, bring your legs together and push gently downward with your arms. You'll be able to raise your head and take another breath. Relax again and jellyfish float until you need more air, then repeat the cycle. You may have to fight the temptation to keep your head above water; lift it only to inhale, then settle back into the jellyfish position and rest until you need to breathe once more.

If you know which direction you must travel to reach safety, you can modify your hand and leg movements to give yourself a slight thrust toward shore each time you come up for air. But remember that the point of survival floating is to conserve your energy with slow, relaxed motions.

Flotation Devices

Your ability to stay on the surface of the water will be greatly enhanced if you're grasping or wearing a flotation device. Of course, the best choice is the U.S. Coast Guard approved personal flotation device (PFD) you wear whenever you go out in a boat, but in an emergency there may be no PFDs around. As you go into the water, grab anything that will help keep you afloat—a log, a boat seat cushion, a water cooler, a beach ball—and hang on.

1

2

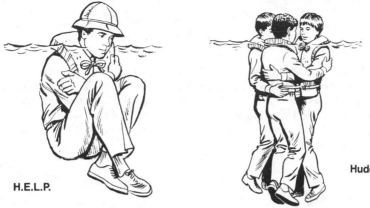

H.E.L.P.

Huddle

You can convert articles of clothing into flotation devices. As you float in the jellyfish position, slip off your pants, tie an overhand knot in each leg, close the fly, and inflate them by using your hand to cup air and push it under the water and into the pants. Hold the waist closed beneath the surface of the water, and rest your head between the pant legs.

(For more on personal flotation devices, see "Canoeing" and "Kayaking and Whitewater Rafting.")

When you are thrown into cold water, hypothermia may endanger your life as much as drowning. The colder the water, the more serious your situation. Quickly get into or onto a watercraft or swim for shore if you must. If you are wearing a personal flotation device, you can assume a heat escape lessening posture, or H.E.L.P., that will keep you a little warmer, and you can huddle with others in the water, sharing your body heat.

(For more on hypothermia, see "Outdoor First Aid.")

SAVING OTHERS

Helping a swimmer in trouble can be dramatic, but it must be done carefully and correctly. Drowning people may panic, grabbing with all their strength at anything, including other swimmers, they think will help save them. As a rescuer, you must act in such a way that you do not unduly risk your own safety. The best way to perfect your lifesaving skills is to enroll in courses taught by qualified lifesaving instructors. They'll teach you to follow proven guidelines, including four ways to save a victim, and the order in which those four should be considered: reach, throw, row, and go.

Reach

The farther you stay from a victim you are aiding, the safer you will be. If you can, remain on shore and reach for the person. Use a tree branch, a fishing pole, a canoe paddle, the sleeve of your jacket, or whatever else is handy. If the victim is close enough, hang onto a tree or lie on a dock and grasp him or her with your free hand, taking care not to let yourself be pulled in.

Throw

Most aquatic accidents occur within a few yards of safety, close enough for you to reach the victim without leaving dry land. Should a victim be too far from shore for that, throw out a line. At established swimming areas, there ought to be rescue lines attached to ring buoys. Otherwise, use your bear bag rope, a climbing rope, canoe and kayak painters, or a rescue rope you've prepared especially for an emergency.

Almost any light line can be thrown a moderately long distance. One of the best ways to weight a line for practice and actual use is to tie one end to a plastic jug containing an inch of water. Another good device is the rescue bag, a cloth sack full of rope that can be thrown very accurately, paying out the line as it flies. During activities such as kayaking and whitewater rafting when you expect participants to end up in the water, station rescuers with heaving ropes or rescue bags at the end of stretches of rough water where they can help floundering paddlers ashore.

(For more on rescue lines, see "Canoeing" and "Kayaking and Whitewater Rafting.")

Row

If you cannot quickly find a branch or pole with which to reach or a rope to throw, or if the victim is far from shore, consider a rowing rescue. Maneuver a rowboat toward the person stern first, a canoe bow first. Talk as you approach, calming the victim so he or she can help with the rescue. When the shore is not too far away, have the person grasp the stern of the rowboat or the bow of the canoe and hang on as you propel the craft to safety. If it will be a long trip or if the victim is too exhausted to hold on, help the person over the stern of the rowboat or the side of the canoe, being very careful to do it in a way that will not cause the craft to capsize.

ROWBOAT RESCUE

CANOE RESCUE

MOTORBOAT RESCUE

Go

As a last resort, swim out to rescue a victim. However, don't rush into the water without first looking around the shore. Is there a surfboard nearby? A personal flotation device? An air mattress, a kayak paddle, a towel, a shirt, or a pair of pants? Take with you anything that will let you reach out to the victim or that will help keep you both afloat.

Enter the water safely, wading in feet first. Never leap or dive into unknown water, for it could be full of submerged stumps or rocks. Use the crawl or breaststroke so that you won't lose sight of the victim, and pace yourself in order to have the strength to make the rescue and get back to shore. Reassure the person by talking calmly, but be very cautious; don't let the victim grab you. If the person is quiet and cooperative, you can toss one end of a towel or shirt to the victim and pull him or her ashore with it by swimming backwards, propelling yourself with the kick of the elementary backstroke or the scissors kick. Some people may let you grasp a wrist and pull them along, or approach from behind and tow them by the collar or personal flotation device. However, never take your eyes off the victim. Be alert for any changes in movements or mood, and instantly back away if the person panics and threatens your safety. Wait until the victim stops fighting, even if that means loss of consciousness, then resume pulling the person ashore.

Strong rescuers with extensive lifesaving training and experience may be able to use a cross-chest carry to control and move a struggling victim,

Hair Tow

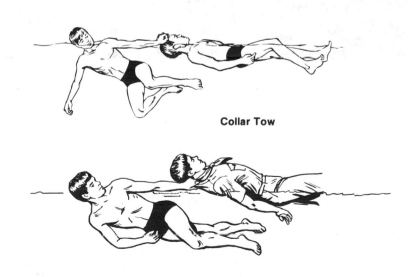

Collar Tow

but attempt it only if you know what you are doing. Otherwise, stay out of the reach of the victim and wait for struggling to cease before you make contact.

(For information on first aid for victims of aquatic accidents, see "Outdoor First Aid.")

You have nothing to fear from backcountry water as long as you respect its power and take the time to learn the swimming and lifesaving fundamentals. The satisfaction of mastering such important recreational and survival techniques will be great, and the security you'll feel on and around open water will be well worth the effort.

"There is an eagle in me and a mockingbird . . . and the eagle flies among the Rocky Mountains of my dreams and flights among the Sierra crags of what I want . . . and the mockingbird warbles in the early forenoon before the dew is gone, warbles in the underbrush of my Chattanoogas of hope, gushes over the blue Ozark foothills of my wishes—and I got the eagle and the mockingbird from the wilderness."

Carl Sandburg, 1918

Chapter 14

Where To Go

Margaret Fuchs
Management Assistant, Land
Management Planning Staff, U.S.
Forest Service

Y ou can't have outdoor adventures unless you have an outdoors in
which to enjoy them. Fortunately, there are millions of acres of
public lands just right for backcountry activities. Some are small,
ideal for a few hours or an evening of activities. Others encompass entire
mountain ranges and the full lengths of wilderness rivers. As an American citizen, you share in the ownership and caretaking of a tremendous
variety of national parks, forests, and wildlife refuges. The state in which
you live has set aside land for parks that everyone can use, and most cities
and towns have recreational facilities where you can sharpen your Scouting skills.

Of course, public lands aren't the only areas you'll want to explore.
Many individuals, organizations, and corporations own territory you can
visit if you first obtain their permission and agree to abide by certain
regulations. Councils of the Boy Scouts of America operate hundreds of
terrific camps all across the country, and the national high-adventure
bases and programs provide some of the best wilderness experiences
anywhere.

There's certainly no lack of places to go. The problem is knowing how
to find out where they are, what they have to offer, and what you can
expect when you get there. Among other things, you'll want to know:

- What services, activities, and facilities are available, and the seasons of
the year during which they can be used.

- If entrance fees are charged, if permits are required, and from whom
you must obtain permission to use private lands.

- The availability of equipment for special activities such as horseback
riding, fishing, and boating.

- The location of the nearest medical services.

This chapter explains ways for gathering all the information you'll
need.

LOCAL AREAS

No doubt you've heard your friends talk about campsites they thought were fantastic. Maybe they've mentioned exciting canoeing and kayaking rivers not far from your home, or shining lakes full of hungry fish. Perhaps members of your family have found interesting hiking trails within easy access of your neighborhood.

Keep your ears open and you'll learn more about local backcountry areas than just about any other way. Most people who are interested in hiking, camping, fishing, and hunting have a favorite haunt they don't mind talking about, and since the information comes firsthand from somebody who's been there, it's usually reliable.

Chambers of commerce, visitors' bureaus, and parks and recreation departments of cities will have detailed material describing the locations and offerings of local areas they're eager to promote. Look for their listings in your telephone book. They'll also be able to tell you about any brilliant displays of foliage or migrations of wildlife to observe during certain times of the year.

Your public library is another rich source of backcountry information. Librarians can guide you to books that list local recreational areas and discuss their geology, animal and plant communities, and social history. Likewise, local outing clubs, wildlife and conservation groups, activities organizations at colleges and universities, and employees of backpacking equipment stores may be able to direct you to unspoiled territory that relates to their own particular interests. Travel and motor clubs often have maps pinpointing recreational areas; they also may be able to help you plan the best ways to reach more distant trailheads.

STATE AREAS

Parks, beaches, forests, historical monuments, wildlife refuges—every state in the nation has reserved some of its best lands for recreational uses. State road maps usually indicate their locations, and you can ask your public library for the addresses of state departments of parks, fish and game, and recreation. Even if the first state officials you contact don't have the information you need, they'll know how you can get in touch with the agencies that do.

FEDERAL AREAS

Scenic and varied, the federal recreation areas of America are so vast almost everyone can reach and enjoy rugged, undeveloped country. As with local and state lands, user fees usually are modest. While most public campgrounds are operated on a first-come, first-served basis, you may need to make reservations to stay in some of the more popular sites during busy times of the year. Permits often are required for overnight stays in the backcountry. Still, when you consider the tremendous opportunities we all have to use public lands, the necessary fees, reservations, permits, and regulations are a small price to pay.

Jurisdiction over federal lands used for recreation is divided among a number of agencies, each with its own function.

National Park Service

A part of the Department of the Interior, the National Park Service (NPS) administers more than 300 areas comprising 79 million acres (54.4 million acres are in Alaska alone). Located in almost every state in the Union as well as Guam, Puerto Rico, and the Virgin Islands, the lands administered by the NPS are fine for camping, backcountry exploration, hiking, mountain climbing, horseback riding, swimming, boating, fishing, bicycling, cross-country skiing, and the study of nature and American history.

The following regional offices can give you plenty of information on a park you may wish to visit. For a small fee, they can also provide you with a national park system map and guide, which give an overview of America's entire national park system.

North Atlantic Region

National Park Service
15 State Street
Boston, MA 02109-3572
617-223-5199

(Connecticut, Maine, Massachusetts, New Hampshire, New Jersey, New York, Rhode Island, and Vermont)

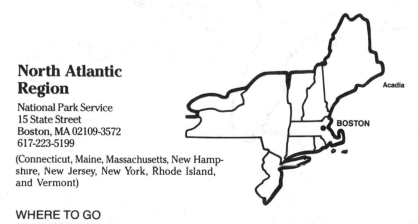

WHERE TO GO

Mid-Atlantic Region

National Park Service
143 South Third Street
Philadelphia, PA 19106
215-597-7018

(Delaware, Maryland, Pennsylvania,
Virginia, and West Virginia)

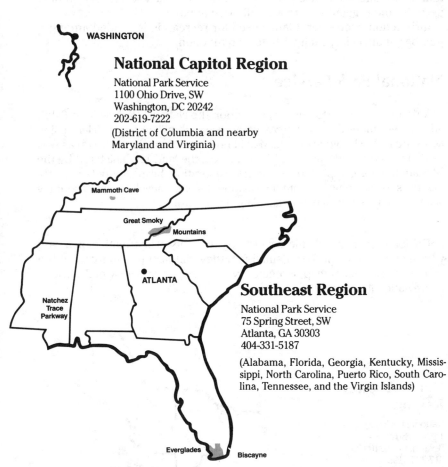

WASHINGTON

National Capitol Region

National Park Service
1100 Ohio Drive, SW
Washington, DC 20242
202-619-7222

(District of Columbia and nearby
Maryland and Virginia)

Southeast Region

National Park Service
75 Spring Street, SW
Atlanta, GA 30303
404-331-5187

(Alabama, Florida, Georgia, Kentucky, Mississippi, North Carolina, Puerto Rico, South Carolina, Tennessee, and the Virgin Islands)

Midwest Region

National Park Service
1709 Jackson Street
Omaha, NE 68102-2571
402-221-3448

(Illinois, Indiana, Iowa, Kansas,
Michigan, Minnesota, Nebraska,
Ohio, and Wisconsin)

Rocky Mountain Region

National Park Service
P.O. Box 25287
Denver, CO 80225-0287
303-969-2000

(Colorado, Montana, North Dakota, South
Dakota, Utah, and Wyoming)

Southwest Region

National Park Service
P.O. Box 728
Santa Fe, NM 87504-0728
505-988-6012

(Arkansas, Louisiana, New Mexico,
Oklahoma, and Texas)

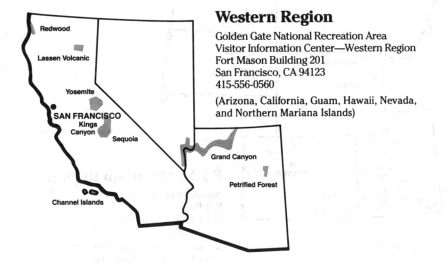

Western Region

Golden Gate National Recreation Area
Visitor Information Center—Western Region
Fort Mason Building 201
San Francisco, CA 94123
415-556-0560

(Arizona, California, Guam, Hawaii, Nevada,
and Northern Mariana Islands)

Pacific Northwest Region

Outdoor Recreation Information Center
915 Second Avenue, Room 442
Seattle, WA 98174
206-220-7450

(Idaho, Oregon, and Washington)

Alaska Region

Alaska Public Lands Information Center
605 West 4th Avenue
Anchorage, AK 99501
907-271-2737

(Alaska)

U.S. Forest Service

The National Forest System contains nearly 200 million acres of bountiful forest lands. A part of the Department of Agriculture, the U.S. Forest Service (USFS) oversees 156 national forests full of mountains, lakes, rivers, and valleys. While most national forests are managed to provide timber for the lumber industry, grazing lands for ranchers, and recreational opportunities for visitors, parts of some forests have been designated as wilderness areas, and are regulated to prevent any acts of man that may disturb the unspoiled quality of the environment. Hikers and campers are encouraged to choose activities that are in harmony with that goal. That may mean using stoves rather than open fires, limiting group size, and packing out all garbage and litter.

(For more information, see "Reducing Our Impact.")

With so many opportunities for adventure, you'll want to be sure to call or write to the national forests you would like to visit. They'll be glad to furnish maps and information to help you plan your trip.

Northern Region

(Idaho and Montana)

Forest Service, USDA
Federal Building
P.O. Box 7669
Missoula, MT 59807
406-329-3511

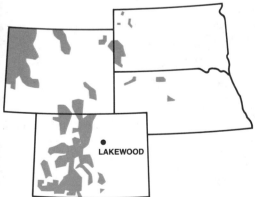

Rocky Mountain Region

(Colorado, Nebraska, South Dakota, and Wyoming)

Forest Service, USDA
11177 West 8th Avenue
Lakewood, CO 80225
303-275-5360

Southwestern Region

(Arizona and New Mexico)

Forest Service, USDA
Federal Building
517 Gold Avenue, SW
Albuquerque, NM 87102
505-842-3292

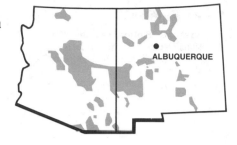

Pacific Northwest Region

(Oregon and Washington)

Forest Service, USDA
P.O. Box 3623
Portland, OR 97208-3623
503-326-2971

Eastern Region

(Illinois, Indiana, Maine, Michigan, Minnesota,
Missouri, New Hampshire, Ohio, Pennsylvania,
Vermont, West Virginia, and Wisconsin)

Forest Service, USDA
310 West Wisconsin Avenue
Room 500
Milwaukee, WI 53203
414-297-3693

Southern Region

(Alabama, Arkansas, Florida, Georgia, Kentucky, Louisiana, Mississippi, North Carolina, Puerto Rico, South Carolina, Tennessee, Texas, and Virginia)

Forest Service, USDA
1720 Peachtree Road, NW
Room 850
Atlanta, GA 30367-9102
404-347-2384

Intermountain Region

(Idaho, Nevada, Utah, and Wyoming)

Forest Service, USDA
Att'n: Information
2501 Wall Avenue
Ogden, UT 84401
801-625-5306

Pacific Southwest Region

(California)

Forest Service, USDA
630 Sansome Street
San Francisco, CA 94111
415-705-2726

SAN FRANCISCO

Alaska Region

(Alaska)

Forest Service, USDA
P.O. Box 21628
Juneau, AK 99802-1628
907-586-8806

JUNEAU

Fish and Wildlife Service

The Fish and Wildlife Service is dedicated to the preservation of all wildlife, especially endangered species. To that end, it oversees 500 national wildlife refuges in the United States, each a protected natural habitat for wild fish, birds, and mammals. Open to the public, the refuges are wonderful places to see animals as small as hummingbirds and as large as bison living in the wild. Many refuges also allow boating, fishing, and hiking, and they are productive sites for photographers, botanists, biologists, and bird watchers.

For an overview of the national wildlife refuges, write and ask for the "Visitor Guide."

U.S. Fish and Wildlife Service
U.S. Department of the Interior
Washington, DC 20240

If you plan to visit a refuge, you can contact the appropriate regional director for current regulations and visitor information.

Bureau of Land Management

Lying mostly in the western half of the United States, the lands of the Bureau of Land Management (BLM) offer rugged desert landscapes, evergreen forests, snowcapped mountains, and an abundance of wildlife. Activities on BLM lands include camping, hiking, backpacking, cave exploration, kayaking and whitewater rafting, nature study, photography, and geology. Since many BLM areas are remote, you'll want to write or call the appropriate office before you embark on a backcountry trek. For information on BLM lands and regional offices, write to:

Bureau of Land Management
U.S. Department of the Interior
Washington, DC 20240

U.S. Army Corps of Engineers

The Army Corps of Engineers was established to serve the needs of America's military forces. The corps' engineers also are responsible for building many of America's trails, waterways, and harbors. The dams they've constructed have created reservoirs and lakes that provide out-

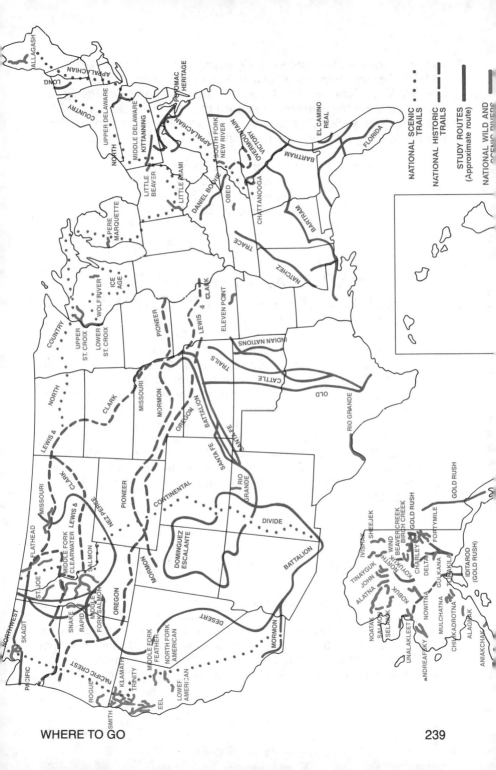

standing locations for outdoor recreation, and the corps takes great pride in offering a wide range of activities to the public. But don't make the mistake of thinking you'll be limited to boating and swimming; the territory beyond the shorelines often is just right for backpacking, bird watching, horseback riding, and bicycling. To learn about various corps projects and to get the details on the ones in your area, write to:

Army Corps of Engineers
Pulaski Building
20 Massachusetts Avenue, NW
Washington, DC 20314

NATIONAL TRAIL SYSTEM AND WILD AND SCENIC RIVERS

Many public and private lands are crossed by trails protected by the National Trails Act of the U.S. Congress. The longest in the system are the Appalachian Trail and the Pacific Crest Trail. Crossing 13 states, the Appalachian Trail winds 2,100 miles from Maine to Georgia, while the 2,600-mile Pacific Crest Trail stretches all the way from Canada to Mexico. Likewise, rivers rich in history and rugged beauty are protected by law as wild and scenic rivers, and some sections are limited to use only by non-motorized boats. The National Trail System and the Wild and Scenic Rivers System are administered by the National Park Service of the U. S. Department of the Interior. For information on specific trails and rivers, write to the National Park Service, Interior Building, Washington, DC 20240.

COUNCIL SCOUT CAMPS

Ever slept on a mountaintop, floated a canoe across a shimmering lake, or spent a week sharpening your wilderness skills? Most councils of the BSA operate at least one camp, and as a member of a Boy Scout troop, Varsity Scout team, or Explorer post, you can take part in activities that range from overnight outings and weeklong summer encampments to extended river runs, backpacking treks, desert and snow survival, and advanced backcountry training. Many councils have developed exciting high-adventure programs that will put you to a real test. Council camp staffs are well prepared to teach the fundamentals of outdoor living, and to help you get the most out of your camp experience.

Get involved with your council's camp programs by asking your Scoutmaster or Advisor for information, or by contacting your council service center. For details on challenging programs for teenagers, check your local Scout service center for *Guidebook to Council High-Adventure Programs,* No. 20-150. Groups planning overnight trips outside the boundaries of their own councils will need to file Local Tour Permits, No. 34426, and a National Tour Permit, No. 34419, if the distance is in excess of 500 miles. Permit forms also are available at local Scout service centers. A booklet titled *Tours and Expeditions,* No. 33734, contains a wealth of information on planning for vehicle trips and outings.

National High Adventure Bases

For real excitement, it's hard to beat the national high-adventure base of the Boy Scouts of America. Designed for older Boy Scouts, Varsity Scouts, and Explorers, and available to other youth groups, each base offers the training, equipment, and support you'll need to embark on a wilderness trek that will challenge your skills, strength, and willpower, and fill you with magnificent memories of mountains, forests, and water. Scoutmasters and local Scout service centers have information and application forms for all the bases, or you may write directly to the ones that interest you most.

Philmont Scout Ranch

Explore the rugged high country of northern New Mexico on a 12-day backpacking expedition, or as a member of a horse-mounted cavalcade, a trail crew, or an advanced wilderness program. Covering more than 137,000 acres of mountains, forests, prairies, and streams, Philmont is a challenging, inspiring backpackers' paradise. Staffed camps in the backcountry offer specialized program opportunities including rock climbing, black powder rifle shooting, living history, horse riding, archaeology, conservation, and many others.

Florida National High Adventure Sea Base

The clear waters of the Florida Keys and Bahamas offer unlimited opportunities for you to explore coral reefs on extended voyages aboard watercraft and sailboats. Snorkel and scuba dive amid pillars of coral surrounded by multicolored tropical fish. Explore a primitive island, search for the wreckage of galleons, fish for sailfish and marlin in the Gulf Stream waters, experience wind surfing, and study the marine life of North America's only living reef.

Northern Tier National High Adventure Programs

The Sioux and Chippewa once traveled this northern lake country. Rough French-Canadians came after them, heavily laden with furs. Headquartered in the beautiful Superior-Quetico boundary waters of Minnesota and Ontario, the Northern Tier offers extensive wilderness canoeing expeditions and the Okpik winter camping program.

For brochures and application forms, write:

Philmont Scout Ranch
Cimarron, NM 87714

Florida National High Adventure
Sea Base
P.O. Box 858
Islamorada, FL 33036

Northern Tier National High
Adventure Programs
Box 509
Ely, MN 55731

"This Indian was justly proud of his race; he had discovered an important secret of success. He knew that as a Douglas fir cannot possibly become a cedar or a sugar pine, similarly he could not be recast into another image. He could only be himself. Once a man accepts that fact, his yearnings become geared to his capacities. He knows his strengths as well as his limitations. He may be unknown and unsung; but being wise, he has found the road to contentment. Like the mountain laurel, or snowberry, or sage, he pretends to be no more than he is. By being just what he is, and no more, he contributes a unique and distinct flavor to his community."

William O. Douglas, 1950

Chapter

15

Planning

Randall Day
Chief Ranger,
Philmont Scout Ranch,
1978–80

One of the real joys of an adventure is planning for it. Anticipation—that's what happens when you and some friends get out maps, talk over routes, think about activities you like, and discuss what you can see and do on a trek. As you write a trip itinerary, you can imagine yourself hiking a woodland trail, casting for bass in a farm pond, or carving graceful turns with cross-country skis. As you package food for each meal, you'll look forward to the flavor of savory dishes cooked outdoors. As you gather your gear, you can almost see your tent pitched in a deep forest, your pack leaning against the summit marker of a high peak, or your canoe paddle dipping into the still waters of a quiet lake. Once everything is prepared, anticipation will turn to action, and you'll be ready to travel. By planning well, you leave little to chance, and that means you can enjoy every outing to the fullest.

WHAT IS PLANNING?

Perhaps you've wondered what it would be like to sleep in a snow cave, bicycle a hundred miles, camp in a desert, or do any of a hundred other exciting outdoor activities. Every adventure begins as a daydream, but transforming daydreams into reality requires a stretch of objective, hard-nosed thinking. The first step is to get a notebook and a sharp pencil. Putting ideas on paper forces you to think them through, and later, when you plan other adventures, you can look in notebooks of past outings and see what worked and what could be done differently. Your first consideration will be deciding what you want to do and who will go with you.

Planning Group Ventures

Most adventures are more fun when friends travel together as a group, and they are safer, too. You probably already have people in mind you'd like to include in your crew. You'll want at least four so that if one of you is injured, a companion can stay with the victim while two others go for help. However, you won't want a group that is too large. A crew of four to six can travel lightly and quickly. You won't require large campsites, you'll see more wildlife, and you'll find it easy to camp without leaving a trace.

Each member of your crew will have certain strengths that will help make the trip successful, but you'll also need to consider limitations when selecting an adventure just right for your group. There are two ways to match a group with an outing. You can decide on the adventure and then find companions who have the necessary ability and interests, or you can decide with whom you would like to share an adventure and then tailor activities to fit the strengths and weaknesses of everyone involved. Normally a crew should have from four to 12 persons, or no more than the maximum specified by land management officials. Find out the limitations so your group can tailor plans accordingly.

Experience and knowledge. The amount of experience a person has is often, but not always, an indicator of how well that person will do on a trip. You'll want your companions to have a mastery of the skills of any activity you plan. It's also valuable for them to have related experience such as first aid training, backcountry navigational expertise, swimming and lifesaving abilities, and an understanding of weather, wildlife, and botany.

Still, abundant experience does not necessarily create abundant wisdom. People in the habit of using poor camping practices are not better campers if they repeat the same mistakes many times. Experience must be tempered with good judgment, a concern for the environment and the members of the group, and a willingness to learn from anyone who can teach you better outdoor skills.

Leadership. Every group that ventures into the wild outdoors should have a leader and an alternate. The leader is responsible for monitoring the needs and desires of the group and for making decisions to ensure safety and enjoyment. A good outdoor leader learns the abilities and limitations of each individual in the group and delegates task accordingly.

Maturity. The more mature the members of the crew, the more demanding the adventures they can enjoy. Mature backcountry travelers can take care of themselves in the wilderness and help others when they require assistance. They use good judgment and, rather than waiting for someone to tell them what to do, they keep their eyes open and pitch in wherever they can to make an outing run smoothly and well.

CHAPTER 15

Attitude. When difficulties arise while a group is away from home, the attitudes of crew members will determine the success of an adventure. Sometimes it's easy to let anger and depression spoil a trip, but even the worst weather and the silliest mistakes can be overcome if the group takes adversity in stride and endures. Cheerfulness is infectious. Keep your spirits high; treks with the most miserable conditions may create the fondest memories.

(For more on maturity and attitude, see "Reducing Our Impact.")

Interests. Each member of your crew will have definite likes and dislikes. One might love kayaking but dislike mountain climbing. Another might enjoy camp stew and hate freeze-dried chili. Still another might like to spend time alone while a fourth person might thrive on the company of others. As your group discusses what it would like to do on an adventure, each person probably will make personal interests known. All will want to do the things they like best. Are you willing to try something new? Does a crew member have a skill to teach the rest of you once you're in the field? Can you satisfy several different interests with one trip, or do you need to focus on a single activity on this trek, and do something different next time?

Physical capabilities. Different adventures require different degrees of exertion. Therefore, be certain the activities you are considering are not beyond the physical capabilities of your group. An exhausted hiker is not only miserable, but also is more likely to become injured, lost, or ill. A clue to the fitness of your companions is the amount of exercise they get during a typical week. If they regularly engage in sports, walk a lot, bicycle, or go camping on weekends, they probably are in good shape. Even so, make a crew's first treks short and easy. You'll have time to get acquainted with one another, practice using your equipment, and hone skills while you're giving your body a chance to become accustomed to the rigors of the outdoors. Gradually extend the length and duration of your outings so the physical development of crew members can keep pace.

(For more on getting in shape, see "Becoming Fit.")

Planning the Duration of a Trip

Determine how much time you have for a trip. It could be an afternoon excursion, an overnight campout, or a wilderness trek lasting several weeks. Include in your plans sufficient time to travel to and from points where your adventure will begin and end, and give yourself a few hours' leeway in case the weather is bad or the terrain is more rugged than you had expected.

Available time is a factor that helps you determine the shape of an adventure, as do the physical conditions of your crew and the amount of energy you wish to expend. There will seldom be complete agreement since some crew members may want to travel long and hard, while others would rather spend more time studying the surroundings and photographing wildlife, or making camp early so they can fix gourmet backcountry meals. Before you leave home, decide how strenuous a trip will be so that once you're underway, no one will be caught by surprise. Take the desires of everyone into consideration and see if you can work out compromises. Perhaps you will want to hike hard one day and take it easy the next, or plan one leisurely outing followed a few weeks later by a more ambitious trek.

CHAPTER 15

See the sights along your way.

Planning What to Do

Hiking, kayaking, fishing, cooking, orienteering, skiing, swimming, bird watching—there are hundreds of great outdoor activities. There are so many, in fact, your group may have trouble agreeing on what to do during an adventure. Of course, the interests of crew members will have the most weight in determining your activities, though sometimes the area in which you'll travel makes the choice obvious. If your destination is a fishing hole hopping with hungry trout, you'll have no trouble deciding what to do once you get there! The season of the year also may help you decide. In snowy conditions, for instance, cross-country skis or snowshoes will get you into the backcountry. In the autumn, you can comfortably travel areas that in the spring are thick with black flies, mosquitoes, and mud.

Planning Where to Go

Deciding on a general area in which to conduct your activities is usually not difficult. You probably already know of interesting parks, forests, mountain ranges, grasslands, waterways, and historic landmarks, and when you've heard other adventurers tell about territories they've enjoyed, their descriptions may have whetted your appetite to see those places yourself. While exotic, distant locations are appealing, don't overlook areas close to home. Transportation arrangements will be easier and you'll be surprised how exciting familiar territory can be. Also, it's a good idea to practice your outdoor skills in lands you know well, saving more remote destinations until you're confident you have the experience to handle new country.

(For more on selecting an area, see "Where to Go" and "Planning.")

As you evaluate the suitability of an area, consider the following:

Terrain. Is the land rugged or gentle? What activities does the terrain suggest? Will it demand special equipment or training?

Weather. Anticipating weather conditions, including high and low temperatures, wind velocity, and precipitation, is crucial to successful trek planning. Not only should you plan for the probable weather of the are a and terrain where you are going, but also for the possibility of unusually severe weather. If you plan for freak storms that occur perhaps once in 10 years, you probably will be able to survive a storm that may occur only once in 100 years. Good judgment must be exercised in weighing the amount of clothing, food, and gear to be carried against the likelihood of extremely severe weather. The National Oceanographic and Atmospheric Association and the Environmental Data and Information Service publish weather statistics that are valuable for planning treks, particularly in areas unfamiliar to you. Television, radio, and newspaper weather forecasts will give you a general idea of current weather conditions to expect. In mountainous areas, forecasts for cities at low elevations may have little in common with conditions high among the peaks.

(For more on understanding the elements, see "Weather.")

Wildlife. Animals will enrich your adventures. In much of the country you may want to carry a bird identification book and a pair of binoculars. In bear country you'll need 50 feet of nylon line and a bear bag so that at night you can suspend your food from a tree.

(For more on animals, see "Wildlife and Fish.")

Vegetation. Forests heavy with underbrush may be impossible to travel, beds of nettles can make you more than a little miserable, but plump raspberries and wild strawberries make hiking in the summer worthwhile.

(For more on vegetation, see "Plants.")

Potential hazards. Are you planning a route that will take you near steep cliffs? Snow slopes that could avalanche? Swift rivers that must be crossed? Dry woodlands susceptible to forest fires? The more you know about possible dangers, the easier it will be to deal with them.

(For more on avoiding hazards, see "Outdoor Safety.")

Necessary permission. Find out if agencies overseeing the areas you wish to use require permits or fees. If you plan to cross private property, contact the owners and get permission to enter their lands.

Make an Itinerary

Once you've decided where you want to go and what you want to do, work out an itinerary in your notebook. Here's a sample of an itinerary for an overnight trip:

Lark Mountain Trip Itinerary

Thursday

7 p.m.	Shakedown at Scott's house. Everybody brings equipment and food and checks it over.

Friday

4 p.m.	Meet after school at Scott's house. Have all gear and provision ready to go.
4:15 p.m.	Tom's dad drives us to beginning of Lark Mountain trail.
5 p.m.	Start hiking.
6 p.m.	Reach Lark Mountain pond. Make camp, cook supper, have evening campfire, and use star charts to identify constellations.

Saturday

7 a.m.	Start breakfast.
7:30 a.m.	Eat, clean up, and break camp. Pack gear.
9 a.m.	Fishing in Lark Mountain pond.
12 noon	Lunch
1 p.m.	More fishing, and maybe a walk up Lark Mountain if the weather is clear.
3 p.m.	Start hiking toward the road.
4:30 p.m.	Meet Tom's dad at the trailhead for ride home.

An itinerary is a blueprint of your outing, and once you have it on paper you'll discover it's easy to see what meals you'll need to prepare and what equipment you'll want to take. You won't be likely to forget important details like arranging transportation to and from the area, and you can have the adult leaders of your group look over your plans and make their own suggestions.

Planning a Budget

Using your itinerary as a guide, figure the cost of the trip. Usually it won't cost much; on a day-hike near home or a quick bike ride, you can make a few sandwiches, pick up a candy bar, and be on your way. An overnight campout will require a little more food and maybe a dollar or two to help a driver pay for gas.

However, the finances of adventures that entail more than a few meals, require special equipment, or begin a long distance from home need to be planned with care. You might want to go to several grocery stores to compare food prices, and you can call a motor club to learn about travel costs. Estimate all the expenses including those for permits and campground fees, and then divide the total by the number of members in your group. Can you each afford your share? If not, you may need to alter your plans, though for exciting, extended opportunities such as the wilderness treks offered by high-adventure programs, you can organize weekend and summer work projects to earn the funds you need.

Planning Gear and Provisions

Other chapters of the *Fieldbook* discuss in detail what you'll need in the way of food, clothing, personal equipment, and group gear. As you and your companions plan an adventure, go over the *Fieldbook* lists of gear and provisions, and in your notebook write down exactly what items you'll need for the trip you're planning, then divide up the responsibilities of gathering them together.

(Use the lists in "Gearing Up," "Hiking," and "Camping Know-How." For suggestions on food, see "Trail Menus and Cooking.")

Personal gear. Each member of the group should bring personal clothing suitable for the season, and the gear each will need along the way and in camp.

Group gear. Determine what equipment your group will need and where it is stored, then assign a couple of members to gather and prepare it for the trip.

Food. You can handle food preparation as you do group gear, working together to select recipes and determine how much of each ingredient to buy, and then assigning a couple of people to purchase the provisions and repackage them for the trip. For a long trek there will be lots of food, and you'll all want to pitch in to get it ready.

Shakedown

A day or two before you leave for an adventure, conduct a thorough shakedown. The members in charge of group equipment and provisions should bring the items they have gathered, and each person should have all the necessary personal gear. To begin a shakedown, spread everything on the floor or on a ground cloth outdoors. Read aloud the list of personal equipment, and as each item is mentioned be sure everyone has it and puts it into a pack. When you've finished the personal equipment list, there may still be a few items left on the floor. Some, such as cameras, binoculars, fishing gear, and nature books, may be worth their weight in the backcountry, while other items are unnecessary and should be left at home.

Go through lists of group equipment and food in the same way until you have everything your crew will need and nothing more. Divide the group gear and provisions among the members so that everyone carries a fair share. Load your packs, swing them onto your backs, and adjust them until they ride easily on your shoulders. When you're done with the shakedown, every detail of your trip preparations should be done except one, and that is the most important of all—leaving a trip plan.

Trip Plan

A trip plan lets people know where you're going and when you intend to be back. If you are late in returning, they must assume you have encountered difficulties, and they should begin search and rescue operations. Leave copies of your trip plan with your parents, a member of your unit committee, and any park officials, forest rangers, or law enforcement agencies whose jurisdictions include the areas in which you'll be traveling. When you return be sure to notify everyone with whom you have left a trip plan so they know you're back and don't report you missing.

SAMPLE TRIP PLAN

Trip plan of _____

Date and time of departure _____

Date and time of return _____

Adults who will go along _____

Destination _____
_____

Route (going) _____
_____
_____

Route (returning) _____
_____
_____

Permits required _____

Special equipment _____
_____
_____

Special clothing _____
_____
_____

II.
OUTDOOR
ADVENTURES

"The object of your mission is to explore the Missouri River, and such principal streams of it, as, by its course and communication with the waters of the Pacific Ocean, whether the Columbia, Oregon, Colorado, or any other river, may offer the most direct and practicable water-communication across the continent, for the purposes of commerce."

President Thomas Jefferson's instructions to
Lewis and Clark, April 1803

"Coulter . . . with a pack of thirty pounds weight, his gun and some ammunition, went upwards of five hundred miles to the Crow nation; gave them information, and proceeded from them to several other tribes. On his return, a party of Indians in whose company he happened to be was attacked, and he was lamed by a severe wound in the leg; not withstanding which, he returned to the establishment, entirely alone and without assistance, several hundred miles."

Manuel Lisa, 1818

Chapter 16

Backpacking

David L. Caffey, Ed.D
Chief Ranger, Philmont Scout Ranch,
1974–77; Author, *Head for the High
Country;* Director, Harwood
Foundation, Taos, New Mexico

B ackpacking has long been a part of the American tradition. Native Americans were able to carry enough food and gear to sustain themselves during long periods of travel, and many explorers, trappers, and settlers owned nothing in the world except what they could tote in bags slung over their shoulders. Through trial and error they learned what to take along, what to leave at home, and what skills were essential for living in the wilderness. They were ready for any situations that might arise, and because they were prepared, they traveled in relative safety.

Today you can share with those early Americans the great adventure of backpacking. Trails can carry you away from the demands of school and jobs, from the blare of televisions and radios, from the asphalt and concrete of the cities, and the speed and complexities of modern life. Food will taste better, and at night sleep will come easier. You'll become self-reliant, able to take care of yourself far from the nearest road. You'll learn responsibility, since you must let others know where you are going and when you will return, and you must hike and camp in such a way that the areas you visit will not be harmed by your presence.

Discover the joy of being on a trail for a few days, weeks, and even months. Learn how simply you can live, and sense the passage of time not by clocks, but by the progress of the sun and the stars wheeling through the sky. Revel in the contentment of being warm and dry, and nourished with simple trail foods. Delight in alpine blossoms, fog lifting above snowy peaks, sunlight sparkling on distant lakes, and the quiet observation of wildlife. In the simplicity of backpacking you'll find yourself a little closer to the core of life.

What You Have In Your Head

Backpacking is an adventure that requires a general knowledge of many outdoor skills. What you carry on your back is important, but even more essential is the wisdom you have in your head to keep yourself safe and to fully appreciate and protect the country through which you travel.

The first section of the *Fieldbook* contains information basic to enjoyable backcountry adventures—camping know-how, outdoor first aid, and so on. Read those chapters carefully and learn the techniques they describe. By the time you hit the trail, you should have a pretty good grounding in backcountry lore.

What You Have On Your Back

Part one of the *Fieldbook* also covers the gear you'll need for backpacking. What you put in your pack can go a long way toward making your trips successful.

COMPLETE BACKPACKING EQUIPMENT LIST

_____ Backpack

_____ Boots

_____ Socks

_____ Clothing appropriate for the season

_____ Sweater or jacket

_____ Parka or coat

_____ Rain gear

_____ Hat

_____ Tent

_____ Groundcloth

_____ Tent stakes

_____ Sleeping bag

_____ Foam sleeping pad

_____ Stove

_____ Fuel bottle or cylinders (filled)

_____ Cook kit

_____ Cooking utensils

_____ Cup

_____ Bowl or plate

_____ Spoon

_____ Food

_____ First aid kit

_____ Pocketknife

_____ Matches

_____ Water bottle or canteen

_____ Fire starters

_____ Flashlight with extra batteries and bulb

_____ Watch

_____ Whistle

_____ Toothbrush

_____ Toothpaste

_____ Biodegradable soap

_____ Small towel

_____ Metal mirror

_____ Comb

_____ Pencil and paper

_____ Repair kit

_____ Cord

_____ Bear bag

_____ Bear bag rope

_____ Emergency coins

_____ Protection from insects

_____ Bandanas

_____ Compass

_____ Moccasins, running shoes, or booties

_____ Toilet paper

_____ Camera (optional)

_____ Hiking stick (optional)

(For a discussion of each item, see "Gearing Up.")

CHAPTER 16

SHAKEDOWN

Get together with your crew a day or two before you depart on a trek and conduct a *shakedown*. Spread all your equipment, clothing, and provisions on the floor or on a ground cloth outdoors. Consider each item carefully. Is it essential? If so, pile it beside your pack. If not, put it in a separate pile you'll leave at home.

After you've gone through everything, repeat the process. Check off each item on your lists of food and gear, and be sure you have all the basics but nothing more.

Finally, take a last look through the pile of nonessentials. Some of the items could make your trip more pleasant, and you'll have to decide whether they are worth the extra weight on your shoulders. In the case of a plant identification book, binoculars, or a camera, the answer may well be yes, but don't forget that ounces add up quickly. The more thorough your shakedown, the lighter the load on your back.

LOADING A PACK

Once you've determined what to carry, the next step is to pack it for the trail. Small, frequently used items go in your pockets—your knife, compass, whistle, bandana, some matches, a few adhesive bandages, and perhaps paper and a pencil.

Equipment you won't need until you make camp can go deep in the pack, but rain gear, the first aid kit, a sweater, clean socks, and your lunch should ride just under the main flap. Carry your map, water bottle, sun and insect protection, and trail snacks in the pack's outside pockets, reserving one pocket for your fuel bottle or cylinders so they'll be isolated from the rest of your supplies. Always return each small item to a specific pocket of your pack so you can locate it quickly.

For trail hiking, arrange the contents of your pack so that its center of gravity is high and close to your back. For cross-country skiing, snowshoeing, and mountaineering treks, you can trade a little comfort for a lot of stability by placing heavy gear in the bottom of the pack and thus lowering the center of gravity. In either case, pad the front of the pack's interior with a layer of clothing to provide cushioning against your back.

UPPER LEFT POCKET
Water bottle or canteen
Rain gear

LOWER LEFT POCKET
Protection from sun
Protection from insects
Flashlight with spare bulb
    and batteries

UPPER COMPARTMENT
Cook kit and utensils
Stove
Water bag
Tent or tarp
Tent stakes
Ground cloth
Food and condiments in
    bag

LOWER COMPARTMENT
Hat or cap
Socks
Clothing appropriate for
    the season
Sweater or jacket
Parka or coat
Moccasins, running shoes,
    or booties
Bandana

STUFF BAG
Sleeping bag
Foam pad

CHAPTER 16

FLAP POCKET
  Camping permit
  Maps
  Pencil and
    paper
  Compass

BACK POCKET
  Cup
  Bowl
  Matches and
    fire starters
  Whistle
  Cord
  Bear bag and
    rope
  Emergency
    coins
  Soap
  Toilet paper
  Metal mirror
  Comb
  Toothbrush
  Toothpaste
  Small towel

**UPPER RIGHT
POCKET**
  Stove fuel
  Stove wind
    screen

**LOWER RIGHT
POCKET**
  First aid kit

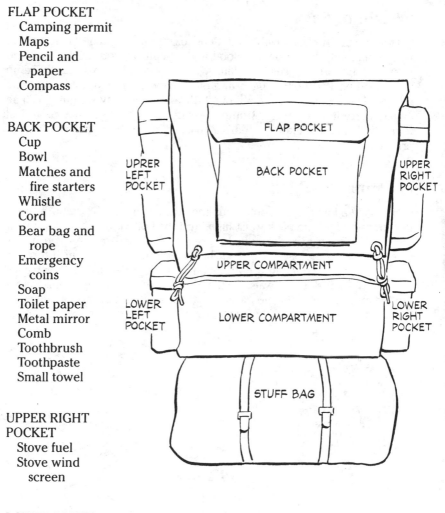

Weight of Pack

How much your pack will weigh depends on the length of the adventure you've planned, the amount of food and equipment you must carry, and your personal preferences. Traveling with a group allows you to divide up tents, food packs, cooking gear, and other crew gear. If you can keep the weight of your pack down to about a fifth your total body weight, you'll be able to carry it pretty well. Strong hikers may be able to haul a good deal more, but the most experienced backpackers keep their packs as light as practical.

Hoisting the Pack

Swinging a loaded pack onto your shoulders is simple. Grasp both shoulder straps and lift the pack waist high. Rest the bottom of the pack on your thigh and slip an arm through the proper shoulder strap. As you do so, smoothly swing the pack onto your back and slip your other arm through the remaining strap. Lean a little forward at the waist to hoist your pack into position, buckle the waist belt, and adjust the shoulder straps so that when you stand upright most of the pack's weight rides on your hips. To remove the pack, reverse the steps.

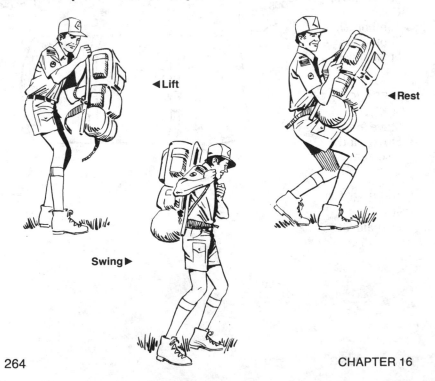

◄Lift

◄Rest

Swing►

HITTING THE TRAIL

Hiking with a pack is much different from walking without one. A pack on your shoulders alters your sense of balance. Its weight puts extra strain on your feet, ankles, and knees, especially when you're pounding downhill. Take it easy at first until you become accustomed to the sensation of carrying a pack, and rest whenever you begin to tire.

Over the course of a long hike, pack straps and waist belts can make your shoulders and hips sore, especially if you're lean and don't have a great deal of natural padding on your bones. To ease the discomfort, occasionally adjust the shoulder straps to shift the weight of the pack. You also can use a couple of socks for padding by folding them over the hip belt or under the shoulder straps.

You may be tempted to slip your thumbs under the pack straps when your shoulders are sore, but that's not a good idea. If you stumble, you may not be able to free your hands quickly enough to break your fall.

Setting a good pace will enable everyone in your group to enjoy a trek. Help ensure the comfort of the slowest members of the crew by position-ing them near the front of the group where they can more easily maintain a steady stride. Stronger backpackers should carry a greater proportion of group gear, though no one should be made to feel inferior for toting a light load, or superior for enduring a pack that is too heavy. Backpacking is a group activity, and everyone must pitch in to do whatever is necessary for the good of the entire crew.

Begin each day's walk slowly, allowing plenty of time for your muscles to warm up and your packs to settle into place. Take brief rest breaks to refresh yourselves and adjust your clothing to meet changing weather conditions, and never hike to the point of exhaustion; you may need those reserves of energy to meet unexpected situations.

EXTENDED TREKS

Have you ever reached the end of a weekend camping trip and wished you didn't have to go home? Have you ever looked out over ranges of mountains that seemed to invite you to hike all the way to the horizon and beyond? Ever wanted a challenge that would put your backcountry skills to a real test? If your answer is yes, you may be ready for a backpacking trek that lasts for weeks and covers hundreds of miles.

Long-distance hiking is becoming increasingly popular as backpackers gain confidence in their abilities and discover magnificent trails that seem to go on almost forever. The chapter "Where to Go" describes some of the most famous of these extended footpaths, including the Appalachian Trail and Pacific Crest Trail. If you wish, you can follow one of them from one state border to another, or even from one border of the nation to the other. Of course, you can plot an extended trek anywhere in the country by studying maps, finding interesting hiking trails, and figuring out ways to connect them into one continuous route.

To become a long-distance backpacker you'll need to make some special preparations. Start with durable gear of the best quality you can afford, and treat it with care. Equipment that would show few signs of wear on a short trek is much more likely to break down or wear out during an extended hike. Stock your repair kit with spare parts to keep your stove in running order, to patch your clothing and tent, and to keep your pack in good shape.

CHAPTER 16

Rhythm of a Long Hike

Unaccustomed to the weight of a pack, the long hours of walking, and the rigors of spending many days and nights living in the backcountry, you may find that the first weeks of a trek are a little difficult. Along with the excitement of the adventure, you'll probably have some doubts about the wisdom of such a massive undertaking, and perhaps even question your ability to make it all the way to your destination.

However, changes will begin taking place in your body and mind from the instant you take your first step. By the third or fourth week of a hike, thick callouses will protect the soles of your once-tender feet. You'll no longer be so conscious of having a pack hanging from your shoulders, and you will be able to complete your camp chores quickly and efficiently. Your legs will be stronger, and any fat on your body will melt away. As your body and mind become accustomed to the demands of the adventure, you'll find that you have fallen into the rhythm of the trek.

Long Hike Nutrition

Accustomed to eating fairly large meals and plentiful snacks, you may find that during the first weeks of a big hike, trail food doesn't fill you up. However, just as your mind and muscles become attuned to the trail, your digestive tract also will become streamlined and efficient. In fact, many hikers find that after a month on the trail they eat less than they would at home.

The food you carry on a long hike differs little from what you would take on any backpacking trek. You may want to scrutinize your food lists with weight in mind, and to make sure nothing in your pack will deteriorate in quality before you use it. Divide your provisions into separate meal packets, and seal them into plastic bags.

(For more on selecting and preparing food for backpacking, see "Trail Menus and Cooking.")

Resupplying

When a hike will keep you on the trail more than a week or 10 days, it's unlikely you'll be able to carry all the provisions you'll need. Two good ways to resupply yourself are trailhead rendevous and mail drops. In a few cases, caches and air drops may be your only options.

Whichever method you choose, gather and pack supplies for the entire trek before you leave home. Get some sturdy cardboard boxes, and reinforce them with strips of strong, wide tape. Line the interior of each

◄ Air rendezvous

box with a couple of large plastic trash bags placed inside one another, and pack your provisions into the bags.

Don't seal the box until absolutely necessary. That way you or your support crew can add any last-minute items that you may need. And be sure to put in some treats and a special meal. A few weeks down the trail, opening a box of supplies is cause for a real celebration.

Trailhead Rendevous

Unless your trek takes you into the heart of a huge wilderness area such as Alaska's Denali National Park, you'll probably cross a road at least once a week. With careful planning, you can arrange to meet with your parents or other reliable adults at points where the trail meets highways. They can bring the food you need for the next leg of your journey.

Mail Drop

Mail drops are particularly effective when you hike a long trail far from home. Research the trail ahead of time and find post offices near it to which you can send parcels addressed to yourself in care of General Delivery. Ask a postmaster to explain the packing and mailing regulations you'll have to follow. You also can contact park and forest rangers who may know of addresses within parks to which you can mail your provisions.

The timing of your mail drops is important since the post office should have several weeks to deliver each of your boxes. Also remember that most post offices are closed on Saturday afternoons, Sundays, and holidays, and those in remote areas may have more limited hours. When you're hungry, tired, and eager to get into your next box of supplies, there's nothing more frustrating than reaching a post office just after it has closed for the weekend.

Caches and Air Drops

It is possible to stow your provisions in plastic or metal buckets with tight lids and then, before you embark on your trek, stash them at intervals along the trail you're going to hike or get a horse packer to bring them in. Usually the buckets are buried to protect them from animals. It's also possible to arrange with a pilot to drop your supplies by parachute at prearranged places and times. If you do use caches or air drops, you must carry containers and parachutes out of the wilderness and dispose of them properly.

PACING A LONG TREK

With so much trail lying ahead of them, many long-distance hikers set off at a blistering pace. Unfortunately they've forgotten that the real joy of any adventure is not in the destination, but in the journey itself. Too much haste for too many days can sour hikers, making them irritable and susceptible to illness and injury.

As you plan a long hike, allow yourself plenty of time to delight in every aspect of the trip. Don't be in such a hurry that you can't stop to watch the wildlife, study the flowers, and take in the beauty of the land through which you're passing. Give yourself an occasional day off to sleep late, wash clothes, sit in the sun, and rest.

As with any backcountry activity, circumstances may arise that make it prudent for you to stop and go home. An injury, a lingering illness, or the depression that sometimes afflicts long-distance hikers can make a trip so miserable there's no reason to go on. But consider your decision carefully. The rainy weather that spoils the adventure for a few days may suddenly clear, leaving blue sky and warm breezes to lift your spirits and urge you on.

"In a canoe a man changes and the life he has lived seems strangely remote. Time is no longer of moment, for he has become part of space and freedom. What matters is that he is heading down the misty trail of explorers and voyageurs, with a fair wind and a chance for a good camp somewhere ahead. The future is other lakes, countless rapids and the sound of them, portages through muskeg and over the ledges."

Sigurd F. Olson, 1972

Chapter 17

Canoeing

Thomas W. Johnston
Veteran Staff Member of Maine
National High Adventure Area and
Northern Tier National High
Adventure Programs; District
Executive, Moby Dick Council

For hundreds of years, canoes have plied the waters of the world. Polynesian islanders long have traveled vast distances across the Pacific in swift, narrow outrigger canoes packed with provisions. Indians of the Pacific Northwest shaped cedar logs into magnificent war canoes large enough to hold a dozen paddlers or more. On the Great Plains, braves stretched buffalo hides over wooden frames to make round boats, and the Indians of the Great Lakes and eastern woodlands fashioned light, graceful canoes covered with birchbark. As explorers and fur trappers worked their way into the American interior, they often used canoes to wander the rivers and lakes of the new land.

Today, the canoe still opens a special world of adventure. Whether you embark on an afternoon of easy paddling, a week of canoe camping, or a month of wilderness exploration, a canoe offers you a fresh way to enjoy territory and wildlife you might otherwise miss. You can glide silently along a forested shore, hear the cries of loons and see deer, moose, and bear. You can feel the power of a fast stream, and maneuver your craft through the foam of a small rapids. You can strengthen your body and sharpen your mind as you master the fine art of canoeing. Indians, islanders, explorers, and Scouts have long known that canoeing is one of the best ways to travel. Give it a try and you'll agree.

KINDS OF CANOES

Selecting the right canoe for your outings is a matter of finding the proper size, materials, and design to fit your needs. Beginners will do well to borrow or rent canoes to learn the advantages of various kinds before investing in craft of their own. Most canoes today have skins of canvas, aluminum, fiberglass, or plastic.

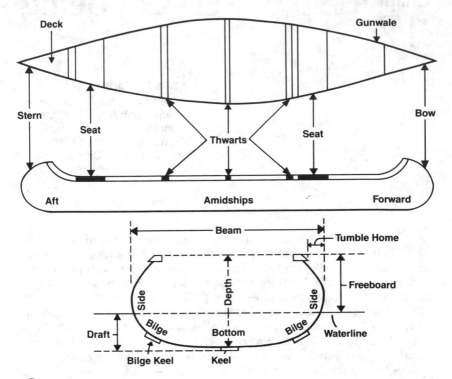

Canvas

The early birchbark canoes were quick and responsive, but they were also fragile, easily torn by rocks and snags. In the 19th century, craftsmen began building canoes by stretching specially treated canvas over wooden frames. Layers of paint and lacquer toughened the skin, yet the canoes retained the fine handling characteristics of their birchbark ancestors.

Some canvas canoes are still in use today, though they require extra care in the water and in storage. On long excursions, the canvas and wood can absorb water. The skin is susceptible to tearing, and the wooden frame can crack and rot. Still, a well-built canvas canoe can light up the eyes of any serious canoeist.

Aluminum

After World War II, several aircraft companies turned their expertise in building planes to constructing lightweight metal canoes, and soon the aluminum canoe dominated the market. It is light enough to be portaged by one or two people, and it requires little maintenance. However, although it is tough, an aluminum canoe is not indestructible. The metal skin can be dented and torn, the thwarts broken, and the ribs cracked. Rivets can pop loose and, in extreme cases, a strong current can wrap a canoe around a boulder. The misconception that fiberglass, plastic, and aluminum canoes can't be damaged may cause inexperienced paddlers to use poor judgment and attempt to navigate waters too rough for their skills. Treat every canoe, regardless of the materials from which it is made, with care.

Fiberglass

Fiberglass is a fabric made of woven strands of fine glass. Layers of the fabric can be saturated with various polyesters, then stretched over a canoe frame and allowed to harden into a strong, durable shell. Chopped fiberglass can be sprayed into molds along with polyester resins and a catalyst to create rugged canoes complete but for the addition of gunwales, seats, and thwarts.

Plastic

The latest canoe materials are strong plastics layered over a foam core and reinforced with a vinyl skin. Light and flexible, a canoe made of plastic has no seams or ribs. It can bend back into shape after serious warping or creasing but, like any canoe, it has its limits. Do not abuse it.

With four materials to select from and a host of companies eager to sell you their current model, you'll need some experience before you buy a canoe. Learn all you can from seasoned canoeists about different designs and brand names. Try out a variety of canoes so that you'll know just what you want. Deal with reputable merchants and manufacturers, and be ready to pay enough to get a quality canoe rather than a second-rate product. You'll be happier in the long run.

One way you might save money and get a canoe with special meaning is to make one from a kit. Follow the same guidelines in purchasing a kit as you would for buying a ready-made canoe, and be sure you'll have the help of someone who has experience with the kit you want.

STORAGE

Canoes spend most of their time out of the water. You can greatly extend the life of your canoe by storing it properly. If you have room in a shed or garage, keep your craft indoors, turned upside down and stored on supports. Water, sunlight, and abrasion are the enemies of any boat so if you keep your canoe outdoors, build a rack that will keep it off the ground and shelter it from the elements.

EQUIPMENT

No canoe is complete without equipment to propel it and to protect its passengers. A good canoeist puts as much thought into the choice of gear as into the selection of the right canoe.

Paddles

Paddles are made of wood, aluminum, plastic, and combinations of all three. Like canvas canoes, wooden paddles have a classic feel that synthetic models lack. Ash, maple, spruce, and cedar make fine paddles, well worth the careful sanding and refinishing they require between long trips. Take care not to grind the tips into gravelly lake bottoms or the handles against rocky shores, and in porcupine country stow them out of reach of animals eager to gnaw wood salty with perspiration.

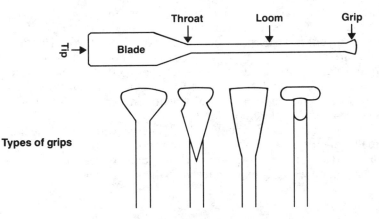

Types of grips

Before you use a paddle, check it for size. A blade width of 6 to 8 inches is fine for most canoeists, and the shaft should be long enough so that the grip reaches just about to your nose when the tip of the blade is touching the floor. Since you may be swinging it all day, a light paddle is preferable to a heavy one.

Personal Flotation Devices

Each canoe must have one approved personal flotation device for every person on board. In most states this is a law, and it is good common sense everywhere. Select flotation vests or jackets from the United States Coast Guard list of acceptable PFDs, and wear one whenever you are on the water. For general use, the BSA model 01675, a type-III vest, is a good choice.

Painters

A painter is a rope, and you'll find a multitude of uses for it. Nylon rope ¼- or ⅜-inch in diameter is ideal. Tie a painter 12 feet long to the bow of your canoe, and another to the stern. Coil them and keep them out of the way by taping the coils with duct tape to the bow and stern plates, or by tying them to the thwarts. Include in your gear an extra painter 25 feet in length, and use the painters for tying up along shore, guiding your canoe through shallow streams, and for rigging up a sail.

Ropes called *heaving lines* are used for rescuing stranded canoeists. A heaving line should be 50 feet long and at least ⅜-inch in diameter, and it should float. Depending on the expected roughness of the water conditions, each canoe in a party should carry one or two heaving lines.

Bailers

Canoes are bound to take on water, no matter how calm the surface of a lake or stream. You can make a bailer for emptying your canoe by cutting a section out of a 1-gallon plastic jug. Use a large sponge to sop

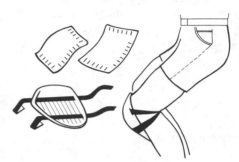

up puddles in the bottom of a canoe. To prevent them from floating away if you capsize, attach each bailer and sponge to a thwart with a 5-foot length of light line.

Knee Pads

A little cushioning under your knees will keep them comfortable during a long day's paddle. You can improvise a pair of knee pads by cutting up an old closed-cell foam sleeping pad, or you can buy gardener's knee pads or whitewater kneeling pads with nonskid surfaces.

Yokes

If you intend to portage your canoe, a padded yoke will make your job easier. Some canoes have built-in yokes made of aluminum or wood. If your craft doesn't have one, you can bolt a temporary yoke onto the center thwart, or you can make your own yoke by lashing two paddles between the stern and midship thwarts.

Duct Tape

Duct tape is handy for everything from repairing torn canoes and splintered paddles to securing painters, plugging holes, reinforcing worn vinyl, and patching the seat of your pants. Wrap a length of duct tape onto a blunt pencil and keep it in your pocket for quick access. Stow the rest of the roll in your repair kit.

LAUNCHING AND LANDING

Much of the success of canoeing depends on a canoe in tip-top shape. Protect your canoe as you launch and land it by wearing sneakers or lightweight boots you don't mind getting wet. That may sound a little strange at first, but in practice you'll find that if you carry your canoe into the water before you climb in, and if you hop out of it before the prow can scrape against the shore, you can launch and land without allowing the least scratch to mar the skin of your craft.

To launch a canoe, put on your PFD and carry the canoe into water that is at least 6 inches deep, taking care not to catch your foot under a log or between rocks. Stow your gear in the canoe, then have one person hold the craft steady while the bowman gets in first. Place your hands on opposite gunwales for support and keep your weight centered and low while moving gracefully into the canoe. Then the stern paddler climbs aboard and paddles the boat away from the shore. Do not use a paddle to shove off, since rocks and gravel can roughen the blade or grip.

Land a canoe by reversing the steps of the launching procedure, stepping out of the canoe and into the water before the prow grinds into the bank. No landing is complete until the canoe is tied securely to a tree or boulder, or has been carried ashore and overturned. Currents, winds, and tides have a way of making off with poorly protected canoes.

LOADING A CANOE

If you'll be out in a canoe for long, you'll want to take provisions and extra clothing, and for trips involving overnight camps you'll need all the gear a backpacker would use. No matter what you carry, make it watertight. Pack as if you are certain your canoe will be swamped, even though you hope it won't. That way, your gear will always be dry and safe.

There are many watertight containers on the market, but plastic bags are just as effective and much less expensive. Pack all your items into small, heavy-duty plastic bags. Close each one with a *gooseneck* by twisting the top and then bending it over and wrapping it with a strong rubber band. Put the small bags into packs lined with larger plastic bags such as trash can liners. If you're taking a sleeping bag, jam it into a "stuff sack" lined with a plastic bag before you slip it into a pack. Gooseneck the large bags, and your packs will be waterproof and they'll float.

Of course, you'll want to have some gear handy all day. Stow cameras, binoculars, maps, compasses, lunches, and the like in surplus waterproof ammunition boxes, or in heavy plastic bags you can gooseneck and keep close to you as you paddle.

Float a canoe in the water before you load it with gear. Keep the load low. In most cases, you'll want to distribute the weight of the packs evenly in the center of the canoe, though sometimes moving gear forward or backward will help you more effectively manage your craft as you paddle in strong winds, high waves, or rapids.

Attach each pack to the canoe by tying it to a thwart with a 10-foot length of cord. Do the same with ammunition boxes and loose bags. That way, if you capsize, the packs, boxes, and bags will float free

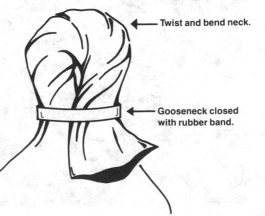

Twist and bend neck.

Gooseneck closed with rubber band.

CHAPTER 17

of the canoe, making it easier for you to recover your equipment and get the swamped canoe to shore.

Paddling

The real joy of canoeing comes when you glide quietly across the water, the canoe responding to every dip of your paddle. To maintain a good pace over a long distance, you'll need to master the general principles of paddling, as well as a few of the basic strokes.

Good position leads to effective paddling. Whether you canoe with a partner or alone, kneel in the canoe, wedge your knees against the sides of the craft, and rest your weight against a thwart or the front edge of a seat; or sit solidly on a seat and brace your knees against the gunwales. Think of yourself as a part of the canoe, locked securely in place.

When you travel with a partner, work as a team paddling in unison on opposite sides of the canoe. Maintain a smooth rhythm, keeping your strokes steady and light, and relying on the strong muscles of your shoulders and back. Keep your eye on your destination and paddle directly for it. The straighter your line of travel, the less energy you'll have to expend.

There are a number of effective paddle strokes, and you'll want to learn them all. For starters, become familiar with the *forward stroke* and J-*stroke* for traveling forward, the *backstroke* for reversing the course of a canoe, and the *drawstroke* and *prystroke* for moving a canoe sideways.

Forward Stroke

Bow and stern paddlers can both use the forward stroke. Holding the paddle by the grip and shaft, lean forward, dip the full length of the blade into the water, then pull with your lower arm, push with the upper one, and draw the paddle through the water parallel to the canoe. As it comes out of the water, flip the blade sideways, or *feather* it, so it will cut through the wind as you swing it forward to begin the next stroke.

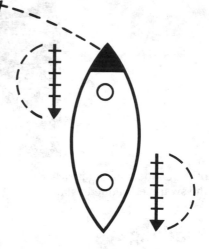

Because of the stern paddler's position in the craft, the strokes of that person will have more effect on the direction a canoe travels than will those of a paddler in the bow. The stern paddler can remedy that by using the J-stroke, one of several effective steering strokes.

J-Stroke

Begin a J-stroke as you would a forward stroke, but when the paddle is even with your hip, rotate it so that the edge of the blade nearest the canoe turns back and out (away from the canoe). At the same time, use your lower arm to push the paddle away from the canoe. The whole stroke makes the shape of the letter J, and the hook in the J that forms as you push the paddle away will keep the canoe on course.

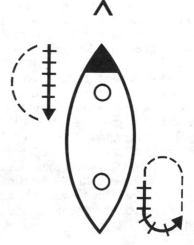

Backstroke

To stop the forward motion of a canoe and to move it backwards, dip your blade into the water close to the canoe and push it forward until it breaks the surface, then feather it back to the starting point and stroke again. Stopping a moving canoe requires a powerful stroke, so throw your shoulders and back into the work. By altering the angle of the blade and adjusting the motion of the paddle, the stern paddler can steer the canoe as it moves backwards.

Drawstroke

A drawstroke will move your craft sideways toward your paddle. Keeping your paddle vertical and the blade parallel to the canoe, lean out and dip the blade into the water. Pull with the lower hand, push with the upper one, and slip the blade out sideways just before it touches the canoe. Feather it underwater, and stroke again.

Prystroke

The prystroke will move your canoe sideways away from your paddle. Essentially it is a reverse drawstroke. Hold the paddle as you would for a drawstroke but instead of dipping it into the water away from the canoe and pulling toward yourself, slip the blade into the water next to the canoe and push it away. Increase your leverage by firmly holding the paddle just above the blade with your lower hand and pulling the top of the shaft toward you with your upper hand.

SPECIAL TECHNIQUES

In addition to practicing the basic strokes, a good canoeist knows special ways to get a canoe through any water. Among these are *sailing, poling, lining,* and *portaging.*

Sailing

When the wind is at your back and the lake is open and smooth, nothing beats the thrill of flying across the water under sail. Since a canoe is very light and draws little water, it won't take much sail to push you along, but it also won't take much wind to tip you over if you mishandle a turn. Keep that in mind as you decide when and where to give sailing a try.

Use a sturdy pole for a mast and another lashed to it to make a spar. Raise the mast toward the bow of the canoe, stabilize it by tying a painter between the top of the mast and the stern thwart, then tie a poncho or trail tarp to the spar so that it catches the wind. The person in the stern steers with a paddle while the bowman tends the sail and navigates. Be ready at a moment's notice to drop the sail and stop the canoe.

For better stability, lash two or three canoes side by side by tying a couple of poles across their thwarts. Raise sails in each canoe, or devise a framework that will straddle several craft and hold a single dining fly. Hang on!

Poling

In shallow streams, you can maneuver your canoe by poling it. Stand sideways in the center of the craft with your feet spread and planted directly over the keel. Push yourself along with a flexible pole 9 to 14 feet long and up to 2 inches in diameter. Poles made of wood, aluminum, and fiberglass are fine. Many have a soft iron shoe on the bottom end to protect the pole and grip the bottoms of rocky stream beds.

Poling takes practice, but since you can use the pole for balance as well as for locomotion, it is safe and efficient.

When a stream is too shallow for paddling or poling, you may have to wade, pulling the craft by its painters or gunwales. When a stream is too rough, your options are lining or portaging.

Lining

Whenever you suspect there is rough water ahead, land your canoe and scout ahead on foot before paddling on. Make sure you know what's coming up before you drift into it. If the stream appears to be unsafe or if you're tired of fighting upstream against a strong current, you'll want to line your craft through the difficult stretch of water, or portage around it.

To line a canoe, you'll need a couple of nylon cords 50 to 100 feet in length. Tie one just behind the bow and another ahead of the stern. (You can use painters as lines. Stow them properly as soon as you reach waters safe for paddling.) As you walk along the shore, guide the canoe by lengthening or shortening the lines to adjust the angle of the canoe so that it stays clear of the bank and maneuvers around obstacles. Never

Note position of line. Keep one end of canoe away from shore.

wrap a line around your hand or tie it to your waist; a swamped canoe weighs more than enough to drag you into the water.

Portaging

When lining is impractical and in territory where dry land separates the lakes in which you wish to paddle, portaging is the answer. Land the canoe safely, then unload it. Consider the length of the portage, the amount of gear you have to carry, and the strength of your crew; you might be able to carry everything at once, or you may want to make two trips, toting the gear and then coming back for the canoes.

You can carry a canoe by yourself if it is equipped with a yoke. With a partner nearby to assist you, stand alongside the middle of the craft with your knees slightly bent, grasp the nearest gunwale with both hands, and pull the canoe up onto your thighs. Reach across the canoe with your bow hand and grasp the far gunwale, slip your stern arm under the canoe to cradle it, then with a smooth motion lift and turn the canoe and let the yoke settle gently onto your shoulders. Balance the canoe with a hand on each gunwale. Have your partner lead the way as you walk, warning you of obstacles or turns in the trail. If you tire before the end of the portage, ease the bow of the canoe into the crotch of a tree and duck out from underneath for a rest.

Canoes also can be carried by two persons. Stand alongside the thwarts and, working in unison, lift the canoe onto your thighs, then lift and flip it so the thwarts rest on your shoulders. Walk in step, the taller person in front to navigate.

CHAPTER 17

When you reach the end of the partage, reverse the lifting procedure, place the canoe gently on the lake or stream, and wade it into water at least ankle deep before loading your gear and shoving off.

SAFETY

Safety is the most important word in canoeing. Every water sport has its hazards, but if you are aware of the dangers and are prepared to handle common mishaps, you can enjoy a lifetime of adventures without undue worry. Prevention is more effective than any rescue, so learn to anticipate and avoid trouble.

For starters, you should be a good swimmer, and training in lifesaving and first aid will give you added confidence. While you are on the water, wear a personal flotation device (PFD). Stay within shouting distance of other canoes in your party, don't venture too far from land, and be aware of sky and water conditions. If a storm is brewing or if the wind whips up waves that make you uneasy, get to shore.

On rivers, tie up your canoe and scout ahead on foot if the water downstream is rough or you have the slightest suspicion there are snags, rapids, or falls. Before running a rapids, gather all the canoes in your group and plan not only how to navigate the stretch of white water, but also how to support one another should a canoe overturn. Plan to run short stretches of rapids one canoe at a time. You may need to station crew members with heaving lines at the end of the rapids. If in doubt about any stretch of water, portage around it.

Rescues

Every canoeist manages now and then to swamp a canoe, so it's important that you know what to do. Intentionally swamp your craft in calm water and practice various kinds of rescues until they become automatic. That way you'll know just what to do when you upset accidentally.

A prime principle in any rescue is this— *life is more valuable than gear.* Be absolutely certain you get yourself and your partners to safety regardless of what happens to your canoe and equipment. They can be replaced; you can't.

A second principle is that, even full of water, a canoe will float. Usually your best bet after upsetting is to stay with the canoe. Sit in the bottom and use your hands or a paddle to propel yourself to shore.

When there are other canoes nearby, you have more rescue methods from which to choose. Yell, "Swamped!" as you go over or if you see another canoe in distress. Other paddlers can bring their canoes alongside the swamped craft, aid the wet canoeists, retrieve floating gear, and help get their canoe to shore. If the canoes are far out in open water, a canoe-over-canoe procedure to empty the water our of the swamped canoe may be in order.

Should you overturn in a stream with a swift current, you're pretty much on your own until you reach quieter waters. Work your way hand-over-hand to the stern of the canoe and hang on. That way you won't be pinned between the canoe and any boulders the bow may strike.

If you are thrown clear of a canoe in a rapids, flip onto your back and ride out the white water feet first. Your PFD will keep you afloat, and your legs will act as shock absorbers, protecting you from obstructions in the stream. Keep your body at a slight angle to the current and back-stroke with your arms; the force of the water may push you ashore. If someone with a rescue line is stationed at the end of the rapids, watch for it to be thrown to you.

The techniques of safe paddling and rescue methods are constantly improving, and you'll want to keep your skills up to date. To find out about good training courses for canoeists, check with your local Scout service center, and with organizations such as the American Red Cross, American Whitewater Association, and American Canoe Association.

Come alongside capsized canoe on the side away from the person in the water, if possible.

Hold capsized canoe and direct canoeist in water to hold onto your canoe.

CHAPTER 17

Many colleges, universities, and outing clubs also provide water sport instruction.

(For information on cold-water safety, see "Outdoor Safety")

Swing capsized canoe at right angle to yours. then raise it up quickly and turn it bottom up in one motion, if you can.

Ease the other canoe across the gunwales of your canoe until it is balanced. This will help to get all the water out.

Roll the capsized canoe over on the gunwales of your canoe in preparation for putting it safely back into the water.

Ease the other canoe back into the water, sliding it carefully off the gunwales of your canoe.

Hold the other canoe by its gunwales alongside yours as the rescued "victim" climbs back in.

CANOE CAMPING

Once you feel at home on the water and can handle a canoe proficiently, you'll want to try a canoe camping trip. Never go alone; a crew of about half a dozen youth and two adult leaders can travel quickly, safely, and well. Whether you decide to start your trek near your home, at a local council camp, or at one of the BSA high-adventure bases, you'll learn plenty about managing a canoe over a long period of time. You can practice using a map and compass to find your way, discover how to read a river, and understand when it is wise to turn back because of bad weather or dangerous water. Nature will speak to you in terms of head winds and tail winds, currents and eddies, white water and pools as smooth as glass.

Plan a canoe camping trip just as you would a backpacking adventure, but load your provisions and gear into goosenecked plastic bags to protect them from the water. Even though you'll be paddling rather than walking, don't take anything more than you need. The smaller and lighter your load, the less time you'll devote to equipment and the more time you'll have for fun.

"The craft barely misses huge rocks close to the surface as it shoots down narrow channels through which the river points. Submerged logs reach out clawlike to rip expanses of calm below the roaring falls or cascades. And then comes a rapid, giddy run through flat water in which the boat bounces like a cork along a current. These experiences fill every moment on our western streams with tenseness. Then man is not only pitted against fish; he matches wits with a river. There are few greater exhilarations in the woods."

William O. Douglas, 1950

Chapter 18

Whitewater Rafting and Kayaking

Ken Horwitz
Board of Directors,
American Whitewater
Affiliation; Outdoor Writer

Tumbling down mountain valleys, foaming through sandstone canyons, heaving, boiling, and swirling between the sheer walls of narrow gorges, the great wild rivers of America were once the bane of travelers. They were to be avoided rather than relished, gone around rather than down. Today, however, that has changed. Boating enthusiasts have learned the safe uses of rafts and kayaks, and they are discovering in those wild rivers flowing fluid wilderness paths into some of the finest unspoiled country anywhere. Furthermore, as they challenge the sweep and power of whitewater, they find that their skills and stamina are tested as never before.

If you've ever seen a paddler riding a raft through the roar and spray of thundering rapids or watched a seasoned kayaker hold a tiny boat motionless in the trough of a standing wave, you've no doubt wanted to try whitewater boating yourself. It's not nearly as hard as you may think. With some guidance from experienced whitewater enthusiasts and a lot of practice, you can master the arts of rafting and kayaking too, and soon you'll be in the middle of a sport full of more excitement and thrills than just about anything you can imagine.

WHITEWATER SAFETY

There is a right way to enjoy any sport. The opportunities and possible dangers of rafting and kayaking make knowing the right way extremely important. With proper training, equipment, and planning, you can embark on a whitewater adventure confident you will come home happy and in one piece. The first step in developing that confidence is outfitting yourself with the necessary skills and safety gear.

Swimming

Every rafter and kayaker should be a good swimmer. You can count on falling off a raft once in awhile, and out of a kayak plenty of times, so be sure you can take care of yourself in the water.

(For pointers on survival in the water, see "Swimming and Lifesaving.")

Personal Floatation Device

Whenever you venture onto the water, wear a personal floatation device (PFD) approved by the U.S. Coast Guard. Use a type-III PFD; designed specifically for river running, it isn't very bulky and won't restrict the movement of your arms.

Helmet

The rocks and boulders that make running a rapids so exciting can be lethal to an unprotected boater thrown overboard. Always wear a good helmet, preferably one made especially for kayakers and rafters.

Clothing

In any but the warmest weather conditions, boaters face the threat of hypothermia, so protect yourself by dressing appropriately. When the water is cold (below 70° F), you may need a neoprene wet suit. Kayakers and rafters often use synthetic nylon or polypropylene underclothing covered by a thin waterproof nylon shell. This combination keeps the body warm in much the same way as layers of wool clothing, but it is much lighter than wool and cannot absorb water and become heavy in case of capsizing.

(For more on hypothermia, see "Outdoor First Aid.")

Just as your head needs a helmet to protect it from the rocks, your feet need protection, too. Tennis shoes and plastic river sandals are fine for rafters, but kayakers should use molded sole wet suit booties.

RAFTS

Shortly after World War II, adventurers set out in large army surplus rafts to challenge the Colorado River rapids in the heart of the Grand Canyon, and the sport of whitewater rafting was born. Made of tough rubberized or neoprene materials resistant to abrasion and puncture, the rafts used today to navigate wild rivers are descendants of those military rafts. Most are constructed with several inflatable chambers, any one of which can keep the raft afloat even if the others are damaged. Large rafts may have rigid frames to provide increased stability, and those used in

To fully get the illustrated effect of the Eskimo Roll in progress, fan the corners of this page and the next eight right-hand pages.

heavy rapids are encircled on the outside waterline by a rope to provide a handhold for rafters thrown into the water. Floorboards, oarlocks, and d-rings complete the configuration of most river rafts.

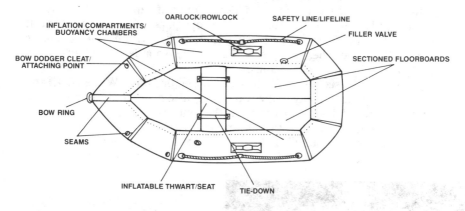

Propelling a Raft

Once on the water, rafts can be propelled in two ways: with oars or with paddles. Your choice of power will depend in large part on the kind of trip you are planning.

WHITEWATER, RAFTING AND KAYAKING

Paddle rafts. Paddling a raft is a group activity requiring the cooperation of everyone on board. Facing forward, several rafters sit on each side of the boat and use canoe paddles to guide the raft. A group leader sits in the rear of the craft and use a paddle as a rudder to steer the raft down the river while shouting commands to the paddlers, instructing them how to stroke to best maneuver the boat.

In rock-strewn rivers with channels too narrow for oar-maneuvered craft, paddling rafts have a distinct advantage. A skilled leader can direct the power and flexibility of many paddlers to keep the raft under control.

Oars. A raft equipped with oars can be steered efficiently by a single experienced oarsman. Perched atop a platform in the middle of the raft, he or she can see the river ahead and control the motion of the raft by pulling on long oars secured to the raft's frame by pins and clips or by oarlocks. Pins and clips are best for novice oarsmen since they permanently set the blades of the oars at the best angle to the water and make it difficult for a big wave to jerk the oars out of the hands, while experienced rafters find that with oarlocks they can pull in their oars when navigating swift, narrow passages.

Since a raft with oars needs only one well-seasoned boater on board, passengers can sometimes go along for a ride down a river even if they don't have much whitewater experience. Of course, they'll need to know how to swim and must wear helmets and floatation devices. As they splash and churn down the river, they can watch the oarsman and learn some of the basics of handling a raft in rough water.

Rafts come into their own when large groups of people want to travel a river together, especially if they have lots of equipment to carry. A big raft can become a veritable truckload of people and provisions, the oarsman's perch often an ice chest full of food. Even heavily loaded, rafts can carry a party safely through most rapids.

Of course, the size of a raft places certain limits on it. While width and length give a raft stability in the water, they also make the craft difficult to maneuver with finesse. Furthermore, the shape of a raft means it can only lumber downstream, riding the current through whatever water lies ahead. Traveling sideways, standing still in the current, and darting through wild water in weightless, splendid solitude is the stuff of kayaks.

KAYAKS

Eskimos have built kayaks for centuries, stretching sealskins over frames of wood and bone to make light, streamlined craft. Modern sport kayaks, while similar in outward appearance to the sealskin boats of old, are constructed of plastic or fiberglass, their shapes refined by modern engineering. Because of their light weight and great speed, fiberglass kayaks are used today for competition and slalom events. However, fiberglass is susceptible to breakage. Plastic kayaks are generally tougher, and thus have become the norm for most recreational use, especially in shallow rivers. Their only drawback is that they are heavier and slower than fiberglass craft.

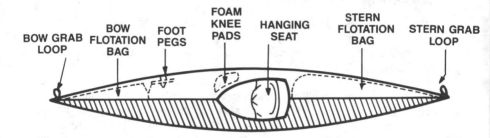

There are plenty of good kayaks on the market. The best way to find the one right for you is to paddle borrowed boats until you get a feel for what you want, and then to save your money until you can purchase a quality kayak that will meet the largest range of your paddling intentions. On even the most difficult rivers, you'll be able to trust the kayak in which you learned.

As you gain whitewater experience, you'll discover that the boat is an extension of your body, responding to your every move. You don't sit in a kayak so much as wear it, and so the fit must be snug. Adjust the foot pegs so that you can brace your knees against the underside of the kayak's deck.

To prevent water from filling your kayak, slide flotation bags into the bow in front of the foot pegs, and another into the stern. Between the bags, vertical braces made of waterproof foam will help keep the deck of the kayak from collapsing onto your legs when the boat is under the extreme pressure of rough water. *Always* equip a kayak with braces and flotation bags. They are just as important to your safety as your helmet and life vest.

You'll also need a spray skirt and a paddle. Made of nylon or neoprene, a spray skirt fits tightly around your waist. When you're seated in your boat, attach the skirt to the lip of the kayak cockpit and it will prevent water from flooding the craft while you negotiate rapids or roll upside down. A quick-release tab at the front of the skirt allows you to bail out of the boat safely.

A kayak paddle is long and double bladed, the blades turned at a 90° angle to one another. Flat blades are best for beginners, while advanced kayakers find that cupped blades give them more speed, especially as they paddle upstream to play in a wave. The instructions below assume you are using a paddle with flat blades.

Propelling a Kayak

With a few basic strokes, you can make a kayak dance. The best way to learn them is in quiet, safe water such as that in a swimming pool. Practice until the strokes are automatic. That way when you get on a river, you'll know just what to do.

At first, you may find it difficult to get into a kayak without tipping it over. Provide some stability by placing your paddle across the back of the cockpit and resting one blade on the shore or swimming pool deck. Grasp the center of the paddle and the back edge of the cockpit with one hand, and ease yourself into the boat. Attach the spray skirt to the lip of the cockpit and hold the paddle in front of you, your hands evenly spaced.

If this is the first time you've been in a kayak with a spray skirt attached, you may be concerned about how to get out if the boat overturns. Find out by leaning away from the shore until the kayak capsizes and you're hanging upside down in your seat. As soon as you pull the quick-release tab on the spray skirt, you'll drop free of the cockpit. This is called a *wet exit*, and you'll want to repeat it a few times until you're at ease bailing out of the boat.

Forward stroke. To move a kayak forward, extend the right paddle blade as far toward the bow of the boat as you can, twisting your torso to increase your reach. Dip the blade into water close to the kayak. In this position, your right arm will be straight while your left arm will be bent back near your shoulder. Begin the stroke by punching the left arm forward. Twist your torso to keep the face of the blade moving smoothly through the water, and pull with your right arm. When your shoulders are fully rotated to the right, knife the blade out of the water, cock your left wrist toward you to turn the left blade of the paddle into proper position, and begin a forward stroke on the left side of the kayak.

Stroke power comes from the push of the upper hand, the twist of the torso, and the pull of the lower hand. Use all three rather than relying just on the pull of an arm, and your strokes will be smooth, quick, and strong.

Reverse stroke. To slow a moving kayak or move it backwards, employ a reverse stroke by exactly reversing the steps of the forward stroke. Begin by twisting to the right and dipping the face of the right paddle blade into the water behind you and close to the boat. Push forward with your right arm, twisting your torso to the left as you do, and when that arm is straight, pull with your left arm until the blade breaks the surface of the water. Rotate your shoulders to the left, cock your left hand toward you to position the blade, and begin a reverse stroke on the opposite side of the kayak.

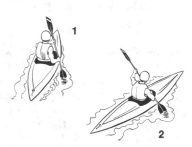

Sweep stroke. A sweep on the right side of a kayak turns the bow to the left as it pushes the boat forward, while a sweep on the left side turns the bow the other way. Sweeps are useful for moving around obstacles, especially when forward momentum is important. A sweep is easiest to perform when the ends of the kayak are out of the water, as they are when the boat is riding the crest of a wave.

Begin a sweep by holding the paddle horizonally over the boat. Extend one arm and rotate your shoulders, and insert a blade into the water as far forward as possible, the face of the blade turned away from the bow of the kayak. Pull the paddle in a wide half circle that continues all the way

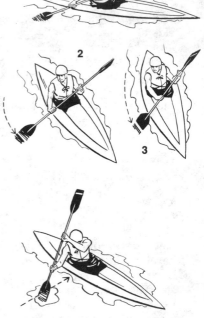

to the stern. Power the stroke with the twist of your shoulders and torso.

Reverse sweep. A reverse sweep slows the forward motion of a kayak as it turns the boat toward the side on which the stroke is performed. Use it when a quick, forceful stroke is needed to avoid an obstacle. Holding the paddle horizonally, twist sideways and insert the blade into the water behind the cockpit, the face of the blade turned away from the boat. Sweep the paddle in a quarter circle toward the bow, rotating your shoulders as you do. For best results, sweep wide.

Draw stroke. The draw stroke pulls a boat sideways with little effect on forward motion. Executing a draw with the paddle at midship will move the entire boat sideways, while a draw with the paddle closer to the bow will turn the boat to the stroke side, making the bow draw a good turning stroke.

To perform a midship draw, hold the paddle nearly perpendicular to water, your upper hand reaching out across the boat. With the blade face turned toward the kayak, dip the blade into the water and pull it toward the center of the boat, knifing it out of the water before it touches your craft. For a bow draw, reach out and dip the blade into the water as far forward as possible, then draw it toward the bow of the boat.

Braces. In rough water you can use your paddle to balance a kayak in much the same way outriggers give stability to Pacific island canoes. To understand how this is possible, think of the wing of an airplane. When the wing is tilted up, flowing air lifts it so well it can support the weight of the entire plane. If you hold a canoe blade flat in the water with its leading edge tilted up, the flowing water will lift the paddle.

Apply this principle to kayaking or whitewater canoeing by trying a *low brace*. It is similar to a reverse sweep, but instead of holding the paddle

blade perpendicular to the surface of the water, tilt the top edge forward and lean hard on the paddle while you make the sweep. As long as the paddle is moving forward or fast water is rushing toward it, the blade will support all the weight you can put on it.

To execute a *high brace*, hold the paddle at eye level, then lower one blade until it touches the water and draw the face of the blade toward the boat. Water forced against the flat of the blade will support your weight, and if the kayak was about to tip over, the brace should right it. In moving water, tilt the leading edge of the blade as it enters the water and hold it steady. You'll have a virtual three-point stance.

Duffek stroke. The Duffek stroke turns a kayak sharply to the stroke side even as it continues the forward motion of the boat. Effective only when the boat is moving, the stroke is chiefly used for entering and leaving eddies that form behind boulders.

Begin the Duffek stroke by dipping the paddle into the water as you would for a bow draw stroke and hold it there, the blade face turned toward the boat or angled slightly forward. In still water, nothing will happen, but if the kayak is moving forward, the paddle will act as a pivot point around which the kayak will turn. Lean toward the paddle during the turn, pulling the blade toward the bow as you finish the Duffek stroke to keep the craft upright.

ESKIMO ROLL

Before you leave the safe waters in which you're practicing the basic strokes, learn the principles of rolling a kayak. Remember how you bailed out of an overturned kayak by pulling the quick-release tab on the spray skirt? That's an effective way of getting out of trouble should your boat upset, but with an eskimo roll you can right a kayak without having to get out of it—a real advantage when you're running a rapids.

As your boat tips, lean forward against the bow deck and your head will be less likely to hit the bottom of the stream. Extend one arm across the kayak deck to position the paddle parallel to the boat. Take a second to slide a hand to the forward blade and make sure it is flat against the surface of the water, then use your shoulders and arms to move the blade in a smooth sweep stroke that continues all the way to the stern of the boat. Keep your eye on the paddle as it moves, and when the force of the stroke rolls you toward the surface of the water, snap the boat upright with your hips.

Learning the eskimo roll requires lots of trial and error and help from a veteran kayaker, but once you've mastered the technique you'll find it is one of your most important whitewater skills.

RIVER SAFETY

The power of a river is remarkable, especially if the stream is squeezed between narrow banks. An obstacle such as a boulder will force the water to go around and sometimes over it, causing rough rapids, eddies and

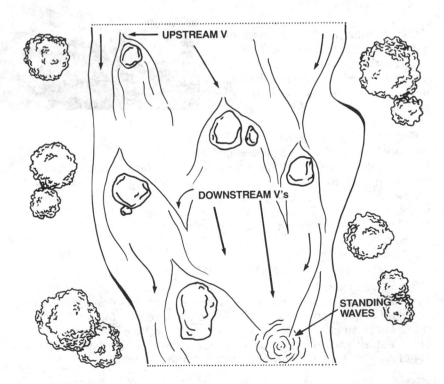

danger for whitewater enthusiasts.
The key to rafting and kayaking such
water safely lies in understanding
the dynamics involved as a river tumbles along, and then managing a boat so
it works with the stream rather than fighting against it.

Before you run any section of whitewater, land your boat and scout
ahead along the shore with someone who knows the stream well so that
you can see the lay of the river and be certain there is safe water at the end
of the rapids. *Never* raft or kayak any river unfamiliar to you unless you
have a knowledgeable guide; the chances of encountering a waterfall,
dam, or other deadly trap are too great.

As you survey the rapids ahead, you can pick a route through them in
much the same way a rock climber plots an ascent. A stretch of river that
may at first appear to be a frightening run of foam and spray may be
broken down into a half-dozen carefully controlled maneuvers. One
feature to look for is an eddy.

Eddies

A boulder in a river takes the brunt
of the river's force on its upstream
side. Just downstream, however, the
water may be calm for a short distance, or even swirl back toward the
obstruction in the opposite direction of the prevailing current. Good boaters
can slip into an eddy and be momentarily protected from the full impact of
the current. Sometimes they run a rapids gradually by moving from eddy to
eddy rather than racing the full length of the wild water in a single dash.

As you look over a river, pay special attention to the real dangers of
whitewater—strainers, drops, and heavy hydraulics.

Strainers

One of the most dangerous of river
obstacles is created when a tree
leans out over the water with its
trunk or some of its branches submerged. Water can flow under and
around them, but they'll trap anything carried by the current in the

same way a net catches fish. Cracks in rocks can also act as strainers, allowing water to pass, but trapping an unwary paddler.

Avoid strainers by studying every stretch of river before you run it, even those you've boated before. A tree may have fallen since your last visit, or the water level may have dropped and exposed rock strainers that were no threat before. If you do see a strainer, plan a route through the rapids that will keep you far away from the danger.

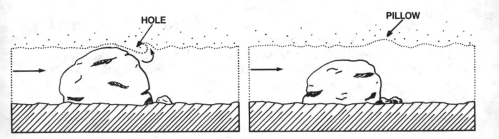

Drops

Places where a stream falls over a ledge seem like obvious dangers, but even experienced boaters can be surprised by them if they haven't scouted ahead. As with strainers, changing water levels may expose drops that even the day before were invisible. Stay away from rapids with large drops, though low drops can be run if you are with an expert rafter or kayaker who will show you exactly how it should be done.

Heavy Hydraulics

When the waves, currents, and eddies of a river are not overpowering for your abilities as a boater, you can have a great time challenging a rapid. However, when those forces are too great, you should avoid them altogether. The whirlpools, backwashes, and giant waves that make up *heavy hydraulics* are no place for wise rafters and kayakers. Be especially wary of large submerged boulders and of man-made structures such as low, wide dams. Many smooth, inviting streams have low head hydroelectric dams to divert water for irrigation or power generation. While the peacefulness of the river may beckon beginning paddlers to test their skills, the spinning reversal of current just below a small dam can be totally inescapable. Under no circumstances should you ever flirt with drowning by boating or swimming near a dam.

Horizon line indicates dangerous waterfall.

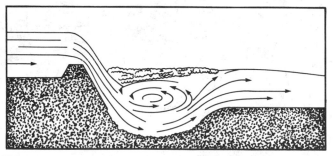

This typical low head dam with souse hole is dangerous.

Broaching

Broaching occurs when a swift current pushes a raft or kayak against the upstream side of an obstacle in the river. A broach that involves only a momentary bump against a rock is called a *pin*. In a true broach, the boat is caught solidly against a boulder by a raging torrent. Make every effort to keep your craft far away from obstacles upon which it may

VELOCITY DIFFERENCES WHERE IRREGULAR OBSTACLES OCCUR

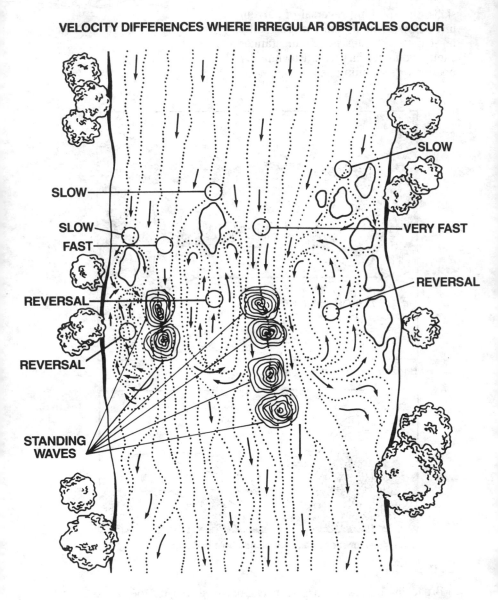

SLOW

SLOW

SLOW

FAST

REVERSAL

REVERSAL

VERY FAST

REVERSAL

STANDING
WAVES

broach. If a broach is imminent, you must exit the kayak or raft at once. Never consider for a second the idea of riding out a broach.

If you do find yourself trapped in a broached boat, immediately lean downstream directly onto the obstacle and await the assistance of a partner using a safety rescue throwline. Never lean upstream—that will instantly cause the boat to be pulled underwater and wrapped.

Wrapping

If a broached boat capsizes, tons of pressure from the current will wrap it around the obstacle. For a rafter, the danger is being caught between the raft and the boulder. For a kayaker, the threat is being trapped inside an overturned and crushed kayak.

Like snakebites and lightning strikes, actual wraps are rare. However, since there is almost no chance of survival for a kayaker trapped underwater, bail out of your craft at once if there is the slightest indication you are about to be caught in a permanent broach. The chance of injury while swimming the rest of a rapid is minimal compared with the danger of a broach and wrap.

Retrieving a broached kayak

EMERGENCY PROCEDURES

From time to time, every whitewater boater experiences a capsizing. Whenever that happens, the most important rule is that the safety of the boaters comes first. Retrieve kayaks, rafts, and equipment only after everyone has been brought ashore.

When you do capsize, follow these steps:

1. If there is a danger of broaching or being trapped by strainers, bail out of the boat immediately.

2. If there is no imminent danger, right your kayak by using an eskimo roll.

3. If you are in the water, hang onto your boat. It will float, and it's easy for rescuers to spot. Work your way to the upstream end of the craft so you will not be crushed against onrushing obstacles.

4. If it will increase your safety, release your grip on the boat. In very cold water, in the face of worsening rapids, and when no rescue is imminent, it may be best for you to swim hard for the nearest shore.

5. If you must swim in rough water, use a backstroke. Aim your feet downstream and use your legs as shock absorbers to bounce off rocks. Stroke hard to avoid strainers, watch for eddies and calm pools that will protect you, and be careful not to wedge your foot between rocks in the streambed.

6. If you are on shore and see others capsize, throw them a rescue line. Each kayak and raft should be equipped with a 50-foot length of floatable nylon line at least ⅜ inch in diameter. Coil it neatly and use duct tape to secure it within easy reach. In rapids where upsets are likely, station several people with rescue lines on the shore at the end of the section of rough water.

7. If you are using a line to retrieve a boat, do not tie it to your body. A current that can wrap a kayak can just as easily pull you into the river.

PUTTING IT ALL TOGETHER

Once you've learned the basic skills of whitewater boating and have given plenty of thought to ways to avoid possible hazards, you're ready to join some experienced river runners for a try at a real stream. Start with easy trips on relatively calm waters, moving on to more rugged conditions as your abilities improve. Combine boating with your expertise in camping for some extended river treks, and look into the sport of whitewater kayak racing. Finally, see if there are any whitewater boating clubs in your area. Its members will already know what you're about to discover—that when the whitewater bug bites, it bites hard.

RIVER DIFFICULTY CLASSIFICATION

I   Easy Sand banks, bends without difficulty, occasional small rapids with waves regular and low. Correct course easy to find, with only minor obstacles like pebble banks, riffles at bridge piers. River speed less than hard backpaddling speed.

II   Medium Fairly frequent but unobstructed rapids, usually with regular waves, easy eddies, and easy bends. Course generally easy to recognize.

III   Difficult Maneuvering in rapids necessary. Small falls, large regular waves covering boat, numerous rapids. Passages clear though narrow, requiring expertise in maneuver. Scouting usually needed.

IV   Very Difficult Long extended stretches of rapids, high irregular waves with boulders directly in current. Boiling eddies, broken water, abrupt bends. Scouting mandatory first time. Powerful and precise maneuvering required.

V   Extraordinarily Difficult Extremely difficult, long, and very violent rapids, following each other almost without interruption. River bed extremely obstructed. Big drops, violent current, very steep gradient. Scouting necessary but difficult; extensive experience necessary.

VI   Limit of Navigability Grade V carried to the extreme. Nearly impossible and very dangerous. Only for teams of experts, at favorable levels and after close study with all precautions.

One of the most useful ways to classify whitewater is by the international rating system sanctioned in this country by the American Whitewater Affiliation. Rapids are graded from I (very easy) to VI (risk to life) according to the scale we've reprinted in the accompanying table. While it tells nothing of the river's individuality to say that Racehorse Rapids below the Hook is grade II-III in medium water and grade III at higher levels, it does give the next paddler down a rough idea of what he can expect.

"If a burro is taken into training early and treated with kindness, it is very responsive and cooperative. The burro has ideas of its own which should be respected. Mistreated and abused burros are the hard ones to deal with, and they show their disrespect in many clever and often amusing ways."

William G. Long, Superior Court Judge (Ret.), 1969

Chapter 19

Riding and Packing

Stephen Zimmer
Veteran Trail Rider and Packer;
Director of Museums, Philmont Scout
Ranch; Western Historian

Indians, explorers, mountain men, cowboys, miners, soldiers, and settlers all used horses and pack animals, and for good reason. They increase by many miles the distances travelers can cover, and allow them to haul heavy loads over rough terrain. Today, you can slip your foot into a stirrup, swing into the saddle, touch your heels to a horse's sides, and know the joy of riding. You can feel the confidence that comes with knowing how to groom a horse, saddle it, and care for it in the stable and on the trail. You can learn to manage mules and burros, getting to know their habits as you use them to carry your provisions and gear on extended treks.

Much of America's backcountry may still be explored by adventurers on horseback or leading pack animals. A successful pack trip requires sound planning, good, dependable animals, and your ability to handle your mounts. If you're a stranger to trail riding, you'll need plenty of practice under the watchful eyes of experienced riders and horse packers before you hit those dusty trails. Then, once you've mastered the basics of riding, try a few short trips of one or two days. Before long you'll be ready to tackle just about any riding adventure.

Veteran horse handlers can give you the guidance you need to learn the ways of saddle and pack stock, and to get you properly equipped. A good place to start is with the right clothing.

CLOTHING

The traditional clothing of the American cowboy evolved over a period of many years to serve the needs of horseback riders. The pointed toes and slick soles of Western boots make it easy for you to slide into and out of saddle stirrups, while the high heels prevent your feet from slipping through. A long-sleeve shirt and long denim pants will guard you against the sun and dust. Add a pair of leather chaps if brush is dense. A wide-brimmed cowboy hat will shade your face and keep rain from running down your collar, and one fitted with a hard plastic shell can protect your head should you fall from the saddle. Carry a rain slicker to ward off sudden downpours, and if the trail becomes too dusty, the bandana around your neck can be pulled up over your mouth and nose.

THE SADDLE HORSE

The horse you ride probably belongs to your family, neighbors, a summer camp, or a riding stable. As you become acquainted, you'll discover that the horse has preferences and habits just as you do. Perhaps it's shy about gates, doesn't want to be approached from a certain direction, or likes to have its nose rubbed. A horse responds to the way you treat it and, like every animal, deserves your best. The way a horse acts toward you will be determined in large part by how you act toward it.

The behavior of horses, mules, and burros is influenced also by the way in which they perceive the world. Because their eyes are located on opposite sides of their heads, they see two different visual fields at the same time. In addition, they are color blind, seeing everything in white, black, and shades of grey. Moving objects alarm them until they are able to identify them, usually with their keen senses of smell, hearing, and touch. When they feel threatened, their first instincts are to take flight or to fight.

A calm, reassuring voice is your best asset in dealing with trail animals. When they are unsure of themselves, they will respond favorably to your confidence, kindness, and quiet authority.

Equipment

Saddle. The western stock saddle is the most versatile saddle for trail riding. Its heavy construction makes it rugged enough to take hard pounding, and its shape helps a rider stay in the seat on steep climbs and descents.

Bridle. Consisting of a headstall, bit, and reins, the bridle is used to control and guide a horse. Bits come in various shapes and sizes to match the age, experience, and training of different animals.

Halter. A halter with a strong lead rope is sometimes used in the stable to control an unsaddled horse. In the backcountry, leave the halter on your horse and slip the bridle over it. When you need to tie the horse to a tree or post, you can use the halter's lead rope. Tie it high enough and short enough that your horse cannot step over the rope and injure itself. Never tie a horse with the reins; if the animal spooks and jerks its head, it may break them.

Breast collar. As a horse climbs steep trails, a breast collar keeps the saddle from slipping backward.

Saddle blankets. Two heavy, woven blankets or pads are placed beneath the saddle to cushion and protect the horse's back.

Saddle bags. Tied behind the saddle, a couple of saddlebags hold your lunch, camera, jacket, and other personal gear.

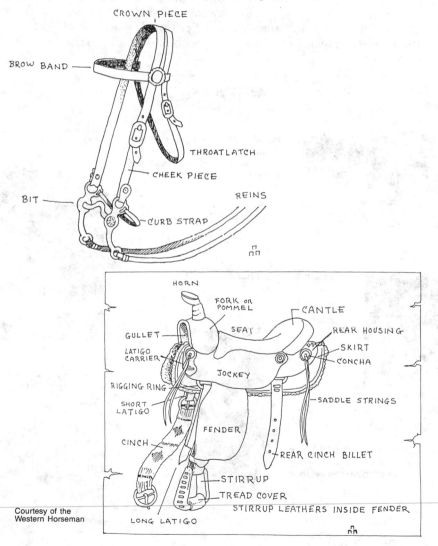

Courtesy of the
Western Horseman

BRIDLING AND SADDLING

When you go to a stable to ride, wranglers will match you with a horse on the basis of your weight and riding experience. They'll help you catch your mount, slip the halter over its nose, and lead it to a hitch-rail near the tackroom or saddle shed.

Tie your horse up short with a quick-release knot in the lead rope, and then use a curry comb and brush to groom the horse's back, sides, and underside. As you remove all dirt, sweat, and matted hair, comb in the direction that the hair naturally lies. After brushing, lift and inspect all four hooves, cleaning them if necessary with a hoof pick and checking for loose shoes.

BRIDLING

◄1. Always work from the left side of a horse. Put bridle reins around the horse's neck.

2. Hold top of bridle in right► hand with bit in left.

◄3. Hold bit in left hand.

4. Gently ease the bit into► the horse's mouth without bumping the teeth.

5. Pull headstall up► over head.

◀6. Be gentle with horse's ears.

◀7. Pull out forelock and straighten browband.

8. Buckle throat latch. ▶

SADDLING A HORSE

1. Brush horse thoroughly with curry comb and brush.

2. Position saddle pads well forward on the horse's back, making sure the hair beneath lies flat.

◀3. Gently lift the saddle onto the pads and shake it into position.

4. On the far (right) side of the horse, straighten the cinches. ▶

 ◄5. On the near (left) side, put stirrup over saddlehorn and reach under for front cinch ring.

6. Thread latigo through ► cinch ring.

7. Run latigo through cinch ring again. ▼

8. Pull it snug and buckle. ►

◄9. Buckle rear cinch.

10. Reach in front of horse for ► breast collar.

11. Buckle breast collar
    into near-side rigging
    ring.

12. Snap lower strap into ▶
    center ring of cinch.

13. Retighten the cinch ▶
    before mounting.

MOUNTING A HORSE

Standing on the horse's left side, remove the halter lead rope from the bridle and put the reins around the horse's neck. Hold them in your left hand short enough so that you can control the horse if it should move while you're mounting. You may find it easier to manage the reins if they are tied together. With the same hand, grab some of the horse's mane. Use your free hand to twist the stirrup and guide your foot into it, then grasp the saddlehorn, bounce a few times on your right foot, and spring into the saddle, easing yourself down and slipping your free foot into the empty stirrup. The balls of your feet should rest in the stirrups with your heels slightly lower. That way, you'll be able to free your feet quickly if you must. Have a wrangler help you adjust the length of the stirrups if they are too long or too short.

RIDING

Once mounted, use reins to control the direction and speed at which your horse travels. Hold the reins lightly with one between your thumb and index finger and the second between your index and middle fingers. Squeeze the horse with your legs or tap with your heels and the animal should move out. Many horses used in the backcountry are trained to neck rein, responding to the pressure of reins against their necks. To turn left, move the reins to the left and touch the horse's neck with the right rein. For a right turn, move the reins the other way. To stop, pull back lightly on the reins. Remember that the bit serves only to cue the animal. Too much force on the reins will cause pain and perhaps injury. Always put slack in the reins after a horse has turned or stopped properly; otherwise your mount will continue to turn or back up, and certainly become confused.

Match the speed at which you ride to the terrain you're covering. Let your horse walk when the grade is steep or rocky, and whenever you're leading a pack horse. To ride up a steep grade, stand in your stirrups and shift your weight forward over the saddlehorn so that your horse bears your weight with his front legs and shoulders. When riding downhill lean back in the saddle to cause your horse less fatigue. On level ground where the footing is sure, you can let the horse lope. On a long day's ride over difficult terrain, get off your horse and walk awhile to give the animal a rest.

PACK ANIMALS

No history of the American West is complete without the image of old prospectors coming down from the hills, their pack animals loaded with shovels, hardtack, beans, and, if the prospectors had been lucky, maybe even a poke of gold. Trustworthy, stubborn, smart, and independent, mules and burros provided the power needed to move settlers across the continent, pull the plows of farmers, and transport the supplies of soldiers and trappers as well as prospectors.

You'll probably get your first taste of working with burros, mules, and pack horses under the guidance of veteran packers. They may begin by explaining that a burro is a species that can reproduce its own kind, while a mule is a sterile cross between a male burro and a female horse. Because they are part horse, adult mules usually are larger than burros, though burros tend to be better adapted to the rigors of wilderness travel.

SADDLING A PACK HORSE

◀1. Brush horse, position saddle pads same as for saddle horse. Lift saddle onto horse's back. Shake by front buck so saddle settles to its natural position.

2. On the far side, ▶ straighten cinches.

▼3. Adjust both cinches so they are under horse's belly.

◀4. On near side, tighten front cinch first. Pull snug.

▼5. Secure latigo with girth hitch.

◀6. Tighten rear cinch snug, but not as tight as front.

◀7. Place back breeching over horse's rump. Standing away, gently pull out horse's tail.

▲8. Adjust connecting straps of breeching.

◀9. Buckle breast collar in front. Now pack horse is properly saddled and ready for loading.

LOADING A PACK HORSE

◀1. Hook panniers from the sawbucks so they hang evenly.

2. Place bedrolls, tents, and other▶ soft baggage on top of saddle.

◀3. Throw tarp over load.

4. Tuck tarp ends under panniers. ▶

◀5. Tie diamond hitch. Throw lash cinch over load, under horse's belly.

6. Twist ropes on top to▶ form a diamond.

◀7. As hitch progresses, keep rope taut.

8. Secure excess lash rope with a▶ series of slip knots.

LEADING A PACK HORSE

◀1. On the trail with a pack horse, rider holds lead rope in right hand.

2. Two turns of the lead rope around the saddlehorn▶ may be used to lead pack horse.

◀3. When at rest, leather hobbles are buckled on horse's front legs.

TO PACK A BURRO

◀1. The equipment (left to right): tarp, lash rope and cinch, saddle, halter and lead rope, saddle pad, and two box panniers.

◀2. Catch and halter burro from left side.

3. Brush burro thoroughly.▶

◀4. Place saddle pad in correct position.

5. Lift saddle on burro's back.▶

CHAPTER 19

6. Tighten front cinch first with two passes through cinch ring. Secure with a girth hitch.

7. Put end of latigo through front rigging ▶ ring.

◀8. Pull tight.

9. Put latigo end underneath right side▶ of rigging ring.

◀10. Pull through.

◀11. Put latigo end down through loop and pull tight.

▼12. Tighten rear hitch.

◀13. Finished hitch.

14. Pull breeching over rump and adjust connecting straps. ▶
    Buckle breast collar in front.

◀ 15. Properly saddled burro

◀ 16. Hang panniers evenly. Place
    soft baggage (tents, bed
    rolls) on top.

17. Throw tarp over load. Tuck ▶
    in edges.

◀ 18. From left side of burro,
    throw lash cinch over pack.

◀ 19. Reach under and hook
    lash rope to cinch.
    Draw tight.

◀ 20. From right side, twist ropes
    three times, forming dia-
    mond in middle.

21. Take end of lash rope from rear right side ▶
    of pack to front. Hold diamond open.

CHAPTER 19

322

◄22. Put lash rope through diamond and go to the front of the pack on the left side.

23. Go under the left side of pack and up► through diamond.

◄24. Pull tight.

25. End with series of slip knots.►

◄26. Properly balanced pack

Equipment

Burros and mules need saddles if they are to carry heavy loads. The saddle most frequently used for pack animals is the *sawbuck,* named for its resemblance to the wooden stand used to hold logs in position for sawing. Each saddle is shaped to fit a particular size of animal, and it's rigged with a double cinch to hold the saddle and its load on the animal, a breast strap to keep it from moving backward, and a back breeching to prevent it from sliding forward.

A pack animal is groomed and saddled in much the same way as a saddle horse, the saddle resting on two or three saddle pads and the cinch strap pulled tight. The breast strap and breeching should be snug, but not so tight that they hamper the animal's movement. A pack animal doesn't wear a bridle, but a hiker or horseback rider can control it with a halter and a strong lead rope ⅜ inch in diameter and 20 feet long.

PACKING

Pack horses and mules can carry up to 175 pounds each while a burro can haul 75, but even though pack animals are able to bear much more weight than you can, keep their loads as light as possible. There's no reason for them to haul equipment you don't really need, and a lighter load will make it easier and safer for them to travel rugged trails.

Pack your tools, food, tenting, and cooking gear into *panniers*—wooden or plastic boxes, or large leather or canvas bags designed to fit on a sawbuck. Place soft items on the side that will rest against your animal's body. Evenly distribute your gear between each animal's two panniers, using a small scale hung from a tree branch or fence rail to check the weight of each. Since an unbalanced pack can cause the sawbuck to slip or rub sores into the animal's back, each pannier in a pair should weigh about the same. Pad loose items with groundcloths or clothing and pack everything in such a way that the load doesn't rattle. Strange noises coming from a pannier can spook even the steadiest trail animals.

CHAPTER 19

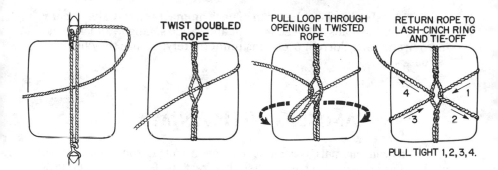

TWIST DOUBLED ROPE

PULL LOOP THROUGH OPENING IN TWISTED ROPE

RETURN ROPE TO LASH–CINCH RING AND TIE-OFF

PULL TIGHT 1, 2, 3, 4.

DIAMOND HITCH

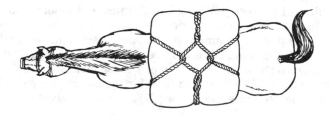

ON THE TRAIL WITH A PACK ANIMAL

An experienced rider with pack horses or mules can cover 15 miles a day over rough terrain. Burros move more slowly, and are preferred by many hikers.

Pack animals go at a walk. They use less energy, and the gait is easy on their feet. The leisurely pace will give you plenty of time to take in the surrounding countryside.

If you'll be riding, you may find it convenient to mount your horse, get settled, and then have a partner hand you the lead rope of your pack animal. When you're leading an animal, hold the rope in your hand or give it one loose wrap around the saddlehorn, but *never* tie it to any part of the saddle or wrap it in such a way that it will not easily come loose.

When leading several pack animals, you can tie the lead rope of one to the pack saddle of the animal in front of it. Tie the lead rope short enough that the animals cannot step over it, but not so short that they impede one another's motion. Make sure the animals you put together are compatible.

One rider should follow the string of pack animals and stay alert for any signs of shifting loads, loose equipment and saddles, fatigue, or lameness in your animals. Correct problems immediately, before they become serious.

CAMPING WITH ANIMALS

Tend to your animals as soon as you reach your destination. They've worked hard for you and have earned their rest and feed. Since your pack animals still have weight on their backs, unload them before you unsaddle your riding horse. Untie the diamond hitches and set the panniers in a convenient location for making camp, then loosen the saddles and fold the cinches, breast straps, and breechings over the top. Set the saddles on a log or pole, place the saddle pads on top, wet side up, and cover everything with the tarps.

Your guide will instruct you on feeding times and amounts; usually about a gallon of oats per animal per day, and the addition of hay for roughage in areas without ample grass. After each animal has been cooled, brushed, fed, watered, and checked for saddle sores and foot damage, tie them by their lead ropes to a picket line on level ground where there is ample forage. Use your lash rope for the picket line, stringing it 4 feet above the ground between two large trees. Space the animals

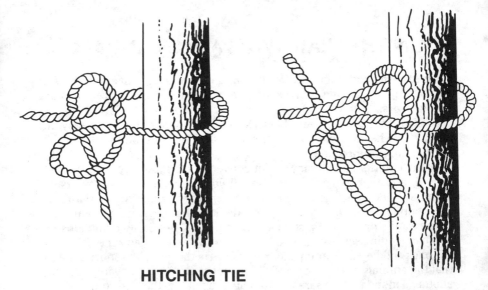

HITCHING TIE

CHAPTER 19

about 8 feet apart, and alternate them on opposite sides of the line. Each lead rope should be long enough to enable the animal to graze and lie down comfortably, yet short enough to prevent it from becoming entangled. Check the picket line from time to time to see that the animals do not become fouled in the ropes.

Another way to restrain livestock during the night is with *hobbles*—strong leather or nylon straps buckled onto the lower front legs of animals so that they may graze and yet not stray too far from your camp. Some animals are not accustomed to hobbles, so follow your packer's advice on how and when to use them.

CARE OF TRAIL ANIMALS

Animals used in the backcountry deserve special attention and care beyond basic feeding and grooming. Sometimes they may appear to be unusually obstinate, stubborn, or spooky, but they very likely have good reasons for their actions. Be patient with them and help them overcome their strange behavior by discovering the causes for it and correcting the problems.

On long trips, be especially alert for saddle sores, lameness, or illness. Horses and mules taken into rough country should have their feet trimmed

For more security, put another bight on the running end through the loops.

and fitted with shoes before the start of each trek. Burros' hooves are harder and do not need shoes, but you must check their feet daily, just as you do those of horses and mules. Use a hoof pick to keep each animal's feet free of mud and stones.

CARE OF THE BACKCOUNTRY

When you take animals into the backcountry, you accept the responsibility for using them wisely and for protecting the land through which they travel. Because of their weight, sharp hooves, and grazing needs, saddle horses and pack animals have the potential for unwittingly harming the land. It's up to you to see that they don't.

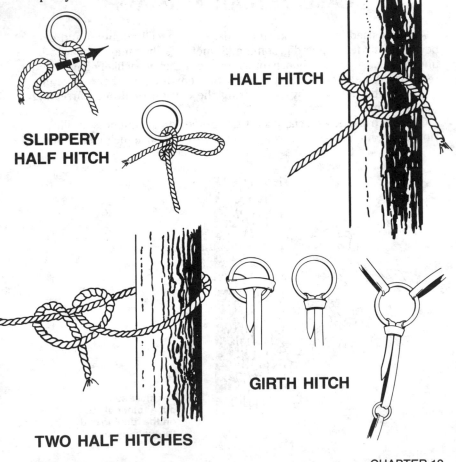

SLIPPERY
HALF HITCH

HALF HITCH

TWO HALF HITCHES

GIRTH HITCH

In addition to the low-impact hiking and camping techniques you always use, take the following precautions as well:

- Tie an animal's lead rope only to strong trees at least 8 inches in diameter. Ropes twisting on the bark and branches of smaller trees may injure them.

- If you can, hobble your animals rather than tethering them. Since hobbled livestock can graze over a large area, they are less likely to trample and paw at the ground.

- Since the hooves of animals can churn up damp soil and fragile vegetation, hobble or tether them only on dry ground.

- Except while traveling or watering, keep your animals at least 200 feet from springs, streams, and lakes, and hobble or tether them away from sites campers will use in the future. Scatter accumulations of manure to discourage flies.

"One has to lie deep in the snow to learn how warm and protective it is. A den in the snow confines the body heat like a blanket or overcoat. It is a snug place, no matter how the wind may howl. One who holes up in the snow understands better the mysteries of the woods in the winter. He knows why the severe weather grouse squirm their way under soft snow and be quiet. He understands why deer bury themselves in drifts, lying a half-day or more with just their heads sticking out. He learns something of the comfort of the bear in hibernation."

William O. Douglas, 1950

Chapter 20

Winter Camping

Tom Johnston
Former Staff Member, Maine National
High Adventure Area and Northern
Tier National High Adventure
Programs; District Executive, Moby
Dick Council

James Gilbert Phillips
Silver Beaver Scouter; Snow Camping
Instructor, University of New
Mexico; Widely Recognized Authority
on Snow Camping

W inter camping is one of the most advanced and challenging of outdoor adventures. It will take you into a magnificent frozen wilderness sparkling with snow and ice. Temperatures are cold, and the usual watering holes, campgrounds, and trails of summer are buried beneath drifts. On still nights a fragile, magical beauty blankets the land beneath the dance of the stars, and when the weather turns bad, howling winds and driving snow make a familiar meadow seem as awesome and alien as any arctic landscape. Living under such strange and demanding conditions requires a high degree of skill and plenty of experience, but if you learn the ways of the Eskimo, you'll know the backcountry as only a master camper can.

Winter Camping Step by Step

Just as there are many degrees of proficiency necessary for warm weather treks, the levels of winter camping demand increasing mastery of backcountry skills. Since each level builds on previous ones, winter campers need a solid foundation of basic camping and survival techniques, and they should not attempt more advanced treks until they have the knowledge and experience they need for safe and successful outings.

- BEGINNING WINTER CAMPING
  Cabin or hut with fireplace or stove
  Permanent lean-to shelter with fireplace

- BASIC
  Two-man tents
  Large wall tents

- ADVANCED
  Snow shelters   Snow caves, igloos, snow domes,
  No heat   thermal shelters

- FULL ARCTIC
  No shelter   Clothing and food are used to maintain
  No heat   body heat. This is excellent survival
                         training if you are prepared.

MISCONCEPTIONS ABOUT
WINTER CAMPING

Winter camping requires more than a heavy coat and a rugged attitude. Frozen campgrounds pose special challenges and dangers that allow only slim margins of error. Before a winter trek, campers must familiarize themselves with the best cold-weather techniques, equipment, and advice. Even persons with some experience in snowy conditions may have a faulty understanding of winter camping. Among the most common misconceptions are these.

Leather hiking boots will keep your feet warm.

FALSE! The snug fit of most hiking boots can limit the circulation of blood in the feet, especially if you're wearing extra layers of socks. Mukluks, booties, and overboots cut generously enough to hold your foot and plenty of insulation and still allow moisture to escape are much more effective.

An open fire is the best way to stay warm.

FALSE! If the heat of a fire warms you while you're wearing winter clothing, the insulation effectiveness of the clothing may be suspect. Clothes able to protect you from the cold will also shield you from heat. Wearing the right clothing, eating plenty of energy-rich foods, drinking large quantities of water, and bedding down in a cozy sleeping bag are much more dependable ways of staying warm than standing near a fire.

In cold weather, tasks can be done just as quickly as in warm weather.

FALSE! Every effort in cold weather takes much longer to complete than it would under warm conditions. Eskimos move with patient, sure motion, allowing plenty of time to conduct their activities.

Waterproof clothing is ideal for cold weather camping.

FALSE! To keep you warm, your clothing must allow body moisture to escape. Moisture trapped close to the body wicks away heat through conduction and evaporation. Waterproof clothing is preferable only in wet, rainy weather.

Sugary and starchy foods provide sufficient cold weather energy.

FALSE! Sugar and starch burn too quickly to keep you warm hour after hour. Foods high in fat, complex carbohydrates, and protein release their energy more slowly.

Drinking liquids is not important on winter treks.

FALSE! Cold air is very dry, and it draws moisture out of your body each 1time you breathe. Winter temperatures may trick you into believing you're not thirsty, even though your body needs plenty of fluids to ward off the dehydration that can upset your metabolism and increase your susceptibility to hypothermia. Most people need 2–3 quarts of water per day.

Winter camping does not require much preparation.

FALSE! Arctic conditions exist when the wind is blowing and the temperature is 20° F or colder. There are only seven states in the U.S. that do not experience weather this cold at least part of the year, and so it is extremely important to prepare adequately—and in fact to overprepare—whenever you camp in the winter. Learn what to expect in severe weather, and then take positive steps to acquire the necessary knowledge, skills, and equipment to meet the challenge.

Mental attitude has little to do with winter camping.

FALSE! A positive mental attitude is the most important ingredient in the success of cold-weather trips. The demands of winter will occasionally drain your energies, and you'll have to rely on yourself to keep your spirits high.

PLANNING FOR WINTER CAMPING

The best time to begin preparing for winter adventures is during the warm months of the year. You'll have the weeks you need to read up on cold weather camping, winter ecology, and survival techniques, and to gather or make equipment and clothing.

As the weather cools, practice your outdoor skills on day hikes and overnight outings. Adult group leaders with training in cold weather living should carefully instruct crew members in every phase of winter camping, and by the time the first snows fall you'll be ready for well-planned winter treks. Need to learn more? Many local outing clubs and universities sponsor public classes in winter survival, and so do some sporting goods shops and units of the military. A number of Scout councils conduct cold-weather camping programs, and the Northern Tier National High Adventure Area offers courses in the best techniques of arctic living.

Buddy System

The buddy system is a great way to ensure everyone's well-being, especially if veteran winter campers are paired with those without much cold weather experience. Buddies can help each other pack for a trek, look after one another in the woods, and watch for symptoms of frostbite, hypothermia, and exhaustion.

Checklist

Make sure you have everything you need by writing down a checklist of essential gear, clothing, and food, and then marking off each item as you load it into your pack. Several miles up a snowy trail is no place to discover you've forgotten your hat and mittens.

Keeping Warm

Without a doubt, keeping warm is the most important task of a winter camper. Chilly weather saps body heat, especially if the wind is blowing. A traveler who does not guard against the cold risks hypothermia and frostbite.

(For information on preventing cold weather health problems, see "Outdoor Safety." For treatment of hypothermia and frostbite, see "Outdoor First Aid.")

There's no mystery about how to keep warm. Think of your body as en efficient, portable furnace. Stocked with fuel and fluids, it will maintain a constant temperature of about 98°F. If that heat escapes from your body too rapidly, you'll feel cold; if it escapes too slowly, you'll feel hot. Just as you would insulate a house containing a furnace to maintain a comfortable indoor temperature, you can insulate your body with adjustable layers of clothing to trap or release heat created by your cells.

(For a discussion of the layer system of dressing, see "Gearing Up.")

Of course, frigid winter conditions make the proper choice and use of clothing more vital than at other times of the year. As you prepare your cold weather clothing, keep warm by following the guidelines that spell the word COLD

C—Clean

Since insulation is effective when heat is trapped by dead air spaces, keep your insulating layers clean and fluffy. Dirt, grime, and perspiration can mat down those air spaces and reduce the warmth of a garment.

O—Overheating

Avoid overheating by adjusting your layers of clothing to meet the outside temperature and the exertions of your activities. Excessive sweating can dampen your clothing and cause chilling later on.

L—Loose Layers

A steady flow of warm blood is essential to keep all parts of your body heated. Wear several loosely fitting layers of clothing and footgear that will allow maximum insulation without impeding your circulation.

D—Dry

Damp clothing and skin can cause your body to cool quickly, possibly leading to frostbite or hypothermia. Keep dry by avoiding cotton clothing that absorbs moisture, brushing snow from your clothes before it melts, and loosening the clothing around your neck and chest. Since body heat can drive perspiration through many layers of breathable cloth and force it out into the air, don't wear waterproof clothes.

(For a comparison of clothing fabrics and insulation materials, see "Gearing Up.")

FOOTWEAR

What you wear on your feet must match the climate and terrain of your treks, and it must keep your feet warm. As with your other clothing, the layer system is the answer. One way is to start with a pair of silk, nylon, or thin wool socks next to your skin, covered by several pairs of heavier wool socks. Next, slip into an insulated bootie or wool felt liner. Place a foam or wool insole in the bottom of an outer boot or mukluk, and slide your foot into it. The whole assemblage must be loose enough for you to wiggle your toes easily, yet not so loose as to cause blisters. Use plenty of foot powder to fight trench foot caused by prolonged dampness.

Mukluks and Foam Foot Wraps

A terrific alternative to layers of socks is the foam foot wrap inside a mukluk. Mukluks are winter overboots of Eskimo design, which, when insulated with foam, provide the warmest footwear possible.

(For instructions for making your own mukluks, see "Making Equipment.")

Shoepacks

Combining a leather upper that breathes with a waterproof rubber bottom, shoepacks are special boots made for use in chilly, wet conditions. Your feet may become damp in them, so carry plenty of extra socks.

Skiing and Mountaineering Boots

Low-cut ski touring boots are designed for speed rather than warmth, but boots for backcountry skiing and winter climbing often are insulated. Worn with gaiters, they can keep your toes warm as long as you're active. In camp, though, you'll want the protection of dry, insulated booties or mukluks.

Booties

Essentially a huge pair of insulated socks with reinforced soles, booties will keep your feet warm when you're not traveling. Put them on over dry socks, and on cold nights you can wear them to bed.

MITTENS

Mittens that allow your fingers to be in direct contact with one another can keep your hands warmer than will gloves that isolate each finger. Select mittens filled with insulation, or pull on woolen gloves and cover them with nylon overmitts to keep them dry. Long cuffs will prevent cold air and snow from seeping in around wrist openings, and a cord attached to each glove and run through the sleeves of your parka or around your neck will keep your mittens close if you have to remove them for a moment.

HEADGEAR

Stocking hats are great for wear outdoors and at night in your sleeping bag. Even better is the balaclava—a stocking hat long enough to cover your head and neck, and all of your face except your eyes. For full arctic conditions, consider wearing a foam hat with long ear flaps. Add to the warmth of your head by pulling the hood of a parka over your hat and drawing it about your face. A scarf will keep warm air from escaping past your collar, and you can wrap it across your mouth and nose.

(For instructions on making a hat from foam, see "Making Equipment.")

PARKA

Eskimos have long used large, insulated parkas as portable winter shelters. Next to your footwear, your parka will be your most important piece of cold weather clothing. The parka should be large enough to cover extra layers of clothing and to allow circulation of air to help move moisture away from your body. A

large, permanently attached hood will prevent heat loss at the head and neck. A wind flap covering the zipper keeps frost off the metal, and buttons hold the parka closed if the zipper should fail.

FOOD

Your body burns calories to produce heat, so you'll need to fuel it with nutritious foods that provide plenty of energy over a long period of time. Start your morning with a hot, hearty breakfast, eat a little at each rest break during the day, and make camp early so you can cook a satisfying supper before dark. Rely on easy, one-pot supper menus full of nourishing, stick-to-your-ribs ingredients, and have a snack before you go to bed. Food may freeze in your pack, so cut items such as cheese, meat, and chocolate into bite-size chunks before you leave home.

(For more information on nutrition and winter meals, see "Trail Menus and Cooking.")

It's fun to carve a kitchen in the snow. Using a shovel or a saw, fashion shelves and benches in a drift or an open-topped snow pit. Erect a wall to block the wind, and use snowshoes to line the benches on which you'll sit.

LIQUIDS

During cold weather activities water is more important to your body than food. Much moisture is lost as you exhale (when you "see your breath" in the winter, you're actually seeing moisture being expelled by your lungs), and through perspiration and elimination. While you may not feel as thirsty as you do in the summer, be sure you drink at least 10 to 12 cups of fluid each day. Cocoa, soup, broth, and warm fruit juices are satisfying ways for you to keep your fluid intake high and avoid dehydration. You may want to carry a vacuum bottle in your pack, fill it with hot water as you cook your meals, and have steaming water for warm drinks throughout the day and evening.

GATHERING WINTER WATER

A good place to replenish your water supplies is a stream flowing too swiftly to freeze. To dip from the stream without risk of falling in, hang a water bottle by a cord from a ski pole or branch. When streams and lakes are frozen, you may be able to cut through the ice with a hammer and auger. Try a spot covered with snow—the ice may be thinner there. Tie one end of a cord through a hole in the handle of the chisel and anchor the other end above the ice so you won't lose the tool when it breaks through. At night, keep the hole from freezing by covering it with a tarp and snow. Purify any water you take from streams and lakes.

(For information on purifying water and on determining the safety of ice, see "Outdoor Safety.")

The snow itself is another good source of water. Melt it in a pot over a flame; if you have it, put a few cups of water in the bottom of the pot first to speed the melting process and to prevent the snow from scorching. Ice and slab snow will produce more water than light powder snow.

Another way to melt snow is with a "water maker." Put handfuls of

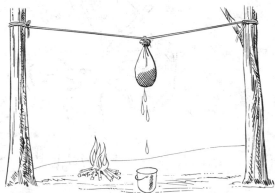

CHAPTER 20

snow into a clean burlap bag and suspend it a yard or so away from an open fire. Put a pot beneath the bag to catch water as it trickles from the bag.

On sunny days, you can position a large sheet of black plastic on a hillside, sprinkle snow on the upper half, and direct the flow of water into a pot placed under the lower edge.

For a personal water supply, tuck a small, wide-mouthed plastic bottle or flask between your underwear and your outer clothing. As you drink water from the container, refill it with snow or ice. Your body's heat will melt the contents and you'll have drinking water throughout the day.

A filled water bottle won't freeze overnight if you take it with you into your sleeping bag. Fill it with boiling water, tighten the cap securely, and slip it into a wool sock for a foot warmer. You can also use the insulating power of snow by burying water bottles or a covered pot of water under a foot of snow. Clearly mark the spot, and in the morning when you dig up the cache you'll have water for cooking breakfast.

OPEN FIRES

A winter camper who knows how to dress, eat, and build a shelter should not need external sources of heat. Still, it's important to be able to build an emergency fire in the snow.

(For information on kindling a blaze, see "Stoves and Fires.")

TOTING YOUR GEAR

Backpacks

Many cold-weather travelers carry all their gear in packs on their backs. Since winter camping requires bulky clothing and sleeping systems, choose a large, comfortable pack. If you'll be skiing or snowshoeing, you may find that an internal frame pack is easier to manage than one with an external frame.

(For more on pack selection, see "Gearing Up.")

Toboggans

Developed by Eskimos to haul loads long distances, toboggans without runners are fine for moving across ice packs and relatively flat land. Stow your gear neatly and low, and lash a tarp over it. Usually two persons maneuver each toboggan, one out front in a pulling harness, the other behind with a snubbing line for downhill braking. In deep snow, other group members can travel ahead of the toboggan to break trail, dropping back now and then to take their turns in the sled harness.

For many winter treks, a combination of toboggans and light backpacks works well. Carry your clothing and sleeping bags on your backs and use toboggans for group gear, one sled per cooking crew. Each crew should carry enough food, water, stoves, and shelters for its members to make a safe camp even if they become separated from the rest of the group.

MAKING CAMP

Night comes early in the winter and stays a good long while. Set up your camp by mid-afternoon to allow time for building shelters, cooking meals, and enjoying the surrounding territory. A lantern will hold back the darkness and help keep your spirits high until you're ready for bed.

When deep snow covers the ground, you can camp places that in the summer would be out of the question. Meadows won't be damaged by your tents, solidly frozen ponds won't give under your weight, and roads and parking lots may be transformed by drifts into delightful clearings in a winter landscape. If you can, place your camp in the protection of a natural windbreak where it catches lots of direct sunlight. Check over-head for tree limbs heavily laden with snow; strong winter winds can blow it onto your shelter.

A WINTER SLEEPING SYSTEM

Ever shivered through a hard winter's night in a thin, damp sleeping bag? Even a heavily-insulated bag tends to become clammy and cold as moisture from your body permeates it night after night. No doubt you wished someone would figure out a way winter campers could sleep warm no matter what the weather.

You're in luck. Using gear you can make yourself, you can sleep cozily at temperatures far below zero. In fact, it's effective even when you have no shelter. Here's what's required.

Plastic Sheet

Use a 12- by 12-foot piece of 4-mil clear polyethylene, the same as that you can use to rig up shelter in milder weather.

(For directions on reinforcing a sheet for use as a trail tarp, see "Making Equipment.")

◄ 1. Spreading
     plastic
     sheet

Deicing Cloth

A piece of nylon fabric about 3 by 7 feet.

2. Spreading deicing cloth ►

Moisture-Handling Pad

A pad of 1-inch-thick low-density polyurethane foam, 3 by 7 feet.

◀ 3. Spreading moisture-handling pad.

4. Spreading sleeping bag ▶

Foam Sleeping Bag

Made according to the pattern in "Making Equipment," the bag is constructed of 1¼-inch foam, lined and covered with breathable nylon.

In addition, you'll need to be dressed in warm, breathable clothing with no waterproof coatings to impede the passage of body moisture through the cloth. Some winter campers fashion pants and vests from the same foam as that used in the moisture-handling pad, and wear them under large woolen trousers and shirts.

◀ 5. Since the fabric and foam of the system are breathable, a plastic envelope is necessary to block the wind. Fold the narrow length of the plastic over the top of the bag.

6. Next, fold the remainder of the plastic over▶ the bag and tuck extra underneath.

◀ 7. Finally, fold the end of the plastic under the foot of the bag. Loose enough to allow you to breath easily, the plastic will protect you from the wind and falling snow.

8. To get into bed, slip off your footwear and ▶ tuck it under the head of the bag for use as a pillow. Slide into the bag, placing your feet inside a foam foot mitten, and when you're all the way in, take off your parka and drape it over your chest between the sleeping bag and the plastic. Snuggle down, pull the parka over your face, slip your hands into your mittens, and you're set to sleep soundly through the coldest arctic storms.

▼9. Drying the system in the sun

CHAPTER 20

Note that the clothing you wore during the day serves at night as one layer of the sleeping system. Because all the fabric and insulation is breathable, the warmth from your body will drive moisture through your clothing and the sleeping bag until it hits the plastic or the deicing cloth and freezes. In the morning you'll find that you are warm and that your clothing is dry, even if it had been damp when you went to bed. Shake the ice off the plastic and the deicing cloth, and you'll be ready to pack up your sleeping system and get on with the activities of the day. If you aren't traveling and the sun is shining, spread out your sleeping gear and let it dry, though the system will keep you warm even if the foam bag becomes very wet.

SHELTERS

Winter shelters help ensure your comfort and safety in the snow. With a little practice you'll be surprised how quickly you can prepare a secure, warm shelter.

One warning, however: *never use a stove or heater inside a shelter!* Snow shelters and closed tents can become virtually airtight. A stove will burn up the available oxygen and replace it with odorless, colorless carbon monoxide—a deadly poison. Play it safe and do all your cooking outside.

Shovel

An essential part of your winter gear is a sturdy shovel. In addition to building snow shelters, you'll use it for all kinds of camp chores, and it is an important rescue tool in case of an avalanche. The shovel you choose should be strong, light, and durable. Some of those sold by outdoor equipment stores are fine, but others are too flimsy. Many winter campers prefer an aluminum grain scoop with a shortened blade (you can trim it to size with a hacksaw and round the edge with a file). Weighing about 3 pounds, it has plenty of capacity and durability.

Saw

When the snow is deep and well packed, use an ordinary carpenter's saw to cut the blocks of snow necessary to construct igloos and snow houses. A stiff ripsaw is ideal. Guard the blade with a length of split garden hose and carry it whenever you travel in snowy country.

Tent

While it provides the least insulation of any winter shelter, a good tent goes up fast and provides protection from wind and snow. Even if you intend to build a snow structure, you may want to carry a tent as a backup shelter in case your wilderness excavations fail.

Stamp out a tent platform in the snow with your snowshoes, skis, or your boots. Use dead-man stakes or snow flukes to hold the guy lines taut; in stormy weather, back them up with ice axes or skis placed through loops in the ropes and driven into the snow.

As soon as your tent is up, crawl inside and use your hands to smooth the snow under the floor. By nightfall the snow will freeze solid, and it will be too late to do much about the bumps and depressions beneath your sleeping bag.

You may want to erect a wall of snow on the windward side of the tent to protect it from gusts. If snow is swirling around your camp, you might need to shovel it away from the tent several times a day.

SNOW STRUCTURES

Shaping a house from a tub of water—that's essentially what happens when you build a shelter from snow. It will require several hours or even a full day to construct, but it is a much better insulator than a tent and it won't flap in the wind. The colder the temperature, the more successful your shelter-building efforts will be. On flat terrain or in snow that's not too deep, the best snow structure is the snow dome.

Snow Dome

Begin by shoveling up a mound of snow 6 feet high and 10–12 feet in diameter at the base. Push several dozen 1½ foot-long sticks into the mound at regular intervals, pointing them toward the center of the floor. Leave

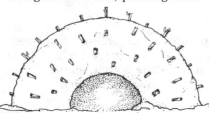

the pile alone for at least 2 hours (overnight, if possible) to give the snow a chance to settle and consolidate. Then, using a shovel, cut a 24-inch-high entrance into the mound and hollow out the inside of the dome, piling the snow near the low entrance to form a wind barrier. Dig until you've exposed the ends of all the sticks, and you should have a roomy, secure shelter. Fashion a door by piling snow on a ground cloth, gathering up the four corners, and tying them with a cord. The snow will crystallize into a hard ball that can be pulled with the cloth into the entryway to block the wind and trap warm air inside the dome. Punch out a couple of ventilation holes with a ski pole or stick. Never burn a stove or lantern inside because they may give off poisonous carbon monoxide gas.

Snow Cave

Built on some of the same principles as a snow dome, a snow cave is dug into deep drifts or steep, stable snow slopes. Architecturally sound, it provides perfect protection in the worst winter storms. In fact, you'll be so warm and snug you won't even know the wind is howling outside. Begin by digging a tunnel into the drift, angling it upward several feet. Next, excavate a dome-shaped room at the top of the tunnel, judging the thickness of the roof by uncovering 1½-foot long sticks poked in from outside, or by watching from the inside for the light blue color of the snow that indicates the wall thickness is about right. Smooth the curved roof to remove sharp edges that may cause moisture to drip onto your gear, and carve niches in the walls for candles. Finally, use a ski pole or shovel handle to punch a couple of ventilation holes in the ceiling at a 45° angle to the floor, and you'll be ready to move in. Since the entrance tunnel slants upward, rising warm air won't escape through it and heavier cold air can't come in.

You may find it easier and drier to build a cave if you dig an entry the size of a closet door into a snow bank and stand upright as you carve out a room at waist level. When everything else is done, use snow blocks to close off the top of the doorway and fashion it into an entrance tunnel.

Eskimo Igloo

Although you'll need some practice to build a proper igloo, the finished structure can be as tight and safe as it is attractive. If the snow is so hard that your boots leave no prints. it needs no preparation. The best snow is that on open, gentle, windswept slopes. For the snow to be firm, temperatures must be no higher than 10° F at night, and no more than 25° F during the day. Subzero temperatures assure snow of the best quality. Test it by pushing a ski pole into it; there should be firm resistance for at least 36 inches. For an igloo large enough to sleep five campers comfortably, clear away soft surface snow from an area about 20 feet by 40 feet in size. This will be the "quarry" from which you'll take blocks for the igloo.

Using a full-size carpenter's saw, cut from the quarry blocks measuring 6 inches by 30 inches by 36 inches. The first block or two won't come out cleanly; use a shovel to clear away the debris until you can hop into the hole left by the removal of the initial blocks. From then on, you can cut each block cleanly along its back, sides, and base, and carefully lift it from the quarry. Line up blocks on edge on the slope above the quarry. As you work, keep the sides of the quarry square and accurate, and take care to make the blocks uniform in size. Good igloos require 40 to 50 large, well-shaped blocks, not random pieces of snow.

◀ Cutting the blocks

◀ Stacking the blocks

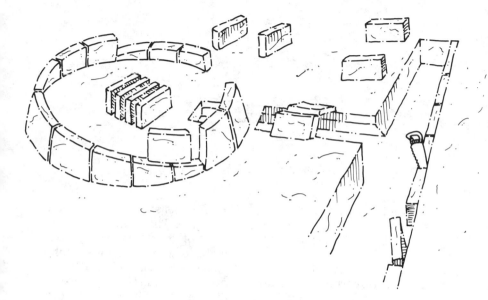

After the blocks are cut, use a ski pole to draw a perfect circle with a 10½-foot diameter. The outside of the circle should be about 8 feet up the slope from the quarry. Use your feet to tramp down the snow just outside the line marking the circle, and set snow blocks side by side along it to form the first tier of the igloo. Using the saw for precision shaping, taper each block slightly and lean it inward just a little so all the blocks lock solidly against one another. Pack snow against the outside of the blocks.

Next, remove one of the blocks to create an opening in the tier and carry as many blocks as possible into the igloo; it's much easier to build with them if you and the blocks are inside. Replace the entrance block and use the saw to cut two slopes about 5 feet long in the first tier of blocks. These slopes are called spirals, and they are essential to the success of your igloo-building efforts.

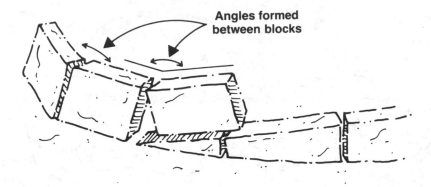

Angles formed between blocks

Now use the saw to trim the top of the first tier's blocks so they are banked inward toward the center of the igloo. That done, begin the second tier by placing a block at the low point of a spiral. If the spiral rises from left to right, note that the upper left-hand corner and lower right-hand corner of each second-tier block bear the weight of that block. When those two corners are secure, gravity will lock the block in place on the sloping spiral and banked surface of the first tier. Lift the next block into position, again taking special care to lock the upper left-hand corner and lower right-hand corner in place. Use the saw to trim the edges of the block for a perfect fit.

Continue to build your way up the spirals, leaning each tier more sharply toward the igloo's center than the one below it. As the blocks near the top, they'll be almost horizontal. Trim every block so that the critical two corners fit properly. The last few blocks may require extensive shaping before you ease them into place, but the shell of the igloo will be strong by then, and you shouldn't have much trouble securing the blocks. The final block is known as the keystone.

To get out of the igloo, create a maintenance entrance by removing a block from the first tier on the side away from the quarry, but save the block so you can replace it later. Using a saw and a shovel, cut a trench from the quarry to the base of the igloo. The trench should be as deep as the quarry, about 24 inches wide at the top, and 36–48 inches at the base. Burrow under the igloo wall and up through the floor to create an entrance, then lean blocks of snow against one another over the trench to form the gabled roof of the entrance tunnel. Use snow to fill the gaps between all the igloo blocks.

Finally, add a few last touches to make your winter house a home. Cut a ventilation hole near the top of the roof, bring your sleeping bags and pads in through the maintenance entrance, and then close it off by replacing the snow block. Stow the rest of your equipment in the entrance tunnel.

An igloo is a very effective winter shelter, one that will last for months if temperatures remain low. Correctly built, it is tremendously strong and can easily support the weight of a Scout standing atop the keystone. Cold air will drain out of the igloo and into the quarry below it, and even when the outside temperature is well below zero the inside of the igloo will be a relatively comfortable 25° to 30° F. The quarry also serves as a patio and kitchen, and you can use your saw to carve benches and tables on which to do your cooking and eating.

Snow trench, tree pit, thermal shelter—knowing how to construct quick snow shelters is a vital survival skill for every winter camper. Practice building them after you've already erected a secure shelter for the night.

(For information on survival shelters, see "Survival Preparedness.")

WINTER CAMPING HINTS

- It's easy to lose equipment in the snow. Keep everything stored on your toboggan or in your pack, tent, or pockets. Tie your pocketknife to a length of cord attached to your belt or belt loop.

- Tie brightly colored cord or ribbon to small pieces of gear so they can be retrieved easily if they're dropped.

- Colorful outer clothing will make you more visible, too.

- Carry a 6-inch square of ¼-inch plywood, and place it under your stove to insulate it from the cold.

- Since winter nights and storms can be very long, take along a good book and a few candles to pass the hours in your shelter.

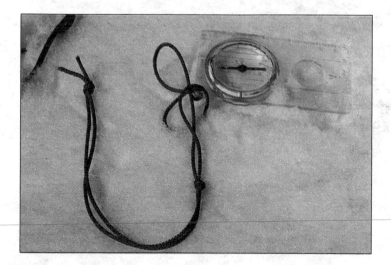

"Come, ye maids of the vanity box,
Come, ye men of the stifling air;
The white wind waits at your door and knocks;
The white snow calls you everywhere.
Come, ye lads of the lounge and chair,
And gird your feet with the valiant skis
And mount the steed of the winter air
And hold the reins of the winter breeze."

Wilson MacDonald, 1880-1967
"The Song of the Ski"

Chapter 21

Cross-Country Skiing

Clyde S. "Sandy" Bridges
Director of the Northern Tier
National High Adventure Programs and
Founder of the Okpik Winter Camping
Program

Carved on a rock in Sweden is the image of a man traveling across snow. The carving is 4,000 years old, and the man is wearing skis. Older than memory, faster than the wind, and quieter than the hush of falling snow, cross-country skiing is a magnificent winter adventure. The equipment is simple, durable, and easy for a beginner to use, yet the challenge of the sport keeps even the best skiers interested year after year. Combining vigorous exercise with agility and endurance, cross-country skiing can be an ideal addition to your physical fitness routine, and you need no more space than an empty field or a snowy park near your home. Once you've mastered the basics, skis may well become an essential part of your cold weather camping gear, carrying you deep into remote wildernesses for the best winter treks of your life.

To get started, you'll need skis, bindings, boots, and poles. It's wise to rent gear from an outfitting store the first few times you go skiing. That way you can learn about quality, fit, and design before investing in equipment of your own.

CROSS-COUNTRY SKIS

Unlike downhill skis, skis for cross-country use are long, narrow, and often quite flexible. A century ago they were sometimes 10 or 12 feet in length and very heavy, but your skis should be just long enough to reach from the floor to the wrist of your arm stretched overhead—anywhere from 170 to 220 centimeters.

The materials from which skis are made also have changed. Those long skis of the past were carved from pieces of hardwood, primarily ash, maple, and birch. While some very good skis are still shaped completely from wood, most modern skis are constructed of fiberglass layered around cores of foam or wood.

Bindings

Attached to the top of each ski is a binding to hold a ski boot in place. The majority of cross-country skiers use a three-pin binding consisting of three pins protruding upward from a metal plate screwed onto the ski, and a movable bail. Holes near the front of the sole of a boot made to fit the binding slip over the pins, and the bail snaps down to bind the sole in place. The heel of the boot is free to move up and down as a skier kicks and glides across the snow.

Some wilderness skiers prefer a modified cable binding similar to that used by downhill skiers. Designed to hold a leather hiking boot or special plastic skiing boot, the binding is hinged at the toe to allow foot movement as skiers make their way up a snowfield. To descend, they can clamp down the heels of their boots and make their runs in much the same manner as downhill skiers.

Boots

The boots you'll use with three-pin bindings may be as low and light as running shoes, or as stiff and heavy as mountaineering boots. Your choice will depend on the kind of skiing you intend to do. For most recreational skiing, lighter boots are just the thing, while treks into rugged mountain country can't be done safely without sturdy, insulated boots. Check the fit of ski boots as you would hiking boots, making sure they match the bindings on your skis. Break in new boots on short trips before attempting any extensive touring, and wear gaiters to keep the snow out of your boots.

Universal ski bindings fit all kinds of boots.

Poles

Made of bamboo, fiberglass, or aluminum, ski poles should be long enough to reach from the floor to fit snugly beneath your armpit. Adjust the length of the wrist strap until you can put the weight of your arm on the strap without gripping the pole. The basket near the point of the pole provides the surface you need to push against the snow. Wrap a little duct tape around the pole beneath the basket to prevent it from slipping off and becoming lost as you ski.

Correct length of pole

Correct length of ski

HOW CROSS-COUNTRY SKIS WORK

Perhaps you've seen a good cross-country skier skimming over the snow. The traveler kicks forward with one ski, glides on it a moment, then kicks the other ski out in front. One motion flows into the next, and in a few moments the skier is out of sight.

But how can this be? How can a ski that slides forward so smoothly provide the traction the skier needs to kick along a track? The problem has two solutions—waxless and waxable skis.

Waxless Skis

Look at the underside, or base, of a waxless ski and you won't find a smooth surface. You'll probably discover that the middle third of the base is molded with a pattern that resembles overlapping fish scales, diamonds, half-moons, or ripples. Notice that the pattern edges face the tail of the ski, and that it's much easier to run your hand over the ski from tip to tail than it is to go the other way.

Now place the ski flat on the floor and look at it from the side. It's slightly bent, and with no weight on it the patterned middle third doesn't touch the floor at all. However, when you have someone stand squarely in the binding, the ski flattens out until nearly all the pattern is in contact with the floor.

This flexible bend of a ski is called its "camber," and it combines with patterns in the base to provide traction and glide. The weight of a skier pushing off on a ski flattens it, pressing the pattern down where it can grip the snow. When the skier glides, there is less pressure on the ski, allowing it to flex and lift the pattern clear of the snow. The ski slides on the smooth areas of the base.

Waxless skis can be noisy on downhill runs and a bit slow, but they're great for beginners, for changing snow conditions, and for any skier who doesn't want to deal with waxes.

Waxable Skis

The bottom of a waxable ski has no pattern. Instead, a skier applies a thin layer of special wax to the bottom, especially to the middle. As the skier's weight presses the ski down, microscopic crystals of snow dig into the wax and hold the ski steady. During the glide, the waxed portion of the base rises a little above the snow, allowing the tip and tail of the ski to slide.

Waxable skis are swifter and quieter than waxless models, but learning to use waxes takes some experience. Different snow conditions require different waxes for maximum efficiency, and you'll need to know the approximate temperature of the snow in order to choose the appropriate wax. Packed in metal tubes marked with effective temperature ranges, waxes can be rubbed directly onto the base and then smoothed with a block of cork. New skis may require the application of pine tar or a glider wax to seal the pores in the base and protect against wear. To choose the best waxes for your area, ask the advice of outdoor equipment salespeople, and watch to see what waxes experienced skiers are using.

Track Skiing

A good way to learn to ski is to follow the tracks of other skiers over gently rolling terrain. The tracks will help guide your skis while you practice the skills you'll use later for backcountry treks, and low hills will give you a chance to try gradual ascents, easy downhill runs, and plenty of kicking and gliding.

Kick and Glide

You've dressed for the weather, clamped your boots into the bindings of your skis, and pointed the tips down the track. Now, use your knowledge of the way skis work to kick and glide over the snow.

Begin by striding forward, putting your weight on your left ski while you slide the right one out in front. Shift your weight to your right foot just as if you were taking a step and, as the right ski grips the snow, slide the left ski ahead of it. Repeat the sequence rhythmically—kick and glide, kick and glide, using your skis as platforms from which you propel yourself along.

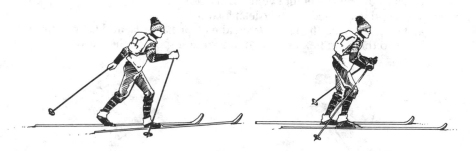

As you get the knack of kicking and gliding, improve your balance and control by leaning forward as you ski. Check the way you use your poles; rather than gripping the handles, let your wrists press against the straps. As the right ski comes forward, plant your right pole ahead of yourself and push backwards with it. Do the same with the left pole as the left ski glides ahead. The power of your arm and shoulder muscles will enhance your speed, and the smooth, rhythmic use of the poles will help you master the basic forward motion of cross-country skiing.

Skiing Uphill

The pattern or wax on the base of
your skis should grip the snow well
enough for you to kick and glide
up gradual slopes. But when a hillside becomes steeper, switch to the
herringbone step. Spread the tips
of your skis until they form a 90°
angle, plant your poles behind the
skis with each step, and walk up
the snow.

Skiing Downhill

Practice downhill techniques on gradual
slopes until you can control your speed and
direction. The easiest method of descent is
to distribute your weight evenly over both
skis, bend your knees slightly, lean forward,
and let gravity do the rest. Watch ahead for hazards, and keep your legs
loose so they can flex as you go over rough spots in the snow.

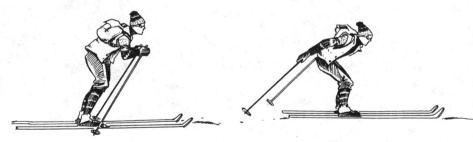

Double Poling

On slopes too gentle for a downhill run, you can make headway by
double poling—that is, using both poles in unison to push yourself along.
Leaning forward at the waist with your knees flexed and feet together,
plant both poles a little ahead of your boots. With a light grasp on the
poles, push against the wrist straps and let your skis slide down the track.
Recover the poles by swinging your arms like pendulums and plant the
poles again, repeating the sequence with a relaxed, steady rhythm.

CHAPTER 21

Kick Turn

While you're standing still, you can reverse your direction with a kick turn. Lift one ski above the snow, raise its tip, and carefully rotate your leg until you can put the tip down beside the tail of your other ski. Shift your weight off the remaining ski, then lift it and twist around to place it in the normal position alongside the first ski.

Step Turn

Make small route changes while you're in motion by lifting a ski and turning the tip in the new direction you wish to travel. As you put your weight onto that ski, lift and turn the other ski. For sharp turns you may need to make a series of small step turns.

Snowplow Stops and Turns

Control your downhill speed with a braking technique called the snowplow. As you make a run, spread the tails of your skis apart, forming the skis into the shape of a V. Bend your ankles inward a little, and the edges of the skis will bite into the snow and slow your progress.

To make a snowplow turn, go into the snowplow V but instead of coming to a full stop, shift your weight onto your right ski. The edge of that ski should bite into the snow, causing you to turn to the left. Weight the left ski, and you'll turn right.

Recovering From a Fall

Every skier falls, and beginning skiers fall a lot, so it's important to know how to untangle yourself from your skis and get back on your feet. However you land on the snow, twist around until your skis are on your downhill side, parallel to the slope. Using your poles for balance, get onto your knees, then stand up and brush yourself off. You'll be ready to go.

BACKCOUNTRY SKIING

Like snowshoes, cross-country skis allow you to move swiftly over snow that would be nearly impassable were you on foot. With them, you can take winter treks far into the backcountry. Of course, you'll want to observe all the usual precautions for safe cold weather travel and be aware of the dangers of avalanches, but with proper preparation and plenty of common sense backcountry skiing can add exciting dimensions to your wilderness activities.

(For more on cold weather living, see "Winter Camping" and "Survival Preparedness." For a discussion of avalanche hazards, see "Mountain Hiking and Climbing.")

Gear

Skiers who spend a lot of time exploring mountainous, untracked territory have special equipment requirements that can be met with backcountry ski gear. Since wilderness skiers often carry heavy packs or

pull sleds laden with gear, their skis are a little wider than skis used on gentle terrain. The extra width gives a skier more stability on powdery snow, and metal edges running the length of the skis bite into hard snow for smooth turns and quick stops. Bindings may be stronger, too, in order to withstand the strain of hard use. Rising above a skier's ankles, sturdy boots provide plenty of lateral stability, and for warmth they may be insulated or lined with inner boots.

Breaking Trail

One of the most important skills of backcountry skiing is breaking trail. When the snow is hard, making headway is no problem—kicking and gliding, double poling, and downhill running will get you where you want to go. However, when you sink into fresh powder with every step, the situation changes. Then it's best for skiers to travel in single file, the leader making a track in the snow that those behind can follow without much effort. Breaking trail can be exhausting, so group members will want to take turns; the leader simply steps to the side of the track, waits for the line to go by, then falls in at the rear. Rotate every few minutes to give each skier opportunities to lead and to rest.

Uphill Travel

The herringbone step will carry you up short ascents. For longer climbs you may find it less tiring to zigzag up a slope, using kick turns to connect the switchback legs.

In rugged country, climbing skins can get you to the top of steep snowfields in no time at all. Once made of animal hides, modern climbing skins are manufactured by attaching mohair or nylon fibers to a tough, narrow strap about as long as a ski. A loop on one end slips over the ski tip, and a sticky adhesive holds the skin on the base of the ski. The fibers are angled toward the tail of the ski, gripping the snow in a manner similar to that of the pattern on the base of waxless skis. Skis with skins will slide enough for you to kick and glide a little, but they really come into their own on tough climbs. For descents, all you need do is remove the skins, roll the sticky surfaces against one another for packing, and head down the slope.

Downhill Travel

You can influence the direction and speed of your descents with step and snowplow turns and with snowplow stops, but for sure control try the telemark turn, the most graceful maneuver in all of skiing.

It's possible to ease into the telemark from the snowplow turn. The basic difference between the two turns is one of position; in a snowplow turn, the skis form a V shape, while in the telemark the skis are parallel and one is a bit ahead of the other. During a telemark turn, you may imagine you're on a single long ski, similar to the slalom board used by a water skier.

As you make a series of snowplow turns on gentle slopes, gradually adjust the position of your skis from the V of the snowplow to the single line of the telemark. Put your weight on the forward ski, twist it a little with your ankle to begin the turn, and as you come around the corner shift your weight to the back ski. To turn the other direction, slide the back ski forward, twist it with your ankle, and let the inside edge carve an arc in the snow.

Two important considerations for successful telemark turning are hip position and downhill lean. You'll find you can balance best if you always keep your hips pointing down the slope (in skiing jargon that direction is known as the fall line). In perfect telemark form, this means you'll twist your torso to the right to turn left, and to the left to turn right. Finally, lean down the fall line as you turn. Skiers learning to telemark have a tendency to lean backwards, causing their skis to slide out from under them. If you lean forward, you'll be surprised how solid a telemark turn can feel.

CHAPTER 21

Carrying a Pack

With good skis underfoot and packs on your backs, you and your buddies can discover tremendous freedom in the backcountry. At first you may fall frequently, however, for skiing with a pack is different from skiing without one.

On day trips, a small pack on your shoulders or a fanny pack strapped around your waist will hold the food, water, and extra clothing you'll need, but it won't interfere with your skiing. For overnight treks you'll want a large backpack. Those with interior frames are easier to manage than ones with frames on the outside. Load the pack so the center of gravity is a little lower than usual, and adjust the straps so it fits securely against your back and doesn't sway from side to side.

Getting up from a fall is sometimes difficult when a heavy pack is pushing you against the snow. Use the same technique as you would if you had nothing on your back, and if that doesn't work, slip out of the pack, get up, then put your pack back on.

CARING FOR SKI EQUIPMENT

If something goes wrong with your skis miles from civilization, you could be in for a long, weary trudge home. Avoid that possibility by always carrying a pouch with any waxes you may need, a cork to spread the wax and a scraper blade to remove it, a screwdriver that will fit the screws on your bindings, and a pair of pliers. It's also a good idea to have an emergency ski tip that can be slipped over the end of a broken ski.

During a trek, pay attention to the surfaces over which you ski. Beware of rocks and sticks poking through the snow; they can gouge the bases of your skis and cause them to become sluggish. Keep your speed under control, especially as you ski through forests, and go around sharp depressions that could severely bend your skis.

In camp, store your skis upright against a tree or a fence, or by sticking the tails into the snow. Face the bottoms east before you bed down so the morning sun will warm them and make waxing easier.

When you get home, let your gear dry at room temperature. It's a good idea to use a wax remover to clean the bottoms of waxable skis. If you have wooden skis, see that they get the treatment recommended by their manufacturer. Recondition ski boots as you would any hiking boots, and stow your equipment where you can get at it quickly. It won't be long before you glance out the window on a cold winter's day and yearn for the joy of strapping on your skis and heading for adventure in snows of the backcountry.

"There is only one way to learn to walk on snowshoes, and that is to put them on and try. After stumbling around and falling down, standing on the heel of one shoe with the other shoe, so that it is impossible for you to lift your first foot, and getting into all manner of ridiculous scrapes, you will learn the knack of shuffling along as a person does in slipshod slippers, and after this it will be only a short time before you become an expert snow-shoer."

Daniel C. Beard, 1925

Chapter 22

Snowshoeing

Clyde S. "Sandy" Bridges
Director of the Northern Tier
National High Adventure Programs and
Founder of the Okpik Winter Camping
Program

Have you ever trudged along a trail deep with snow, your boots sinking out of sight with every step? After a few hundred yards you were probably exhausted, and wished there were a way you could stay atop the drifts.

Now think of traveling that same wintry trail while wearing snowshoes. Instead of wallowing thigh-deep in the snow, you can stride across the surface. Instead of struggling to make headway, you can move forward with smooth, steady speed.

Snowshoes have been around for a long time. In fact, the earliest humans to inhabit North America may have used primitive snowshoes to help them travel the snowy regions of the continent. By the time European settlers arrived, the Indians of the northern woodlands had developed snowshoe making into a highly perfected art, shaping wood and rawhide into snowshoes that were as efficient as they were beautiful.

Since then, wanderers of the winter wilderness have found snowshoes to be an invaluable part of their gear, allowing them to move over snow that would be impassable otherwise. With a little practice, you, too, can master the quiet, rhythmic stride of the snowshoe.

HOW SNOWSHOES WORK

When you hike in the winter with only boots on your feet, all of your weight presses down on the relatively small surface area of your boot soles, causing them to punch deep into the snow. Snowshoes put a larger platform under your feet, spreading the weight of your body over a surface many times greater than that of your boot soles alone. As a result, you'll stay on top of the snow, your snowshoes floating on the drifts in much the same way wide, flat-bottomed boats float on a lake.

SNOWSHOEING

369

As with different kinds of boats, the shapes of various models of snowshoes give them different handling characteristics. Some are designed for fast, straightforward travel. Some will carry heavy loads. Others are made for quick turning and steep climbing. Before you invest in a pair of snowshoes, try to rent or borrow several kinds so you can get a feel for the differences. Then you'll be able to match the right pair of snowshoes to your needs.

KINDS OF SNOWSHOES

Bearpaws

Flat, wide, and oval, bearpaw snowshoes have no tails. That makes them easy to turn, and so they are good for use around a cabin where you'll frequently need to change direction. For that reason, snowshoes without tails are referred to as *cabin models*. On the other hand, the flat toes of bearpaws tend to dig into powdery snow, and their shape forces a traveler to maintain a wide stance that can strain inner thigh muscles. Bearpaw snowshoes are not for long treks.

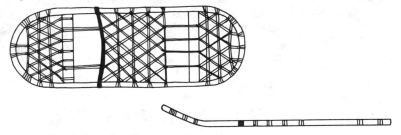

Green Mountain Bearpaws

The most versatile of all snowshoes, Green Mountain bearpaws solve many of the problems of the standard bearpaw variety by being longer, narrower, and slightly upswept in the toes. Their narrow width is useful for climbing slopes because the edges can be dug into the snow. Lacking the stability of snowshoes with tails, they are a bit awkward for traveling long distances over flat, open terrain.

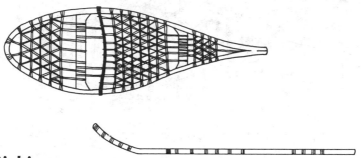

Michigan

Shaped like a teardrop a bit wider than a Green Mountain bearpaw, a Michigan snowshoe has a short tail. Acting in much the same manner as the keel of a boat, the tail helps keep the snowshoe moving in a straight line. That makes the Michigan model better than bearpaws for traveling moderate distances.

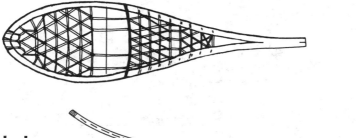

Alaskan

Similar to Michigan snowshoes, Alaskans have long tails that increase their stability but lessen their turning capabilities. Their great surface areas and distinctly upturned toes make them ideal for negotiating deep snow, though their long tails make them unsuitable for traveling through heavy timber or up steep hills.

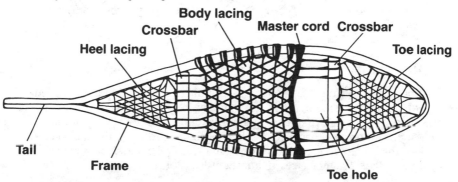

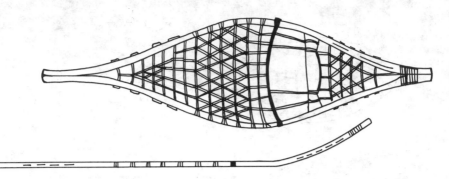

Ojibwa

Take an Alaskan snowshoe and give it a pointed toe, and you've got the Ojibwa. Rather than the one-piece frame of most snowshoes, the Ojibwa is constructed of two pieces of wood joined at the tip and the tail. The advantage is a frame that is in some ways stronger. The disadvantage is that the pointed toe tends to knife into the snow rather than gliding over it.

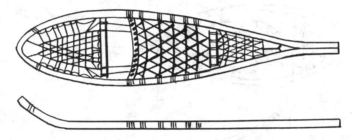

Trail

Trail snowshoes are the largest and longest of all. Narrow and equipped with long tails, they are difficult to turn but superb for adventurers embarking on long treks across flat, open country. Their large surfaces afford plenty of flotation for carrying heavy loads, and their sharply upturned toes enable them to glide atop the snow without exhausting the traveler. Because of their long length and, hence, wide turning radius, trail snowshoes are not effective in thick brush, heavy forests, or on steep terrain.

Aluminum

Showshoes with frames constructed of aluminum tubing and neoprene webbing are extremely tough and lightweight. Usually shaped like Green Mountain bearpaws, they have generously upturned toes and are narrow enough for edging on sideslopes. They also require less care and maintenance than their wood and rawhide counterparts. Their only real drawback is their relatively small size, giving them less flotation than other models.

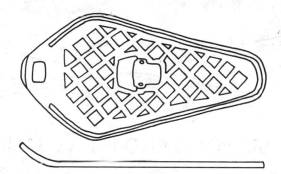

Plastic

While unsuitable for long treks, plastic snowshoes may be useful in the immediate vicinity of a cabin. However, a snowshoer who intends to enjoy any but the shortest, least adventurous outings would do well to avoid plastic snowshoes altogether and depend instead on more durable wood or aluminum models.

BINDINGS

Bindings do just what the word implies—they bind a traveler's footgear to the snowshoes. There are dozens of bindings on the market, but the best have several things in common. They grip your boots or mukluks firmly, but need not be cinched so tightly that they restrict circulation in your feet. With each step you take, they allow the easy up and down motion of your heel. They also prevent lateral movement of your snowshoes, which keeps them from flopping about and gives you more precise control of your footing. Some bindings have flaps that bend back over your toes and keep them from sliding forward—a desirable feature when you're traveling downhill. In any case, your bindings should be adjustable to fit your feet no matter what you're wearing.

◄ Shoe pack with bindings

Mukluk with ► snowshoe

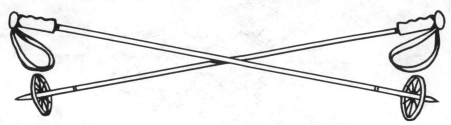

SKI POLES AND ICE AX BASKETS

Many snowshoers use one or two ski poles to help them maintain their balance as they travel over the snow. You'll find that a pole is especially helpful as you make turns and get up from falls.

A mountaineer traveling on snowshoes may attach a special basket to the end of an ice ax and use it for balance in much the same manner as a ski pole.

(For information on stopping a fall with an ice ax, see "Mountain Hiking and Climbing.")

USING SNOWSHOES

The width of snowshoes often causes beginners to spread their feet far apart, putting unnatural tension on their thigh muscles. In addition to being in good condition and using snowshoes designed for the trip you're undertaking, you can alleviate some of that strain by using good technique. As you stride forward, let the inside edge of the snowshoe in motion pass over the inside edge of the stationary snowshoe. Swing your foot far enough forward so that the snowshoes don't touch when you step down. Firmly plant the leading snowshoe to create a stable platform on which to place your weight, and pause an instant after each step. That will allow the snow to consolidate a bit beneath the snowshoe and give you a momentary rest.

Turning

The easiest way to change your direction of travel is by using the *arc turn*. Simply turn your snowshoes a little with each step, gradually curving around until you're lined up on your new course.

A *step turn* alters your direction more quickly. While standing in one spot, lift and turn your snowshoes one after the other, repeating the motion until the toes are facing the direction you want to go. Your movements should be made smoothly and precisely with your legs spread apart far enough to prevent the tail of one snowshoe from being pinned beneath the edge of the other.

For a fast 180° turn, use the *kick turn*. Leaning on a ski pole for balance, lift one snowshoe, twist around until you're facing the way you just came, and plant the shoe firmly beside the stationary one. Lift the second snowshoe, rotate around and plant it beside the first, and you're ready to go.

Traveling Uphill

Climbing gentle slopes is easy if you negotiate them with the same stride you use on level ground. As hillsides steepen, however, you'll find that the shape of your snowshoes and their tendency to slide backwards require that you use different methods to make your ascents. On short pitches in soft snow, you may be able to kick the toes of your snowshoes into the slope. You can also use a herringbone step much like that employed by skiers; point the toes of your snowshoes outward and use the inside edges of the frames to bite into the snow.

On long grades and steep ascents, switchbacking is often the best method. Zigzag up the slope with long, diagonal traverses connected by step turns or kick turns.

Traveling Downhill

Surprisingly enough, downhill travel is one of the more difficult snowshoeing techniques. Your bindings must be snug to handle the increased downward pressure of your footwear, and you'll have to alter your stride to keep your snowshoes flat on the snow.

On gradual grades you can do that by leaning back a bit to put pressure on the tails of your snowshoes. On steeper slopes you may need to tie a cord to the tip of each snowshoe and hold the loose end in your hand. By pulling up on the cord as you plant your snowshoe, you can keep it in the best position. This method is not recommended for long snowshoes or for those with long tails. However, it is quite practical to use with bearpaws, Green Mountain bearpaws, or Michigan snowshoes.

For long descents, use a reverse of the uphill traverse, zigzagging down the snowfield. If the pitch is steep, the snow is firm, and the runout at the bottom of the slope flattens gradually and is free of obstacles, you can place one snowshoe ahead of the other, sit on the rear shoe, and slide down. You'll have little control over your speed or direction, so you must be certain there is no possibility of colliding with trees or rocks, or of slipping over the edge of a cliff.

Breaking Trail

As you snowshoe into the backcountry, you'll soon discover what cross-country skiers know—travel is much easier if you have a track to follow. The tracks of snowmobiles, tires, skis, or of other snowshoers will pack down the snow ahead of you and you'll be able to make good time.

If there are no tracks, break your own trail. Travel in single file, shortening your steps and keeping the tips of your snowshoes high to prevent them from becoming loaded with snow.

(Snowshoes with sharply upswept toes are better for breaking trail than are the flatter models.)

Breaking trail can be tiring work, especially in deep powdery snow, so organize your group so that the lead changes every few minutes. After you've had a turn at leading, step to the side of the trail, allow everyone to pass, then fall in at the rear. The new leader breaks trail for a while, then drops to the back and allows the next person in line to take the lead. Gradually everyone will have a chance to lead, and no one should become too tired or overheated.

HAZARDS

Familiarize yourself with the causes of avalanches and check with local officials before snowshoeing into the backcountry to find out if you should avoid certain avalanche-prone areas. Once on your way, you'll travel with the least difficulty if your route keeps you on open, smooth snow. Be cautious crossing sharp depressions, since a snowshoe bridging a dip may crack under your weight. Frozen, snow-covered lakes can be especially inviting to winter trekkers, but venture onto them only if you are absolutely sure the ice is safe.

(For more on winter travel safety, see "Outdoor Safety" and "Mountain Hiking and Climbing.")

SNOWSHOE CARE AND STORAGE

When you return from a winter outing, inspect your snowshoes for signs of wear and tear. Hard use can chip the finish protecting wooden frames and abrade rawhide lacing. Aluminum frames may become dented or bent, and even neoprene webbing can be nicked and cut. Take care of minor damage before it becomes severe, and your snowshoes will be in top condition whenever you're ready to head for the hills.

To touch up the finish on wooden frames, clean the bare areas and sand them lightly. Blow away any dust and then use a brush to apply a light coat of marine spar varnish. After it's had a day to dry, sand the new coat just enough to roughen it slightly and brush on a second layer of varnish.

Heavily used snowshoes may need more extensive refinishing at the end of the winter. It's also a good idea to apply a coat of varnish to rawhide webbing, and to dab varnish into the holes through which the laces pass. Neoprene webbing should not be varnished. Just keep it clean. Rinse your brush in turpentine after every use, and tightly seal varnish cans.

An advantage of aluminum frame snowshoes is that they require little maintenance. Still, you'll want to check them for cracks and dings, and repair or replace any worn parts of the frames, webbing, and bindings.

Finally, store your snowshoes in a dry, out-of-the-way place that's rodent-proof. Mice love to chew on rawhide lacings, and some animals will gnaw frames for the salt they contain.

"Climb the mountains and get their good tidings. Nature's peace will flow into you as sunshine flows into trees. The winds will blow their own freshness into you, and the storms their energy, while care will drop away from you like the leaves of Autumn."

John Muir, 1838-1914

Chapter 23

Mountain Hiking and Climbing

Caroline S. Munch
Ranger, Philmont Scout Ranch,
1973–76; Veteran Mountain Climber

C limb far above the meadows and valleys of the wilderness and stand on the roof of the backcountry and feel the cool wind blow through your hair. There you'll find a lofty, magnificent world of summits, ridges, and talus slopes, and fields of boulders and snow. Mountains fall away for miles, or pile up, range against range, clear to the horizon. There you'll discover a remarkable ecology adapted to harsh, alpine conditions, and in yourself you may find a keen sense of confidence in your ability to travel safely through even the wildest terrain. While your backpacking and camping skills can carry you along trails deep into the backcountry, the final ascent from your camp to the crest of a mountain range may involve plenty of cross-country travel over tough terrain.

That's where the skills of mountain hiking and climbing pay off. They can take over where the trail ends, lift you far above the lowlands, and let you explore that great, solitary realm where the summits meet the sky.

WHAT MOUNTAIN HIKING AND CLIMBING IS

The skills employed in mountain hiking and climbing bridge the gap between basic trail hiking and technical mountaineering. Unlike rock climbers who intentionally seek out steep, difficult routes, mountain hikers and climbers strive to reach their destinations with a minimum of difficulty or exposure to potential danger. The techniques described in this chapter will help you make your way across difficult wilderness terrain and climb safely to the tops of mountains. Often done on a day-hike basis from established base camps, it's an advanced form of backcountry travel that demands participants have first mastered the basics of hiking. Among

other things, that means always carrying sufficient rain gear, extra clothing, food, and water as well as a first aid kit, matches and fire starters, a map and compass, and sunglasses.

(For more on the basics, see "Ready for Hiking.")

WHAT MOUNTAIN HIKING IS NOT

Whenever there's a danger of falls or the steepness of a climb threatens hikers with injury should they slip, they've gone beyond the outer bounds of mountain hiking and climbing and ventured into territory that requires the skills of a mountaineer. Roping up for climbs is an exacting art, ruthlessly unforgiving of mistakes. Steep and exposed ascents should be attempted only by technical climbers who have the training, leadership, and gear to protect themselves from falls. Everyone else must find safer routes by which to make ascents, and be wise enough to leave alone those peaks beyond their abilities.

(For information on climbing safely with ropes and hardware, see "Mountaineering and Technical Climbing.")

The variability of conditions in the high country increases the importance of knowing when to turn back, and that involves more than simply realizing you've run up against an impassable cliff, a dangerous gulley, or a yawning snow crevasse. You must also be aware of the physical condition and emotional state of each of your companions. Unfortunately, climbers are sometimes reluctant to let others know when they are becoming weary or frightened, or when they feel an ascent is beyond their limits. When group members show signs of fatigue or fear, it's time to switch to an alternative route, or to turn around and go back the way you came. Under no circumstances should someone be ridiculed for expressing an uneasiness with a high route; it's far better to encourage members of a crew to speak openly about their feelings than to discover too late someone is paralyzed by panic on a mountainside where retreat will be difficult.

(For more on when to stop and turn back, see "Outdoor Safety.")

FINDING A ROUTE

Take advantage of every opportunity to talk to other hikers and climbers and to read about the peak you plan to climb well before your trek. Mountain guidebooks contain a wealth of information about trailheads, campsites, the easiest routes up a peak, and areas of particular hazard, as well as the history of the area. You may be able to benefit greatly from the experience of other people.

Mountain hikers do share one thing in common with mountaineers: they climb first with their eyes. Take the time to look over the slopes you plan to ascend, imagining what you'll find along the way. Can you see trails leading to the top? An established path is usually your best route up a mountain, but don't be confused by game trails that may wander about a mountainside and get you nowhere near your destination.

If there is no trail, consider running a ridge to the top. Though you may walk farther than if you went straight up the face of a mountain, the ridge will probably not be as steep. Ridges are sometimes jagged, and may drop off steeply on one or both sides—factors that may make you avoid or skirt around them.

The rounded face of a mountain often offers a clear route to the summit. Couloirs (mountainside gorges), draws, and stream beds, while occasionally climbable, may prove to be rough going, and in their upper reaches can become too steep or narrow for safe passage.

As you study a mountain and determine your route, make a rough sketch of the way up and include prominent landmarks on it. Your perception of a route may change drastically as you work your way up the mountain, and a sketch can come in handy to remind you which way you should be going. A sketch will be especially helpful during a descent if foul weather has moved in and obscured your view of the route.

ZIGZAGGING AND THE REST STEP

Mountain climbing can be as exhausting as it is exhilarating. Long, steep ascents put terrific demands on leg muscles and cardiovascular systems. You can ease the strain by zigzagging your way up slopes, going at a 45° angle to the line of travel, then switching back and crossing above the way you just came. The steepness of the climb will be lessened, and on severe slopes you'll be able to walk on the edges of your boots rather than your toes.

During long climbs, the rest step will give your body a moment to recover after every stride. As you ascend, move your right foot ahead and place the sole of your boot flat on the ground. Swing forward and lock your knee; for an instant the bones of your leg and pelvis will support your weight, allowing your thigh and calf a brief rest. Then swing your left foot forward and repeat the sequence. Even though you may be moving slowly, a rhythmic, even pace will lift you steadily up a mountainside. Breathing should be synchronized with your step to save energy. On moderate slopes, take a breath per step; on steep slopes, take two or three breaths per step to take in more oxygen.

TRAVERSING DIFFERENT TYPES OF TERRAIN

Surrounded by heavy brush, deep forests, rushing streams, tumbled rocks and snowfields, many mountains seem to defy hikers' attempts to climb them. However, overcoming the difficulties of an ascent makes the view from the top all the sweeter. Here are some pointers on dealing with the most frequent of mountain obstacles.

Brush

Brush is the bane of cross-country travel. Brambles and briars sometimes choke hillsides and stream beds. Mountains scarred by fires or logging operations may become covered with dense, low, second-growth timber. A mass of snow can roar down a mountainside and scour an avalanche chute clear of trees, leaving it inhabitable only by low, impenetrable masses of tangled scrub.

Obviously, the best way to deal with brush is to avoid it altogether. Look for a clear route around thickets, perhaps one leaving a valley floor and leading directly to the top of a ridge, or ascending at least high enough to pass above the fringes of the heavy vegetation. When you must wade into the brush, wear clothing that will protect you from snags and scratches, and if you'll be in tall tangles for a while, take a compass reading so you can come out where you want to on the other side of the thicket. In an overgrown watercourse, you'll occasionally find the going easier if you walk right up the stream itself.

Forests

Once again compass navigation can be invaluable, since a forest may be without memorable landmarks. Dead and fallen branches are a major obstacle. Downed trees can be very slippery, and an incautious hiker hopping onto a fallen log may be in for a wild tumble. While it's best to go around them, take special care if you must climb piles of logs pushed up like giant jackstraws by storms, avalanches, or loggers. There are voids between the logs into which your foot may drop, and occasionally a log or two is balanced precariously enough for your weight to start it rolling.

Streams

Stream crossing is always serious business. Twisting your foot on a mossy rock, soaking a sleeping bag in the current, or falling in on a chilly day can quickly complicate your best laid backcountry plans. A little forethought and caution will get you safely across the streams that block your way.

Unless it's a brook you can step over or a stream with a bridge you can walk, take plenty of time sizing up the situation before you embark on a crossing. First, consider the depth, swiftness, and temperature of the water. Water more than knee-deep can make you a bit buoyant, and when there is a swift current you may have difficulty keeping your footing. During a wide crossing through cold water, your legs can become numb and weak before you reach the other side.

Next, look downstream. If you should fall into the water, is there a chance you could be swept into a rapids, against rocks, or over a falls? If so, don't tempt fate by challenging a stream that may not give you a second chance.

When fording streams, always take the essential precaution of unbuckling the waist belt of your backpack and loosening the shoulder straps. Weighed down by packs they could not shed, more than a few unfortunate hikers have drowned in water less than waist deep.

In mountainous country where snowfields blanket the high peaks, snow melting on warm spring and summer afternoons can cause streams to swell. A raging torrent at midday may, after a cool night, be tame enough to cross at dawn. When you come upon such a stream late in the day, camp nearby and wait until morning when the crossing can be made safely.

　　　　　　　　　　　　　　　　　CHAPTER 23

STREAM CROSSING TECHNIQUES

Stepping Stones

Before you step off the bank, decide which rocks you'll step on and in what order. Plant your feet squarely in the center of large stones, and move smoothly from each one to the next. Are the rocks wet or mossy? Expect them to be slippery. Sometimes you can toss a handful of sand on them to improve your traction, and a walking stick will help you maintain your balance.

Fallen Logs

Beware of loose bark and wood slick with sap, spray, or rain. While it's usually not difficult to walk the backs of large logs close to the water, the safest way to cross is to straddle the log and scoot your way to the far bank.

Wading

Always wear shoes when you wade streams. You'll have better footing on wet rocks, and your feet will be protected from cuts and bruises. If you're carrying running shoes to wear around camp, you can pull those

on for the crossing and keep your boots dry. If not, wear your boots without socks, and when you're across dry your feet before you put your socks and boots back on. Long-distance hikers expecting to wade many streams sometimes take along neoprene diving booties to wear in the water.

Members of a crew usually can wade shallow streams one at a time, but when the water is deep or the stream wide, they'll do better to cross in pairs or groups of three. By facing one another and locking their arms around their companions' shoulders, they can lean together and form stable human tripods. More difficult crossings may require a belay, and some must be bypassed entirely.

SCREE, TALUS, AND BOULDER FIELDS

As mountains break down over the centuries, solid cliffs fracture, fall, and cover slopes with broken rock. The largest of these stones are boulders heavy enough to wedge together. Smaller rocks prone to moving under a hiker's weight are known as *talus*. If the material is very loose and no larger than the size of gravel, it's called *scree*.

Climbing on scree is similar to walking on snow. Sometimes you can make headway by kicking toeholds into it, or by pointing your toes out and herringboning up the incline like a cross-country skier. Think of snow as you descend, too. Lean forward far enough to keep your weight over your feet, and dig in with your heels as you take long, plunging steps.

Many rocks on a talus slope are large enough to hold the sole of your boot, but their size makes them easy to tilt and dislodge. Watch carefully

as you take each step, choosing the largest, flattest rocks and placing your weight in the center of each rather than near the edge. As with rocks in stream crossings, be ready for a seemingly stable stone to move underfoot, and if it should begin tumbling down the slope, shout "Rock!" to warn anyone below. Members of a crew traversing a scree or talus slope should stay on the same horizontal plane so that rocks loosened by one of them will not endanger the others.

Negotiate boulder fields by stepping carefully from one rock to the next. Don't leap from rock to rock; the chances of slipping and twisting an ankle are too great. Point out loose boulders to those following you so they can go around them or be prepared for unstable footing. Tighten loose clothing, equipment, and boot laces that could catch on the sharp corner of a boulder and upset your balance.

(For safe ways to climb on large boulders, see "Mountaineering and Technical Climbing.")

ALPINE TUNDRA

Ground cover near and above treeline is often composed of vegetation that's tough enough to survive short growing seasons and long, vicious winters. It cannot, however, tolerate crushing by hikers and campers. Stay on trails whenever you can, and if there are none, try to step from stone to stone to avoid trampling fragile plants. Groups of hikers should walk abreast 5 or 10 feet apart to minimize the effects of their passing.

(For more on walking without leaving a trace, see "Reducing Our Impact" and "Hiking.")

SNOWFIELDS

In the winter and at high altitudes during much of the summer, snowfields can be inviting routes to mountain summits. However, you don't want to venture onto steep mountain snow unless you know how to stop yourself if you lose your footing and begin to slide. For that you need an ice ax and plenty of practice using it.

MOUNTAIN HIKING

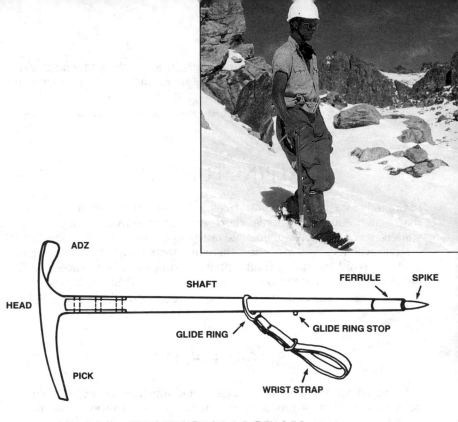

ADZ

HEAD

SHAFT

FERRULE   SPIKE

GLIDE RING

GLIDE RING STOP

PICK

WRIST STRAP

USING AN ICE AX

An ice ax can greatly enhance your security as you travel on steep, snowy slopes. Have an experienced snow hiker demonstrate the safe use of an ice ax, and master its use before you need it.

The main parts of an ice ax are the *shaft*, *spike*, and *head*. For many decades shafts were made of wood, but modern shafts made of metal or fiberglass are much more durable and reliable. Wrap the lower half of your ice ax shaft with duct tape to protect it from abrasion.

The spike on the end of the shaft allows it to be driven into snow and ice, and to act as a brake during *glissades*, skillful glides over snow and ice. The head of the ax has a sharp blade called the *pick* used for self-arrests, and a shorter, wider blade called the *adz* designed for chopping steps in hard snow.

Many hikers choose axes with shafts long enough to reach from their palms to the trail—about 85–90 centimeters—so they can be used as walking sticks between snowfields. Mountaineers usually select axes of 65–80 centimeters, since the shorter length is easier to handle on steep slopes.

To be effective, the pick of an ice ax must be sharp. Unless you are on steep snow where a self-arrest may be necessary, keep the pick and adz of the ax covered with a leather sheath or with rubber guards made especially for that purpose. On the trail carry your ax with the adz pointing forward, or slip it through an ice ax loop on your pack and lash the shaft to the pack itself.

When you hike on snow, unsheathe the ax and handle it prudently. Wrap one hand around the head and hang on. Your chances of injuring yourself with an ax are slight as long as you maintain your grip. Whatever else happens, *don't let go of the ax!*

Crossing Snowfields and Glaciers

The primary purpose of an ice ax is to stop you if you fall down a snow slope. With one hand gripping the head and the other holding the shaft, you'll be in position to make a self-arrest. Falls on snow usually occur when you lose your footing and begin sliding feet first. When that happens, roll *toward* the pick of the ax until you're on your belly. The pick will embed itself in the snow and stop you in a surprisingly short distance.

If a slip turns into a head first tumble, roll toward the pick and, as it bites the snow and begins to slow your descent, swing your feet around until they are below you on the slope. Closely tuck your elbows to your body.

Obviously, self-arresting is a technique that requires expert instruction and plenty of drilling. You can practice by purposely sliding down a slope with a safe runout at the bottom. Slide in every imaginable position—even headfirst on your back—and when you can automatically make the right moves to arrest your fall you'll be a master of one of mountain hiking's most effective safety tools.

The consistency of the snow affects the speed with which you can climb. Deep, powdery snow may engulf your feet and make you feel as if you're wading, while hard, windblown slabs can be as slick as ice. When a slope is not too steep, you can zigzag your way up. While it's possible to follow the same course on more severe inclines, you may also need to kick steps with the edges of your boots. Holding your ice ax in your uphill hand, drive the shaft of the ax into the slope and use the momentum of your stride to kick a step with each of your feet. Settle into your new stance,

then move the ice ax forward and plant it again. Having made the ax a solid anchor before you move your feet, you'll have something sturdy to grip if your boots slip. Keep your weight directly over your feet. If you lean too far into the slope, your feet are likely to slide out from under you.

Sliding, however, is exactly what glissading is all about. If a snowfield is free of boulders and fallen limbs, and if it has a safe runout at the bottom (that is, it flattens gradually and there are no cliffs or crevasses), a glissading descent will get you down a mountain in no time at all. Holding your ice ax in the ready position, aim your toes down the slope and ski on the soles of your boots. Keep your knees bent and drag the point of the ice ax shaft in the snow if you want to slow yourself. It's better to avoid sitting glissades; banging into a snow-covered boulder won't do much damage to the boots of a standing glissader, but it can badly bruise the tailbone of one who's sitting.

The *plunge step* is another effective descent technique. Facing down the fall line and leaning far forward, kick out with your foot, lock your knee, and goose-step down the snowfield. The farther forward you lean, the more stable your footing. If you fall and begin to slide, roll into the self-arrest position and stop yourself with your ice ax.

SNOWFIELD HAZARDS

Although all backcountry travel demands caution, snowfields present unique dangers. The most obvious is a drop-off at the base of a snow slope. To self-arrest with an ice ax, you've got to have a little sliding distance; traveling too closely to the lip of a cliff doesn't give you that leeway. Plan your route accordingly.

Snow bridges over streams may be thick enough to hold your weight as you cross, but if you have doubts don't try it. The fall itself may not be very dangerous, but wet clothes and cool weather are a ready invitation to hypothermia.

Darker than snow, rock tends to absorb more warmth from the sun. Where a snowfield and rock meet, that warmth can melt a little of the snow, sometimes undercutting the edge. An unwary hiker stepping from rock onto a snowfield may plunge through. Make your first step onto a snowfield a big one, and when you return to the rock, be aware that your boot soles will be momentarily wet and slippery.

On large snowfields you may want to mark your route with wands. Usually made of bamboo and topped with strips of flagging, wands will show you the way home even if bad weather makes visibility difficult.

AVALANCHES

Avalanches are a serious concern for all backcountry travelers whose outings take them into snowy, mountainous regions. An avalanche occurs

when snow that has built up on a steep slope tumbles down the mountain. Big avalanches can carry away trees and boulders, and even a small snowslide can bury a hiker.

Being aware of the likelihood of avalanches is your best protection against them. New, unstable snow loading a slope is far more likely to avalanche than are drifts that have had time to settle, and snow frozen hard by a cold night is less likely to break loose than a slope warmed by the afternoon sun. Avalanche warnings are posted in many parks and forests when the danger is high. Rangers sometimes close certain areas, so check with officials before you journey into snow-ladened backcountry. When the slopes are unstable, don't be reluctant to change your plans. The mountains will still be there after conditions have improved.

Avalanche cords, beepers, and shovels will enhance your safety. Around their waists, members of your party can tie brightly colored cords 50-100 feet in length, and let the free ends drag behind them. If someone in a widely spaced group is buried, the cord will usually "float" to the surface, allowing others to follow it to the victim.

Battery powered beepers worn by each hiker emit a radio signal that can be received by the beepers of his companions. As they near a buried traveler, the signal will become stronger, enabling them to pinpoint the spot.

Adventurers who spend much time in the snow usually carry sturdy, short-handled shovels made of plastic or metal. Invaluable for freeing avalanche victims, they also can be used in camp to throw up windbreaks, carve snow caves, and shape drifts into customized kitchens. (For more on snow camping methods, see "Winter Camping.")

Tumbling snow acts somewhat like an ocean wave, complete with undercurrents. If you see an avalanche roaring toward you and you can't get out of its path, shuck your pack. When the snow hits, move your arms and legs in a swimming motion to keep yourself upright and your head above the snow. As the avalanche slows and the snow begins to settle, push it away from your face to form an air pocket so you'll be able to breathe until your companions dig you out.

Should others in your party be caught in an avalanche, keep your eye on them as long as you can, and if they disappear beneath the surface note the exact place you saw them last. Hopefully they'll be wearing avalanche cords and beepers, but if not, probe the area with a ski pole from which you've removed the basket, listen for their voices, and don't give up hope. People have survived under the snow for hours before being rescued. Treat avalanche victims for shock and hypothermia.

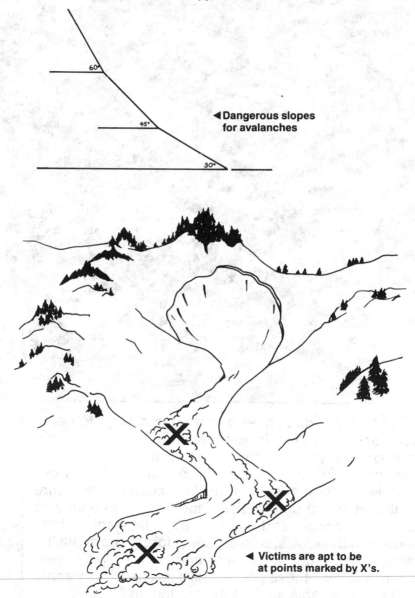

◄ **Dangerous slopes for avalanches**

◄ **Victims are apt to be at points marked by X's.**

"The mountains . . . offer a fighting challenge to heart, soul, and mind, both in summer and winter. If throughout time the youth of the nation accept the challenge the mountains offer, they will help keep alive in our people the spirit of adventure. That spirit is a measure of the vitality of both nations and men. A people who climb the ridges and sleep under the stars in high mountain meadows, who enter the forest and scale the peaks, who explore glaciers and walk ridges buried deep in snow—these people will give the country some of the indomitable spirit of the mountains."

William O. Douglas, 1950

Chapter 24

Mountaineering and Technical Climbing

**Mark Parsons, Michael Mosier, and
Steve Kostka**

Former Head Rock Climbers, Philmont
Scout Ranch

When asked why he was attempting to climb the highest peak on the face of the Earth, the early Everest mountaineer George Leigh-Mallory responded, "Because it's there." Perhaps he was in a hurry when the question was posed and so did not explain any further, or perhaps he knew that people who do not climb would never really understand, no matter how lengthy his answer. Of course, those who were climbers would need no explanation at all.

Every climber and mountaineer has reasons for exchanging the security of flat ground for the lofty world of the climb. A few see a mountain as an adversary to be subdued, and thrive on the challenge of overcoming the forces of gravity and fear in order to conquer a summit. On the other hand, many alpinists feel great contentment and ease as they climb, sometimes sensing that they have become almost a natural part of the rock they are ascending. Others climb for the view from the top, or to master the fluid motion of moving from one hold to the next, or to experience the mystical wonders of playing in a vertical realm of wind, rock, and sky.

Whatever their reasons for going up, climbers find themselves engaged in a most democratic sport. Women can climb just as well as men, and a small, agile person can be as successful as a muscular athlete. Basic climbing requires almost no equipment, and it can be practiced anywhere there is a boulder, a cliff, or even a stone wall a couple of yards high. Granted, it does demand a degree of physical prowess, but climbing primarily requires self-discipline, mental toughness, and concentration.

"Because it is there" was Mallory's way of explaining why he climbed. Give climbing a try and perhaps you'll discover what he meant. Better yet, you may come up with an explanation of your own.

BOULDERING

Learn to climb by doing it near the ground where slips and falls won't result in injury. By scrambling around on boulders and low rock faces, you'll become accustomed to the rock, learn the limits of your abilities, and stretch beyond those limits. Known as *bouldering,* this kind of practice is an essential part of climbing and mountaineering, but the critical difference is the degree of exposure. Boulderers climb no higher than they can safely fall; usually no more than about 5 feet off the ground.

Clothing and Equipment for Bouldering

While mountaineers attempting high peaks may require hundreds of dollars' worth of equipment, a boulderer needs little more than a suitable pair of shoes. Many start bouldering wearing old running shoes or lightweight hiking boots, and for a while that proves satisfactory. As their skills increase, however, they're likely to invest in special climbing shoes. Snugly fitted, they give boulderers the traction and foot flexibility they demand.

Before attempting an ascent, remove any jewelry, watches, and rings you may be wearing, and tuck in the ends of clothing. They'll hinder your ability to use handholds, and they're sure to be scratched or broken. As for clothing, the only requirements are that it be comfortable, allow easy movement, and meet whatever weather conditions arise while you're away from home. A climbing helmet will protect your head from falling stones.

Bouldering Precautions

Bouldering is a relatively safe activity as long as you take a few simple precautions:

1. **Inspect the area**. Before you start scrambling around on any rock face, check the ground below it. There's a good chance you'll take a few falls, and you'll want a landing area that's free of sharp rocks, holes, or anything else that could cause a laceration or twisted ankle.

2. **Determine how you'll get down before you go up**. You won't want to ascend a difficult route on a boulder only to discover you don't have the expertise to get back down again. If you can't see an easily manageable retreat route, do your climbing somewhere else.

3. Don't climb too high. Staying no more than a few feet off the ground, you can work your way around the face of a boulder all day long and learn a tremendous amount about climbing, yet never be more than a step from safety. Even then it's always a good idea to have spotters on the ground below you, both to share in the joys of bouldering and to help ease you down when you slip.

Learning to Boulder

Starting barefoot. Much of your success in rock climbing will be determined by your sensitivity to the rock on which you climb, and by an instinctive awareness of where you've placed your feet. Begin developing that sensitivity by spending a few hours barefoot on the rock. Start on a gently sloping slab, and let your toes get a feel for the stone. You'll notice that rock warmed by the sun feels different—more "stickable"—than cold rock. Sandstone feels different from granite, damp rock different from dry, bare rock different from that encrusted with lichens. You'll also be very conscious of exactly where you're putting your feet. The little nubs, ledges, and cracks you feel under your soles are the irregularities that will provide the holds you'll need to scale a rockface.

The three-point stance. With your shoes on, move to a steeper face, find some toeholds just off the ground, use your hands for balance, and take a step upward. You may discover a natural inclination to press your body close to the rock, but that tends to put your weight a little ahead of your feet and push your toes off their holds. Instead, lean away from the rock at nearly an arm's length. Your weight will press your feet securely against the toeholds, and you'll be in a good position to study the rock around you as you plan your next move. Avoid the temptation to climb with your elbows and knees; at best their round shapes make them unstable on holds, and at worst they'll become bruised and abraded.

Whenever you're on rock too steep to be walked, use a three-point stance. You've actually got four possible points of contact—two hands and two feet. With three of those four points placed on good holds, you can move the free hand or foot toward a new hold. Should one of the three points of contact slip, you'll still have two holding you on the rock.

One by one the hands and feet take their turns moving to new holds. You can often place each foot horizontally against the rock and support yourself on very small nubs (this is known as *edging*), or you can place the flats of your soles on the rock and friction will keep your feet in place (a technique known as *smearing*).

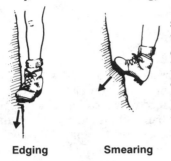

As you become comfortable with the sensation of traveling about on a rock, try to connect several moves with smooth, easy grace. Rather than tiring your arms, let your legs do the work of lifting you. Stay as relaxed as you can, and use finesse instead of brute force to make your moves.

Edging   **Smearing**

Descending. Since you can't see where you're going when you're coming down as easily as when you're climbing, descending a boulder can be difficult. Still, regular practice will help you learn to find good toeholds and use the three-point stance in reverse to ease your way down.

To descend a rock slab that is not steep enough to warrant a three-point stance, point the toes of your boots directly down the rock, bend your knees and place the full surface of your soles on the slab. Keep your

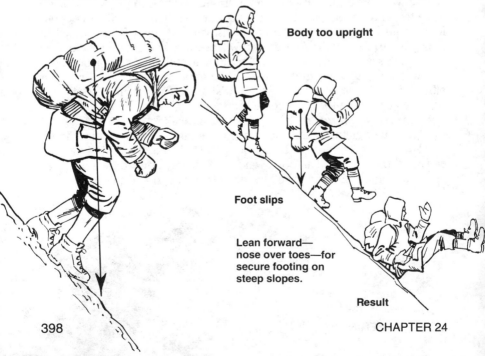

Body too upright

Foot slips

**Lean forward—
nose over toes—for
secure footing on
steep slopes.**

Result

weight directly over your boots and the friction of the soles will prevent you from slipping. Roughly textured surfaces are the safest; avoid stepping on rocks that are wet, loose, or covered with lichens or moss.

Bouldering Techniques

While the most obvious way to climb a rock face is by pulling on holds with your fingers and edging and smearing with your feet, practiced climbers have a whole range of techniques for dealing with various kinds of problems. To climb a crack in the rock, they may hold themselves steady by pulling apart in opposite sides of the fissure (an *opposition hold*). If the crack is wide enough, they can wedge fingers, fists, feet, arms, or even a portion of their bodies into it and create *jam holds*. *Laybacks* allow climbers to walk up overlapped fissures by pulling on one side with their hands and pushing hard against the other with their feet. In huge cracks the size of chimneys, climbers may work their way up by forcing their backs against one wall and their boots against the other (called *chimneying*), or by pressing a hand and foot on each wall (*stemming*). Climbers using the palms of their hands to lift themselves onto ledges are said to be *mantling*.

It must be stressed again that no matter how proficient you become at bouldering, you must never climb any higher than you can safely fall. Above that you must employ the equipment, training, and attitudes of technical climbing.

Down pressure for mantling

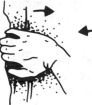
Opposition hold

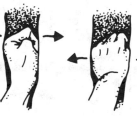
Fist jams

Foot jams

CLASSIFICATIONS OF CLIMBING DIFFICULTY

Most climbing routes are rated with a *class* and a *grade* to indicate their difficulty. The class of a climb will tell you the technical difficulty of the hardest move you must make in order to complete the ascent. Grade suggests the effort required to complete all the technical portions of a climb. A short climb with one hard move would have a high class rating but a low grade, since the ascent could be done in a short time. A climb of many pitches but relatively easy technical moves could have a high grade rating due to the greater effort climbers must expend. Both class and grade are determined under good weather conditions. Rain, snow, and cold can increase the difficulty of any ascent.

Class 1— Hiking. Hands are not needed for balance.

Class 2— Scrambling. Rope not needed, though one may be carried. Hands used occasionally for balance.

Class 3— Easy climbing. Advanced scrambling, using hands and some basic climbing abilities. A rope is carried and used to belay any party members uncomfortable with the exposure.

Class 4— Roped climbing with belay. Pitches are belayed, the rope secured to climbing hardware or anchored around trees or outcroppings of rock.

Class 5— Roped climbing with protection. In addition to a belay, climbers protect themselves from long falls by using chocks, runners, pitons, and other devices. Class 5 climbing is further divided into 13 categories of difficulty ranging from 5.1 (very easy) to 5.13 (extremely technical.)

Class A— Roped climbing with artificial assistance. Ascents on a smooth, steep face or overhang requiring artificial aids such as climbing stirrups.

GRADES OF CLIMBING

Grade I — No more than a couple of hours required to complete technical sections of a climb.

Grade II — Half a day required for technical sections of a climb.

Grade III— The majority of a day required for technical sections of climb.

Grade IV— There are technical moves of at least class 5.7, and the entire climb requires a full day.

Grade V — With pitches of at least class 5.8, the climb requires 1½ to 2 days.

Grade VI— With an abundance of difficult pitches, the climb requires 2 days or more.

TECHNICAL CLIMBING

When climbers ascend above the relative safety of low-level bouldering, they must use ropes and climbing hardware to secure themselves to the rock. All climbers occasionally slip; proper protection will prevent a fall from becoming a tragedy. The information below is intended only to give you a taste of the excitement and adventure of technical climbing. Under no circumstances should you attempt such a climb without proper adult supervision.

Your first and perhaps most important step in learning the craft of technical climbing is to find competent instructors. Although many people say they are climbers, not all of them have the qualifications to instruct novices. Even some phenomenally able mountaineers may not have the patience to impart their knowledge to others. Outdoor equipment stores, especially those handling climbing gear, may be able to direct you to experienced teachers. Many colleges and universities offer mountaineering courses, and mountaineering clubs all over the country provide members with a full range of climbing instruction.

Clothing and Climbing Helmets For Technical Climbing

Climbers should carefully match their clothing to the conditions they expect to encounter. Climbers spending an afternoon scaling a cliff near home may need nothing more than what they might wear bouldering, while members of an extended alpine expedition might require all the clothing and camping gear of winter campers.

Every climber must wear a climbing helmet secured with a chin strap. A falling rock or piece of equipment can put a real dent in your head unless you wear a helmet whenever you're anywhere near the area of a climb. It's also a good idea to bind up long hair and tuck in shirttails so they won't become tangled in ropes and hardware. Belayers and rappellers can protect their hands with leather gloves.

Rope

Most mountaineering instructors will want you to spend a lot of time bouldering. Still, it probably won't be long before you're introduced to a climbing rope, the piece of equipment that most symbolizes the difference between bouldering and mountaineering.

Modern climbing ropes usually are 150 or 165 feet in length. The most frequently used is the nylon *kernmantle* rope, $\frac{7}{16}$-inch in diameter (11 mm). A woven or braided core (the *kern*) gives the rope its strength and resilience, while an outer sheath called a *mantle* protects the core from abrasion.

Since your life may depend on it, carefully inspect a rope before and after every use by running its full length through your fingers. Dents, lumps, or other irregularities in the feel of a rope, or worn spots in the sheath are warnings that the rope should not be used. Furthermore, every rope is designed to stop only a certain number of falls before it can no longer be trusted. As a rule of thumb, after catching three hard falls of any length, a rope should be retired and indelibly marked with dye so it will never again be taken on a climb.

Protect your rope by keeping it dry and clean, and don't step on it. Grit working into the fibers can seriously weaken the core. At home, store ropes loosely coiled in a place far removed from the damaging influences of direct sunlight, dampness, excessive heat, chemicals, and petroleum product fumes.

Belaying

Climbers and mountaineers can ensure the safety of their partners by *belaying* them as they make class 4, class 5, and class A ascents, and whenever any member of a party is uneasy about his or her safety on a mountainside. In short, a belayer controls the amount of slack in the rope connected to the climber, and if the climber slips the belayer uses time-tested techniques to hold the rope fast and arrest the climber's fall.

In order to belay effectively, you'll need to tie in to an anchor point and then take a comfortable stance, usually sitting facing in the general direction of the climber. To avoid being yanked from the belay perch, it is essential for the belayer to be positioned in a direct line between the anchor and the direction of the climber's potential fall.

Each section of a climb is called a *pitch*. For a *top belay*, you'll be situated above the pitch to protect a climber coming up from below. Pass the climbing rope behind your back below your belt. The *guide hand* holds the part of the rope leading to the climber while the *brake hand* stays ready to arrest a fall. Run the rope through a carabiner called a *keeper* attached to your waist opposite the brake hand. It will prevent you from spinning if the climber falls.

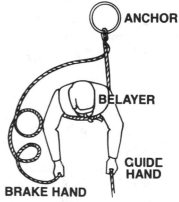

BELAYING—TAKING UP ROPE

Top view of body

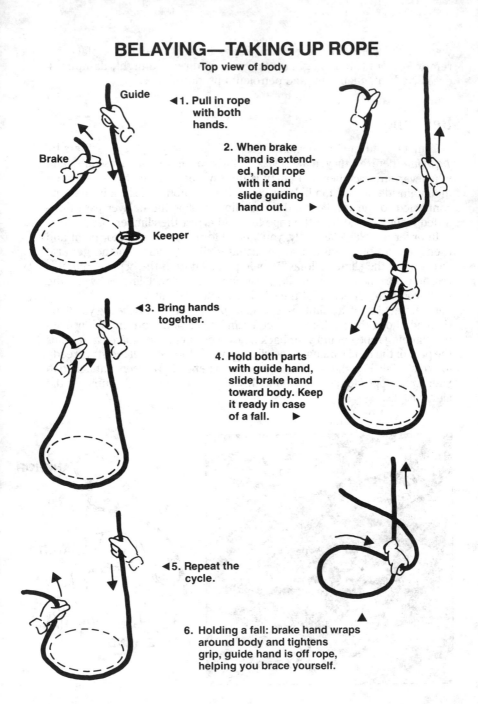

◄1. Pull in rope with both hands.

2. When brake hand is extend-ed, hold rope with it and slide guiding hand out. ►

◄3. Bring hands together.

4. Hold both parts with guide hand, slide brake hand toward body. Keep it ready in case of a fall. ►

◄5. Repeat the cycle.

6. Holding a fall: brake hand wraps around body and tightens grip, guide hand is off rope, helping you brace yourself.

Guide

Brake

Keeper

CHAPTER 24

CLIMBING SIGNALS

Communications between climber and belayer are so important they have become formalized into a set exchange of commands and responses:

CLIMBER	BELAYER	MEANING
	"On belay."	"All set. Your belay is ready."
"Climbing."		"Here I come."
	"Climb."	"Come ahead."
"Slack."		"I need some slack in the rope."
"Up rope."		"Take up the loose rope."
"Tension."		"Hold the rope tightly. Brace yourself for a fall."
"Falling!"		"I'm falling! Hold the rope tightly!"
"Rock!"	"Rock!"	"Look out for falling rocks."
"Rope!"	"Rope!"	"Rope being thrown down."
"Off belay."		"I'm in a secure position and no longer need a belay."
	"Thank you."	"I heard you and understand your signal."

If the day is too windy or the area too noisy for climbers and belayers to hear one another clearly, postpone your ascents or move to another area.

Begin a top belay by grasping the rope with your guide hand fully extended toward the climber and your brake hand holding the rope just in front of your waist. As a climber begins an ascent, pull in slack rope by drawing your guide hand toward yourself and extending your brake hand; the rope should be snug against your lower back as it slides around your body. Slide your guide hand forward along the rope until it is slightly ahead of your brake hand, grasp both lines of the rope with the guide hand, and slide your brake hand back to its original position just in front of your waist. Repeat this sequence as many times as necessary to take in slack as the climber ascends. *Never* let go of the rope with your brake hand until the climber signals "Off belay," and be prepared at any instant to arrest a climber's fall. Practice belaying under the watchful eye of a qualified instructor until you can do it automatically.

Arresting a fall depends on friction. The instant you sense that a climber is slipping, grasp the rope tightly and cross your brake hand across your stomach. The rope will tighten around your body, and you'll be able to hold the climber.

Roping Up

Before beginning a technical ascent, the lead and end climbers in your team should tie themselves to the ends of the belay rope. While you can use a bowline-on-a-coil knot to tie yourself directly to the rope, it's safer to use a climbing harness. A harness more comfortably distributes your

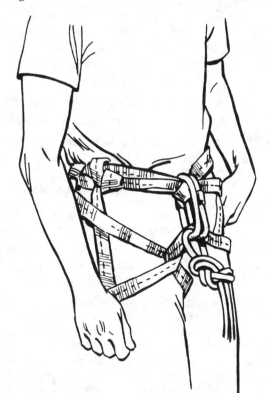

weight and may help prevent internal injuries in case of a fall. Tie a figure eight follow-through in the rope which is looped through the webbing of your climbing harness.

TYING A SEAT HARNESS

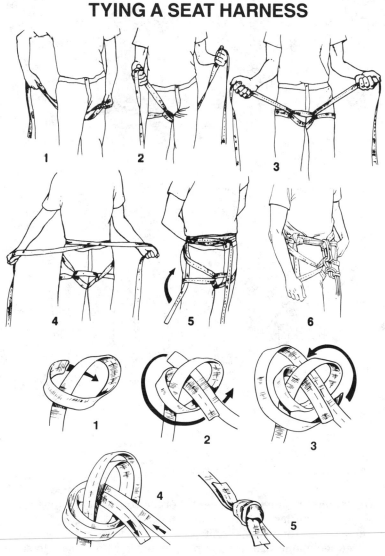

Water knot

Figure eight on a bight

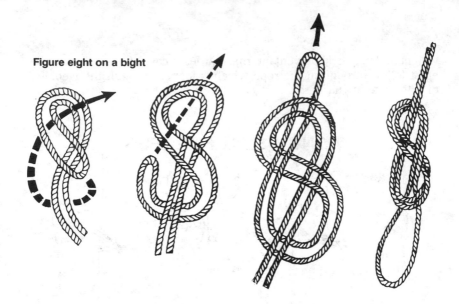

Mountaineers Coil

Coiling a rope

A third climber may tie into the center of the rope by clipping a locking carabiner through his or her climbing harness and a figure eight on a bight tied in the rope. While quite safe when done properly, this is a specialized technique that, if attempted incorrectly, may lead to serious injury.

CHAPTER 24

Placing Protection

Properly belayed from above, you can climb knowing you'll be caught should you fall. Where top belays are not possible, however, a *bottom belay* can be just as effective, but it requires the first climber up a pitch to place climbing hardware on the rock. Here's how it's done.

A belayer establishes a secure anchor at the base of the pitch. When your belayer's ready, he or she will shout, "On belay." As soon as you're set to go, reply, "Climbing!" and the belayer will acknowledge by responding, "Climb!"

Rather than gathering in rope as during a top belay, the belayer will reverse the technique and play out rope as you work your way up the pitch. When you've gone up a few feet, you'll need to find a crack in the rock in which you can fit a *chock,* an odd-shaped piece of hardware attached to a metal or nylon loop. Under tension, it will jam tightly against the sides of the crack. Clip a carabiner to the loop, snap your rope into the carabiner, and you've established a *point of protection.* If you slip now, you'll fall twice as far as the length of rope between you and the carabiner.

CHOCKS AND THEIR USES

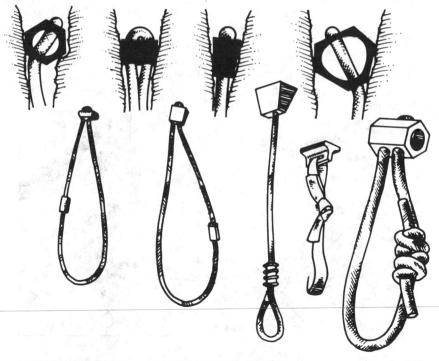

To continue, climb a little farther up the rock and place another piece of protection, and then another and another until you've reached the top of the pitch and tied yourself to a belay anchor from which you can top belay your partner. When you are completely out of any danger of falling, shout, "Off belay!" Your partner will answer, "Thank you!" and you can relax.

Good instruction and plenty of experience will teach you how and where to place your chocks. On the way up, the last member of your party to climb the pitch can retrieve the chocks. For a climb involving several pitches, it's best to wait until everyone has completed the first pitch before moving on to the second, using the same methods of belaying, leading, and placing protection for every section of the ascent.

The use of chocks epitomizes the modern mountaineering philosophy of *climbing clean* and leaving no trace of one's visit to the backcountry. Pitons, the flat or angled metal pins once widely used on routes requiring protection, have fallen into disfavor among climbers. Forcefully hammering pitons into and out of cracks can disfigure rock and spoil some of the pleasure for climbers who come along later. Chocks, on the other hand, pose little threat to the integrity of the rock. Many mountaineers also believe that chocks are more aesthetically pleasing in that climbers using them must be more attuned to the shape, texture, and feel of the rock.

Rappelling

A *rappel* is a controlled slide down a climbing rope, and it's a useful way to descend from a climb. Like every other aspect of mountaineering, rappelling must be attempted only under the watchful eyes of qualified instructors.

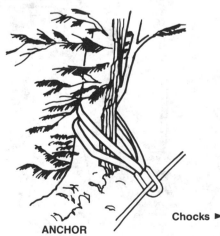

ANCHOR

Chocks ▶

CHAPTER 24

The safety of a rappel depends in great part on the rappel anchor. A large tree, a rock outcropping, or several solidly placed chocks make good anchors, though there must be no question that they'll stay in place.

Before a rappel can begin, a figure eight on a bight is tied in one end of the rappel rope and is clipped through two carabiners (with gates reversed and opposed) attached to the anchor. For added security, a second rope is used to belay rappellers during their descents.

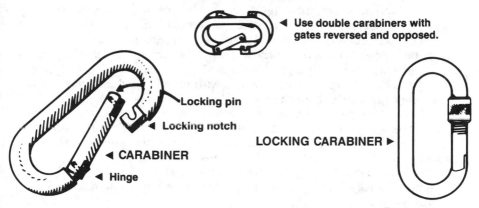

◀ Use double carabiners with gates reversed and opposed.

Locking pin

◀ Locking notch

◀ CARABINER

LOCKING CARABINER ▶

◀ Hinge

As with belaying, friction against the rope is what gives mountaineers control over their descents. A rappeller can create that friction by passing the rope in special ways around his or her body, or by running the rope over carabiners or a figure eight descender clipped to a climbing harness. While quite safe when done properly, both are specialized techniques that, if attempted incorrectly, may lead to serious injury.

To begin rappels, climbers must make the unnatural move of leaning backwards over a ledge or the lip of a cliff. Intimidated at first, they soon discover they can trust the rope to hold them, and that by leaning far back into thin air they can plant the soles of their boots flat against the cliff and walk down the rock. It's best to descend slowly and smoothly, avoiding the temptation to bound down the cliff. Rapid rappels are hard on equipment and points of protection, and ignore the margin of safety every climber and mountaineer strives to maintain.

Figure eight descender ▶

Harness

To brake hand.

▲ Carabiner brake

Mountaineering

To understand the difference between rock climbing and mountaineering, think for a moment of soccer players and football players. Participants in both sports play upon similar fields, attempt to reach a goal, and display plenty of endurance, agility, and teamwork. Yet soccer and football are very different games requiring different abilities and attitudes. Soccer players in shorts and jerseys rely on smooth motion, deft footwork, and quick action. Football players gird themselves in pads and helmets and set out on long, often laborious drives toward the end zone. A good soccer player is not necessarily a good football player and a football player may never get the hang of soccer, though with practice and experience an athlete could master both games.

Now consider rock climbers and mountaineers. The ascents of rock climbers are usually made on boulders and cliffs not far from roads or campgrounds. Even at its most demanding, rock climbing seldom requires its participants to spend more than a few hours or at most a long day completing a climb. The challenge is in the mastery of motion and body control. Usually the act of climbing is far more important to a climber than is reaching a physical goal.

Mountaineers also are interested in efficiency of motion and the finesse of graceful ascents, but they are more driven to stand atop distant summits. For them, climbing technique can become a tool in their quests to reach the tops of mountains. Unlike the cliff and boulder playgrounds of rock climbers, mountaineers seek out peaks that frequently require long approach hikes, strong skills of cross-country navigation and route finding, and a thorough understanding of snow and glacier travel and avalanche hazards. Mountaineering treks usually involve a night or two of camping, often at high altitudes. Exposed to severe weather, mountaineers must be properly clothed, equipped, and trained to cope with miserable conditions.

Competent rock climbers are not necessarily qualified mountaineers, and many mountaineers have never made difficult rock climbs. Yet, like soccer and football players, they have many skills in common. Most importantly, they share a constant concern for safety, and they know that to stop and turn back in the face of unfavorable conditions is always the sign of experienced backcountry travelers.

"The memory of a cave I used to know at home was always in my mind, with its lofty passages, its silence and solitude, its shrouding gloom, its sepulchral echos, its flitting lights, and more than all, its sudden revelation of branching crevices and corridors where we least expected them."

Mark Twain, 1869

Chapter

25

Caving

C. William Steele
Explorer of More Than a Thousand
Caves; Past Director, National
Speleological Society

Jack S. Hissong
Silver Beaver Scouter and Veteran
Caver for More Than 30 Years

B eneath the surface of the earth lies a strange, magnificent world darker than the darkest moonless night. No rain falls. No seasons change. No storms rage. Other than the rush of hidden streams, this underground world is silent as a tomb, yet it is not without life. Furry mammals rest suspended by their toes along the twisted mazes of tunnels, while ghostly, eyeless creatures scurry along the walls. Transparent fish stir the waters of still lakes, and the floor is sometimes the home of strange insects and microorganisms. This is the world of the cave, as beautiful, alien, and remote as the glaciated crests of high mountains. And just as climbers are tempted by summits that rise far above the familiar ground, cavers are drawn into a subterranean wilderness every bit as exciting and remarkable as any place warmed by the rays of the sun.

There are tens of thousands of caves in North America. Some are at the edge of the sea, carved by the erosive motion of waves, while others are lava tubes created when the surfaces of rivers of molten rock cooled even as lava underneath continued to flow. Most caves, however, formed as rainwater, made slightly acidic by carbon dioxide in the atmosphere and chemicals in the soil over which it ran, seeped into fissures in soluble limestone, and gradually melted out branching networks of tunnels and rooms.

Some caves are too tiny to enter, while others, such as Kentucky's Flint Ridge — Mammoth Cave, are so vast many of their passages extend for miles. Within some caves are rooms larger than the biggest sports arenas, and shafts deeper than the tallest buildings. There are towering pillars, and expanses of colorful stone folded as if they were massive draperies. The forces that shape a cave work with exceeding patience. A drop of water hanging from the point of a stalactite leaves a trace of mineral residue when it finally falls, lengthening the stalactite ever so slightly. Then it splashes on a stalagmite rising from the cave floor and deposits a hint of minerals there, too. Centuries may pass before seeping moisture widens a chamber by even an inch, or lengthens a tunnel at all.

Most caves are solid enough to survive earthquakes, yet much inside a cave is fragile. Fine needles of rock, graceful columns, and unmarred walls are today just as they have been for eons. Bats, snakes, frogs, insects, and other cave visitors, all known as *trogloxenes,* form webs of interdependency near a cave's entrance. Deeper down, permanent cave dwellers called *troglobites* make up delicate, specialized ecosystems. A cave is timeless, little touched by the world above. Massive and fragile, living and stony, it remains unchanged and unseen by every living creature save one, and that is man.

(For more on cave formation, see "The Earth.")

Prehistoric peoples took refuge in caves, making them their homes. Ancient hieroglyphics still cover some caves, attesting both to man's early presence and to the permanence of marks drawn on a cave wall. The ancient Greek word for cave is *spelaion.* In the last century, subterranean explorers called *speleologists* have ventured farther and farther underground. By the 1940s, spelunking had become a popular pastime in the United States, and as cavers spent more time beneath the earth, they refined their equipment, safety practices, and techniques.

If you're interested in becoming a caver, you're in for some exciting adventures and you'll want to prepare yourself as carefully as you would for the ascent of a mountain. A cave is no place to get hurt or lost. Underground rescues are difficult, and a caver must do everything possible to prevent dangerous situations from arising.

The best way to become acquainted with the basics of caving is by getting to know members of a chapter (known as a *grotto*) of the National Speleological Society, Inc. Cave Avenue, Huntsville, AL 35810. They'll help you learn to enjoy caves without harming them. One of the first lessons will deal with a caver's clothing and equipment.

CLOTHING

The temperature in a cave is always that of the average annual temperature of the region. Most caves are humid, and because their temperatures remain fairly constant, they seem cool in the summer and warm in the winter. In the U.S., cave temperatures range from just above freezing in the northern Rocky Mountains to the high 70s in Texas. You'll need to consider a cave's temperature as you dress for it.

Old, rugged clothing is a must underground. A caver walks, crawls, climbs, and squirms through passages that may be sloppy with mud, water, and bat guano. Some caves are quite chilly and damp, conditions conducive to hypothermia, so you may need to pull on some layers of woolen clothing to keep warm. Boots with lugged soles will give you traction as you work your way through slippery tunnels, and knee and elbow pads will protect you if you do extensive crawling. Leave a set of clean clothes outside the cave for the trip home. When you change, stow your muddy clothing and shoes in a plastic trash can liner.

(For more on hypothermia, see "Outdoor First Aid." For more on layering clothing, see "Gearing Up.")

GEAR

Even though you'll always travel in caves with several companions, equip yourself to function independently. The most important gear is that which lights your way.

Light

The only illumination in a cave is what you take in, so you must carry dependable sources of light that will last as long as you are underground. Nothing is more vital to your safety, for a caver stranded in the dark without a light has no choice but to sit still and wait to be rescued. To be sure that won't happen to you, carry at least three lights. Even if two go out, you can still find your way to the cave's entrance.

The best caving lights are electric or carbide headlamps that can be attached to hard hats. Electric lamps need fresh flashlight batteries for power, while carbide lamps use chunks of calcium carbide. When controlled amounts of water mix with carbide, it gives off acetylene gas that burns more intensely than many electric lights. Take along spare batteries, and store extra carbide in a watertight container such as a baby bottle with a snug lid. All spent carbide residue must be carried out of the cave so it will not pollute underground water or poison cave life.

Carry a second source of light as dependable and bright as your primary lamp, and back it up with a third source — a good flashlight or a candle and matches in a waterproof match safe.

Hard Hat

When you think of low cave ceilings, you'll realize the importance of always wearing protective headgear. Helmets made for rock climbers are ideal, though construction hard hats, hockey helmets, and even football helmets will shield your head. Use a chin strap to keep headgear securely in place.

Water and Food

Carbide lamps need water, and so do cavers on lengthy jaunts. Subterranean water is rarely safe to drink, so bring water from home in a canteen or plastic water bottle, and tuck a plastic container of water purification tablets into your pocket. Depending on how long you'll be underground, you may want to take along a can of fruit or meat and a candy bar or two for quick energy, but don't expect to camp in a cave. The fragile environment can withstand neither litter nor the disposal of human waste.

Knapsack

Carry your provisions and extra gear in a durable knapsack that won't hamper your movement. Since you may need to wiggle through tight passages, you'll want to keep your load as small and flat as possible.

First Aid Kit

Wear gloves to avoid scraped knuckles. Since a complete first aid kit is bulky, narrow it down to a compact one containing: gauze dressing, adhesive tape, bandaids, steristrip closures, and an antiseptic ointment.

WHERE TO GO

There are two kinds of explorable caves, commercial and wild. While proprietors of many commercial caves offer public tours along well-lit passages, some may also lead novices on crawls into more remote tunnels, and that's a great way for you to get a taste of real caving. Wild caves are those untouched by developers. If you venture into them, do so in the company of experienced cavers, and then only after learning what passages have been explored, what maps can be obtained, and whether special equipment and techniques will be necessary.

If the entrance to a cave is on private land, get the owner's permission before crossing the property, and when you finish your wanderings let the owner know what you found. If a cave is on public land, register with officials in charge of the area, and abide by any restrictions they may place on your activities. Maintaining friendly relations with landowners and managers will do much to keep the cave open for other spelunkers.

CAVING TECHNIQUES

The goal of every caving expedition is to get in and out of the cave safely, to enjoy yourself while you are underground, and to leave no trace of your passing. The first step toward that goal is to file a detailed trip plan with a responsible adult before you embark on any cave exploration. Write down the exact location of the cave entrance, where you intend to go while you're underground, and when you expect to come out. Then, stick with the itinerary. If you have not returned by the time noted on your trip plan, the person expecting you must assume you have encountered difficulties and should notify authorities to begin search and rescue operations.

(For a sample trip plan, see "Planning.")

Never enter a cave alone. Include a minimum of four cavers in every party so that if one of the members is injured, a partner can render aid while two others go for help. As the group travels in a cave, have the most experienced cavers go first and last, a technique known as *caboosing*. Should the party become scattered, the caboose can bring the stragglers along. The first few

times you go caving, take along an experienced guide.

Most animals you'll see underground will be near the cave entrances. All are beneficial and some are endangered; take care not to disturb them. Hibernating bats and those nursing their young cannot tolerate any kind of intrusion, so you'll want to learn how to recognize and avoid caves containing them. Cave creatures would rather flee than confront a human, but in the unlikely event a spelunker is scratched or bitten, cleanse and bandage the wound. If the injury is caused by a bat, a physician must decide whether rabies treatments should be administered.

When you descend into a cave, move slowly and deliberately. Avoid jumping and be especially cautious as you cross ledges and work your way over loose rocks and alongside streams. Keep in mind that a cave is a wilderness and that the responsibility for your safety rests primarily with you.

Experienced cavers can give you pointers on finding your way into and out of a cave. Many popular caves have maps showing the main passageways, and you can plot a course just as surely as you can navigate with a map above ground. You'll also learn to look over your shoulder as you explore, becoming familiar with the natural features you'll see as you retrace your steps. Should several tunnels converge, take a compass reading on the passage that leads back to the entrance and make a note on your map.

CAVE MAP SYMBOLS

Surveyed passage

Underlying (dotted) passage

Vertical drop in passage with depth

Passage ceiling height

Large breakdown

Small breakdown

MAP SYMBOLS CONTINUED

Sketched passage	- - - - - - - - - - - -	Clay	
Sloping passage		Sand	
Stream and pool		Bedrock pillar in passage	
Flowstone		Survey station	△
Rimstone dam		Cross section	

BEAR-WALKING   CRAWLING   CROUCHING   DUCK-WALKING

   Getting lost is a rare occurrence in a cave, but should you be separated from your group, or if the entire crew is unsure about its location, respond in much the same way as if you were lost anywhere else. Don't panic. Sit down, have a bite to eat and a sip of water, and assess the situation. Light a candle and shut off your primary light source to save its power. You'll probably soon remember which way you came and how to get out. If not, sit still, listen, and wait. When you are overdue in reaching the surface, searchers will be on their way to find you.

   As you work your way into a cave, you may come to a cliff, ledge, hole, or stream that is beyond your abilities to negotiate safely. You may find rotten ropes or rickety ladders you don't trust. A sign of a wise adventurer is a willingness to turn back rather than pressing on when doing so could end in getting hurt. Leave the difficult passages and shafts to speleologists specially trained in the uses of ropes and caving hardware. There is plenty for you to see and do in less hazardous sections of a cave. For instance, you can try subterranean photography, a challenging skill to master. You might examine the geology of a cave, finding evidence of the creative forces at work. You may be able to study tiny inhabitants of the darkness whose skins are white because of generations spent away from the sun. You might even draw maps of tunnels and rooms never before recorded on paper, for there are still thousands of caves whose hidden interiors have yet to be brightened by the piercing beams of headlamps.

The more caves you explore, the more time you'll want to spend underground. One day you'll come to the surface tired and covered with mud and gook, but there will be a smile on your face and you'll know you've become a caver. You will have realized that a caving's happiest moments come when you can explore a cave and then leave it as you found it. A caver's creed is this:

TAKE NOTHING BUT PICTURES;
LEAVE NOTHING BUT FOOTPRINTS;
KILL NOTHING BUT TIME.

Make that your creed, too.

"After six days alone, I abandoned the tent and oilstove and started down. Midway to the next camping place I saw my companions coming up to search. The sight of humans in that vast solitude was so strange that I watched them for some time before shouting."

Israel C. Russell, 1890

"I'll bring help to these famishing people or lay down my life."

Charles T. Stanton, 1846

Chapter 26

Wilderness Search and Rescue

Jon Wartes
Veteran Explorer Search and Rescue
Leader; Search and Rescue Author;
Recipient of the Hal Foss Award
Bestowed by National Association for
Search and Rescue

At 6 P.M. on a cold January evening, an Explorer search and rescue post was notified that two hikers, ages 9 and 10, were lost on a mountain. The sky was dark, and a light mist was beginning to turn to snow. The Explorers knew that the hikers probably were wet, and as the temperature fell below freezing the risk of hypothermia would increase.

By 8 P.M., 17 well-trained and well-equipped searchers were in the field. Their initial task was to follow the trail and look for places where the hikers might have made a wrong turn. Around 9:30 P.M., a team member found a footprint on the ground alongside the trail, and for the next hour searchers slowly followed scuff marks and footprints through the trees. At 10:30 P.M. they heard a response to their shouts, and a few minutes later they came upon the huddled and shivering hikers. Within moments they had the hikers in dry clothing and were warming soup for them to drink. By midnight everyone was safely down from the mountain.

The happy ending to this potential tragedy is one of many demonstrating that with proper preparation, leadership, and dedication, Explorers and older Scouts can make genuine contributions to the efforts of search and rescue teams.

A search and rescue (SAR) unit is a highly disciplined group of people who clearly understand the serious nature of their missions. They also are aware of the legal limits to their activities, and will attempt only those rescues that are within the scope of their abilities.

This chapter is an introduction to some of the main concepts and techniques of search and rescue teams. It is not intended to teach you all you need to know to take part in searches, but it may spark your interest enough to find an SAR organization that can train you and then draw on your strengths in emergency situations.

THE SAR TEAM

Teamwork is the glue that holds together every SAR effort. The searcher finding and following footprints in the snow is no more important than the food service officer at the base of the mountain making sure there will be sandwiches and hot soup for the rescued hikers as well as all the members of the SAR team. A search and rescue mission is no place for glory seekers unless, of course, they see the glory of serving in quiet but absolutely essential ways.

The organizational plan of any SAR unit will depend upon the needs of official state and local agencies, the kinds of operations the unit will be expected to handle, and the existence of other SAR organizations with whom it can coordinate its efforts. The organizational chart of a typical SAR group looks like this:

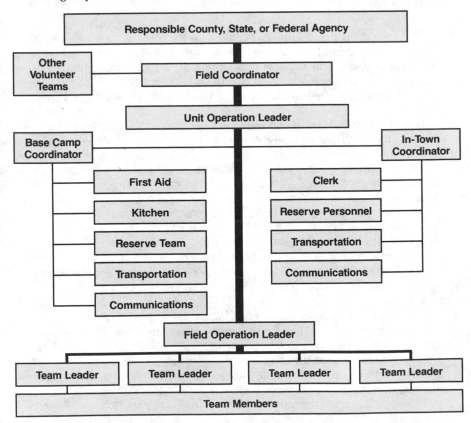

In many cases, one person can handle more than one job.

It may surprise you to discover that a search and rescue operation requires the participation of so many people. However, the vast expanses of wilderness territory SAR teams must cover and the extreme effort required to carry injured people to a road requires many people. Teams in the field must be backed by an extensive support staff to do everything from supplying warm blankets and dry clothing to organizing transportation home after the rescue is done.

Personal Equipment

The personal gear that SAR members should carry in the field will vary with the environment in which they expect to operate and the season of the year. In most situations, though, they can't go wrong with a 24- or 48-hour pack.

The 24-hour packs contain everything searchers will need to support themselves for 1 day in the backcountry — food, rain gear, extra clothing, water, first aid supplies, flashlights, etc. A 48-hour pack includes the contents of the 24-hour pack, plus a sleeping bag, shelter, stove, and extra food. In either case, searchers should carry more than they expect to need; they may be out longer than intended, or they may need to share their food and equipment with the subjects of their search.

Call-out

To be effective, a search and rescue unit must be able to mobilize speedily, but only when asked to help by an agency legally authorized to request aid. An unauthorized mission by an SAR unit is poor manners at best, and at worst can create sticky legal problems. It's essential that SAR units and official agencies meet and clarify their exact relationship long before an emergency arises.

To facilitate a call-out, unit members should have and understand how to use charts similar to the one shown here.

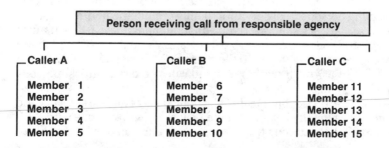

Person receiving call from responsible agency		
Caller A	Caller B	Caller C
Member 1	Member 6	Member 11
Member 2	Member 7	Member 12
Member 3	Member 8	Member 13
Member 4	Member 9	Member 14
Member 5	Member 10	Member 15

The first person to receive word of a call-out telephones callers A, B, and C. They, in turn, each call the five members on their lists. In this way, 3 team leaders and 15 team members will be quickly notified, yet the initial caller need only contact the three team leaders.

DEVELOPING A SEARCH PLAN

It is the responsibility of the agency in charge to develop a search plan. Usually that is done in two stages, beginning with the gathering of information about the subjects of the search, and details that pertain to the current situation. Witnesses will be interviewed and the terrain and weather evaluated. If others have previously been lost in the same area, their cases may be reviewed.

The second stage of plan development involves decision making as each member of the agency staff assesses all the available information and theorizes where the lost persons might be found. A knowledge of statistics about the probable behavior of lost persons is essential.

Most frequently a missing person will follow the way of least resistance by traveling downhill on a road or trail. The entire staff evaluates all the possibilities, including estimates of the probability of finding the missing persons in each area, the size of each area, hazards, the number of searchers available, and other contingencies. The areas of greatest need will be searched first.

SEARCH TACTICS

Confinement

Once a search area has been determined, an SAR team doesn't want the subjects of their search wandering elsewhere. *Confinement* is an attempt to prevent that from happening. Methods include trail and roadblocks, and assigning persons to observation points around the perimeter of the search area. Barriers such as rivers or mountains may act as natural barricades. In wooded areas, two-person teams can unroll a string around the search area and attach tags to the string at 200-foot intervals. Each tag should have an arrow drawn on it to indicate the direction lost persons can go to reach help.

To be effective, this technique must be done quickly and surely, since the unconfined area in which people could be lost will grow in size with each passing moment. Presuming they stay together and that they're capable of

Tagging the string line.

roaming up to 3 miles an hour on an unobstructed road or trail, missing persons theoretically could be anywhere within 28 square miles 1 hour after becoming lost, 113 square miles after 2 hours, and 452 square miles after 3 hours. The area of highest probability for finding a missing person will be much smaller, but prompt confinement of all areas of reasonable probability is crucial.

Segmentation

Once an area has been confined, small teams can use string and arrow tags to further mark off segments of the search area. The additional string lines will give searchers definite boundaries within which to conduct their activities, and the subjects of the search are more likely to find a string line and follow it to safety.

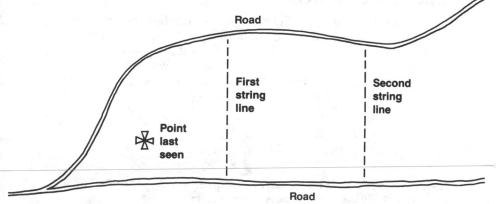

Clue Finding

It is impossible for lost persons to travel without leaving signs of their passing. While it takes considerable skill to recognize many of these clues, some signs are obvious even to untrained observers, provided they are looking for them. Tracks on a steep, sandy bank or in patches of snow are not hard to see, and a candy wrapper in the brush had to be left by someone. The emphasis should be to look for clues, not just for the lost person. By recognizing only a few clues, a team can substantially reduce the potential area of search.

Searchers engaged in tracking can increase the likelihood of success by using a *tracking stick*. A tracking stick is a rod about 4 feet long and ½ inch in diameter. When trackers find two footprints in a row, they can measure the distance from the heel of one print to the heel of the next and mark that distance on the stick with a rubber band. Then, by measuring the same distance ahead and slightly to the side of the forward print, they'll know approximately where the next track should be. At night, a lantern held near the ground will produce shadows that make tracks more visible.

Rubber band

Hasty Search

In the early stages of a search, there often are several areas that are probable locations of the lost persons. A child who has wandered away from a campground, for instance, may have gone up a trail, across a meadow, or down to a beach. Teams of three or four persons can be assigned to go to each of these areas and conduct quick, informal searches.

Open-sweep Search

Rapid but systematic searches of large areas can be very productive. As with the hasty search, the emphasis is not upon thoroughness, but rather upon covering a large area quickly. The usual technique is to employ three-person teams spaced far from one another. Two three-person teams engaged in an open-sweep search can be shown in a diagram like this:

Flanker Compass bearer   Flankers   Compass bearer Flanker

Compass bearer — Provides parallel directional control
Flankers — Guide upon the compass bearer and do most of the searching

Since visual contact among the members of each team is essential, the distance maintained between the compass bearer and the flankers will depend upon the density of the brush. However, teams need not remain in sight of other teams, and in fact they should stay fairly far apart. Even in forests with heavy undergrowth, teams with compass bearers 300 feet apart have a 50 percent probability of finding the subjects of their search.

If, after covering the search area, the teams have been unsuccessful, search coordinators may determine that a second sweep is advisable, and perhaps even a third. Search authorities reason that it is more efficient (in terms of the number of people and the time required) to conduct non-thorough sweep searches and to repeat them as needed, rather than to conduct a single thorough search of an area.

Close-sweep Search

In a close-sweep search, the emphasis is upon thoroughly inspecting an area for clues that may have been left by the missing person, even though it can be a very time-consuming effort that may not most efficiently use available personnel.

Rather than using small teams spaced far apart, the five to nine members of a close-sweep search team stand abreast at intervals of no more than 10 to 25 feet. The team moves forward along a control line (a fence, a string, or a ribbon marking the boundary of the search area), and the searcher farthest from the control line lays down a string to mark the inner edge of the first sweep. When the searchers reach the far end of their initial pass through an area, they wheel around and come back along the new string line. Once again the innermost searcher lays string to control the direction of the next sweep.

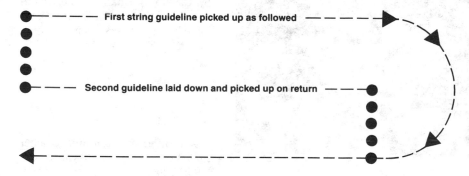

SEARCH METHODS

Some search methods require expertise or equipment beyond that usually possessed by Scouts and Explorers. Among them are the following:

Trailing Dogs

No doubt you've seen movies of dogs tracking lost people. Certain breeds of dogs, notably bloodhounds, have such keen senses of smell that once they've become familiar with a person's odor (usually by being allowed to smell an article of the subject's clothing), they can follow the scent trail right to the person. Success is dependent on many things, including training of the dogs, temperature of the air, humidity, and wind.

Air-scenting Dogs

Unlike trailing dogs, air-scenting dogs are not held on leashes. They are not as discriminating, and will follow to its source any human scent they find in the search area. That means they may locate the subject of the search, though they also are likely to follow the scent of an SAR team member or a passer-by. Usually German shepherds, air-scenting dogs work best when there have been few persons in the territory they are to search.

Tracking

A trained and talented tracker may be able to follow the tracks left by a lost person. It is very important to prevent other people from entering the search area if a tracker is to be successful.

Vehicle Search

Using four-wheel drive vehicles, searchers can travel backroads to gather information about the terrain and to set up roadblocks to prevent lost travelers from wandering away from the area of the search.

Aircraft Search

Most air searches from fixed-wing aircraft are conducted by the Civil Air Patrol. Helicopters usually are supplied by the military, or by municipalities or corporations. Searches from the air can be very effective, but they are highly dependent upon weather and the density of ground cover.

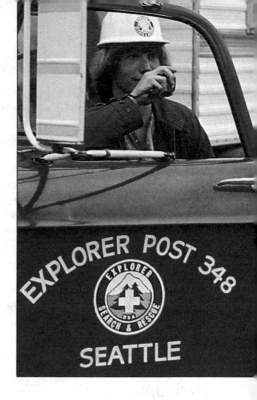

EVACUATION

Searching is only half the duty of an SAR unit. Once the subject of a search has been found, the team must be prepared to do whatever is necessary to effect a rescue. If there have been injuries, the search team should immediately administer first aid and stabilize the victim. The searchers also will report by radio to the unit coordinator, who will determine the best way to bring the victim out of the backcountry. Among the evacuation methods that may be employed are these.

Foot Power

Evacuees who can walk without endangering or further injuring themselves should be encouraged to do so. However, even though an individual seems fine, constant monitoring by team members trained to recognize the signs of exhaustion and shock is necessary.

Hand Carry

If the subjects are not seriously injured, they may be carried short distances piggyback or with some kind of two-person carry.

Pack Animal

Gentle horses, mules, and burros can be used to transport victims who have not sustained serious injuries. Team members may need to ride double or walk alongside the animals to steady the evacuees.

Vehicle

When there are convenient roads, vehicles generally will provide the easiest and most efficient means of evacuating subjects of searches. In some areas, specially equipped backcountry ambulances can bring out seriously injured parties.

Helicopter

If a helicopter is available and there is a suitable landing site for it, an air evacuation can pluck a seriously injured person out of the backcountry and fly directly to a medical facility.

Litter Carry

Carrying an accident victim is demanding and difficult, and it requires a large, well-drilled team. If the terrain is rough or if the accident site is far from a road, a litter carry ordinarily is the evacuation method of last resort. Because of the complexity of a litter evacuation, many SAR units have special litter teams to handle the procedure. A litter team organizational chart looks like this:

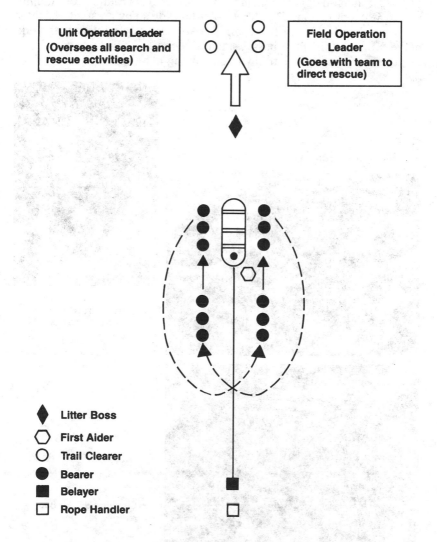

The field operation leader is responsible for the mission and the safety of all personnel. The litter boss supervises the carrying of the litter. In matters pertaining to the well-being of the evacuee, the first aider has the last word. Trail clearers lead the way and prepare the route for the litter bearers. Belayers and rope handlers are required if there may be a need for a technical evacuation. Any additional personnel can help carry rescue equipment and take their turns bearing the litter. Paired by height and positioned on opposite sides of the litter, bearers rotate every minute or two at the direction of the litter boss. They do so by grasping the litter hand over hand while the front pair of bearers lets go and steps to the side of the trail to let the litter pass. Using this technique, the litter constantly moves forward along the trail without having to be set down.

▼Securing the victim in a litter.

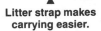

▲
**Litter strap makes
carrying easier.**

◄Carrying a litter over
rugged terrain.

CHAPTER 26

Litter Carrying Techniques

The best litters for backcountry evacuations are made of fiberglass or aluminum. Some are roomy enough to accommodate the victim of a spinal injury strapped to a backboard. Padded with sleeping bags and equipped with straps to hold its passenger in place, a good litter can provide a relatively comfortable ride.

END CROSS SECTION OF A LITTER

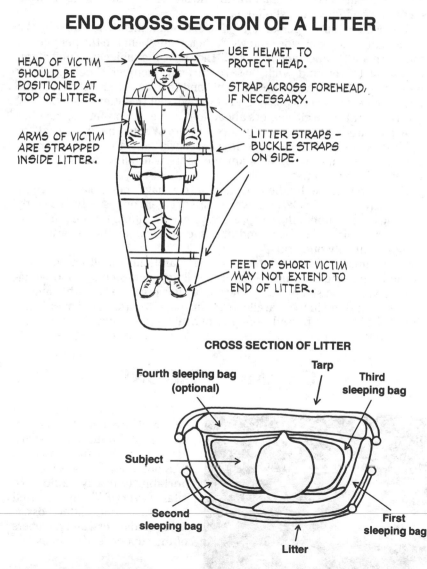

HEAD OF VICTIM
SHOULD BE
POSITIONED AT
TOP OF LITTER.

USE HELMET TO
PROTECT HEAD.

STRAP ACROSS FOREHEAD,
IF NECESSARY.

ARMS OF VICTIM
ARE STRAPPED
INSIDE LITTER.

LITTER STRAPS –
BUCKLE STRAPS
ON SIDE.

FEET OF SHORT VICTIM
MAY NOT EXTEND TO
END OF LITTER.

CROSS SECTION OF LITTER

Fourth sleeping bag
(optional)

Tarp

Third
sleeping bag

Subject

Second
sleeping bag

First
sleeping bag

Litter

To pack an injury victim in a litter, spread half of a tarp across the bottom of the litter and pad the litter with a couple of foam pads or sleeping bags, then put the victim inside a third sleeping bag and nestle him or her into the litter. In weather that may cause hypothermia, cover the evacuee with a fourth sleeping bag. Wrap the other half of the tarp over the top of the load and secure the litter straps. The resulting cocoon will be extremely comfortable, warm, and protective, exactly the environment an accident victim should have.

To place an injured person on a litter, six team members kneel by the subject, three on each side, and work their hands beneath the person. On the command, "One, two, three, lift!" they raise the subject as a unit about a foot off the ground while a seventh team member slides the litter underneath. "One, two, three, down!" and they ease the victim into the litter, the person's head positioned at the head of the litter.

Having sent the trail clearers ahead to remove any obstacles, the litter boss in charge of the carry will have bearers of equal height pair off on opposite sides of the litter. The first aider will take a position near the victim's head, and all other team members will follow behind, out of earshot of the victim.

The bearers kneel by the litter and, if they have them, place carrying straps across their backs and over their shoulders opposite the litter. By holding onto a knot in the strap, a bearer can distribute the weight of the load across his or her back and opposite arm, rather than bearing the weight with only one arm.

On command from the litter boss the bearers lift the litter, and on a second command they move forward, walking out of step to avoid swinging the victim. In steep areas where footing is precarious, both teams of bearers can stand in two parallel rows and pass the litter hand over hand. When the litter has passed each pair of bearers, they should peel off and move to the front of the lines.

COMMUNICATIONS

With so many people in the field and in support positions, reliable communications are essential to the success of an SAR operation. Because of this, portable two-way radios are vital to every SAR unit. Carried by team leaders, litter bosses, field coordinators, and members of the support staff, radios will

◀ Command Post

give the operations director control over the entire search and evacuation, allowing the most effective use of people and equipment.

For the clearest radio operation, follow these guidelines:

1. Keep the radio protected inside a pack. A remote microphone passed over the shoulder provides easy access for communications.
2. Keep the antenna vertical during operation.
3. Think of your message *before* you talk.
4. Depress the transmit button for 1 full second prior to talking.
5. Speak slowly and use common, one-syllable words.
6. Break long messages into segments.
7. During training, agree upon a code word to be used to report the finding of a deceased subject, so as not to alert other listeners to situations involving fatalities until proper authorities have been notified.

EVALUATION AND TRAINING

At the conclusion of every SAR mission, unit members should review and evaluate everything that happened. This is not a fault-finding session, but rather an objective attempt to pinpoint weaknesses in a team's performance and discover ways to rectify them. Good SAR units make few errors, and with honest evaluations and effective training, they'll seldom repeat a mistake.

SAR training must include instruction and practice in search methods, evacuation, wilderness navigation, first aid, and maintaining personal and team equipment. Field exercises and simulated searches and rescues should be conducted on various terrain in all sorts of weather conditions. Finally, thorough training *must* precede a team member's participation in any actual SAR mission; on-the-job training simply will not do.

"Fishing brings meekness and inspiration from the scenery of nature, charity toward tackle makers, patience toward fish, a mockery of profits and egos, a quieting of hate, a rejoicing that you do not have to decide a darned thing until next week.

"And it is discipline in the equality of man—for all men are equal before fish."

Herbert Hoover, 1963

Chapter

27

Fishing

Charles Most
Chief, Branch of Resource
Information, Bureau of Land
Management

P ick a lure from your box, tie it to the end of your line, and make your way to the edge of a still pond. All is quiet except for the buzz of dragonflies hovering above the lily pads. Confidently cast toward a submerged log. The lure arcs through the air, and just as it touches the water the surface explodes as the biggest bass you've ever seen hits it. You set the hook and your heart races, for you know the fight to bring your catch ashore will take all the fishing skill you can muster.

Exciting? You bet! Few activities can match fishing for instant fun and a lifetime of pleasure. The excitement can start right now as you learn something about the anatomy of fish and how their feeding habits influence their behavior. Think of these bits of information as clues that will lead you to the places where the big ones hide.

FINDING FISH

Fish are cold-blooded animals, which means their body temperatures match that of their surroundings. They'll try to find water that is comfortable for them, and if the surface of a lake is too warm, they'll descend to cooler depths or lurk in the shadows of logs, weeds, and lily pads. During the winter, schools of fish swim beneath the ice, adjusting their living and eating patterns to the cold conditions.

Fish breathe by pulling water into their mouths and expelling it past gills that remove oxygen from the water as it passes. Many species will gather just below waterfalls, at the mouths of tumbling tributaries, and near any other bubbling rush of water containing extra air. These are also good places for fish to snap up insects and minnows that float by on the current.

Many fish have excellent vision, and they are especially attracted to bright, flashing colors. Sometimes they can even see a fisherman on the shore, so you may need to stay low. Fish don't have ears like those of mammals, but a series of nerves running the lengths of their bodies will pick up faint vibrations in the water, allowing them to home in on a swimming frog, a struggling minnow, or a fishing lure wiggling toward shore.

If you know what fish eat, you'll have another valuable clue that will help you find them. Predator fish such as bass and northern pike will hover near schools of the small fish that make up their diets. Trout often will position themselves in the current of a stream and feed on insects that drift toward them. Bluegills and crappies mill about in ponds and lakes, skimming insects from the surface, while catfish, bullheads, and other bottom-feeders nose along muddy riverbeds smelling out their meals. Many kinds of fish feed at dawn and at dusk, while others are active in the middle of the day. Some change their feeding schedules depending on weather conditions and the season.

Put together all the information you have about the habits of fish, and you'll discover that in streams they tend to rest in still pools and eddies, darting out into the faster current to feed. Fish congregate below waterfalls and dams, and they'll find protection in the darkness below cutaway river banks and under fallen trees. Fish like to gather around downed trees in ponds and lakes, too, and they'll feed near lake shores in shallow, weedy water rich with insects, frogs, and fingerlings. Drop-offs and holes where the water suddenly becomes deeper are gathering places for predator fish feeding on schools of minnows, and the gravel bars that serve as hatching grounds for many insects and fish will attract schools of deep swimmers eager for a meal.

FISHING METHODS

When you have an idea where you can find fish and when they're likely to be hungry, you're ready to do some serious angling. Of course, you'll want to check local and state fishing regulations first and get any licenses and permits you're required to have.

One of the easiest ways to catch fish is to get a cane pole or a straight, light tree branch, tie one end of a fishing line to it, and to the other end of the line attach a bobber, a sinker, and a hook baited with a worm, grasshopper, grub, or other natural food of the fish you're after. You can probably gather all the bait you need in the grass and brush along the shore. For bottom feeding fish with acute senses of smell, load the hook with a stink bait such as rancid liver, chicken entrails, or cheese balls, and use a line long enough to reach the depths in which they live. Then just toss your line into the water, prop your pole in the crook of a tree, tilt your hat over your eyes, and sit back to enjoy the day and wait for that bobber to jiggle.

Pole fishing consists of brief moments of excitement interrupted by long periods of patient waiting. Fishermen eager to take a more active role in the outcome of their efforts find that by using rods and reels they can cast and retrieve all kinds of lures that, when pulled through the water, simulate the shape and motion of live baits. For these anglers, fishing becomes a game of wits as they try to guess which lure to use, where to cast it to attract a fish, and how to retrieve it to entice a big one to strike.

CASTING SYSTEMS

There are four basic casting systems, each with its own appeal: spin casting, open faced spinning, bait casting, and fly casting. You'll want to become proficient in several of the systems, since some are more appropriate for certain kinds of fish than others.

Spin-casting

The easiest system to master is the spin-casting rig. The equipment you'll need includes a fiberglass rod and a reel with a line spool enclosed in a plastic, cone-shaped housing. The line comes out of a hole in the point of the cone, and its release is controlled by a push button mounted on the back of the reel. The spool is equipped with an adjustable brake, or drag, to slow a running fish and prevent the line from snapping. Since the spool is enclosed, the system is difficult to tangle. This is a great outfit for beginning fishermen.

To cast a lure with spin-casting gear, thread the line from the reel through the line guides of the rod and tie on a lure. (For practice on dry land, you can use a hookless rubber casting weight instead of a lure, and an old tire, a bucket, or a circle drawn on the ground as a target.) Hold the rod in front of you

with the reel up, the tip of the rod pointed toward the target, and the push button depressed beneath the thumb of your rod hand. While holding the button in, swing the rod back and up until it is nearly vertical, then smoothly snap it forward. When it is about halfway back to its starting position, lift your thumb from the button to release the line and send the lure flying. If it goes too high, your release was early; if it goes low, the release was late. It will take you a few casts to get a feel for the instant to release the line, and then you can work on using just the right amount of power to arch the lure into the center of your target.

Spinning

An open-faced spinning reel has no cone covering the line spool. The reel hangs below the rod, and the wire bail that holds the line on the spool can be spun by turning a crank on the side of the reel to wind the line back onto the spool after each cast. The line guides on a spinning rod are large in order to control the line as it spirals off the spool. Rods vary in length from less than 5 feet for ultra-light models, to 15 feet for those used for fishing ocean surf.

Known as spinning, casting with open-faced gear takes a little more practice than spin casting. Grasp the rod by putting two fingers in front

and two behind the leg of the reel. Catch the line in front of the spool with your index finger, and hold it while you use your free hand to open the bail. With the bail in the open position, your finger controls the line in a manner similar to the push button of a spin-casting reel. Make a casting motion as you would with spin-casting gear, and straighten your index finger at the instant you want to release the line. As the lure approaches its target, drop your finger near the spool so that the moving line brushes it and slows, causing the lure to drop gently. This is called feathering, and it will make your casts very accurate.

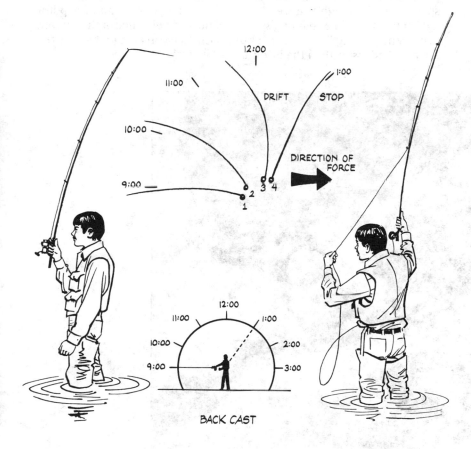

BACK CAST

Bait Casting

In spin casting and in spinning, the line peels over the rim of the spool but the spool itself does not turn. In a third casting system, however, the spool rotates during the cast, unwinding the line. Called bait casting, it's often used to fish with live baits such as minnows and small frogs, as well as with artificial lures.

To use bait-casting gear, wind the lure to within a few inches of the rod tip. Most bait-casting reels have a button that disengages the crank and allows the spool to turn freely, or freespool. Grasp the rod and place your thumb against the back of the spool. Depress the freespool button with your free hand, and you're ready to cast.

The casting motion is basically the same as with spin-casting and spinning rigs, though you free the line by lifting your thumb. Keep it in light contact with the spinning spool to control the distance of the cast and to prevent the tangling overrun, or backlash, that can occur when the reel releases line faster than the lure can pull it away.

Fly Casting

The fourth casting system is the oldest and, in many ways, the most complex. While other systems rely on the weight of the lure to pull line from the reel, fly casters use nearly weightless lures made of bits of feather, fur, hair, and thread, and the line itself is the weight that carries a lure through the air.

CHAPTER 27

Becoming a proficient fly caster takes plenty of coordination. First, slowly whip the rod back and forth over your head as you feed out line from the reel. When you've got enough line looping through the air, swing the tip of the rod toward your target, and let the line curl out over the water, placing the fly just where you want it. In still water, you can drop the fly directly over the fish. In moving water, cast upstream and let the lure drift near feeding trout and bass as they lie in wait.

STANCE

45°

DIRECTION OF CAST

1

2

3

4

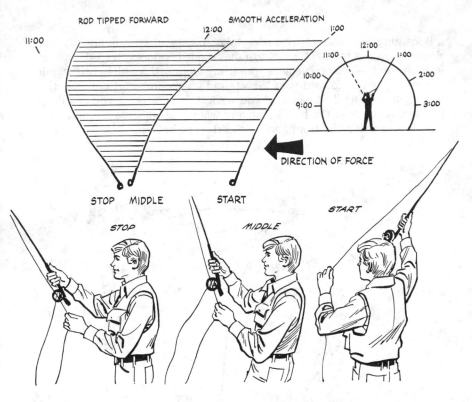

The forward cast

FISHING LURES

Knowing how to cast will help make you a good fisherman. Knowing what lures to use can make you a great fisherman, since you'll be able to select baits that fish can't resist. Here's a brief rundown of the major types of lures and the best ways to use them.

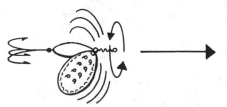

Spinners

Spinners are shiny metal lures that do just what their name implies — they spin through the water as you reel them in. There are many kinds of spinners, some shaped and colored to attract certain species of fish, some designed for special conditions such as underwater weeds and logs. Bass go for spinners, and so do crappie and other panfish. As you retrieve a spinner, reel it in smoothly and steadily to make the blades twirl, or reel and stop, reel and stop, allowing the lure to sink a little with each pause. Always be ready for a strike; there should be plenty.

Spoons

You might think of a spoon as a spinner that doesn't spin. Often painted red with diagonal white stripes, spoons flutter through the water, tempting big fighting fish like northern pike. Spoons with hooks shielded to prevent them from becoming tangled in weeds will reach fish that hide beneath lily pads. Add a bit of pork rind to the hook to increase its effectiveness.

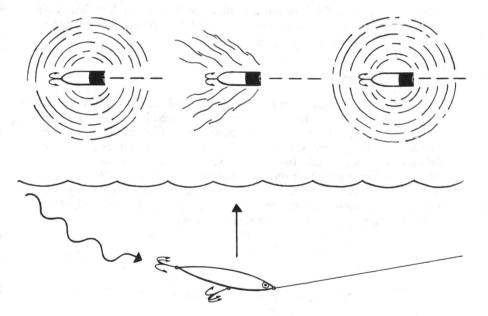

Plugs

Designed from wood and plastic to look like little fish, crawdads, or frogs, plugs give you plenty of opportunities to fool the fish. Some plugs always float. Others float when they are still, but dive as they are retrieved. Some wobble and gurgle, some make a popping sound, and some travel through the water slowly and quietly. Your goal is to manipulate a plug so that it attracts the attention of a hungry fish.

Floater/Diver Lures

Other than plugs, lures that both float and dive are usually shaped like small fish or frogs. If you retrieve them slowly, they'll stay on the surface. Retrieve them quickly and they'll swim a few feet under the water.

Injured Minnows

Another effective lure is shaped like a small fish with shiny propellers on one or both ends. Retrieve it in fits and starts, causing the lure to struggle along like an injured minnow trying to escape a hungry predator.

Crank Baits

Resembling a small fish or a crawdad, a crank bait will dive deeply as you reel it in. It may vibrate or rattle to attract fish up to 20 feet below the surface of the water.

Soft Plastic Lures

While some soft plastic lures are molded to mimic insects, grubs, and small aquatic animals, the most popular is shaped like an earthworm. Hooks embedded in the worm and attached to a leader provide the bite of the bait, and a small lead sinker may give extra weight to increase casting distance. A good way to fish with a plastic worm is to cast it near a submerged log or stump, or into the shallows close to shore. Reel in slack line and then, without reeling, raise the tip of the rod. The motion will drag the worm along the lake or river bottom. Lower the rod, reeling just enough to take up the slack, then raise it again.

Jigs

A jig has a heavy, blunt body embellished with skirts made of hair, feathers, rubber, or plastic. It is designed to sink quickly to the bottom of a stream or lake, and to bounce along as you raise and lower, or jig, your rod. Jig lures come in many sizes and styles, and are effective for catching everything from small panfish to big trout, bass, walleyes, and pike.

TROUT FLIES

Types of dry flies

Midges

**Up wing
hackle**

Fan wing

Bi-visible

Folded wing

**Up wing
no-hackle**

Types of wet flies

Midge nymphs

Quill

Steelhead fly

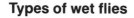

Nymph

Muddler

Bee

Wooly worm

Atlantic salmon fly

Bass bugs

Fly rod popper

**Deerhair
bass fly**

Deerhair frog

RIGGING YOUR TACKLE

Securing a lure or leader to your line is easy if you use the improved clinch knot. You can tie a lure directly to the line, or you can use the clinch knot to tie on a swivel into which you can snap lures. Use the blood knot to join two strands of leader. When you're going after fish that have sharp teeth, it's wise to use a wire leader rather than a swivel; a fish will be less likely to bite through it. Snell a hook that will be baited with a worm for trolling or drifting.

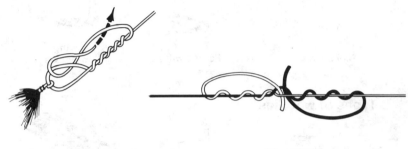

Improved clinch knot   **Blood knot**

PLAYING A FISH

Imagine you've picked a good lure, cast it in the right place, and suddenly discovered you've got a mad fish fighting on the end of your line. What now?

Your first instinct may be to haul in your catch as fast as you can, but that could be the last you'll ever see of that fish. A strong fish can snap a light line with a twist of its body. It can dive beneath sunken logs, or hopelessly tangle the line in a bed of weeds. To prevent that and to enjoy every second of the fight, you'll need to play the fish, letting it swim and fight until it tires enough to be brought ashore or into your boat. As the fish battles, keep enough tension on the line to prevent the fish from spitting out your lure, but don't hold the line so tightly that it's in danger of breaking. Keep the tip of your rod upright, and do what you can to steer the fish away from underwater obstructions. When the fish is finally played out, scoop it up with a net or grasp it behind the head and lift it from the water. Many fish have sharp spines and teeth, so handle them with care.

If you don't intend to eat your catch, release it by gently removing the hook and returning the fish to the water. If a fish you wish to release has swallowed the hook, cut the line and leave the hook in place.

CLEANING YOUR CATCH

Before you can cook any fish, you'll have to clean it.

First, scale the fish. Use a knife with a special saw-toothed scaling edge or regular knife blade. Scrape from tail to head.

Next, remove dorsal fin and belly fin. Run tip of the knife along each side of fin and lift it out—with bones attached.

Note small bones removed with fins. If the fins are cut off with knife instead of lifted out, these bones remain in the fish.

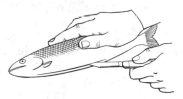

Gut the fish by making a slit from throat to vent. Strip the entrails from cavity with fingers, then wash it out thoroughly.

You can filet fish by slicing along each side close to backbone from tail to head. This results in two boneless pieces of fish.

FISHING TIPS

Every angler has a bag of tricks that make fishing easier and more fun. Here are a few.

- Spinner blades and spoons can be polished to a high luster with damp campfire ashes.

- In camp, store a rod by leaning it against a tent or standing it up in a bush to keep it out of the way of careless feet.

- If a cast accidentally goes into brush or weeds, an extremely slow retrieve may bring it back without snagging. Should your line go over a tree branch beyond your reach, slowly reel in the line until the lure is hanging several inches below the branch, then give the line a sharp pull to swing the lure up and over the branch. Don't pull too hard, though; you don't want the lure to fly back and smack you.

- Sunglasses with polarizing lenses will enable you to see beneath the surface of the water even when the sun is bright.

- Since fish in a swift current usually face upstream, they won't see you if you approach from downstream. Cast over the pools in which they swim and let your lures float toward them.

- Fish slow down as the temperature of the water becomes colder. Tempt them with smaller lures than you would normally use, and retrieve them more slowly.

FISH CONSERVATION

Fishing is a great sport, and once you've been bitten by the bug you'll want to spend all the time you can with a rod in your hand. However, responsible anglers know that in addition to catching fish, they must do all they can to protect the lakes and streams where fish live. Help keep the waters and shorelines clean, and find out from fish and wildlife departments how you can volunteer to do waterway improvement projects. Before fishing on private property, get permission from the owner, and wherever you fish, never catch more than your license allows.

Following wise conservation practices now means that there will be plenty of fish and plenty of great fishing adventures for years to come.

"Biking is freedom—freedom from the city, from your cares, from the humdrum. It invigorates and brings muscles to your legs. It brings you in touch with what's happening around you and in tune with nature. Experience the romantic changes of a day—a crisp dawn, a sunny noon, a starry night. Feel the breezes, taste the salt sprays from the ocean, touch a redwood. Enjoy the best things about being alive."

Sue Browder, 1974

Chapter 28

Bicycling

Robert Morgan
Veteran Touring Cyclist; Former
Consulting Engineer, Boy Scouts of
America

T he road is smooth and empty, the wind is at your back, and the bicycle beneath you rolls smoothly along with every turn of the pedals. Your senses are full of fresh sights, sounds, and smells, and you feel the joy of motion, of physical exertion, and of the freedom to travel anywhere you want to go. Perhaps you're just a few miles from home, riding for an hour or two in the afternoon. Maybe you're on a weekend tour, visiting parks and historical sites 40 or 50 miles apart. You could even be starting a 2- or 3-month coast-to-coast bike trek that will take you through some of the most scenic territory on the continent.

Outdoor adventures don't happen only in forested wildernesses and on untamed rivers and lakes. In fact, backroads and bike paths can be just as inviting, just as strenuous, and just as exciting as any hiking trail. You may already use a bicycle for commuting to school and to work, and you may have taken some day-long rides that gave you a hint of the pleasures awaiting a serious cyclist. If so, you're probably ready to try bicycle touring, a sport that combines bicycling with camping, navigation, mechanics, and physical fitness, and offers as much fun and satisfaction as any adventure you've ever tried. Of course, as with every outdoor activity, you'll want to prepare yourself ahead of time by learning what to expect and by equipping yourself properly and safely. For starters, that means having a good bicycle.

THE RIGHT BICYCLE

Most bicycles around these days are BMX bikes, road bikes, or mountain bikes. Each style is designed for certain kinds of riding.

BMX Bikes

BMX stands for "Bicycle Moto-Cross." With their stocky frames and knobby tires, these small, rugged bikes are built for banging around neighborhoods, empty lots, and the jumps and ruts of BMX courses. They'll get you to school and back, but their small wheels and lack of gears make them unsuitable for long rides.

Road Bikes

Bicycles designed for touring or racing on paved surfaces have lightweight frames and 10-speed derailleur gear systems. Narrow, high-pressure tires

barely touch the ground, and quick-release hubs allow you to remove wheels easily for repairs. Downturned handlebars offer a variety of hand positions to increase your pedaling efficiency and ease fatigue. Toe clips help you pull up as well as push down on the pedals.

Mountain Bikes

These all-terrain bicycles combine the toughness of BMX machines with the full size and gear systems of road bikes. Large tires and stiff frames provide extra stability on uneven ground. A wide range of gears gives you plenty of power for climbing hills and a fair amount of speed on smooth roads. Wide, straight handlebars increase steering control. Mountain bicycles are heavier and slower than road bikes, but have the versatility for rides in cities, on long-distance tours, and along rough backcountry roads.

Cost

Hundreds of bicycles are available on the market, so do some research to get the best value for your money. Ask bicycle salespersons to help you find a bicycle that fits your body as well as it fits your riding needs. You might also discuss bicycles with experienced riders, check consumer reports in bicy-

cling magazines, and call local bicycle clubs for additional information. Then, get the best bike you can for the money you have.

Tires

The wheels of most touring bicycles are equipped with narrow (1½-inches), high pressure (80–90 pounds per square inch) clincher tires.

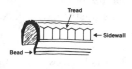

Their narrow width makes them fast and efficient, and the way they clinch onto the rims of the wheels make them easy to remove and repair when they are damaged. BMX and mountain bikes use clincher tires with wider, thicker tread. The knobby shape of some mountain bike tire treads increases traction on rough rides but decreases speed on smooth roads.

Gears

Gears can make bicycle riding a pleasure rather than a chore. Mounted on the hub of the rear wheel of a bike with gears are toothed disks in a cluster known as a *free wheel.* Two large gears, which make up the *chain wheel,* are attached to the pedal crank. Controlled by levers on the frame, a rear shifter called a *derailleur* moves the bicycle chain up and down the gears of the free wheel, while a front derailleur moves the chain back and forth on the gears of the chain wheel. Use the derailleurs to shift the chain into any of 10 to 18 different gear combinations, depending on the configuration of the free wheel and chain wheel. The lower gears make pedaling easy, but the bike won't move forward very far with each revolution of the pedals. In the higher gears, each turn of the pedals propels the bicycle a long distance, but it also requires more effort.

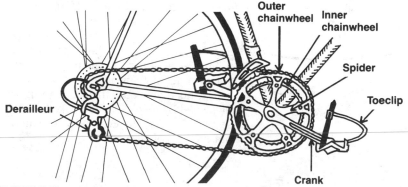

When you're on a ride, you'll be able to shift gears until you find one that allows you to pedal at a rate that will get you where you're going without exhausting your energies. This steady pedaling rate is known as a *cadence*, and you'll find that your body works most efficiently when your legs push the pedals around at about the same cadence all the time — usually 60 to 80 revolutions a minute. When pedaling becomes sluggish because of a hill or headwind, maintain the cadence by shifting to a lower gear. Likewise, if pedaling becomes too easy and the cadence too fast, shift to a higher gear to slow the pace of pedaling and increase the speed of the bike.

Handlebars

The turned-down handlebars on road bikes allow you to lean over the frame in the most efficient position for pedaling. Straight handlebars on mountain and BMX bicycles give maximum control for steering through tough territory.

Saddle

For long rides you'll need a seat on which you can sit for hours at a time, and that allows plenty of clearance for your legs. Wide, padded seats can chaff your thighs, and the hard, narrow saddles used by racers may be

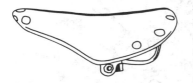

uncomfortable for day-long riding. A touring saddle is a compromise between the two—not too wide or narrow, and not too hard or soft. Women may find that a slightly wider saddle fits them better than the touring saddles used by men. Mountain bike and BMX saddles are usually cushioned to smooth out the jolts of off-road riding.

Toe Clips

Because you may need to put out your foot for balance during off-road riding, BMX and mountain bikes don't have toe clips. Road bikes, however, often feature toe clips to position your feet on the pedals and allow you to apply force to each pedal by pulling up as well as pushing down. To get into the toe clips, straddle the bike, slip one foot into its clip, and pull the strap snug. Push off, and when the bike is rolling nicely and you're well balanced, use your other foot to flip the remaining pedal upright, then slide your toe into the remaining clip. Reach down carefully and tighten the strap. Reverse the procedure to get out of the toe clips, and try to anticipate your stops far enough in advance to give yourself time to loosen the straps.

Shoes

Shoes made especially for road bikes contain steel shanks on plastic soles that prevent the edges of metal pedals from digging into a rider's feet. Expert cyclists may use cycling shoes equipped with cleats that fit tightly into the pedals and allow them to ride with tremendous power. Cleated shoes are difficult to remove quickly from toe clips, however, and you'll want to feel very confident on your bike before you try them. Sneakers or running shoes will do if you do not have cycling shoes or are riding a BMX or mountain bike.

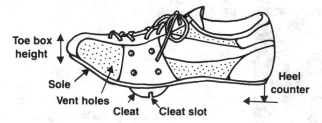

Toe box height

Sole

Vent holes

Cleat   Cleat slot

Heel counter

Fitting a Bike to Your Body

Like shoes, a bicycle must fit properly if you're to get the best use out of it. An experienced bicycle salesperson can help you select a bike that is exactly the right size for your body. In general, with your feet flat on the ground you'll want to be able to straddle the top tube of your bike frame with just a couple of inches to spare, and you'll need to be able to reach the handlebars when you're seated on the saddle and leaning forward at a 45° angle. Another way to determine your bike size is to measure the inside of your leg from your crotch to the floor and subtract 10 inches. The figure you get is the approximate frame size of the bike you should have. When riding the bike, your legs should be nearly straight at the low point of each pedal stroke.

SAFETY GEAR

Cycling is not dangerous as long as you do it wisely and equip yourself and your bicycle with the right safety gear.

Helmet

In a bicycling accident, your head is very vulnerable to injury. Protect it by always wearing a helmet made especially for bicyclers. Helmets constructed of hard plastic and lined with foam cushioning are ideal. Wear a helmet every time you ride a bicycle, even on short trips around the neighborhood.

Gloves

Fingerless cycling gloves with padded palms will cushion your hands from the constant jarring of rough roads, and if you fall off your bike, they'll keep your hands from being chewed up by pavement and gravel.

Clothing

Whenever bicycles and automobiles collide, the cyclist loses. To help prevent that from ever happening, wear brightly colored clothing that makes you highly visible. Fluorescent orange vests like those worn by highway construction workers will catch the attention of most motorists.

Bicycle Visibility

You can make your bike more visible by flying a colorful pennant above it on a flexible fiberglass rod. Add reflectors to the frame and wheel spokes, and stick strips of fluorescent adhesive tape to your pedals and panniers. On dark days, let oncoming traffic know where you are by attaching a flashing bicycle beacon to your helmet, belt, or the back of your seat, or by strapping a cyclist's flashlight to your arm or leg. After dusk bicycles become nearly invisible regardless of the lighting system. Avoid night riding.

Rear View Mirror

To help you keep an eye on the traffic approaching from behind, clip a small rear view mirror to your handlebar, or try one of the special mirrors that can be attached to your bicycling helmet.

Repair Kit

Keeping your bicycle in good repair will enhance your safety. It's a good idea to have a repair kit with you whenever you go riding so you can take care of any mechanical problems when they arise. Contents of a basic kit are:

- 6-inch adjustable wrench
- Phillips screwdriver
- Blade screwdriver
- Tire patching materials

- Tire iron for removing clincher tires from wheel rims
- Tire pump

Your bike will get quite a workout on extended tours, and you may have to make more extensive repairs. Before you embark on a long bike trek, supplement your repair kit with some or all of the following spare parts:

- Inner tube
- Tire
- Spokes and a spoke wrench
- Derailleur
- Brake cables
- Brake shoes
- Small can of lubricant

Protecting Your Bicycle

Discourage theft by securing your bike to a bike rack or other sturdy object with a cable, chain, or u-shaped bar lock. Thread the cables and chains through the wheels as well as the frame so that they cannot be removed.

RIDING SAFELY

As a cyclist on a road, you are part of the traffic, not separate from it. You must obey the same laws and use the same good sense as any motorist. Yet because you and your bike are smaller and slower than the cars and trucks whizzing by, your responsibility goes beyond traffic regulations. You must do all you can to let drivers know where you are and what you are going to do. You'll need to use your ears to listen for oncoming cars, and use your eyes to spot dangers up ahead. Ride single file in the right-hand lane, about 2 feet from the curb or shoulder. You'll be visible to drivers, and you'll avoid any broken glass and storm sewer grates at the very edge of the road. Be courteous, though, and if a car can't get around you, pull over and let it pass. When a road has a wide, paved shoulder, ride on it away from the traffic.

Travel in a predictable manner and use hand signals to indicate turns or stops. Intersections can be hazardous, so try to make eye contact with drivers approaching on side streets, and anticipate what they are going to do. Large trucks and trailers present a special danger, for although they usually give a cyclist plenty of room, the blast of air they generate as they pass may be enough to blow you over if you don't realize it is coming.

Finally, watch for chuckholes, bumps, railroad crossings, sewer grates, bridge joints, loose gravel, and other road conditions that could cause you to lose control. Slow down before you reach a problem area and, if necessary, walk your bike to safety.

RIDING RESPONSIBLY

Right turn

Just as you camp and hike in ways that do no harm to the environment, ride your bicycle only in appropriate places. Touring bicycles perform best on hard-surfaced roads where they leave little trace of their passing. BMX and mountain bikes can be used on paved roads, but they are also designed for riding on dirt roads, trails, and open country.

Choose your off-road routes with care. Bicycles ridden up and down steep hillsides or across meadows may destroy vegetation and scar the ground with ruts that will erode into gullies. Riding on walking paths can bring you into conflict with hikers, horseback riders, and other trail users.

Many cities have set aside bicycle lanes along streets or built separate byways especially for pedallers. Parks and forests often designate which of their trails can be used by bicycle riders and which are off-limits. Fragile environmental conditions such as seashores, alpine vegetation, or the presence of wildlife may warrant barring bicycles altogether.

Obey the rules concerning bicycle riding. They are almost always made in the best interests of the environment, all resource users, and everyone's safety. You may want to become involved in helping land managers of a park or forest determine whether a trail can be opened for bike riding. Your willingness to assist in the upkeep of such a trail could make a strong impression upon those who make the final decisions.

Stopping

Left turn

TOURING

Once you and your friends have mastered the art of riding in traffic and learned to handle your bikes well in various situations and weather conditions, you'll be eager to try some extended, overnight tours. You'll probably want to camp along the way, and that means carrying your equipment and provisions with you.

Panniers/Handlebar Bags

There are three guidelines for carrying gear on a bicycle — keep it light, attach it securely to the frame, and carry the weight low so you can more easily balance the bike. Most riders do that by using luggage racks bolted to the front and rear of the bicycle. The racks should be strong and rigid. Tents and sleeping bags, protected inside plastic trash can liners, can be strapped atop the rear rack, while almost everything else should go inside saddlebags, or *panniers,* mounted on the sides of the carriers. Use a handlebar bag to carry maps, compasses, a first aid kit, and other items you may need to grab quickly. Some handlebar bags have clear plastic map pockets on top so you can quickly refer to your map.

A loaded bicycle handles differently from one without any camping gear on the frame, so take short practice rides near your home until you become accustomed to cycling with the added weight of full panniers. Since you'll want to keep your load as light as possible, try to chart your route so that every day or two you'll pass a store where you can replenish your provisions. And when you stop for the night, use the same low-impact camping techniques as you would for any other adventure.

(For more on camping equipment, see "Gearing Up." For information on camping well, see "Camping Know-How" and "Reducing Our Impact." For suggestions on high-energy meals and snacks, see "Trail Menus and Cooking.")

Sag Wagon

For some trips you might arrange to have a parent or adult Scout leader follow your cycling group with a car or van. Called a *sag wagon*, the vehicle can be used to carry camping gear, food, spare bicycle parts, and even weary riders. Freed of the weight of loaded panniers, you'll be able to cover more distance each day, and you'll have the security of a vehicle close at hand should you run into difficulties on the road.

Touring Clothing

Just about any rugged, brightly colored clothes are all right for your first tours. As you become more experienced, you may want to investigate cycling shorts and jerseys. Shorts with chamois-lined crotches are sheer heaven on long rides. Jerseys are made with large, convenient pockets in which you can carry candy and fruit for quick energy on the road.

Bicycle Maintenance and Repair

Proper bicycle maintenance and a pretrip overhaul will almost guarantee you a trouble-free tour. Dirt and friction are a bicycle's worst enemies, so keep your machine clean, and once a month put a drop of lightweight oil on each of the moving parts and cables. Chains are especially susceptible to grime, and as it builds up, your pedaling will become noisy and difficult. Scrub the chain occasionally with a toothbrush dipped in kerosene, or remove the chain from the bicycle with a chain-link remover and soak it in kerosene overnight. Replace the chain, lubricate it lightly with oil or with a graphite lubricant made especially for fine machinery, and wipe off any excess with a rag.

Increase the stopping power of your brakes by wiping the brake pads and wheel rims with a clean cloth dipped in rubbing alcohol, then turn the bicycle upside down and give each wheel a good spin. Watch the rim, and if you see a bump or a bend, you may need to have a bicycle mechanic straighten the wheel on a truing jig.

The finish on a bicycle frame is similar to that of an automobile. You can clean it with soap and warm water, or with rags and window cleaner, but don't use kerosene. Wipe the frame dry, apply a good automobile wax, and buff it until it shines.

Occasionally check the cables controlling your brakes and derailleurs. If they are becoming frayed, replace them, greasing the new cables before you thread them through the cable housings. Once or twice a year, depending on how much you ride, repack the grease in the wheel hubs, crank set, and head set. You'll need some special tools and instructions to do this properly. Members of cycling clubs can teach you what you'll have to know, or you may find a bicycle mechanic who will let you watch as he overhauls your bicycle. The more you understand about what makes your bike work, the easier it will be for you to repair it on the road, and the more you'll enjoy touring.

Fixing Flat Tires

No matter how careful you are, one of your tires will go flat now and then. To repair a puncture in a clincher tire, take the wheel off the bike, release any air still in the tube, and use bicycle tire irons to pry one side of the tire off the rim. Take care not to pinch the tube with the irons, since that can cause more punctures.

Next, push the tube valve through the hole in the rim and pull the tube from the tire. If you have a spare tube in your repair kit, use it and wait until you make camp in the evening to patch the damaged tube. If not, find the puncture and fix it by following the directions on your patch kit. Inspect the tire inside and out for any nails, thorns, or bits of glass still sticking through the tread, then push the tube valve back through the hole in the rim and slip the tube back into the tire. Use your hands to force the tire bead over the rim, check to be sure the tube is not pinched beneath the bead, and then inflate the tire. Remount the wheel on the bike, check your brakes, and be on your way.

Where to Go

With good maps, you can plan a trip that takes you along scenic routes that avoid heavy traffic. Plot a course through the countryside along little-used backroads, and pinpoint interesting rest stops, resupply points, and campsites. When you want to ride in a city, obtain maps from cycle shops or chambers of commerce. They'll show you which streets are designated as bicycle routes, and where you can find paths set aside solely for cyclists. You'll know which streets to avoid during busy commuter hours, and you can design tours that weave through the city from one interesting landmark to another.

Finally, consider the direction of the wind. Near the end of a long, strenuous ride, there's nothing quite so nice as a steady tail wind to blow you home. Weary and a little hungry, but full of satisfaction and memories, you'll know you've found adventure bicycling the backroads of America.

(For more on preparing for bicycle touring, see "Where to Go" and "Planning.")

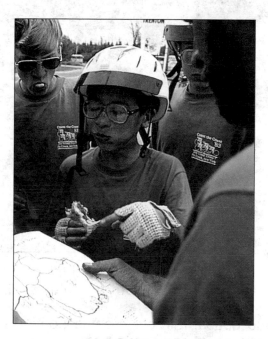

"The next time you pick up a camera think of it not as an inflexible automatic robot, but as a flexible instrument which you must understand to properly use. An electronic and optical miracle creates nothing on its own! Whatever beauty and excitement it can represent exist in your mind and spirit to begin with."

Ansel Adams, 1980

Chapter 29

Outdoor and Nature Photography

Fayanne Teague
Recognized Outdoor Photographer and
Writer; Veteran of Many Outdoor
Treks; Employee, National Office,
Boy Scouts of America

D uring the last century, photographers traveling the American frontier discovered that Indians refused to allow themselves to be photographed, fearing that the camera would somehow steal a part of their souls. In a way they were right; a good photograph does seem to possess the very essence of its subject. However, a picture only records, it does not steal. It freezes an instant in time, capturing for the future a special moment of the past.

Backcountry travelers know that the moments worth saving are many, for the outdoors is a visual feast rich with action, color, wildlife, and spectacular vistas. With a skillful eye, a photographer can use a camera to freeze the frenzy of action-packed adventures, capture the quiet of a windless forest, hold the howl of a storm, bring home the summit of a distant mountain, or possess forever the fleeting glory of a sunset. But photography is more than just a technique for recording people, places, and events; it is an art as well. A camera provides a new way of seeing the world, of studying the relationships of shadows and light, and of discovering both the spacious grandeur and the finest details of the world in which we live.

To a newcomer, taking pictures may seem an imposing mystery full of f-stops, film speeds, meter readings, and complex equipment. At its heart, though, photography is simply a matter of seeing well and knowing when to trip a shutter.

CAMERAS

You can learn the basics of photography with almost any camera, and even a simple camera without variable focus or adjustable lens settings can produce a pleasing photographic record of a trek. However, if you have a choice of cameras, the best for outdoor photography is the 35 millimeter single-lens reflex camera, or SLR. Light in weight, compact, and easy to use, it will allow you to create clear, sharp photographs, and as your skills increase you can expand its capabilities by adding accessory lenses and attachments.

FILM

Almost as important for fine photographs as the camera is your choice of film. Of course you'll want to choose film that will fit your camera, but beyond that you'll need to decide whether you'd like your finished work to be black and white prints, color prints, or color slides. Professional wilderness photographers often choose color slide film because it creates such a realistic representation of a scene. Furthermore, slides can be projected onto a screen for presentations before groups, and prints can be made inexpensively from slides; making slides from prints is a good deal more costly. On the other hand, black and white film gives photographers a great range of opportunities to explore the interplay of light and darkness, and a photographer able to employ the tricks of the darkroom can produce striking black and white prints.

Film is rated according to its speed—that is, how quickly the emulsion on the film reacts to light. The speed is noted as an ASA/ISO number printed on the film carton. The higher the number, the faster the film. For the time being, you need to know only that a very good speed for outdoor color slide photography is ASA/ISO 64. Use ASA/ISO 100 for color print film, and for black and white photography start with ASA/ISO 125.

In addition to the ASA/ISO number, film cartons also will show an expiration date after which the quality of the film may deteriorate. Always buy fresh film and, if you keep it at home awhile, store it in your refrigerator. Have exposed film developed promptly so you'll be able to enjoy the photographs right away, and the film will be in the best possible condition. When you get prints or slides back from a processor, label each one with a brief description of the scene it depicts and file it in a safe place. Special storage boxes will hold hundreds of slides, or you can slip them into plastic sleeves that fit into three-ring binders. Black and white negatives and prints of any kind can be arranged in plastic pages, too.

Experienced photographers take plenty of film with them whenever they head for the outdoors, and professionals may shoot a hundred exposures a day. While you may not take that many pictures during an entire trek, it is wise to pack along more film than you think you'll need. Photographic skills develop with practice, and the more pictures you take the better you're going to be. Also, there's always the chance that you'll come upon a magnificent vista or a rare glimpse of nature that demands to be photographed from several angles or with various camera settings. If you've got the film, you may come away with a prized once-in-a-lifetime shot.

Load film into your camera by following the instructions in the owner's manual. Since film is sensitive to light, it's best to handle it and your camera in the shade. Most cameras have an ASA/ISO dial or gauge that must be set to match the ASA/ISO number of the film.

PHOTOGRAPHIC TECHNIQUES

The basis of all good photography is the photographer himself. No matter how simple or complex the equipment he owns, the quality of his pictures depends on how skillfully he uses it.

Setting Shutter Speed and Aperture

Some modern cameras are so automated you need only point them at a subject and shoot. However, most cameras require that you decide how long the shutter will be open to allow light to fall on the film, and how large that opening, known as the *aperture*, will be. The shutter speed can be as quick as 1/1000th of a second, or as long as several hours. The faster the speed, the greater the camera's ability to freeze action (at 1/1000th of a second, the spinning blades of a helicopter in flight would appear to be almost motionless). The slower the speed, the more light the camera will capture (exposed at a shutter speed of several hours, film can register the light of stars).

**Shutter
speed
1,000 ▶**

Lens Opening (f-number)	Shutter Speed	
5.6	1/30	
8	1/60	More light
11	1/125	
16	1/250	
22	1/500	

The settings at the top of each column expose the film to more light. As the setting in one column is increased, the setting in the other column must be decreased to maintain the same exposure. For example, suppose the correct exposure setting is 1/125 second at f/11. To help stop fast action, you can change the shutter speed to 1/250 second, but you must also change the lens opening to f/8 in order to maintain the same exposure.

The size of the aperture is measured in f/stops, and it can be adjusted by turning a ring that encircles the camera lens. The smaller the f/stop number, the larger the aperture opening. At f/4, a great deal of light will strike the film, while at f/22, much less light will enter the camera. Aperture size will also affect the *depth of field* of a photograph. Depth of field is a term used to describe the distances away from the camera between which objects will appear in sharp focus. A high f/stop number such as f/22 can put in focus objects between 4 feet from the camera and infinity when the camera is focused on a subject 25 feet from the camera. A low f/stop number such as f/4 will sharply focus only those objects between 15 and 30 feet when the camera is focused on a subject 25 feet from the camera.

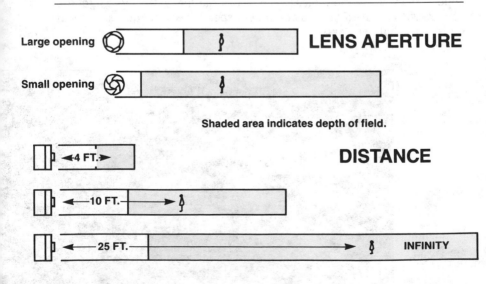

LENS APERTURE

Large opening

Small opening

Shaded area indicates depth of field.

DISTANCE

◄4 FT.►

◄─10 FT.─┤ →

◄─ 25 FT.─ →   INFINITY

FOCAL LENGTH

Medium

Short

Courtesy of Kodak

If your camera has adjustable shutter speeds and aperture openings, look through the viewfinder and you'll see the indicator needle or signal lights of a light meter. They'll let you know when the f-stop and shutter speed are properly set to permit the right amount of light to strike the film. (Using ASA/ISO 64 color slide film, an average outdoor exposure on a sunny day could be shot at a speed of about 1/250th of a second with the aperture at f/8.)

Bracketing

Even when the light meter indicates an exposure will be perfect, variations in the brightness of a scene can cause the resulting photograph to be a little too light or too dark. To be sure you've gotten a good exposure, take one shot with the camera adjusted to the speed and aperture setting indicated by the light meter, then *bracket* it by shooting another photo one f-stop higher and a third one f-stop lower. That way you will have covered all the f-stops most likely to produce a properly exposed photograph.

Shooting a Photograph

The way you handle a camera and release the shutter also can contribute to the quality of your photography. Hold the camera comfortably and securely in both hands, your feet slightly apart and your body relaxed. Better yet, brace yourself against a tree or boulder, or mount the camera on a tripod to keep it absolutely still. Take plenty of time to set up a shot, and then hold your breath as you squeeze the shutter release.

It's a good idea to keep a notebook in your pocket and write down the shutter speed and f-stop of each photograph as you take it. After your pictures are developed, you'll be able to see how the photographs were affected by your camera settings, and you'll have a better idea of how to correct poor exposures.

COMPOSITION

In the excitement of an adventure there's a tendency to simply point a camera at a subject and shoot. On the whole, however, your pictures will be much better if you take time to study what you see in the viewfinder, and adjust the camera and your position until the exposure is a fine photograph rather than just a snapshot. Known as *composition*, this involves considering the effects of lighting, the placement of the subject, the nature of the background, and the existence of framing.

Lighting

Light makes photography possible, and using light well can make you an expert photographer. Outdoors, your subjects often will be bathed in sunlight, though the diffused light of overcast days and shaded forests can be just as effective.

When the sun is bright, try to position yourself so that it is coming over your shoulder from behind. For portraits, though, direct sunlight may cast shadows on the faces of your subjects, or cause them to squint. Sometimes you'll have better luck taking their pictures in the shade.

Placement of the Subject

There is a tendency for amateur photographers to place the subjects of their photographs exactly in the center of the viewfinder. That may be fine for close-up portraits, but in many outdoor shots a viewer's eye will find the composition more pleasing if the subjects are off-center.

Experts often do this by mentally dividing a scene into thirds both vertically and horizontally, then composing the photograph by placing the most important part of the scene at one of the four points where the vertical and horizontal lines cross. As you study photographs in books and magazines, and as you look at great paintings, you'll be surprised how frequently this *rule of thirds* is used to help compose a picture.

Background

You've probably seen photographs where a tree seemed to be growing out of someone's head, or the foliage behind a doe was so close in color to the animal's hide that the deer seemed almost to disappear. The background of a photograph can often make or ruin a picture. When you look through a viewfinder, notice what is behind your subject, and imagine how that background will affect the finished photograph. You may have to take a moment to move a piece of camping gear out of the way, or step a few feet to your left or right. And remember how the f-stop setting on your camera determines the depth of field of a photograph? With a low f-stop number, you may be able to blur the background, causing a sharply focused foreground subject to become even more distinct. A higher f-stop number will bring into focus both the subject and the background.

Framing

A good photographer may enhance the appeal of a scene by framing it, perhaps by bordering one or two sides of the picture with the branches of trees. Not only will the frame direct the viewer's eyes toward the subject, it also can increase the feeling of depth in a photograph, hide unattractive portions of the background, and fill in empty spaces above or alongside the subject.

While the basic rules of good photography apply anywhere, a photographer in the outdoors will find a variety of special situations that both test his talents and expand his opportunities.

Waterfall...framed by dead tree...and close up.

Photographing Landscapes

Jagged mountains, endless prairie, surging rivers, still glades—the backcountry is a landscape photographer's paradise. In addition to framing your photos and using the rule of thirds to compose them, notice where you place the horizon. It, too, will usually look best if it is a third of the way from the top or bottom of the picture. Letting it cut through the center tends to create the feeling of a picture split in half.

Vary the distances from which you shoot. Perhaps you're hiking toward a tumbling waterfall. Take a picture when you're still a long way off, another when you're halfway there, and a third close up. Try different times of the day, too; a waterfall that's pretty at midday may be absolutely stunning when the light of a sunset dances in its spray.

Photographing People

The greatest photographic subject of all is the human face. While a posed group shot is fine now and then, concentrate on capturing shots of people in natural situations, and use their activities and facial expressions to show the emotions of an adventure. A close-up of a weary hiker sipping from a water bottle, or of a jubilant climber celebrating the ascent of a mountain can energize a photograph.

Lighting faces is sometimes tricky. Subjects looking into a bright sun may squint, and hats can cast dark shadows across their eyes. Try composing sunlit shots with the subject in profile, or move into shade. Bright overcast days are ideal for portrait shots. The time of day affects the quality of the light. Sunlight early in the day and late in the evening is softer and casts more photogenic shadows than the harsh, direct rays of midday.

Photographing Action

Backcountry activities are full of action. What better way to show it than with photographs of kayakers shooting rapids, cyclists cranking hard up a hill, or a camp cook flipping flapjacks? To capture action on film, set up a shot ahead of time. Get downriver of that kayaker, pedal to the top of the hill ahead of the other cyclists, and get out your camera while the cook's still stirring batter. Anticipate where the action will be the most exciting, set the shutter speed and f-stop for that spot, then watch through the viewfinder and be ready to trip the shutter the instant the action peaks.

Photographing Wildlife

Imagine using your stalking skills to slip close enough to a deer to take its portrait, or of making a series of pictures as a bird builds a nest and hatches its young. Photography is the best way to bring home wild animals. In fact, you may find wildlife photography so satisfying that you'll plan entire treks around it.

One way to catch wildlife on film is by keeping your camera loaded and the shutter speed and f-stop set for average conditions. You'll be ready to swing your camera into position to photograph an elk running across your trail, or a hawk alighting for a moment on a fence post.

However, as with most photographs, the best wildlife pictures come not from quick shots, but rather from well-planned exposures. First of all, you've got to get close enough to an animal for it to fill a good share of your viewfinder. If you have a telephoto lens, you can pull distant animals right into your camera. Otherwise you can stalk them, or wait quietly near a salt lick, watering hole, or bird feeder. Try sitting in a blind or on a branch in a tree, and you may find that animals won't notice you at all. And don't forget to look for small wildlife; a well-crafted photograph of a frog or ground squirrel can be just as dramatic as any depicting larger animals.

▼ Elk

▼ Moose

Toad portrait

Toad at home

Of course you'll want to take precautions to protect the animals and yourself. Don't frighten birds away from their nests or handle small animals, and be especially careful not to come between an adult animal and its young.

(For more on approaching wildlife, see "Observing Nature.")

Photographing Plants

The blossom of a wildflower may wilt soon after it opens, but if it's on film the image will last for years. Plants add color and beauty to landscape shots, and you can successfully shoot forests and fields of flowers as you would any scenic vista. Don't limit yourself, though; the details of leaves, petals, needles, moss, and bark are rich with photographic potential.

Backgrounds are important in close-up shots of plants. By using a low f-stop number, you can blur the background so the plant itself is more distinguishable. Place a sheet of dark paper behind a plant and you'll have a neutral background that won't interfere with the subject of your photograph.

Foul-weather Photography

When the skies turn dark and wet, it's tempting to put away your camera until the sun comes out again, but that's a mistake. The splash of rain on a trail, delicate droplets hanging from leaves, mists rising from a forest, and the fantastic shapes of clouds can all become magic on film. Watch for the tiny, unusual shot as well as the spectacular vista. You can keep your camera dry inside a plastic bag, and perhaps even cut a lens hole in it so you don't need to remove the camera in order to shoot.

Photographing on Snow

The intense brightness of sunny mountains and snowfields can cause your camera's light meter to give faulty readings, resulting in photographs that are too dark. To compensate for the extra light, hold the sunlit palm of your hand in front of the lens in such a way that it fills most of the viewfinder field. Adjust the shutter speed and f-stop until the light meter indicates you would have a proper exposure if you took a picture of your hand, then move your hand and shoot a photograph of the snowy scene beyond. The camera should let in just about enough light to make a good picture. To be sure you've gotten the right setting, bracket your first shot by making another exposure at a setting one f-stop higher, and a third at one f-stop lower.

(Cameras with automatic shutter speed settings may need to be adjusted differently. Consult your owner's manual or camera instruction booklet.)

TELLING A STORY IN PICTURES

A photographic record of a trek is a real treasure. With it, you can relive an adventure time after time, and share the excitement with your family and friends. The best trek photos will tell an interesting, complete story, and that takes a little planning and plenty of careful camera work. Imagine how the photos will appeal to friends and members of your family who aren't going on the trip. What will they need to know to understand and appreciate the experiences you've had?

Start by shooting pictures at home as you shop for provisions, prepare your equipment, and load gear into your pack. Take close-up shots of maps so you can show where you're going, and at the trailhead photograph signs displaying the name of your destination.

During the trek, work for variety. Get close-ups as well as medium range and distance shots. In addition to action photographs, landscapes, and pictures of wildlife and plants, take photos of yourself and your companions engaged in routine activities. After all, making camp, cooking, hanging bear bags, and crawling out of a sleeping bag are all memorable moments in the backcountry.

Before showing your photographs in public, go through and edit them to remove those that aren't very well exposed, and any that just aren't interesting. Arrange the rest in an order that best tells the tale of your trek. Some photographers choose phonograph records or tape some music to use as sound tracks for their presentations.

◄ Signs help tell your story . . .

along with the images you have ► captured on firm.

ADDITIONAL EQUIPMENT

As your skills increase, you may want to add a few accessories to your camera to expand its capabilities. Veteran photographers, members of camera clubs, and books and magazines on photography are all good sources of information about the gear you would like to have. Among the most useful additions for an outdoor photographer are filters, lenses, flashes, tripods, and clamps.

Filters

Made of coated glass, filters screw onto the ends of many lenses and alter the quality of the light falling upon the film. For most basic outdoor color photography, the filter you're likely to use most is a polarizer that darkens the blue color of the sky and heightens the dramatic appearance of clouds and snowfields. That's especially important when you're shooting in bright sunlight that would otherwise wash out the sky. In fact, a polarizer can improve your pictures so much you may consider it a necessity. Use a larger f/stop to compensate for loss of light, however. For black and white photography, a red filter enhances contrasts in much the same way. Other useful filters for color film include skylight and ultraviolet haze filters.

50mm

35mm

200mm

Lenses

Most SLR cameras are sold equipped with a lens of about 50 millimeters that produces photographs with approximately the same field of vision as the human eye. It's suitable for most general photography, but there are other lenses as well. The smaller the focal length of a lens, the wider its field of view; a 28mm lens can encompass much more of a mountain range in one shot than would a 50mm lens. The greater the focal length of a lens, the more powerful its magnification and the narrower its field of vision. Thus a 200mm lens will make a small portion of a distant scene seem quite close. Zoom lenses have variable focal lengths. For instance, a 35–70mm zoom has the capabilities of both a wide angle lens and a normal lens, while a 70–200mm zoom offers a broad range of telephoto possibilities.

Lighter and less expensive than lenses, teleconverters and close-up rings can double or triple the telephoto or close-up powers of lenses to which they are attached.

CHAPTER 29

**FOCAL LENGTH AND ANGLE OF VIEW
COMPARISONS OF COMMON LENSES**

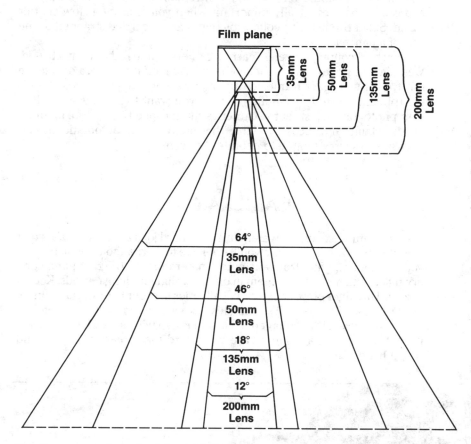

This line represents angle of view/picture area at equal distance from subject to film plane.

Flash Attachments

For taking photographs in dim light and at night, or for filling in shadows during the day, slip a flash attachment onto your camera. Different camera models require different flashes, so get the advice of a reliable camera dealer before you buy.

Tripods and Clamps

A camera mounted on a tripod will remain perfectly still during an exposure. That's especially important when you're using a slow shutter speed. Small tripods with collapsible legs can be carried strapped to the side of a backpack.

Many backcountry travelers carry a camera clamp rather than a tripod. Weighing only a few ounces, it can be used to mount a camera on a fence rail, tree branch, pack frame, ice ax, or any other convenient object. Like the tripod, it's nice to have along when you want to include yourself in your photographs; just set the camera's shutter speed and f-stop, mount it on the clamp and focus the lens, then activate the automatic shutter release and scurry around to get into the scene.

CAMERA CARE

Temperature extremes, water, dust, and hard jolts are a camera's worst enemies, but with a little care you'll not have to worry about them. Protect your camera and film from extreme temperatures. Store them in a cool, dry place, and never leave them in direct sunlight for long periods. Keep a haze or U/V filter on your camera at all times in order to protect the finely ground glass of the lens. It's much less expensive to replace a scratched filter than to repair a damaged lens. A lens cap will shield the lens when it's not in use, and a camera case can guard the camera from dirt and rough handling.

On the trail you can carry your camera on a strap around your neck, though you may want to consider using a harness that will hold the camera snugly against your chest as you walk and yet keep it instantly available for use. Another practical method is to tote your camera in a small padded camera pack strapped around your waist. Your camera will be out of the way while you travel, and you'll need just a few seconds to get it out of the pack and into shooting position. Nonetheless, before crossing streams it's wise to stow your camera gear in a plastic bag and place that deep in your backpack.

CAMERA MAINTENANCE

In addition to extra film, your camera kit for a backcountry trek should include a packet of tissues made especially for wiping camera lens glass and a fine lens brush for removing dust and lint. Put in a spare set of camera batteries and flash batteries and you should never be stuck with an inoperative camera in the midst of marvelous scenery.

◀Packing the gear

Hitting the trail▶
on horseback...

and on foot▶

"I shall be telling this with a sigh
Somewhere ages and ages hence;
Two roads diverged in a wood, and I —
I took the one less traveled by,
And that has made all the difference."

Robert Frost 1980
"The Road Not Taken," 1916

Chapter 30

Trail Building and Maintenance

Bob Birkby

Former Conservation Director for
Trail Building, Philmont Scout Ranch;
Fieldbook Rewrite Editor; Outdoor Writer

As a hiker, you know there's no sight more inviting than a ribbon of trail winding into the backcountry. It can lead you high among jagged peaks, deep into bayous, or far across rolling prairie. You can spend an hour strolling on paths near your home, or days following them miles into a wilderness. As a horse rider, you can use a trail for sightseeing or for leading a pack train of supplies to a distant camp. Perhaps you'll heft a canoe onto your shoulders and follow a portage trail around rough water, or you might race on foot into remote territory with rescue teams and fire fighting crews, depending on good pathways for quick passage. In the winter, you can strap skis or snowshoes to your boots and explore the high country on trails blanketed with snow.

A good trail is a gateway to adventure, and it also helps protect the backcountry by reducing our impact on the land. Of course, good trails don't just happen. They must be properly designed, constructed, and maintained, and that involves a lot of planning and effort. If you understand how trails are built and cared for, you'll be able to recognize the craftsmanship that goes into the paths you walk. You'll know how a switchback works, what water bars do, and why a trail is located where it is. Before long you'll have the basic knowledge you need to help protect trails, complete minor repairs, and perhaps even assist a trained crew building a new path in the backcountry.

PLANNING A NEW TRAIL

Water is a trail's greatest enemy. Melting snow, pounding rain, and the relentless forces of freezing and thawing combine to loosen and wash bits of soil from pathways. Over time, erosion can eat into a trail bed and eventually destroy the usefulness of the route. You've probably walked on eroded trails that had become deep trenches rather than paths, and the experience probably wasn't very pleasant.

To counter the effects of snow and rain, members of a trail crew incorporate special design features as they build new trails. Let's follow a crew through the construction of a trail and discover what you can do to help.

Surveying

Whether a new trail section will be 20 feet or 20 miles in length, deciding exactly where it will go is the most critical factor in its construction. Surveying a location is part science and part art, and when it's done well the results can be absolutely spectacular.

For a major project, crew member begin the task of choosing a location by gathering topographical maps and aerial photos of the area through which the route will pass. They know where the trail must begin and where it will end, so they study the maps and photos and explore the countryside between the starting and ending points until they are completely familiar with the lay of the land. They note the valleys, passes, cliffs, soil types, vegetation, and anything else that may affect the placement of the trail, and they try to incorporate in the trail location the following features:

- **Scenic vistas.** Hikers enjoy seeing the countryside through which they are traveling, and appreciate glimpses of distant mountains, lakes, and valleys.

- **South-facing slopes.** Since hillsides that face south get the most direct sunlight, trails covered with snow and those wet from heavy rains will dry out sooner on south-facing slopes than will trails located on slopes with northern exposures.

- **Solid, well-drained soils.** These make the best foundations for hiking trails.

A good trail location avoids the following:

- **Crossing meadows.** A trail in the trees located away from the edge of a clearing will not harm fragile meadow grasses.

- **Overly steep grades.** The steeper the grade of a trail, the faster water will run down it. Water moving quickly can carry large particles of soil and rock from the trail tread.

- **Creek or gully bottoms and swamps.**

- **Loose, boggy, and unstable soil.**

The crew also must find a way to build the trail around major *control points.* Rock outcroppings, mountain passes, canyons, and streams are all points that control the trail's location because it must pass above, below, or directly through them. On a map, the crew marks a possible route around each control point, and then draws a line connecting them to one another. This line is a potential location for the trail.

The crew surveys the trail sections between the control points with an *abney level* or clinometer, precision instruments used to determine the grade or steepness of a path. Using strips of brightly colored flagging tape, crew members mark a route that smoothly connects the control points.

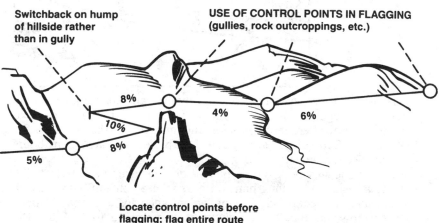

Switchback on hump of hillside rather than in gully

USE OF CONTROL POINTS IN FLAGGING (gullies, rock outcroppings, etc.)

8% 4% 6% 10% 8% 5%

Locate control points before flagging; flag entire route before construction begins.

(Trial specifications used in many Scout camps require that the steepness of most new trails not exceed 10 percent, i.e., no more than a 10-foot vertical gain for every 100 horizontal feet of trail . If the grade is much steeper, water may rush down the trail and turn it into a gully.)

After the preliminary surveying is complete, crews mark the center of the proposed trail at regular intervals with wooden stakes, and use additional stakes and brightly colored flagging to indicate the locations of retaining walls, barriers, switchbacks, and any other special construction features.

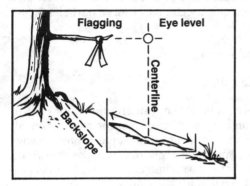

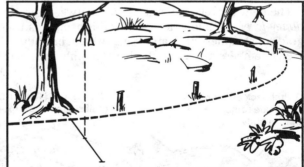

It is vital that crew members completely plan and survey a trail route before they begin any construction. In fact, they'll probably need to consider several different routes before they are satisfied they've found the best location. Extra effort at this stage of the project will save many hours of work once the digging has begun.

Planning and surveying a trail must be done by trained experts; building one takes lots of willing hands. Here's where you can get involved. Local, state, and federal land management agencies and organizations sponsor programs that allow volunteers to work on trails under the supervision of experienced group leaders. Check with them to see what opportunities are available in your area.

TOOLS AND CLOTHING FOR TRAIL WORK

Working on a trail safely and comfortably begins with choosing your clothing wisely. Trail building and maintenance are satisfying endeavors, but they can be strenuous, dusty jobs in the thick brush of steep hillsides. You'll want clothes that can take a beating and still give you plenty of protection. Wear sturdy boots that will support your ankles and protect your toes (never tennis shoes), long pants, a work shirt, a hard hat, and gloves.

The right tools also will help make your work easier and safer. A good kit for a crew includes the following:

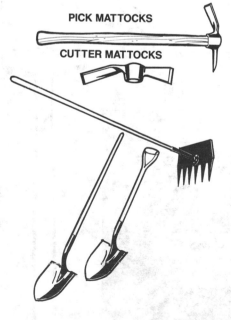

PICK MATTOCKS

CUTTER MATTOCKS

Mattocks. A mattock has a head that combines a pick and a digging blade. It is used to pry rocks, loosen soil, chop roots, and cut slopes.

McCleods. Originally designed as a tool for fighting forest fires, the McCleod is ideal for raking stones and debris, carving away packed earth, and preparing slopes for seeding.

Shovels. Use them to remove loosened dirt and clear it from the trail.

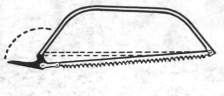

Bush saw. A small bush saw is handy for general brush and branch removal. As with all your tools, keep it sharp and clean, and between uses sheathe the blade with a piece of old hose split down its length.

Crosscut saw. You may need a large saw to cut logs that have fallen across the pathway, and for cutting timbers to make water bars and switchback barriers. Safety training in crosscut saw operation is an important prerequisite to using one.

Axes. Axes are used to peel bark from timbers and in the construction of trail barriers.

Sledge hammer. An 8- to 10-pound sledge is great for knocking the tops off boulders too large to remove from the tread, driving spikes into log barriers, and breaking up stones to plate trails crossing talus slopes. Always wear protective goggles when you use a sledge hammer.

BUILDING A TRAIL

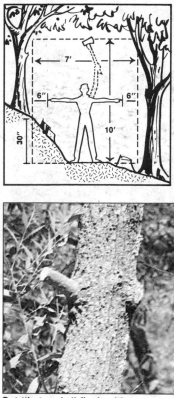

Clearance. Once the route has been surveyed and a properly equipped crew assembled, construction can begin. The first steps involve trailway clearance as the crew removes branches, brush, and trees from the route. (Boy Scout specifications require a minimum clearance of 10 feet in height and 3½ feet on either side of the center of a trail.) Crew members neatly and symmetrically trim branches from standing trees, cutting them close to the trunk to avoid leaving "hat racks," and evenly on all sides to prevent unsightly "haircuts." Always use a saw to prune tree branches; an ax may disfigure the tree. Undercut a branch first to prevent stripping bark from the tree and then finish sawing through from the top. If many branches must be cut from a small tree, it may be better to remove the tree altogether. Stumps are sawed flush with the ground, and all cut material is scattered away from the trail.

Cut "hat racks" flush with tree trunk.

Trail Tread. After the route has been cleared, the foreman will check the location once again to be certain there are no insurmountable difficulties. When he's satisfied the route is exactly where it should be, the crew will shape the *tread* or walkway of the trail. On gentle slopes, trail builders may have to do nothing more than clearly mark the location and let the boots of hikers do the rest. On steeper hillsides, they'll need to dig down along a line marking the inside edge of the trail, and then remove dirt and stone until they have uncovered a tread lying entirely on solid, undisturbed soil. This is called a *full-bench cut,* and is important for the long life of a trail. Loose earth is thrown away from the trail, and the tread is *outsloped* by building the inside edge of the trail about 2 inches higher than the outer shoulder of the trail. Water falling upon the tread will run off immediately rather than coursing down the trail and causing erosion.

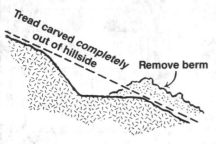

Tread carved completely out of hillside

Remove berm

After shaping the tread, the crew cuts away the sharp *backslope* above the trail, eliminating most of the soil that could wash onto the walkway. Finally they use rakes or McCleods to smooth the backslope and the *downslope* (the area of disturbed soil on the outside edge of the tread), and they sow the disturbed earth with grass seed. Revegetation can stabilize the soil, improve the appearance of the trail, and help heal the scar of new construction. Eventually, native grasses and plants will move back in and take over the slope once more.

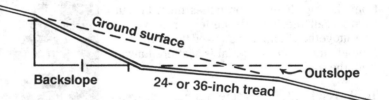

Ground surface

Backslope

24- or 36-inch tread

Outslope

SPECIAL CONSTRUCTION TECHNIQUES

One of the goals of a trail crew is to build pathways that lie lightly on the land, drawing little attention to themselves. The crew tries to camouflage its work so that rock walls, switchbacks, drainage systems, and barriers blend into the landscape as if they were natural parts of the terrain. As you hike well-built trails, keep your eyes open for the following special construction techniques.

Dry Walls

Known as *dry walls,* rock-retaining walls hold trails on slopes where it is impossible to achieve a full-bench trail width. Since no mortar is used, the walls must be built with great care.

Crews begin a dry wall by digging a shelf below and a bit outside the eventual tread location and setting large rocks upon it to form the wall's foundation. These are wedged tightly with smaller rocks, and empty spaces are packed with earth. The wall slopes inward slightly to increase its stability, and the top row of rocks should be flat and fairly large. Behind it, the surface of the fill material acts as the trail's tread.

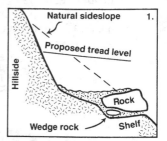

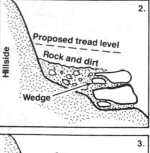

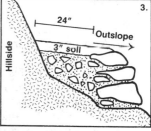

BUILDING TRAILS THROUGH BOULDER FIELDS

Rock slides and boulder fields present special problems for trail builders, and they may try to survey routes that avoid them. On the other hand, the absence of soil on rocky slopes means erosion is practically nonexistent, and once a trail is hammered through the rocks the tread will be extremely durable.

If you're part of a crew building a trail across a talus slope, you'll start by rearranging the rocks as much as you can to form a rough pathway across the slope. Next you'll haul in small stones and gravel to fill the

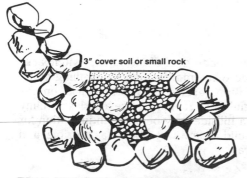

TRAIL BUILDING AND MAINTENANCE

voids between the rocks. A wheelbarrow is good for this, and dirt from trail construction near the rock slide makes ideal fill material. Finally, you'll plate the top of the trail with three inches of soil and fine gravel.

Drain dip at gully crossing

Streams, seeps, and gullies ►

Note drywall and rock spillway

BUILDING TRAILS ACROSS STREAMS, SEEPS, AND GULLIES

As a proposed trail route approaches a natural drainage, a crew will allow the trail to descend gently into the watercourse and then climb back out again. This is called a *drainage dip*, and it prevents stream water from running down the trail and eroding the tread.

A route that passes over a larger stream may require a series of stepping stones or an elevated walkway to allow hikers to cross without getting their feet wet. A large, well-placed log often makes a good bridge. For increased safety, a crew may flatten the top of the log and attach a handrail. More elaborate backcountry bridges often are wonders of wilderness engineering.

Switchbacks

When a trail must quickly gain a good deal of elevation, switchbacks allow it to zigzag up a steep slope while maintaining a prevailing grade that won't be susceptible to erosion. Crews build switchbacks on the rounded faces of slopes, not in gullies or ravines. Since a series of many short switchbacks zippering up a hillside may be an open invitation for hikers to take shortcuts, crews build as few switchbacks as possible, and place them as far apart as they can.

Trail builders usually will try to wrap each switchback around a prominent *turning point* (a large tree or a boulder). The circular turning area where the two legs of the trail meet should be nearly flat, held in place by a dry wall. A log or rock barrier erected between the legs of the switchback encourages travelers to go all the way around the turn.

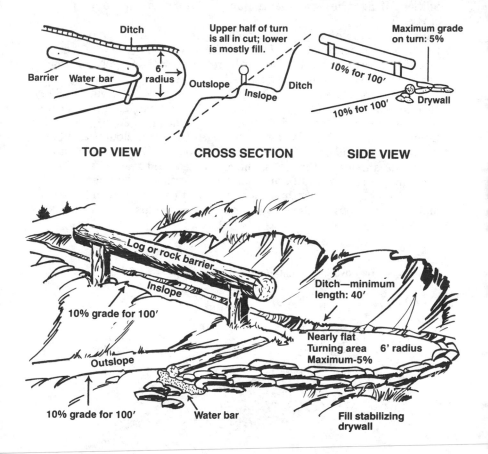

TOP VIEW   CROSS SECTION   SIDE VIEW

TRAIL MAINTENANCE

Once construction is completed, a trail's future depends in large part on regular maintenance. By finding and repairing erosion damage before it becomes serious, a crew can tremendously increase the useful life of a trail. You can help by making it a habit to look after the trails you hike. Without breaking stride, you can kick small rocks to the side of the path. Flick away pine cones and chunks of wood with your hiking stick, and with the heel of your boot scrape the silt from drainage ditches and from behind water bars. Straighten crooked trail signs, replace rocks that have fallen from switchback barriers, and report major trail problems to officials of agencies or organizations that manage the land the trail crosses.

Ideally, a maintenance crew should inspect every trail each spring so that trees and rocks that have fallen on the tread during the winter can be removed. Every 3 years trails should be refurbished thoroughly—brushing, berm and slough removal, barrier replacement, and erosion control.

Brushing involves cutting back vegetation to restore the original trailway clearance of 10 vertical feet and 7 horizontal feet. *Slough* is a composition of soil, leaves, and pine needles piled up along the inner edge of the tread. *Berm* is similar debris on the outer edge. Together, slough and berm narrow a trail and create a shallow trough down which water can run. Maintainers can use McCleods, shovels, rakes, and mattocks to loosen and remove slough and berm and to restore the outsloping tilt of the tread. Switchback barriers and dry walls need to be checked and repaired, and accumulations of silt removed from drainage dips and water bars.

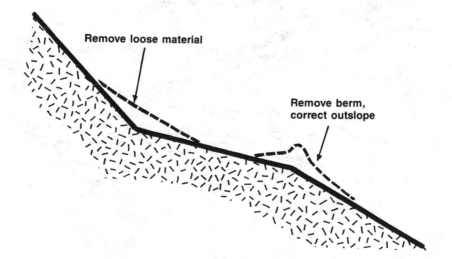

Remove loose material

Remove berm, correct outslope

On badly eroded trail sections, water bars will channel water off the tread and help save the route. To be effective, water bars must be made of large stones or of solid logs at least 8 inches in diameter and 6 to 8 feet long. To use a log, peel off the bark and bury one end of the log in the backslope. Embed the rest of the log across the trail, angling it downhill at 45° and leaving the top few inches exposed above the tread. Pack earth against the downhill side of the log, and scatter stones in the water bar spillway.

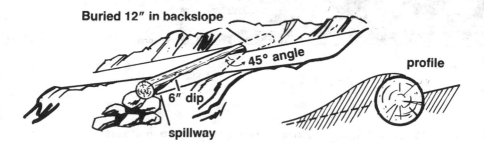

Marking Trails

Hikers with a map, compass, and a few landmarks should be able to pinpoint their location on most trails. However, above treeline, in snowfields, in storms, or at intersections, they may have to depend on trail markers to help them find their way.

Trail marking should be done in such a way that it does not harm the backcountry. The old method of chopping blazes into trees is no longer used since chopped blazes disfigure trees, leave them open to insect infestation and disease, and cannot be erased if the trail location is changed. Better alternatives for marking trails are discussed below.

Painted blazes. The 2,000-mile length of the Appalachian Trail is marked with rectangular blazes of white paint. Where other trails intersect the main route, they are similarly marked, but with blue paint. The paint does not harm the trees, it is highly visible, and it can be removed.

Signs. At trailheads and intersections, rustic wooden signs help hikers choose the proper path. A router can be used to cut letters into the sign,

◄ Cairn

and a dark stain will help new signs more readily blend into their surroundings. Signs should be securely mounted on treated posts set firmly in the ground.

Cairns. Above treeline, piles of stones called *cairns* are good markers. They should be neat and solid, and tall enough to be visible without being so large as to detract from a traveler's wilderness experience. If an area is subjected to frequent stormy or foggy weather, cairns need to be close enough to one another to guide hikers during periods of low visibility.

Surveyor's tape. The brightly colored flagging used to indicate the locations of new routes can also be used to temporarily mark existing trails. For instance, if a rock slide has obliterated a portion of tread, a few strips of flagging tied to branches will show hikers the best way to detour around the obstruction. Flagging should be removed after its purpose has been served.

Closing Abandoned Trail Sections

After building a trail at a new location, crews close any sections of old trail that no longer will be used. They'll scatter logs, brush, and rocks in the tread, dig small drainage ditches across the route at 100-foot intervals, and sow it with grass seed. In a few years, the abandoned trail will melt back into the hillside and all but disappear.

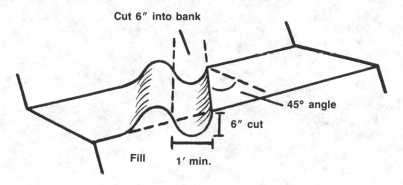

Cut 6″ into bank

45° angle

6″ cut

Fill

1′ min.

TRAIL RESPONSIBILITY

As backcountry visitors, each of us has a responsibility to see that we use trails properly and do all we can to protect them. The simple maintenance we perform as we hike can make a great difference in the appearance and condition of trails, and as volunteer members of properly supervised crews we'll be able to leave a lasting, worthwhile mark.

(For more on ways to use the backcountry wisely, see "Reducing Our Impact.")

III.
APPRECIATING OUR ENVIRONMENT

O beautiful for spacious skies,
For amber waves of grain,
For purple mountain majesties,
Above the fruited plain!
America! America!
God shed His grace on thee
And crown thy good with brotherhood
From sea to shining sea!

Katherine Lee Bates, 1893

"Take the flower that hangs in the morning, impearled with dew, arrayed as no queenly woman was ever arrayed with jewels. Once shaken, so that the beads roll off, and you may sprinkle water over it as carefully as you please, yet it can never be made again what it was when the dew fell silently upon it from heaven . . ."

Henry Ward Beecher, 1813-1887

Chapter
31

Understanding
Nature

Patrick D. Crosland
Interpretive Specialist, National
Park Service

A warm breeze ripples the surface of a mountain pond from which a deer is drinking. Cloaked in lush moss, an old log rots on the moist forest floor. A turkey vulture wheels in the rising midday heat, its sharp eyes scanning a meadow below.

As a backcountry traveler, you may have enjoyed these and thousands of other wonderful wilderness sights. Perhaps you thought of them as isolated incidents—a bird here, an animal there, a wooded glade, the warmth of sun on your back. In fact, the sunlight, the water, the air, and all those plants and animals are important parts of a finely balanced, interdependent system. Without their knowing it, and without our often seeing it, every living thing on Earth must rely on the existence and actions of other organisms to provide the necessities of life.

The globe on which we live spins through a vacuum, and save for the constant beat of sunlight and the occasional smack of a meteor, it is complete as it is. Nature must operate solely with the warmth of the sun and the raw materials that make up the Earth and its atmosphere. There is no source of additional materials. And yet the resources that do exist combine in remarkable ways to create the dazzling variety of life forms that fills the seas and skies and land.

ECOSYSTEMS

A group of individuals of the same kind of plant or animal living together is called a *population*. All the populations of plants and animals in an area make up a *community*. Communities of plants and animals together with their physical environments are an *ecosystem*. For example, a stand of fir trees on a mountainslope is a population. All the plants and animals on that slope live together as a community. Add the physical environment—the sunlight, air, water, soil, climate, and other natural elements of the mountainslope—and you have an ecosystem.

Mountainslopes, ponds, forests, deserts, and grasslands can each be considered individual ecosystems, but they are all linked by sharing components such as wind, precipitation, running water, and migrating animals. In fact, since no area is completely isolated, the entire Earth itself is an ecosystem. Made up of all the seas, the land, fresh water, and air, this global ecosystem is known as the *biosphere*. Two basic patterns by which it and all the lesser ecosystems operate are *cycles* and *successions*.

WATER CYCLE

As rain and snow, as streams and airborne mists, as quiet ponds and lakes, and as the surging waves of oceans, water makes life on Earth possible. No animal can live without it. In fact, more than 65 percent of the human body is composed of fluids necessary for transporting nutrients and minerals through digestive and circulatory systems, for washing away cellular wastes, and for helping control body temperatures.

Plants also require water in order for their seeds to germinate. Moisture drawn from the soil by plant roots carries minerals and chemical com-

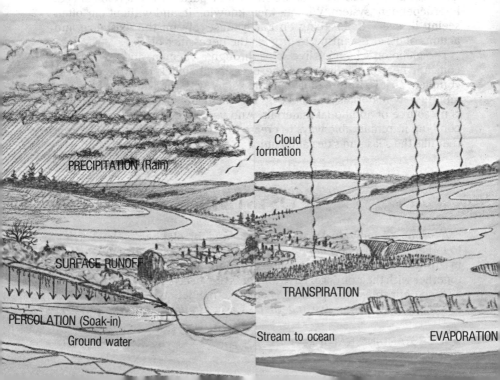

PRECIPITATION (Rain)

Cloud formation

SURFACE RUNOFF

TRANSPIRATION

PERCOLATION (Soak-in)

Ground water

Stream to ocean

EVAPORATION

pounds into stems and leaves for the manufacture of food. A single fir tree will absorb many tons of water in its lifetime, returning most of it to the air in a process called *transpiration.*

Transpiration from plants helps load the atmosphere with moisture. So does the respiration and perspiration of animals, and evaporation from bodies of water. When there is enough dampness in the air, clouds form and the moisture falls as precipitation. Dropping as rain or snow, water hits the surface of the Earth and may run into streams and lakes, soak into the ground, or be absorbed by plants and drunk by animals. In any case, the moisture is soon once again evaporated, transpired, respired, or perspired, and the endless cycle of water movement continues.

THE FOOD CHAIN CYCLE

The path of energy through an ecosystem is a cycle called the *food chain.* The cycle begins with the green plants that are the *producers* for the ecosystem, passes through the *consumers,* and ends with the *decomposers.*

Producers

Green plants are the basic sources of food in the biosphere. They act as factories, making food out of raw materials they take from the air, water, and soil. Using a substance in their leaves and stems called *chlorophyll,* plants draw on the power of sunlight to manufacture sugars and starches from water and carbon dioxide. They store these nutrients in their leaves, roots, stems, and seeds, and animals may eat the plant parts as food. Known as *photosynthesis,* this manufacturing process also produces oxygen to replenish the atmosphere's supply. An acre of healthy young woodland can produce 4 tons of oxygen a year—enough to keep 18 people alive.

Photosynthesis is not limited to plants living on land. In addition to leafy underwater plants such as seaweed, billions of tiny plants called *phytoplankton* drift in the oceans' currents, pumping oxygen into the water and providing food for animals as large as whales.

Consumers

All animals must eat to stay alive. *Primary consumers* are those able to subsist on plants. Know as *herbivores,* this vast group includes rabbits,

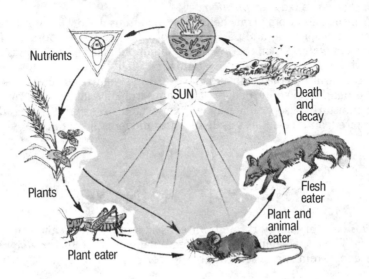

The food chain cycle

mice, squirrels, seed-eating birds, plant-eating insects, grazing animals such as deer and cattle, and many others. Their digestive systems are designed to draw nourishment from the sugars and starches produced in plants by the process of photosynthesis.

Animals that eat other animals rather than plants are called *carnivores*. In the food chain, they are at least one step removed from the plants, and are thus *secondary consumers*. They include hawks, owls, snakes, toads, spiders, sharks, predacious insects, insect-eating birds, wolves, foxes, and other predators, parasites, and scavengers. A few animals, for instance humans, are both herbivores and carnivores.

Food passing through an ecosystem provides sustenance for many animals. For instance, a grasshopper may nourish itself with blades of grass. A bird might eat the grasshopper, a fox could devour the bird, and a hawk may dine on the fox.

Each organism is important to the whole ecosystem since each species contributes to the diversity and stability of the system. Each provides food for the organisms above it in the food chain, and each helps control the populations of organisms below it.

CHAPTER 31

Decomposers

Animals that have eaten plants or preyed upon one another digest their meals and then excrete remnants of plant and animal matter their systems cannot use. Dead animals and plants also fall to the ground or to the bottoms of bodies of water, where the process of decay begins. Carrion eaters such as vultures, hyenas, and crabs may make a final feast. Insects, worms, and maggots also find nourishment, as do microorganisms in the soil. Gradually the organic remains are broken down into simple compounds that can be absorbed by plants able to use them again to manufacture food. The food chain thus connects with itself, and the cycle is complete.

MAINTAINING A NATURAL BALANCE

The arrangement of the food chain is such that it assures naturally balanced ecosystems. Small herbivores living on plentiful plant supplies tend to have lots of young, far more than can ever survive for very long. This surplus goes largely to feed carnivores, which devour most of the excess herbivores and thus keep the size of herbivore populations in check. Likewise, carnivores preying on one another prevent the overpopulation of any single species.

The lower an organism's position in the chain, the more abundant its numbers. For example, aphids, which require the sap of plants for sustenance, are very numerous and very prolific. Ants depending on aphids for food are fewer in number, the birds that eat ants are fewer still, and the predatory hawks and owls that devour small birds make up comparatively small populations.

Starvation and disease also play important roles in maintaining the natural balance. The number of members in any plant or animal population is determined in part by the ease with which they can obtain food and reproduce themselves. When a population becomes too numerous—many deer grazing a mountain valley, for instance—it may exhaust its food supplies and many of its members may die of hunger or illness. When that happens, the demand for foliage will be lessened, plants can regenerate themselves, and the reduced size of the deer population will better fit the natural balance.

The numbers of animals in an area are continually fluctuating. They change due to conditions of various seasons, and of various years. For a while one species may be overly plentiful, then natural limitations will reduce its numbers and another species will predominate. In a way, cycles are at work here, too, as the balance of nature is maintained.

PLANT SUCCESSION

Just as competition among animal populations promotes a critical balance, different plant communities will each take a turn thriving in a single area. This sequence of plants replacing each other as each creates conditions favorable for the growth of the next is known as *plant succession,* and the final stage to grow naturally in any area is called the *climax community.*

Take, for example, a hillside left bare by a forest fire, clear-cutting, cultivation, or overgrazing. Before long, annual seeds carried into the area by the wind will sprout, and tiny root systems will help protect the soil from erosion. Perennial plants and grasses may take root at about the same time, and before long they will crowd out the annuals. Then, depending on the climate and certain local conditions, grasses will become more and more dominant, or shrubs and trees will gradually move in and take over.

Once grasses are established on a hillside in the Northeast, for instance, conditions may be just right for the growth of shrubs such as sumac and trees such as gray birch, black cherry, and aspen. As these plants mature, the shade of their branches would make it difficult for the grasses to thrive. Other trees such as red maples and oaks can then get started in the open shade. When they mature, they'll tower over the birch, cherry, and aspen and take their place as the dominant forest type. The oaks themselves may give way to tall beech and sugar maple trees, which shade the ground so completely that only their own seedlings can survive. When that happens, the last stage of plant succession has been reached—a *climax forest.*

In other parts of the country, different combinations of plants make up that final stage of plant succession. Tough grasses and shrubs dominate the climax grasslands of Midwestern prairie, while pine, spruce, and fir populate the climax forests of the western mountains.

WATER TO FOREST SUCCESSION

Many climax communities are now growing where once there was a pond, lake, or beaver-dammed stream. In almost the same way that vegetation taking root on bare soil will gradually evolve, plants may also take over a body of water and become a forest or prairie.

As plants that live at the edge of the water die, their remains may build up rich, organic underwater layers near the shore. Over a great number of years, if the water is still enough to allow the layers to remain, this nutrient-loaded peat will pile up near the water's surface where plants can root in it. As they live and die, they help build up the layers even more until the water may be displaced altogether.

Next come the plants that form sod. These grasses and sedges grow in such a way that they help transform saturated peat into solid soil. As the soil becomes drier, other plants such as swamp shrubs and lowland prairie grasses take over. Trees may succeed the swamp shrubs until a climax forest has been established.

ANIMAL SUCCESSION

Each animal has its own requirements for food, water, and shelter. Several kinds of animals may eat the same food, but their cover and water requirements will differ. They may have similar needs for shelter, but foods will differ. In short, every native animal occupies a unique position, or *niche,* in the community where it lives.

Because of this, forms of animal life are very dependent on the kinds of plant life an area supports. As plant succession occurs, so, too, are there changes in the species of animals that thrive. For instance, very few animals are found on bare ground, for there is nothing for them to eat. As weeds cover the soil and provide a little shelter and food, small animals such as field sparrows, horned larks, and mice can survive. When perennial grasses and shrubs take over, rabbits and meadow mice, tree sparrows, snow buntings, juncoes, and even occasional pheasant and quail will have the shelter and food they require.

If the climax population consists of long-lived perennial grasses, many prairie birds, jackrabbits, ground squirrels, badgers, coyotes, and red foxes will find ideal living conditions. Where shrubs predominate, many birds will nest. As the trees of the climax forest take hold, tree-nesting birds, bark-boring insects, and larger mammals will find suitable food and cover for their needs.

The boundaries between two plant communities are often good places to observe nature. Since you'll see natives of both habitats, you're likely to find a large variety of animal and plant species where a prairie meets a woodland, where a marsh blends into a timber stand, or along the line between alpine tundra and a forest.

(For more on vegetation, see "Plants." For more on animals, see "Wildlife and Fish." For more on watching animals, see "Observing Nature.")

◄Great Blue Heron

Marmot►

"Nature will bear the closest inspection. She invites us to lay our eye level with her smallest leaf, and take an insect view of its plain."

Henry David Thoreau, 1817-1862

Chapter 32

Observing Nature

Patrick D. Crosland
Interpretive Specialist, National
Park Service

T he backcountry is alive. Animals and plants thrive everywhere in astonishing variety. Microcosmic and gigantic, motionless and swift, camouflaged and brightly colored, the flora and fauna of the out-of-doors create a magnificent, ever-changing feast for the senses of any who seek it out. The trouble is, we seldom take the time. Backpackers hurry along, seeing nothing but dusty trail as they rush to reach their destination. Hikers may marvel at mountaintop panoramas, but fail to notice the small but equally remarkable sights at their feet. Campers spend days in the woods wondering where the wildlife is when in fact they simply do not see that there are animals all around.

Not too many decades ago, people were more attuned to the sights, sounds, and smells of nature. An Indian could glance at a footprint in soft soil and recognize the kind and size of animal that had left it, how long ago it had passed, and where it probably was going. A settler noting the migration of geese and the change in the color of wild hares and ptarmigans would realize spring had arrived and he could begin his planting. It's not that our senses have deteriorated over the years, but rather that most of us have forgotten how to use them in the backcountry. By relearning the skills of careful observation and developing the patience to be watchful and aware, we can all enrich our outdoor adventures.

OBSERVING PLANTS

The next time you're in the backcountry, look around. Look carefully, don't just glance to the side of the trail. Notice the sizes and shapes of the trees, and how close together they are growing. Pick a single tree and examine the color of the leaves. Smell the bark and feel its texture. Have birds built nests in the branches? Has a woodpecker in search of a meal drilled holes in the trunk? Have deer rubbed velvety antlers against the bark, or have hungry rabbits standing on drifts of snow nibbled the

◄ Lily

Lichen ▲

◄ Insect Eaters ▶

Pitcher Plant ▶

◄ Sun dew

low-hanging twigs? Is there evidence of fire, disease, or strong winds? Take one leaf from the tree and study the networks of fine lines crisscrossing its surface. Search the ground for fruit, seed pods, or nuts, and break one open. If you have a plant identification book, find a description of the tree and read about its uses, range, longevity, and special characteristics.

◄ Orchid (Fairy Slipper)

Yucca ▶

Now you're starting to use your senses to observe nature. It's a matter of seeing both the big picture and the smallest details. In fact, the more you notice the less distance you may travel. There are enough plants growing in a few square yards of woodland soil to hold your interest all day long.

OBSERVING ANIMALS

It is a common belief that the senses of wild animals are more acute than those of humans. While some see better than we do, others hear better, and many have superior senses of smell, rarely does one species surpass man in all of these abilities. To get close enough to an animal to observe it well, you'll need to match the strengths of your senses against the weaknesses of the animal's. One of the most important is seeing skillfully.

Sight

Some animals see extremely well, while others are nearly blind. A soaring hawk notices the slight movement of a mouse on the ground far below, and a falcon diving on a smaller bird can identify its prey at a glance, gauge its height and speed, and determine the distance to trees, fences, and other hazards. On the other hand, bears are nearsighted, moles get along by touch alone, and bats navigate with radar. Many animals with their eyes on the sides of their heads have difficulty focusing both eyes on a single object. They can't judge distances as well as you can, and most are colorblind. They see the world as if it were a black and white photograph, which is why they won't notice the fluorescent orange hats and vests hunters wear to warn one another of their presence.

Smell

Most people enjoy the pleasant aroma of flowers and they can detect the pungent odor of a barnyard, but few are able to use their noses to detect

Turtle ▶

the presence of animals. Most wild mammals, however, have such keen senses of smell that many depend more on their noses than on their eyes. A faint, unfamiliar scent in the breeze is all it takes to alert them to danger.

Sound

There are no roaring engines in the backcountry, no honking horns or blaring sirens. Jackhammers don't pound the pavements, and the drone of televisions and radios is far away. We are so accustomed to the noises of cities and towns that the silence of the backcountry may at first startle you. Listen carefully, though, and you'll hear the songs of birds, the splash of water, and the rustle of leaves in the wind. The snort of a deer, the

Moose feeding ▲   **Moose ▲**

rhythmic beat of a woodpecker, the hiss of a snake, or even the snap of a twig may help you locate and identify wildlife you might otherwise never have noticed.

Many animals depend on a keen sense of hearing to warn them of approaching predators. While they are accustomed to the familiar sounds of their home territory, a strange noise can send them scurrying for safety. On the other hand, certain sounds will arouse their curiosity. Blow on a duck call and you might bring a circling flock of birds near your post. Make a kissing sound against the back of your hand, and deer may come to investigate. Whistle softly, and a running rabbit may stop in its tracks, while a shrill whistle in high mountain country can bring a dozen marmots out of their burrows to see what's going on.

Taste

Just as humans enjoy certain foods more than others, animals have their mealtime favorites. In the case of wild berries, you can eat your fill as you watch for birds and bears coming to share in the feasting. You'll probably not find carrion, insects, or worms the least bit appetizing, but knowing what animals do feed on them will give you an idea where to search for the animals you want to watch.

Touch

Insects use their antennae to explore the world around them and to communicate with one another. Fish rely on a system of nerves running the length of their bodies to pick up vibrations in the water. All animals feel heat and cold, and many can feel fine textures. While your sense of touch won't do much to help you find animals and plants to observe, you can certainly enjoy the feel of certain foliage, soils, feathers, and bones. Wild animals often are frightened by the touch of humans, so for their safety and yours, observe them with your eyes but not your hands.

Pronghorn antelope ▲

Ptarmigan ▲

Deer ▼

Mountain goat ▶

READING THE BACKCOUNTRY

Animals seldom wander randomly. They prefer to travel pathways clear of underbrush and fallen trees. If they move from one valley to another, they'll climb through a pass rather than going over the summit of a mountain. They try to stay near food and water. Grazing animals search out open country with plenty of lush vegetation while predators may range far and wide in search of prey. In mountainous regions, many animals will move to higher elevations in the summer, but descend when the first snows of winter blanket the alpine meadows and forests. On hot days, they'll rest in cool woodlands, and chilly afternoons may find them lounging on warm, sunny slopes. Some birds, insects, and fish adjust to seasonal changes by migrating, covering thousands of miles in instinctive quests for warm weather, abundant food, or suitable spawning grounds.

As you plan a backcountry trek, learn all you can about the habits of the wildlife you want to see along the way, and study topographic maps of the area you'll visit. Try to put yourself in the animal's place and imagine what it needs in order to thrive. On the maps, pinpoint ponds and streams, meadows, mountain passes, forests, and any other likely sighting spots.

Once you're in the backcountry, be alert for signs that indicate the recent presence of wildlife. Sharply defined tracks in soft sand, soil, or snow are probably quite recent, and if you find lots of tracks close together, you'll know that many animals have passed or that one has spent a good deal of time in the same place. Like tracks, droppings will help you identify the kinds of animals that frequent an area. If they're dry and bleached by the sun, they've been on the ground for some time. Break apart fresh droppings with a stick and examine the contents to discover what the animal that left them had eaten. Are there small bones, feathers, and fur? Seeds and hulls? Bits of grass?

Study the landscape. Many animals position themselves to take advantage of clear fields of view, sunny slopes, and hidden groves. Keep your eyes open for broken twigs, matted grass, and stripped bark. Watch for burrows, caves, insect mounds, and nests, and when you suspect there are interesting animals nearby, decide the best way to observe them.

◄ Pileated woodpecker holes

GETTING CLOSE TO ANIMALS

Study an animal in its own habitat and you can see what it really looks like, what it eats, and how it reacts to the presence of other wildlife. You'll be able to take photographs or make sketches, and you'll know the thrill of using your woodland skills to observe a wary animal at close range. Three good ways to do that are waiting, tracking, and stalking. Of course, you'll need to use common sense in deciding how safely you can approach, and you'll want to give every animal enough space so it doesn't feel threatened.

Waiting

When you walk in the backcountry, you usually create enough disturbance to send wildlife scurrying for cover, but if you are motionless, many animals will have difficulty seeing you. Use this to your advantage by finding a place to sit and making yourself comfortable. Lean against a rock or tree, fold your hands in your lap, take a couple of deep breaths, and relax. Before long the animals will resume their normal activities, just as if you weren't there. Watch the trees for birds, and the ground for small animals and insects. Near a salt lick, deer may come very close to you, and if you're beside a pond or stream, you may be able to see fish under the surface of the water.

Make yourself even more inconspicuous by building a bird blind. Climb 10 feet up a tree, and animals that might have seen you on the ground will wander underneath with no idea you're watching. Sit in the same place at different times of the day and the year, and don't forget to come at night. With your eyes accustomed to the light of a full moon, you'll see animals that seldom wander about during the day.

Use a magnifying glass to focus your attentions on a tiny spot, perhaps only an inch or two square, and you'll discover an endless variety of life thriving in miniature ways. Extend your range of vision with binoculars and watch distant herds of elk, deer, and mountain goats.

Tracking

Tracking an animal is like solving a mystery. What do those footprints mean? How did this twig get broken? Did an animal rooting for grubs turn over those stones? What made these fresh scratches on the trunk of a tree? One by one the clues appear, each leading you further along the route traveled by an animal. Can you find the spot where it slept? Can you guess where it is headed? What it has been eating? Did it leave any droppings?

Becoming an expert tracker takes practice and patience. The more time you spend at it, the easier it will be for you to decipher signs left by wildlife, and the faster you'll learn to think like the animal you're following. And don't let cold weather keep you at home; on a crisp, clear morning when the ground is covered with snow, you'll be able to trace every move an animal made.

Stalking

Your success in waiting for animals to appear and in tracking them depends primarily on your ability to use your eyes. Stalking an animal will test other senses as well. Let's assume you've been following fresh deer tracks for an hour when you look ahead and catch a glimpse of a handsome buck grazing in a distant meadow. Although the buck is busy eating, he raises his head now and then to sniff the air, listen, and glance around the meadow for signs of danger. You'd like nothing more than to get near enough to watch the deer for a while and take some photographs, so what do you do?

First, make a quick survey of the area. Are there gulleys in which you can hide, or trees and brush that will conceal your presence as you work your way toward the meadow? What is the wind direction? Approach with the wind blowing in your face. If it's blowing toward the buck, he'll smell you long before he sees you. How quietly can you walk? Is the ground covered with crunchy dry leaves, tall grass, damp sod? Is the deer standing still, or moving away? Will mist or fog help conceal your presence and muffle your footsteps? Are there other animals in the vicinity that may startle the buck before you get close to him?

As you creep toward the deer, remember that while his senses are keen, he has trouble seeing things that don't move. Freeze the instant the deer lifts his head, and remain perfectly still until he grazes again. When you reach an observation spot near the animal, enjoy watching for as long as you want, then try to withdraw as quietly and invisibly as you approached.

◀ **Spoonbill**

OTHER OPPORTUNITIES

While we usually think of doing our stalking, tracking, and waiting in woodlands, mountains, and prairies, almost every outdoor environment lends itself to nature observation. Have you ever snorkeled around a coral reef or gone skin-diving to the ocean floor? At low tide many people wander along beaches searching for signs of marine life that have washed ashore, and during certain seasons they may go out in boats and watch pods of migrating whales. The great swamps of the Southern States are full of remarkable plants and animals, and so are the deserts of the Southwest, the prairies of the Midwest, and the forests of the Northeast. In fact, there is hardly a spot on the globe that doesn't support some wildlife community you'll enjoy observing.

(For more on plants and animals, see "Understanding Nature," "Plants," and "Wildlife and Fish.")

◀ Alligator

Bittern ▶

◀ Frog

"Standing here in the deep, brooding silence all the wilderness seems motionless, as if the work of creation were done. But in the midst of this outer steadfastness we know there is incessant motion and change. Ever and anon, avalanches are falling from yonder peaks. These cliff-bound glaciers, seemingly wedged and immovable, are flowing like water and grinding the rocks beneath them. The lakes are lapping their granite shores and wearing them away, and every one of these rills and young rivers is fretting the air into music, and carrying the mountains to the plains."

John Muir, 1868

Chapter 33

The Earth

Lee C. Gerhard, Ph.D.
Exploration Manager, Union Texas
Petroleum Corporation

M any of us are drawn to the wilderness by its timeless tranquillity and beauty. We're quite sure that the mountains we climb this summer will be there next year, too. The tumbling streams that lull us to sleep seem to have flowed forever, and it's difficult to imagine that the deep valleys and broad prairies could ever have been much different than they are now.

Yet the seeming permanence of the backcountry is an illusion, for the land is always changing. The quiet, wooded campsites we like so much may once have been at the bottom of an ocean, or buried under immense fields of ice. The peaceful ridges we walk could have been seared by the heat of volcanic blasts, or ripped apart by earthquakes. And even as we stand on them, granite mountains are slowly dissolving beneath our feet. Creation and decay, eruption and erosion, the Earth is being continually reshaped, cast anew time and time again. It's a relentless, powerful, and fascinating process, and as you explore the backcountry, you'll find evidence of its strength and grace everywhere you look.

FORMATION OF THE EARTH

Perhaps you've seen the blossoming of a flower photographed on time-lapse film. By exposing one frame every few minutes and then running the film through a projector at 16 frames a second, scientists can compress several days of botanical activity into a few moments, allowing us to delight in the delicate, fluid motion of unfolding petals.

Now imagine a time-lapse camera photographing the surface of the Earth from its beginnings to the present. Even at a rate of one frame exposed every 100 years, the finished film would take weeks to screen, and the story it told would as often be one of upheaval and violence as slow, symmetrical beauty. Opening scenes of fire and molten rock would gradually give way to those of a globe dividing into continents and oceans. Mountain ranges heave up through the Earth's crust only to melt

THE EARTH

527

away. Ice fields ebb and flow from the polar caps. Seas cover and then recede from vast continental prairies. Earthquakes and volcanoes abruptly alter the land, and the continents seem to drift about the Earth's surface. Strange plants and animals flicker into view and then are gone, the dinosaurs perhaps the most recognizable. Finally humans appear on the screen, the history of their civilizations taking up but a few seconds at the end of the long film of the Earth.

GEOLOGY

Geo means "earth," while the suffix -*logy* indicates "a subject of study." Many *geologists*, those scientists who study the Earth, believe our planet came into existence about 4½ billion years ago as a flaming, molten ball composed of many elements. Like cream separating from milk, the lighter elements drifted toward the surface of the ball, leaving at the center a dense iron core. The Earth's surface cooled and a crust formed, but even today the thickness of that crust is only about 0–40 kilometers (0–25 miles). Temperatures and pressures beneath the crust are still high enough to keep rock in a fluid form called *magma*. The great slabs, or *plates*, that make up the Earth's crust float upon this mantle of magma like so many gigantic islands able to drift, collide, and overlap. Known as *plate tectonics*, this slow, remarkable motion is a force that can drive mountain ranges into the sky and then bring them tumbling down again.

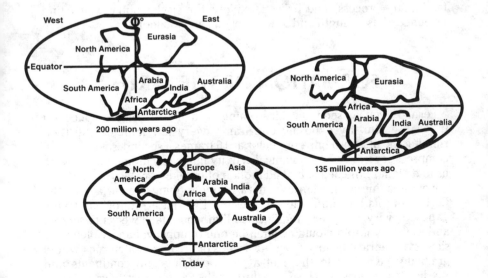

200 million years ago

135 million years ago

Today

Plate Tectonics

The major plates of the Earth's crust are named for the areas of land and sea under which they lie. The North American plate, for example, is the underpinning for most of North America and a good share of the Atlantic Ocean. Bordering its western edge is the Pacific plate extending beneath most of the Pacific Ocean. Other major plates are the Australian, African, South American, Eurasian, Philippine, and Antarctic.

The plates may move only inches a year, but even such gradual migration has far-reaching effects. The motion of adjoining plates takes one of three forms—*separation*, *sliding*, and *overriding*. When two plates separate and pull away from each other, they create a *zone of divergence*. Occurring primarily under the oceans, zones of divergence allow hot magma to rise and fill the gaps between the plates. When plates slide past each other, a *fault zone* can develop, causing earth tremors and horizontal disruption of surface features. A *zone of convergence* develops when the edge of one plate overrides the edge of another. Folded over or thrust upward by the force of the plates, layers of rock may form high mountain ranges.

The pressure of plates jamming against each other and the cracks in the Earth's crust through which molten magma may flow make the broad zones where the edges of plates overlap especially prone to earthquake and volcanic activity. The instability of California's San Andreas fault, the eruption of Mount St. Helens, and frequent earthquakes in the Aleutian Islands can all be traced to the shifting forces along the boundaries of the North American and Pacific plates.

MOUNTAIN RANGES

The center of the North American plate, and thus the center of North America, is geographically relatively stable. Far from the active edges of the plate, the midlands tend to be flat, often layered with the sediment of ancient oceans that once flowed over them. Farther east and west, stress in the Earth's crust has created mountain ranges in four different ways:

Volcanoes

When magma inside the Earth finds passage to the surface, it may erupt skyward as a volcano. In some cases an initial eruption can explode with devastating force, as did Mount St. Helens, and the flow of magma may continue for a long time, as does that from Mauna Loa on the island of

Two years after the May 18, 1980, eruption of Mount St. Helens (Volcano)

Hawaii. The Cascade Range of the Pacific Northwest is volcanic in origin, and the Hawaiian Islands are all the tips of immense volcanoes that, when measured from their bases on the ocean floor, may be the largest mountains on Earth.

Faults

Pressured by plate movement, the Earth's crust may fracture and shift, creating high, sheer walls, zones of broken rock, and disrupted streambeds. Later, lateral movement can jumble these cliffs and create the sharp, angular lines of ranges like the Sierra Nevadas and Tetons.

El Capitan Peak in the Guadalupes of West Texas (Fault)

CHAPTER 33

Adirondacks of northern New York (Folds)

Folds

Instead of fracturing, a plate under stress may fold, the ripples in its surface becoming ranges of mountains. Sections of the Appalachian Mountains were formed this way.

Continental Uplifts

Sometimes large sections of the Earth's crust are forced upward by internal pressures created by plate motion. Although individual mountain ranges may be formed by folds, faults, and volcanic activity, major mountain belts are often the result of this continental uplift. When that happened in western North America, the towering Rocky Mountains came into being.

Denali (Mount McKinley) of Alaska (Uplift)

Water   Chemical   Wind

EROSION

Coupled with the creative force of plate tectonics is the destructive power of erosion. Without erosion, the mountains of the Earth would be extremely lofty. There would be no streambeds, no canyons, and no soil. Without erosion, life as we know it could not exist.

The primary agents of erosion are running water, chemicals, ice, gravity, and wind. Moisture seeping into rock fissures expands as it freezes, gradually breaking the stone apart. The rocks of talus and scree slopes you scramble across on mountainsides were probably shattered by frost. Chemicals carried by water can dissolve stone, or eat away the crystals that hold it together and allow it to crumble into particles. Limestone is particularly susceptible to chemical weathering, as evidenced by old limestone tombstones whose eroded letters have become almost indecipherable.

Falling rain washes away bits of stone loosened by erosion. As these particles are carried along, they act as abrasives. Trickles combine to form rivulets, rivulets unite into streams, and streams combine into rivers, all patiently cutting channels into the Earth. The steeper the grade of the land, the faster and more erosive the movement of the water and the silt in it. When the grade lessens and the streams lose momentum, particles suspended in the water settle to the bottoms of lakes or help create deltas at the mouths of rivers. Winds can carry the dust of decaying rocks long distances, depositing it in slowly growing layers. Whether carried by water or wind, what was once rock is well on its way to becoming soil.

One of the most spectacular forms of water erosion is the glacier. A glacier is a long-lasting body of ice formed where yearly accumulations of snow exceed the amounts that melt. The weight of new snow compresses

Glacial crevasses

that below it, eventually turning it into glacial ice. As more snow falls on the upper reaches of a glacier, it pushes the entire ice field downhill in a motion much like that of a very slow river. Stresses upon the solid ice cause fractures called *crevasses* that may be hundreds of feet deep. When a mountain glacier pushes its way over a cliff, it creates an *ice fall*—high, cold cliffs that may topple without warning. If a glacier reaches the ocean, as many do in Alaska and Antarctica, great chunks of ice shear away and drop into the sea. Called *calving*, this glacial activity is a source of icebergs.

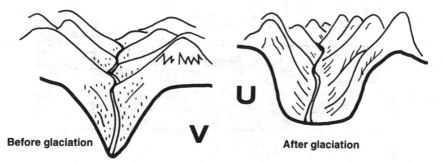

Before glaciation V **After glaciation** U

As a glacier moves across the land, gravel and rocks caught beneath the weight of the ice scour the surfaces over which they travel. Mountain glaciers can carve the sharp, V-shaped canyons cut by streams into U-shaped valleys. If the glaciers melt, they leave behind fields of rocks and debris they may have carried for many miles.

Sometime in the last million years, the climate of the Earth cooled and glaciers crept down from the north to cover a good share of North America. When the weather warmed and the glaciers retreated, they left behind thick deposits of topsoil and, here and there, large, solitary boulders. That soil today makes up much of the rich American prairie.

THE EARTH

Remnants of the glaciers themselves still cover the majority of Greenland, and cloak the summits and high cirques of many U.S. and Canadian mountain ranges.

The power of erosion is astonishing. Over the eons it has carved the Grand Canyon, worn down the Appalachian Mountains, and helped shape every landscape through which you've ever hiked. In fact, you'll find the effect of erosion everywhere you look, but it must be seen in the proper perspective. While erosion did and still does create the soil in which forests, grasslands, and crops can grow, it has an insatiable appetite. Poor management of those lands will allow erosion to take away the soil far more quickly than it can be formed.

(For more on the effects of erosion and ways to avoid its detrimental effects, see "Reducing Our Impact," "Understanding Nature," and "Plants.")

CAVE FORMATION

Occasionally, erosion carves caverns beneath the Earth's surface. Rainwater seeping through the soil may combine with carbon dioxide and form carbonic acid. Over tens of thousands of years, the acid can dissolve rock farther underground, usually limestone, creating water-filled cavities. If

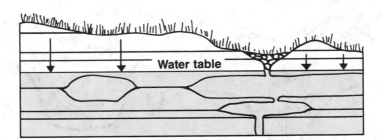

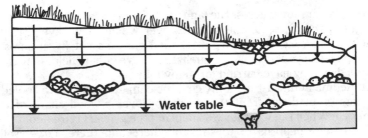

When the water table drops, the ceilings collapse.

CHAPTER 33

Stalactites hang from the ceiling of a cave; stalagmites rise from the floor.

the Earth's surface lifts or the water table lowers, the water will drain from the caves. Where the water once shaped the caverns by eating away at their walls, ceilings, and floors, it now decorates the interiors with deposits of minerals. Drops of moisture loaded with calcium may fall from the ceiling, leave a trace of minerals behind, and gradually create a *stalactite*. Splashing on the cave floor, the minerals in each drop may contribute to the growth of a *stalagmite*. Looking like stone icicles, stalactites and stalagmites grow very slowly, perhaps no more in length each year than the thickness of this page. Other minerals carried by water into the cave color its features and help make this subterranean wilderness as beautiful as it is fragile.

(For information on safely exploring caverns, see "Caving.")

KINDS OF ROCKS

The basic elements that make up the Earth (oxygen, silicon, etc.) bind together to form dozens of *minerals* such as mica, quartz, gypsum, calcite, dolomite, and feldspar. These minerals are the building blocks of rocks, able to combine in myriad ways to create the enormous variety of rock types you'll see in the field. Geologists are able to identify the minerals that compose particular rocks by using such measures as hardness, color, and fracturing qualities as the basis of their classifications. A good rock identification book will give you the information you need to do this, too, and you may find that the delights of being a rockhound are as satisfying as being able to identify many kinds of trees and animals.

To simplify matters, geologists divide all rocks into one of three categories, depending on their origins. Every rock bears signs of the process by which

◀ Granite

it was formed, and by deciphering those clues, you can learn not only how the rocks of the backcountry came into being, but also perhaps better understand the makeup of entire geological areas.

Igneous Rocks

As we've already seen, the Earth was once so hot it was liquid. *Igneous* rocks are those in which minerals form crystals as they cool. The slower the cooling, the larger the crystals. Magma thrown up by a volcano is an *extrusive* igneous rock, meaning it cools on the surface of the Earth. Since it cools quickly, the crystals are very small, and you may need a magnifying glass to see them. Obsidian is magma that cooled so rapidly it became a kind of glass. Granite, on the other hand, is an intrusive igneous rock, meaning it cooled slowly under the surface of the earth. The crystals in granite are large and very easy to see and identify.

Sedimentary Rocks

Sedimentary rocks are formed as eroded rock particles settle out of the water in which they're transported. Layers of this sediment pile on top of one another and become compacted. Gradually, moisture percolating through the sediment deposits cementing substances such as calcium

◀ Limestone

Shale ▶

Dinosaur track in limestone ▶

carbonate, silica, or iron oxide, which act to bind the particles together. Limestone is one of the most common sedimentary rocks, often composed largely from the skeletal remains of ancient plants and animals. Small grains of sand can become sandstone. Pebbles and larger stones may become cemented together to form layers of *conglomerates*, while shale is composed primarily of fine mud. Layers of decayed animal and vegetable matter piling up in prehistoric swamps and lakes were sometimes transformed into coal or petroleum. With a sharp eye you can often find beautifully preserved fossils in sedimentary rock, especially limestone.

Metamorphic Rocks

During the mountain building process, igneous and sedimentary rocks are sometimes heated above the temperature at which their minerals can combine with other elements to form new minerals. The rocks that result are said to be *metamorphic*. For instance, shales are metamorphosed into the slate from which blackboards can be made. Limestone metamorphoses into marble. Granite will change into beautifully banded gneiss. Coal can be transformed into graphite, and graphite into diamonds.

Gneiss ▶

GEOLOGICAL/HISTORY SCALE

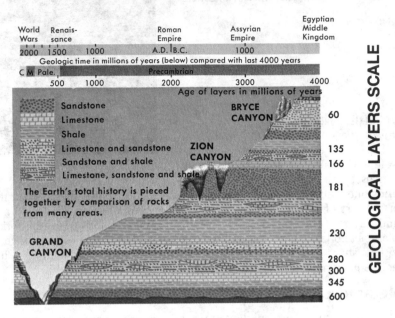

GEOLOGICAL LAYERS SCALE

World Wars, Renaissance, Roman Empire, Assyrian Empire, Egyptian Middle Kingdom

2000 1500 1000 A.D. B.C. 1000

Geologic time in millions of years (below) compared with last 4000 years

C M Pale. Precambrian

500 1000 2000 3000 4000

Age of layers in millions of years

Sandstone
Limestone
Shale
Limestone and sandstone
Sandstone and shale
Limestone, sandstone and shale

BRYCE CANYON — 60

ZION CANYON — 135, 166, 181

The Earth's total history is pieced together by comparison of rocks from many areas.

GRAND CANYON — 230, 280, 300, 345, 600

THE EFFECTS OF HUMANS ON THE EARTH

The forces of nature are astonishing in their patience and power. On the other hand, the impact of humans on the appearance and quality of the planet can be extremely swift. Practices such as dredging rivers, clear-cutting forests, strip mining, the building of highways, farming, and the expansion of cities make changes upon the face of the Earth that would take natural forces thousands of years to equal. Today we are even capable of changing the Earth's climate. Some scientists believe that excess carbon dioxide in the air insulates the Earth and may cause it to become abnormally warm, a process called the *greenhouse effect*.

As users of the Earth, it is essential for us to consider the adverse effects of human endeavors as well as the advantages they may provide, and to use good judgment in the ways we treat the planet. Other chapters of the *Fieldbook* have emphasized the importance of practicing minimum impact techniques of backcountry camping and travel. It's just as important to apply those principles to the rest of our activities, too, and care for all the Earth with the same zeal with which we protect our favorite campsites and wilderness areas.

GEOLOGIC TIME SCALE

ANIMAL TIME SCALE

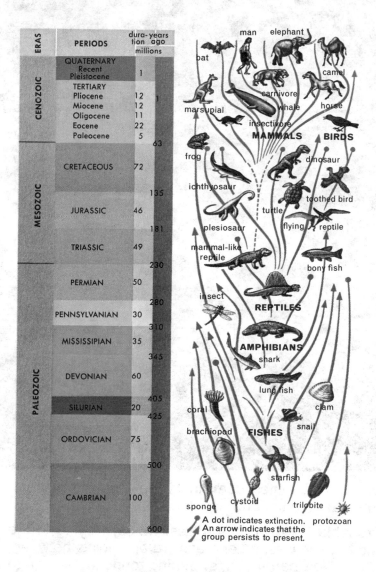

ERAS	PERIODS	dura-tion millions	years ago
CENOZOIC	QUATERNARY Recent Pleistocene	1	
CENOZOIC	TERTIARY Pliocene	12	1
CENOZOIC	Miocene	12	
CENOZOIC	Oligocene	11	
CENOZOIC	Eocene	22	
CENOZOIC	Paleocene	5	
MESOZOIC	CRETACEOUS	72	63
MESOZOIC	JURASSIC	46	135
MESOZOIC	TRIASSIC	49	181
PALEOZOIC	PERMIAN	50	230
PALEOZOIC	PENNSYLVANIAN	30	280
PALEOZOIC	MISSISSIPIAN	35	310
PALEOZOIC	DEVONIAN	60	345
PALEOZOIC	SILURIAN	20	405 / 425
PALEOZOIC	ORDOVICIAN	75	500
PALEOZOIC	CAMBRIAN	100	600

Animal labels: man, elephant, bat, camel, carnivore, whale, horse, marsupial, insectivore, MAMMALS, BIRDS, frog, dinosaur, ichthyosaur, toothed bird, turtle, plesiosaur, flying reptile, mammal-like reptile, bony fish, insect, REPTILES, AMPHIBIANS, shark, lung fish, clam, coral, snail, brachiopod, FISHES, starfish, sponge, cystoid, trilobite, protozoan

A dot indicates extinction. An arrow indicates that the group persists to present.

Courtesy of and from
GEOLOGY by Frank H. T. Rhodes, illustrated by Raymond Perlman
Copyright 1972 by Western Publishing Company, Inc.
Reprinted by permission

THE EARTH

"One of the brightest gems in the New England weather is the dazzling uncertainty of it.

"Probable nor'east to sou'west winds, varying to the southard and westard and eastard and points between; high and low barometer, sweeping round from place to place; probably areas of rain, snow, hail, and drought, succeeded or preceded by earthquakes with thunder and lightning."

Mark Twain
New England Weather Speech
December 22, 1876

Chapter

34

Weather

Donald E. Whiten
Public Affairs Officer, National
Weather Service

The atmosphere above us swirls like a great, restless sea. Jet streams streak across the sky at hundreds of miles an hour. Polar air masses spill off the ice fields and roll toward warmer climes, while hot tropical air stands so motionless a ship's sails can hang limp for days on end. Warm Chinook winds sweep out of the mountains, and thunderheads loom over the prairies like towering, electrically charged anvils.

Thunder and silence, drought and rain, the seemingly random signs of weather are everywhere. Yet weather is not a series of isolated events. It is a single, constantly changing whole as remarkable for its thousand-mile bands of storm and calm as for the narrow paths of tornadoes and lightning bolts. As you travel in the backcountry, you'll want to be able to piece together the weather clues you see, hear, and feel so that you can predict the conditions to come in the next few hours and days. To do that, it helps to understand the big picture.

THE ATMOSPHERE

Breathing it every minute of our lives, feeling it blow against our faces, and watching it move smoke, dust, sailboats, and clouds, we usually take the air around us for granted. The atmosphere rises 60 miles (97 kilometers) above the surface of the Earth, thinning until it vanishes into the vacuum of space. Composed primarily of nitrogen and oxygen, the atmosphere presses down on the surface of the earth with a force of about 15 pounds per square inch (1 kilogram per square centimeter), but we are so accustomed to feeling that weight we seldom realize it is there.

Warm air is less dense than cold air. Because of that, warm air tends to rise while colder air sinks. Think of a hot air balloon. Heated by propane burners, the molecules of nitrogen and oxygen inside the balloon spread apart until the air becomes thinner, and thus less dense, than the air

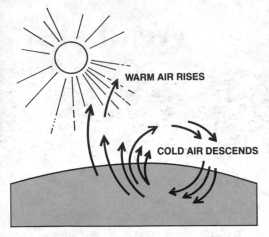

WARM AIR RISES

COLD AIR DESCENDS

outside. The heated air rises, lifting the balloon with it. A similar thing happens over a campfire; as air warms above the flames, it climbs into the sky and carries smoke and sparks high above the ground.

On a much grander scale, sunlight beating directly down heats vast regions of tropical lands and seas and these, in turn, heat the tropical atmosphere. However, the sun's rays strike the polar latitudes at a lower angle, heating ice, sea, and polar land areas to a lesser degree than at the equator. Thus air over the ice caps is colder than that above the equator. As hot tropical air lifts into the sky, cooler air from temperate latitudes moves in to fill the void. As it nears the tropics, the cold air gradually warms enough to rise, and that draws in even more polar air. Meanwhile, tropical air high in the atmosphere cools and sinks as it migrates toward the poles. Warming and rising, cooling and sinking, the cycle goes around and around. That constant, solar-powered motion is the most awesome force affecting the earth's weather. However, it is by no means the only influence; another important force is the Coriolis effect.

THE CORIOLIS EFFECT AND PREVAILING WINDS

While the Earth's great air masses are flowing from polar regions toward the tropics, the earth is rotating beneath them. As a result, the

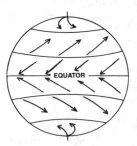

EQUATOR

winds do not appear to travel in straight lines, but rather bend to the right in the northern hemisphere and to the left south of the equator. Named the *Coriolis effect* in honor of its 19th century French discoverer, this phenomenon causes prevailing weather patterns to flow across the face of the earth in easterly and westerly directions, and at times to overlap, collide, and mesh with one another.

Weather watchers have known about these masses of moving air for centuries, and have given some of them names. Sailors since Columbus's time have let the trade winds of the tropical Atlantic push their ships west to America, and then returned to Europe in the prevailing westerlies farther north. Today's transcontinental bicyclists know they'll have the winds of the westerlies at their backs when they pedal from the Pacific toward the Atlantic, but if they go the other way they'll fight headwinds much of the time.

Polar air masses bring cold, northern air into the American heartland, and when they collide with moist air masses drifting in from the Pacific and Gulf of Mexico much of the country can expect rain or snow. Near the equator, warm air tends to rise straight up rather than moving horizontally, creating two areas of great calm called the *equatorial doldrums* and the *horse latitudes*. Sailing ships of old could languish there for weeks, waiting for a breeze to fill their slack canvas, and sometimes horses dying of the heat had to be cast overboard.

Embedded in the prevailing westerlies are *jet streams*, extremely fast currents in the flowing rivers of air. A few miles wide and some 30,000 feet (9 kilometers) above the earth, jet streams can move along at speeds of several hundred miles an hour. Aircraft pilots sometimes seek out these persistent winds and let them push their planes toward their destinations, though if they're traveling the other way they'll be careful to avoid the head-on force of a jet stream.

If the earth were smooth and composed of equal areas of land and water, the prevailing winds would blow in predictable patterns. However, the surface of the globe is irregular. Continents and oceans form ragged shapes, and their surface temperatures vary. Mountain ranges jut into the sky, while plains and deserts lie flat. Some areas are heavily forested, others bare, some light in color, some dark. As a result of all these variations, the atmosphere warms and cools unevenly, and the speeds and directions of the prevailing winds are altered by the drag of friction and by the physical barriers they encounter. Dividing, combining, weakening, and gaining strength, air masses swirl this way and that, responding to local temperature and terrain and to the presence of other air masses.

HIGHS AND LOWS

When warm, high-altitude air cools and sinks, it may form an area of high pressure known simply as a *high*. As highs take shape, barometers will rise, indicating the increase in atmospheric pressure. Since the air in a high pressure region is dense, it keeps other weather systems at bay. The skies affected by a high tend to stay clear.

However, there is only so much atmosphere blanketing the earth, and if the air is more concentrated in high pressure areas, other parts of the sky must be low pressure regions, or *lows*. As indicated by dropping barometric readings, the air in a low is less dense than that in a high, and so tends to draw winds into itself. Those winds often are laden with moisture, and as a result, lows are less stable, cloudier, and stormier than highs.

Meteorologists with access to a widely scattered network of barometers can chart the sizes and shapes of highs and lows by drawing a map with lines connecting points registering identical pressure readings. In some ways the map is similar to a topographical map. While a topo map uses *contour lines* to connect all points in an area that are the same elevation above sea level, a weather map uses lines called *isobars* to show the relationship of locations reporting the same barometric pressure. Just as contour lines expand down a mountainside, isobars ring centers of regions of high pressure, and decrease in value as they move away from the center. Likewise, isobars graph low pressure areas as valleys and deep holes in the atmosphere in much the same way contour lines indicate valleys and lowlands on maps of dry land.

(For more on contour lines and topographic maps, see "Backcountry Navigation.")

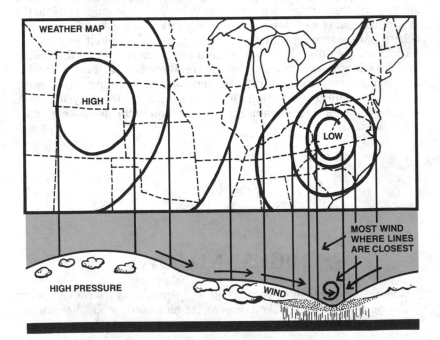

WEATHER MAP

HIGH

LOW

MOST WIND WHERE LINES ARE CLOSEST

HIGH PRESSURE

WIND

CHAPTER 34

FRONTS

If you study newspaper weather maps for several days in a row, you'll see that a continent the size of North America can contain a number of highs and lows. Some may be moving fast, perhaps pushed along by the prevailing westerlies. Others may remain relatively stationary for several days. Those moving up from the Gulf of Mexico often are loaded with moisture, while cold highs moving into the prairies between the Appalachians and Rockies are likely to be dry.

As you examine the isobars on the map, pay special attention to the lines where two air masses meet. These boundaries are known as *fronts*, and it is along fronts that many changes in weather occur. For instance, a region of cold dry air overtaking a warm moist air mass will wedge under the warm air. As the warm air rises, the moisture it carries may cool, condense, and fall as rain. If you are an observer on the ground, you'll probably notice a shift in wind direction and temperature as the front moves through and the new air mass establishes itself overhead. You can also watch changes in cloud shapes and movements, and if you know what to look for you can predict changes in the weather several hours or even a day before they occur. In the backcountry, that can be mighty important.

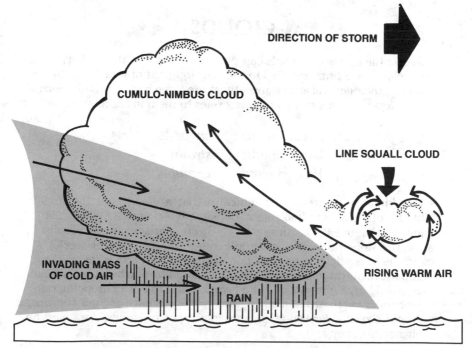

DIRECTION OF STORM

CUMULO-NIMBUS CLOUD

LINE SQUALL CLOUD

RISING WARM AIR

INVADING MASS OF COLD AIR

RAIN

Thunderstorm (cumulonimbus) clouds flattening at the top

CLOUDS

Just as the tracks of animals can give you an idea of the ecology of an area, clouds are primary clues to the development of weather patterns. Based on their general appearance, there are three basic forms of clouds—*streak*, *layer*, and *heap*. Meterologists refer to them in Latin terms.

Streak clouds:	*cirrus*
Layer clouds:	*stratus*
Heap clouds:	*cumulus*

In addition, the prefix *alto* indicates that a cloud is at the middle altitudes of the lower atmosphere, between 6,500 and 23,000 feet (2 to 7 kilometers) above the Earth's surface. (By comparison, an alto vocalist in a chorus sings notes in the middle range of the musical score.) An *altocumulus* is a fluffy heap cloud floating between 1 and 4 miles overhead.

Finally, the term *nimbus* describes any cloud from which precipitation may fall. Thus, a *nimbostratus* is a layer cloud capable of dropping rain.

By combining these Latin terms, meteorologists have devised *The International Cloud Atlas* listing 10 principle types of clouds. Arranged by their heights, they are:

CHAPTER 34

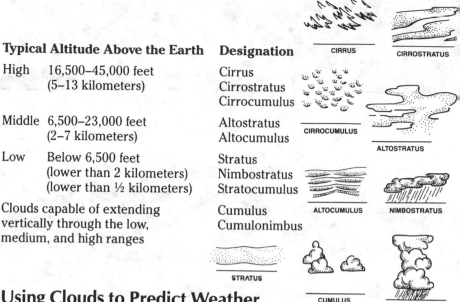

Typical Altitude Above the Earth		Designation
High	16,500–45,000 feet (5–13 kilometers)	Cirrus Cirrostratus Cirrocumulus
Middle	6,500–23,000 feet (2–7 kilometers)	Altostratus Altocumulus
Low	Below 6,500 feet (lower than 2 kilometers) (lower than ½ kilometers)	Stratus Nimbostratus Stratocumulus
Clouds capable of extending vertically through the low, medium, and high ranges		Cumulus Cumulonimbus

Using Clouds to Predict Weather

The movement of a frontal system often is heralded by a procession of different cloud types, each signaling a greater likelihood local weather conditions are about to change. The first sign of an approaching storm may be the appearance in a clear sky of high, feathery cirrus clouds sometimes called *mare's tails*. Over the course of several hours or days, they'll seem to thicken until the sun is hidden behind a thin cirrostratus veil. A grey curtain of altostratus clouds follows, and then a moist blanket of dark stratus clouds rolling close to the earth. Finally, big nimbostratus clouds, black and threatening, bring the rain.

Another, more frightening atmospheric disturbance is the thunderstorm that boils up quickly. Formed when warm, moist air rises very rapidly, gigantic cumulonimbus clouds can produce lightning, hail, or tornadoes. You'll be able to recognize a cumulonimbus cloud by its swift growth as it swells thousands of feet into the air and sometimes flattens out on top.

Of course, not all clouds signal bad weather. Cirrus clouds detached from one another and spaced at irregular intervals across the sky indicate that the weather will stay fair for a while. A "mackerel sky" formed by cirrocumulus clouds that look like the scales of a fish usually promises fair weather, but it may also bring unsettled conditions with brief showers. Backcountry travelers eager for dry trails welcome the sight of cumulus clouds, those huge masses of white fluff. However, on hot days hikers wisely keep an eye on cumulus clouds, and take cover if they begin to swell and darken into cumulonimbus thunderheads, the breeders of violent storms.

(For planning for different kinds of weather, see "Planning." For dealing with foul weather in the backcountry, see "Outdoor Safety.")

Fair weather cumulus clouds

Feathery cirrus clouds—mare's tails

Alto cumulus—mackerel sky

A curtain of altostratus clouds

**Below: A time exposure from a fire lookout tower in the
Dinosaur National Monument in Colorado**

LOCAL WEATHER

Despite these basic principles of meteorology, the conditions in your area may not match the overall patterns of prevailing winds, highs and lows, and fronts. That's because the weather in each part of the country is influenced by local terrain, bodies of water, and a host of other variables. For instance, coastal regions may be cooler and moister than territory a few miles inland. A mountain range may force warm air to rise, wringing out its moisture in the form of precipitation. Flat prairies can allow fronts to roll unimpeded for hundreds of miles.

Learning the patterns of weather in your part of the country takes time, but it can be very satisfying. Glance at the sky whenever you're outdoors, and if you're really interested, keep a daily log of the kinds of clouds you see, the direction of the wind, and the sort of weather you're having. Gradually you'll build up enough observations to see that winds from a certain direction usually indicate rain, and that clouds of a certain type mean the skies will soon be clear.

There is plenty of folklore connected with weather, and some of it contains grains of truth. "Red sky at morning, sailor take warning," goes one old saying, often valid since the brilliance of a sunrise can be caused by moisture in the air that later in the day turns to rain. "Red sky at night, sailor's delight" a sharp red sunset usually indicates that there is clear, dry air to the west, the direction from which many storms come.

Animals also play a part in weather lore. Perhaps you've heard old-timers base their predictions of the severity of an upcoming winter upon

the woolliness of caterpillars, or the thickness of squirrels' coats. Birds, their hollow bones especially sensitive to changes in atmospheric pressure, may alter their flying habits to match certain changes in the weather, and many animals are thought to become irritable, lie down, gather food, or seek shelter long before humans are aware of an approaching storm. Whether or not there is sufficient scientific data to support the claims of folklore adages, old sayings and beliefs provide a fascinating glimpse into the way weather predictions were made before the development of scientific measuring devices. And considering weather's habit of acting on its own despite what meteorologists predict it will do, folk methods sometimes seem just as accurate as any devised by modern science.

FORECASTING RESOURCES

Before embarking on a trek, it's essential to monitor radio and television weather reports and to look at forecasts in the newspaper. A knowledge of probable temperatures, wind speed, and precipitation for an area will enable you to go prepared with adequate clothing and gear. A further source of up-to-the-minute information is the National Oceanic and Atmospheric Administration (NOAA) Weather Radio. Reports are repeated every few minutes to keep listeners abreast of current atmospheric conditions. Operating on high-band FM frequencies (162.40 to 162.55 megahertz), NOAA Weather Radio transmissions can be received by special weather radio receivers and AM/FM radios equipped with a "weather band" feature. Some hikers even carry battery-powered weather radios in their packs.

"We first knew you a feeble plant which wanted a little earth whereon to grow. We gave it to you; and afterward, when we could have trod you under our feet, we watered and protected you; and now you have grown to be a mighty tree, whose top reaches the clouds, and whose branches overspread the whole land . . ."

Red Jacket, Seneca Chief, 1792

Chapter 35

Plants

Edward H. Stone
Assistant Director of Recreation
Management, U.S. Forest Service

John Rumley, Ph.D.
Professor of Botany, Montana State
University

Hiking in open country is an exhilarating experience. The sunlight, the fresh air, and the appearance of the landscape all contribute to the pleasures of a walk. As you stride down a trail, you can fill your lungs with fresh, good air and build a big appetite for that lunch you've got in your pack. Wherever you look you're likely to see green vegetation, and as you become acquainted with the world of plants you'll discover that they're responsible for much of the beauty you see, the clean air you breathe, and the food you eat.

In the leaves and stems of green plants is a substance called *chlorophyll* that reflects the green bands of the sunlight spectrum, giving the plants their color, while absorbing other wavelengths. That absorbed sunlight is important, since plants use it with carbon dioxide and water to manufacture simple, basic foods such as sugars. Called *photosynthesis*, this process also releases oxygen into the atmosphere. In fact, green plants are the only living creatures that replenish the air with significant amounts of oxygen.

(For more on photosynthesis, see "Understanding Nature.")

Despite their importance, we tend to take plants for granted and seldom stop to really appreciate the astonishing variety and complexity of the vegetation all around us. If you do take the time, though, you'll find that the quiet world of plants is full of delightful wonders and challenges. In addition to enriching your hikes, understanding all you can about plants will allow you to better comprehend the important role vegetation plays in the great scheme of the earth's ecosystems. To help identify plants, botanists have organized them into the broad categories shown on the chart.

PLANTS

ALL PLANT SPECIES	
±350,000 SPECIES	
GREEN PLANTS ±310,000	NONGREEN PLANTS ±40,000
VASCULAR ("VEINY") PLANTS ±265,000	NONVASCULAR PLANTS ±85,000
SEED-PRODUCING PLANTS ±250,000	NONSEED-PRODUCING PLANTS ±100,000

FLOWERING PLANTS ±249,000	CONIFERS & RELATIVES ±500	FERNS & RELATIVES ±14,500
MOSSES & RELATIVES ±20,000	ALGAE ±25,000	FUNGI ±40,000

The numbers on the chart indicate the approximate number of species each group contains. For example, there are about 350,000 species of plants, of which 310,000 are green plants and 40,000 are not. The six groups at the bottom of the chart have distinguishing characteristics that make them readily recognizable in the field.

Stamen < Anther
          Filament
Sepal
Receptacle

Petal
Stigma
Style > Pistil
Ovary
Peduncle

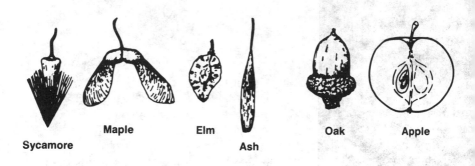

Sycamore **Maple** **Elm** **Ash** **Oak** **Apple**

Flowering Plants

Comprising more than 70 percent of all plant species, flowering plants, or *Angiosperms*, make up the bulk of most vegetation. The seeds of all the members of this group are completely enclosed within a container, or fruit. The fruit varies in form from apples and peaches to cottonwood fluff, cockleburs, and coconuts. Among the flowering plants you're likely to see along trails are grasses, broad-leaved shrubs, and leafy vines and trees that lose their foliage in the winter.

Like several other plant groups, Angiosperms contain *vascular tissues* that act as pipelines conducting fluids throughout the plants. The strings of celery, the veins of leaves, and the rings visible on tree stumps are all evidence of vascular structures.

Conifers

Conifers are *Gymnosperms*, which means their seeds are not enclosed in a fruit. Rather, as their name implies, conifers produce cones of some sort. Seeds in the cones are exposed to the air, and thus can be fertilized directly by windblown pollen. Most conifers are vascular, needle-leaved evergreen trees and shrubs including pines, spruces, firs, junipers, cedars, and yews.

Seed ▶

Cone ▶

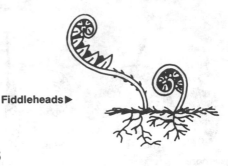

Fiddleheads▶

Ferns

Although they share with seed plants the presence of chlorophyll and vascular tissues and the production of spores, ferns reproduce without seeds. Ferns often have lacy leaves called *fronds*. Uncurling in the spring, fronds resemble the decorative ends of violins and thus are called *fiddleheads*. Boston ferns, bracken ferns, and relatives such as the club mosses, horsetails, and scouring rushes are in this group. Ferns are most abundant in moist forests.

Mosses

Mosses are small plants usually not more than a few centimeters tall, which grow in rock crevices, on forest floors and tree trunks, and along the banks of streams. They often have a small spore capsule at the end of a long stalk that rises above a leafy base. Haircap moss, apple moss, and the closely related liverworts and hornworts typify this group. Most mosses and their relatives live on land.

Fungi

Algae

Unlike mosses, algae are primarily aquatic plants. They are also non-vascular, and though they contain chlorophyll their green color often is masked by red or brown pigments. Some species thrive in fresh water, while others are at home in salty seas. Some are small enough to live in the films of moisture surrounding soil particles. Others, particularly some of the ocean dwellers, are quite large. Freshwater pond scums and marine seaweeds are algae.

Fungi

Fungi are nongreen plants, meaning they contain no chlorophyll and thus cannot manufacture their own food. Still, in their roles as parasites and decomposers they are of great ecological importance.

The bodies of fungi are masses of microscopic threads. Their spore-producing structures are readily visible as mushrooms, toadstools, the bracket-conks on many forest tree trunks, and as molds of all kinds. Many are brightly colored. Some fungi you may discover in the country are puffballs, meadow mushrooms, the death-cup toadstool, and the elfin-shelf of fir trees. Should the bread in your pack get a little old, you may even see the green mold from which penicillin is obtained.

PLANT COMMUNITIES

The chapter on "Understanding Nature" explains that *ecosystems* are composed of all the plants, animals, and natural forces interacting in one area. The plants that predominate in different ecosystems vary greatly. Plant communities you're most likely to encounter on your hikes are forests, alpine tundra, deserts, grasslands, and seashores.

FORESTS

Most forests are composed of distinct vegetational layers called *strata*. The highest stratum is dominated by tall trees whose tops may form a *forest canopy*.

Under the canopy are *intermediate strata* of woody plants shorter than the tall trees. The intermediate strata of complex temperate forests include a low tree layer and one or more shrub layers.

Below these intermediate strata is one close to the ground called the *field layer* composed of grasses and herbs. In addition, some forests have a *moss and lichen layer* on the forest floor and, sometimes, on the trunks and limbs of trees.

Although they all have strata, forests in different parts of the country differ in appearance. For example, a simple lodgepole pine forest in Yellowstone National Park consists of only two strata—the lodgepole pines themselves, and a low shrub layer of huckleberry bushes and similar brush. On the other hand, the complex riverside forests that border large streams such as Arkansas's Buffalo National River often are dominated by a strata of broad-leaved trees including cottonwood, elm, sycamore, and ash. Beneath that stands a tall shrub layer of willows, birches, and sometimes junipers; an intermediate-height shrub layer of dogwoods and short willows; and a short shrub layer of roses and snowberries. The ground may be covered with a field layer of grasses and flowering posies, and there also may be a moss stratum.

Forest Stability

If the tree seedlings and young trees of a forest are of the same species as the tall trees that make up the canopy, the forest is probably self-perpetuating, meaning that it will naturally regenerate itself unless it is destroyed by a catastrophe such as logging or a severe fire.

However, if the young trees are of species different from the tree-canopy stratum, the forest is unstable. In a process called *plant succession*, the

younger species will gradually replace the older as the dominant stratum. Sometimes a third and even a forth stratum take turns as the canopy before the forest stabilizes.

(For more on plant succession, see "Understanding Nature.")

ALPINE TUNDRA

The alpine tundra of the high mountains is a cold, windy, treeless region, its fragile vegetation consisting of low-growing grasses and flowering shrubs and herbs. Snow covers the tundra most of the year, often shortening growing seasons to a single month or two. Since plants can use moisture only when it is in liquid form, they cannot begin growing until the snow starts to melt. When it does melt, it sometimes changes to water so quickly that the tundra becomes saturated. However, relentless winds and intense sunlight quickly dry the stems and leaves of plants. The sun's ultraviolet rays inhibit the elongation of stems and leaves, dwarfing tundra plants.

In addition to surviving the harsh beating of the elements, alpine vegetation must adapt itself to one of three main habitats.

PLANTS

Level Tundra

Scattered with rocks and covered with a thin mantle of soil, tundra that is relatively flat can support meadows and rock gardens of grasses, sedges, and flowers producing a riotous display of color during the short growing season. Although the stems and leaves of these plants are dwarfed, the flowers are full-size and thus seem especially large and striking in the clear high-altitude air. Splashes of yellow often come from buttercups and glacier lilies; blue from bluebells, lupines, harebells, and forget-me-nots; red from Indian paintbrushes and anemones; white from chickweeds and sandworts; and purple from larkspurs and penstemons.

Steep Tundra

Steep mountainslopes rising toward bare, rocky peaks frequently are strewn with large boulders and the smaller stones of talus and scree. The little soil that does exist among the rocks may support communities of cushion plants. Including the pink and white pussy toes, pink moss campions, and blue forget-me-nots, their short stems and compacted leaves form small, rounded pads often bearing bright flowers. In deep clefts among the boulders, plants can grow taller than on more exposed slopes. Look for columbines and relatives of the yellow sunflower in these protected locations.

CHAPTER 35

Alpine Basins

As snowfields melt in the summer, depressions in the mountain landscape often become waterlogged. Large depressions can fill enough to form ponds or small lakes, while others are overgrown with mats of rushes and sedges interspersed with colonies of true mosses. The brownish-green appearance of these plant communities is occasionally punctuated by the white, fluffy, seedpod-tufts of cottongrass.

DESERTS

Deserts are harsh environments for all living creatures, including plants. The majority of desert plants are flowering species, and most cope with the intense heat and extreme dryness in one of three ways.

Short Lives

Desert annuals avoid the stresses of drought by leading their active lives only when moisture is available. They germinate immediately after a favorable rain. In the few days or weeks it takes these plants to use up the water supplied by that one rainfall, they grow to maturity, produce flowers and fruits, and disperse seeds that will remain dormant through

long dry spells. Annual species of fescue, grama, and three-awn grasses follow this growing pattern, as do the annual desert posies that can carpet a desert floor with dozens of species soon after a storm.

Appropriate Shapes

Long-lived perennial desert plants have above-ground parts that last from year to year, so they can't avoid heat and drought as the annuals do. Instead, they may have thin, wiry stems that do not absorb much of the sun's heat, and their leaves are small, or appear only in response to rain. Some of these drought-enduring shrubs, such as creosote bush, blackbrush, flaming sword, and some of the sagebrushes, have thorns or thorny branches protecting them from browsing desert animals.

Water Storage

During rainy periods, cacti store water in their fat, round bodies made waterproof by a coating of wax and protected by spines. Not only do the spines discourage animals, they also reflect sunlight and help maintain a blanket of cool air around each cactus stem. Familiar cacti include the giant saguaro, prickly pears or beavertails, barrels, organ pipes, and chollas.

GRASSLANDS

About a third of the interior of the United States once was covered by native grasslands. While grasslands do not have an obvious vertical strata as do forests, be alert for the patchwork, or *mosaic*, of the plant communities that occupy the prairie landscape. Differences in soil types and the angles of slopes encourage some species of plants more than others, resulting in a comparable patchwork of plant communities. Although separated by considerable distances, slopes with similar angles, exposures to the sun, and soil textures will support similar plant communities.

If you've ever traveled across America, you may have noticed that much of the prairie has been heavily cultivated. As a result, few grassland plant communities appear as they did in their original forms. Still, plant succession can occur when a grainfield is left untouched. For several years it will be colonized by weeds, gradually progressing through mixtures of weeds and meadow plants, which may at last develop into self-perpetuating plant communities.

The patterns of plant succession also are apparent when you examine the small lakes of a prairie region. In the deepest parts of a lake, aquatic plants such as ditchweed and frog's-bit are rooted in the mud. A little closer to shore are two zones of plants with roots beneath the water but stems and leaves in the open air. Pickerelweed and spatterdock grow in the deeper zone, while bulrushes, cattails, cordgrasses, and reedgrasses crowd closer to shore.

A pond shoreline often is occupied by a belt of sedges and grasses such as Kentucky bluegrass, timothy, and foxtails. Farther inland there may be a band of shrubs such as chokecherry, serviceberry, boxelder, and willow. Beyond that, one finally encounters characteristic prairie vegetation, or cultivated fields and pastures. As the pond basin becomes filled with silt, dust, and dead plant materials, the vegetation zones move closer and closer to the center, and ultimately the basin may be covered with prairie plants.

SEASHORES

Like the vegetational strata of forests, seashore plants form distinct bands arranged according to their various relationships with the tides. A good example of this is the zonation of algae.

Different species of algae thrive on different combinations of moisture and open air, and so each species attaches itself to rocks an optimum distance from the edge of the sea. Each of these horizontal algae bands is usually no more than a couple of meters wide, and each reflects the varying conditions of high and low ocean tides. The zones are known as the *tidal-spray region* above the high-tide level, the *tidal zone* located between the upper reaches of high tide and the lowest margin of low tide, and the *underwater zone*. There are also *deepwater zones* accessible to swimmers equipped with diving gear.

Tidal-Spray Zone

On the rock surfaces moistened by mists of the surf, you may find circular dark-green and blackish crusts resembling bits of dried tar. Each crust is composed of millions of microscopic blue-green algae. These hardy plants can withstand the saltiness of the sea, the hot summer sunlight, and icy winter conditions.

Tidal Zone

The tidal zone is divided into an upper and a lower band. The upper band, which is exposed to more sunlight and air than the lower, is conspicuously populated with brown algae, barnacles, and snails. Rockweeds, seaweeds with broad brown fronds, are quite common. Many have spherical flotation bladders that keep them upright when they are under the waters of high tide. At low tide, the plants are sprawled in bunches on the rocks to which they are firmly attached by short, flexible

stems and "holdfast" bases. On Pacific shores, rockweeds often have elongated tubular stems, each bearing a tuft of flat ribbon-like fronds at its tip. These rockweeds look like small palm trees, and are known appropriately as *sea palms*.

The lower band of the tidal zone usually is dominated by low, purplish tufts of red algae called *Irish moss*. This algae produces a gelatin used in making foods, toothpastes, paints, writing paper, and many other commercial items.

Underwater and Deep Water Zones

Look beneath the surface of shallow waters for red algae with very thin, broad, flat fronds purple or red in color. Along sandy beaches, you may discover pieces of deepwater algae washed ashore by waves. Very large brown algae called *kelp* can grow several meters in length and have flat or tubular bodies, often with big flotation bladders near their upper ends. Common varieties are the bullwhip and ribbon kelp, named for their shapes, and the perforated sea wracks.

Algae are not the only plants that make their homes along the sea. Large beds of eelgrass may take root in the sandy bottom, their long, green, ribbon-like leaves swaying in the currents of the offshore waters.

The Indians and pioneers of early America used so many trees, shrubs, and roots as tools, building materials, and food that their well-being often depended on a keen understanding of wilderness vegetation. While we may no longer so obviously rely on plants to fill our day-to-day needs, vegetation will always be essential for our survival. As you spend time in the out-of-doors, carry a plant identification book and use it during rest breaks to learn the names of a few plants. Before long you're likely to become so fascinated with the vegetation around you that you'll want to plan hikes especially for the purpose of studying plants.

"Neither the youngsters nor the oldsters of today are fully aware of the breadth and depth of the wild animal mind, the wonderful scope of its reasoning, or the high quality of its conclusion . . . the wild animal must think or die."

William Temple Hornaday, 1928

Chapter 36

Wildlife and Fish

Daniel A. Poole

President, Wildlife Management
Institute, Washington, D.C.;
Chairman, National Conservation
Committee, Boy Scouts of America

A flight of geese cuts through the wind high above a marsh. A lizard scampers across a dusty trail. Deer slip past a tent, curious, but always alert. Insects crawl in the ground cover and buzz about the foliage of shrubs and trees. The songs of a dozen birds filter through the woods.

They swim, creep, crawl, walk, hop, burrow, and fly. They vary in size from a fraction of an ounce to many tons. They're covered with everything from feathers and scales to skin and fur. Some travel thousands of miles a season; others spend their lives within a few square feet of soil. They are the animals of the city, farm, and backcountry, and the more you know about them the more they'll enhance your outdoor adventures.

It's great to watch a deer bounding along the edge of a forest, or see a mountain goat scrambling up a talus slope. We tend to take wild animals for granted. And yet if you keep your eyes peeled as you travel the out-of-doors, you'll discover an almost endless variety of species, all existing in intricate harmony with one another.

Confronted with such a tremendous variety of living things, zoologists have devised a system of classifying members of the animal kingdom by dividing all animals into two large groups—*vertebrates*, which have backbones, and *invertebrates*, which don't. Mammals, birds, reptiles, amphibians, and fish are vertebrates, while worms, spiders, insects, and crabs are examples of invertebrates.

Mammals

Most mammals have hair on their bodies, bear their young alive, and produce milk with which to nourish them. Mammals are warm-blooded, which means their bodies maintain a constant temperature independent of the warmth of their environment. Hair helps insulate them from the cold. Opossums, shrews, skunks, coyotes, rabbits, deer, squirrels, and mice are mammals.

Roadrunner

Birds

An *ornithologist*, a person who studies birds, groups them according to the structures of their bills, feet, wing shapes, and a variety of lesser differences. The birds you're most likely to see belong in one of two categories—those which perch and those which don't. Perching birds make up the larger group. All its members are land birds, and they vary in size from tiny kinglets to large ravens and crows. Nonperching birds include hawks, eagles, vultures, grouse, quail, waterfowl, hummingbirds, owls, and woodpeckers.

Reptiles

Reptiles are vertebrates with bony, internal skeletons and external coverings of horny plates or scales. They are cold-blooded, which means the temperature of their bodies is about the same as that of the air or water around them. Since they cannot heat or cool themselves, they are unable to function when the weather is too cold or too hot. Most produce their young from eggs, though some bear them alive. They are closely related to the dinosaurs. Lizards, snakes, turtles, and alligators are reptiles.

Amphibians

Amphibians are cold-blooded vertebrates including frogs, toads, salamanders, and newts. Combining the characteristics of both fish and

CHAPTER 36

reptiles, amphibians start life in the water as gilled aquatic larvae hatched from eggs, while the adults breathe air and generally live on land. They have soft skins and internal skeletons.

Fish

Fish are the most numerous vertebrates. Spending their entire lives in ponds, lakes, streams, and oceans, they draw water through gills to extract the oxygen they need. Fins and scales on the outside of their bodies provide mobility and protection. Most produce eggs from which their young are hatched and most are predators.

Insects and Spiders

Spiders and insects are invertebrates. Instead of backbones, they have exterior skeletons that we usually think of as shells. The shells may be very thin, as in the case of mosquitoes, or thick and hard, as with beetles.

Ants, beetles, butterflies—they're all insects. An insect is a cold-blooded animal that, in its adult form, has a body divided into a head, thorax, and abdomen. It also has three pairs of legs and usually possesses a pair of wings. Spiders, which have four pairs of legs, are related to insects but belong to a different invertebrate group. Other invertebrates include mollusks, corals, jellyfish, and worms.

ADAPTATIONS

The categories above may lead you to believe different kinds of animals have little in common with one another, but in fact they all share certain similarities. Unlike plants capable of photosynthesis, animals cannot manufacture their own food. However, many can propel themselves from one place to another, an ability most plants lack. By moving about, they can go to sources of food.

In at least one regard, though, animals are like plants, for each is uniquely adapted to its own niche in a specific environment. Each is perfectly equipped to feed, protect, and reproduce itself as long as the environment in which it lives undergoes no drastic changes.

To realize the astonishing perfection with which animals adapt, you need only think of an animal outside its accustomed niche. Try to imagine a hummingbird diving out of the sky to snatch a fish in its claws and lift it to a nest high on a distant cliff. Now imagine a bald eagle hovering motionless above a field of flowers, sipping nectar from the throat of an avalanche lily.

Of course, the idea is absurd. Eagles are adapted to soaring, diving, and hunting. Their sharp talons are shaped for clutching prey, their beaks for tearing it apart. Their broad wings help them ride currents of air, and the keenness of their vision allows them to spot the slight motions of animals far below. Even the remote locations of their nests help them adapt, for they allow adults hunting for food to leave their fledglings safe from predators.

Hummingbirds, on the other hand, have survived through the ages because they have adapted to fill their own niche in the environment. Their nervous energy, ability to hover, speed in flight, long beaks, and tiny nests are very different from the characteristics of eagles, but just as important to hummingbirds as talons and sharp eyes are to birds of prey.

As you study animals, consider the ways in which each adapts to the conditions of its environment. Among the most obvious things to watch for are color and shape, body covering, mobility, diet, and reproductive habits.

Color and Shape

The walking stick is an insect that mimics the twigs of the trees on which it lives. Unaware of its presence, tiny insects upon which the walking stick feeds come close enough for it to snatch them. Likewise, the walking stick's camouflage keeps it hidden from birds that would feed on it.

Many fish have dark backs difficult to see from above, and pale bellies that, when seen from below, blend with the color of the sky. The tawny color of deer allows them to blend into the underbrush, and the spots on a fawn increase its camouflage. A chameleon changes its color to match that of its surroundings. The ptarmigan is a mountain bird whose brown summer plumage turns white when the snows begin to fall. Also white in the winter, the fur of the arctic hare takes on the earthy hues of the tundra when summer rolls around.

Not all animals are colored to blend with the background. Many birds display brilliant plumage, some insects are quite colorful, and the bright red, yellow, and black bands of the poisonous coral snake may serve to warn the unwary.

◀ An Otter is hard to see on land or on the water.

Mobility

Animals which depend primarily on speed for survival are quick to be startled. Trout in a stream dart so swiftly they seem almost to disappear at a glance. Small animals such as field mice, cottontails, and ground squirrels run broken patterns difficult for a pursuer to follow. Mountain goats and marmots clamber up cliffs other animals cannot ascend. Prairie dogs, badgers, woodchucks, and pikas dive for the safety of their burrows.

Body Covering

A turtle cannot readily flee danger, but it can draw itself into the protection of its tough shell. A porcupine does not move very quickly, but its quills will discourage all but the most persistent pursuers. Although it has a soft underbelly, an armadillo can curl into a ball and present an attacker with nothing but bony armor plate.

Body covering is important for reasons other than protection from predators. The fur of mammals can insulate them against the cold and protect them from the scratches of thorny underbrush. Plumules of down keep many species of waterfowl warm, and outer feathers rich with natural oils shed moisture before it can dampen the down. The scales on the underbellies of snakes allow them the traction they need for motion, and the sleek hides of beavers, seals, and other aquatic mammals help them slip smoothly through the water.

Insect-eating armadillos aren't bothered by stings or bites.

Reproductive Habits

Consider the circumstances under which any species lives and you can make a good guess how prolific it must be to maintain its population. Eaten by the thousand by coyotes, foxes, birds of prey, and other predators, deer mice reproduce in vast numbers to ensure that enough of their offspring survive to breed for the next generation. Grizzly bears, on the other hand, have few natural enemies, and each bear needs plenty of territory in which to roam. Thus a mother bear may give birth to only one or two cubs every other year or so.

HABITATS

If you were to start at sea level and hike to the summit of a distant mountain, you would pass through a number of distinct environmental bands, or zones, composed of plants and animals especially adapted to the conditions that exist in a particular area. The "Plants" chapter discusses zones with vegetation in mind; the animals that inhabit these different environments are as uniquely suited to each area as are the plants.

(For more on zones of vegetation, see "Plants.")

Aquatic Ecosystem

Many animals live their entire lives in the waters of oceans, lakes, rivers, and streams. The most obvious members of the aquatic community are fish, but many other animals make the water their home, too—everything from the tiny crustaceans you see scurrying along the muddy bank of a stream to pods of whales that sometime come near enough a coastline for you to watch them.

Aquatic animals belong to food chains similar to those of wildlife on land. Large animals feed on smaller ones, which, in turn, eat plants. The remains of plants and animals sink to stream and lake beds and the floor of the ocean to become the nutrients on which plants thrive.

▲ Hermit crab

Shore Ecosystem

If you've ever camped near a woodland pond, you've probably heard the deep, rhythmic croaking of frogs. They begin life as eggs in the water, then tadpoles, but as adults they come onto the land. Dragonflies lay their eggs in water, and are aquatic in the larval stage of their development. Beavers come ashore to fell trees for food and building materials, but spend most of their time in and around ponds and streams. Some coastal animals have adapted their habits to the rise and fall of tides. Fiddler crabs, seagulls, and sandpipers feed on morsels washed ashore by incoming tides.

◀Prairie grouse

Between the shores and the mountains, a hiker may encounter grasslands, deserts, forests, chaparral, or combinations of these.

Grassland Ecosystem

Grasslands tend to be open country. There are few trees for climbing or nesting, and visibility is good. Prairie vegetation provides food for grazers such as jackrabbits, prairie dogs, and pronghorns, and the grazers themselves become food for coyotes, hawks, and other carnivores. Many grassland animals rely on their quickness to survive, and some form flocks or herds to increase their safety.

Desert Ecosystem

Just as desert plants cope with heat and scant water, the animals in arid regions must also adapt. Many are nocturnal, active only in the cool of the night. Some, such as the trap-door spider, stay in dark burrows beneath the hot surface of the earth. Lizards hide during the day in the shadows of cliffs and cacti, dashing about at night to feed on insects. The armored

◀Desert peccary

skin of a horned lizard helps slow the evaporation of its body moisture even as it discourages animals that would prey upon it. The open spaces of the desert permit the sidewinder, a snake, its unconventional mode of mobility.

Forest Ecosystem

In contrast to deserts and grasslands, forests offer an abundance of cool shade, moisture, underbrush, and dense stands of trees. A forest is a good place to observe the vertical strata of animals. Birds and some flying and climbing insects inhabit the treetops. Lower, where the tree branches are thicker, squirrels, opossums, honeybees, and many midsize birds thrive. The surface of the earth is home for a great variety of animals including bears, snakes, chipmunks, elk, deer, and grouse. Insects, spiders, and salamanders crawl about in the leaves, needles, and humus on the forest floor, while worms, moles, and quite a few reptiles burrow beneath the soil.

▲ Tree squirrel

Alpine Ecosystem

Above the forests, the alpine zone of mountains is a cold, harsh environment much of the year. During the short summer you're likely to hear the whistles of marmots and pikas, and see them sunning on distant boulders. Swallows, mountain goats, nutcrackers, and dozens of other high-altitude animals thrive in the summer warmth. Some have adapted to the great variations in season by resorting to migration (such as swallows) or hibernation (such as marmots).

MIGRATION

Watch any plant and animal community through a full year, and you'll see a variety of animals moving through it. The environment in which an animal lives is only inhabitable while conditions remain within certain bounds. In the winter, many animals cannot endure the cold and snow of high alpine meadows. However, as the drifts melt and plants make the most of the short growing season, deer, elk, and mountain goats in search of good grazing or browse will move up from the protection of the forests where they have wintered. With them come predators—mountain lions, cougars, bobcats, following their own food sources. Vultures, ravens, magpies and other scavengers drift higher, too, waiting to pick at the remains of the carnivores' meals.

Some animals migrate great distances. Ducks and geese wing their way along the four main continental flyways as they travel from summer breeding grounds in Canada and Alaska to winter havens in the southern United States, Mexico, and South America. Monarch butterflies also migrate, as do whales and bluefish. In order to lay and fertilize their eggs, salmon thrash upstream from the ocean to the headwaters of the same streams in which they were hatched.

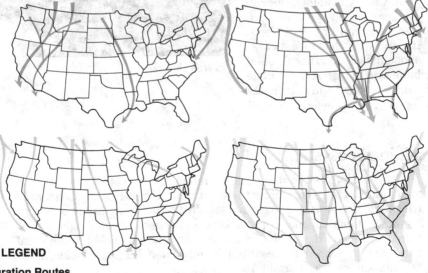

LEGEND

Migration Routes

 Seabirds, Gulls, and Terns

 Shore and Wading Birds

 Waterfowl

 Land Birds and Birds of Prey

HIBERNATION

In the autumn, as the water temperature of a pond drops, cold-blooded frogs burrow into the mud beneath the water. Buried deep enough to be safe from freezing, they undergo complex physiological changes that cause their metabolism, circulation, and other bodily processes to slow until the frogs expend just enough energy to keep themselves alive. They pass the winter in deep slumber, emerging from the mud only when the temperatures of spring have risen high enough for them to again thrive in the water and on shore.

Bears and chipmunks preparing to hibernate eat voraciously through the summer to put on a surplus of body fat before they bed down in their dens and burrows. Ground squirrels and a few other hibernating animals do become active on warm winter days, but most sleep right through the snowy months. By the time they awaken in the spring, they may have lost up to a third of their body weight.

CARRYING CAPACITY

In order to survive, every animal must have sufficient food, water, cover, and living space. The ability of a particular environment to satisfy those needs is called its *carrying capacity*. A given area of land can supply the needs of just so many animals. When the population of one or more species in any area becomes greater than the area can support, some of the animals must move elsewhere or die.

A given land area can support so much wildlife.

More species must leave or die.

The carrying capacity of an area is constantly changing. For example, a plot of rangeland may for several years receive enough sunlight and rain to produce plenty of grass and foliage upon which cottontails thrive. Since their food supplies are plentiful, the cottontail population increases, and so do the populations of coyotes, hawks, and great horned owls, which prey upon the cottontails. For a time the land is able to support larger-than-normal animal populations.

A year of drought can drastically reduce the amount of foliage on which cottontails feed, and many vegetarian animals will die of starvation and disease or leave the area in search of better feeding grounds. The reduction in the cottontail population will soon be reflected in decreases in the numbers of the predators dependent upon cottontails for food.

Even if the production of vegetation remains constant, the rabbit population may grow so large there simply won't be enough food to go around. Those animals that cannot adapt to the crowded conditions must leave or die, for, like a bucket full of water, a natural environment can hold only so many animals.

DISRUPTING AGENTS

Like the drought that limits the food supplies of cottontails, there are many natural occurrences that serve to disrupt the environment to which an animal is adapted. Some are drastic. The eruption of Mount St. Helens destroyed many miles of forest and buried rangelands with ash. Lightning strikes can start forest fires that burn the habitats of many woodland animals. An early winter may catch some animals unprepared for migration or hibernation. A flood will wash away the homes of beavers and the feeding grounds of fish.

While natural disruptions can affect many animals and alter the carrying capacities of different environments, they often play important roles in maintaining the healthy balance of wildlife populations. Unfortunately, the same cannot always be said for the disruptions caused by humans.

In the past, overhunting has severely reduced the numbers of animals such as buffalo. The passenger pigeon, a magnificent wild bird that once thrived in the eastern United States, was driven into extinction by market hunters. While laws today protect many endangered and threatened species, some thoughtless persons still shoot them or destroy their habitat.

A less obvious but perhaps even greater threat to the survival of wild animals is man's destruction of their habitats. Water pollution upsets entire food chains, and lessens the carrying capacity of lakes and streams. Industrial and power plant smokestack emissions may cause rain to become sufficiently acidic to harm vegetation and pollute water far from the source of emissions. Pesticides used by farmers and ranchers sometimes kill harmless insects as well as crop pests. Chemicals may cause the eggs of some birds to become so thin that they break before the chicks are ready to hatch. The reproductive processes of adult animals may also be impaired.

The development of wild lands puts another tremendous strain on the ability of animals to survive. Undisturbed shorelines and timbered valleys become towns and cities with paved streets and seeded lawns. Grasslands turn into fields of corn and wheat. Mountain forests fall to the logger's saw. Dams and irrigation projects flood areas that were once arid, and make dry those which were moist. Animals must adapt to the new conditions or disappear.

Fortunately, there are hopeful signs. In addition to laws protecting endangered species, generations of Americans have had the wisdom to set aside vast tracts of unspoiled land and protect them in the form of parks, wilderness areas, forests, and wildlife habitats. And as people have come to realize the effects their actions can have upon the environment, many have tried to improve the ways in which they dispose of wastes, expand their cities, and use undeveloped lands.

We all have a vital part to play in the future of wildlife. As a species, humans must adapt to new conditions, too, just as other animals do. In a rapidly changing world, a part of that adaptation is seeing with new wisdom the importance of wild animals and healthy habitats. It is up to us to live our lives in harmony with the land and the animals it supports.

(For more on conserving natural resources, see "Reducing Our Impact.")

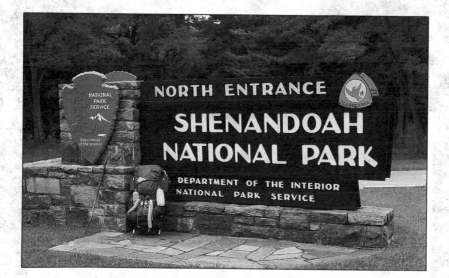

"How hard to realize that every camp of men or beast has this glorious starry firmament for a roof! In such places standing alone on the mountaintop it is easy to realize that whatever special nests we make—leaves and moss like the marmots and birds, or tents or piled stone—we all dwell in a house of one room—the world with the firmament for its roof—and are sailing the celestial spaces without leaving any track."

John Muir, 1838-1914

Chapter 37

The Night Sky

Von Del Chamberlain
Director, Hansen Planetarium, Salt
Lake City, Utah; Former Astronomer,
National Air and Space Museum,
Washington, D.C.

D. David Batch
Astronomer, Michigan State University

Raymond E. White, Ph.D.
Professor of Astronomy, University
of Arizona

Have you ever awakened in the middle of the night in the back-country, crawled out of your tent, and looked at the sky? Far from the lights of cities, the black sheen of the heavens blazes with stars, a few planets, the glowing expanse of the Milky Way, and the occasional fiery streaks of meteors. The great constellations wheel slowly overhead, and if you're lucky you may even see a comet or the pale, luminous veils of the northern lights.

For thousands of years, people have gazed at the night sky with wonder and awe. In ancient times, some believed the sky was a gigantic over-turned bowl, and that the stars were holes poked in it that allowed points of light to shine through. Others thought the stars were lamps suspended by chains from a dark celestial roof. Almost everyone was convinced that the Earth was the center of the universe, and that heavenly bodies revolved around it. As they studied the patterns of the stars, early skywatchers drew imaginary lines from star to star, outlining the shapes of objects, animals, and gods. Some of their names for these constellations are familiar to us today.

Despite their limited resources, there were those among our ancestors who developed a sophisticated understanding of the cosmos. Stonehenge, a ring of mammoth boulders built several thousand years ago on the plains of southern England, may well have functioned partly as a prehistoric observatory used to record important positions of the sun and moon, and perhaps even to predict eclipses. Some Egyptian pyramids were erected with features in line with certain stars, as were some of Central America's Mayan temples.

However, not until about 450 years ago did astronomers begin to agree that the Sun, not the Earth, was the hub of the universe. And it wasn't until well into this century that they realized the Sun was not in the middle of everything either, but rather was just one of billions of stars in but one of billions of galaxies.

While we no longer believe the stars dangle from chains, or that the Sun is a fiery chariot driven by the gods and pulled across the sky by horses, our growing knowledge of what the universe is really like makes the heavens all the more astonishing. The next time you look up at the sky from your darkened campsite, let yourself sense the immensity and magnificent complexity of possible planetary systems amid the countless galaxies, and share humankind's ancient awe and wonder in so remarkable a creation. As you study the stars, you will appreciate their grandeur and more fully treasure our world and the universe through which it spins.

STAR CHARTS

Map makers looking down from a hilltop can be quite sure that the lay of the land before them will appear essentially the same if they come back in an hour or a week or 10 years. Using the north-south lines of longitude and the east-west lines of latitude, they can pinpoint the location of any natural feature on the face of the Earth, and make maps to guide others to it.

The hilltop upon which a stargazer stands is a moving observation platform, rotating and tipping up and down as the Earth revolves around the Sun. Even though most celestial features are far more permanent than terrestial ones, our point of view is constantly moving, and thus different star charts are necessary to reflect the appearance of the sky overhead at different hours of the night and during different seasons of the year.

The 12 charts in this chapter indicate the locations of selected stars as they appear at 2-hour intervals, or for a given time of the night each month. They show the sky as seen from a vantage point of latitude 40 degrees north, and the times on the charts are local standard or daylight savings times. These charts are useful for naked-eye observing in most of the United States, though skywatchers in the extreme southern portions of the country and in nations farther north or south should consult the references at the end of the Fieldbook to learn of charts that will more accurately portray the heavens as seen from their latitudes.

The center of each chart corresponds with the zenith of the sky (the point directly overhead), and is marked with a small cross. Stars are shown as dots, the size of each dot indicating the apparent brightness of the star. Names of selected stars are in lowercase letters, while constellation names and certain shapes within constellations are identified with capital letters. Dotted lines will help you recognize shapes formed by the stars in each constellation (the outline of the Big Dipper, for example), and dashed lines reveal helpful patterns formed by the stars of several constellations (for instance the summer and winter triangles). Solid-line arrows suggest useful ways of moving your eyes from star to star around the sky.

The horizon, that line where the sky appears to touch the ground, is the circle bordering each chart. Silhouettes suggest features commonly seen on the actual horizon. Marked around the margins of each chart are the directions north, south, east, and west.

A few additional labels locate objects of special interest:

Dbl—Double Star

On a very clear, dark night, look at the second star in the handle of the Big Dipper. Known as Mizar, this bright star has a faint companion near it named Alcor. Mizar and Alcor revolve around one another in what is called a *binary system*.

Unlike binary stars, *optical* double stars only appear to be paired. In fact, they may be many light years from one another, but by coincidence are in nearly the same line of sight from Earth.

OCl—Open Cluster of Stars

Open clusters of stars are groups of stars bound loosely together by gravity. They are especially delightful when seen through binoculars or a small telescope. The most famous example is the Pleiades.

Nb—Nebula

A nebula is an enormous cloud of glowing gas and dust. Evidence indicates that these clouds condense to form stars. A portion of the "sword" in the constellation Orion is a beautiful nebula visible to the naked eye

Orion ▶

THE NIGHT SKY

◄ **Milky Way**

Glx—Galaxy

A galaxy is a swarm of billions of stars swirling together through space. The Sun and Earth are part of the Milky Way Galaxy, and when you see the luminous band of the Milky Way overhead you're actually looking through the disk of your home galaxy.

Charting Star Locations

By using imaginary lines called *vertical circles*, astronomers have developed an accurate method of pinpointing the locations of stars. Imagine looking up at the sky from inside a round birdcage; the metal bars rising to meet at the zenith of the cage are similar to the vertical circles arcing from the horizon through the zenith of the night sky.

On flat star charts, vertical circles appear as straight lines radiating from the zenith to the horizon. By tracing such a line through a star, you can state the star's position in the sky according to its *azimuth* and *altitude*.

Azimuth indicates the point at which a vertical circle reaches the horizon, and it is noted in the same manner as the 360° of a compass. An azimuth of 0° corresponds to north on the horizon, while an azimuth of 180° is straight south, and so on. On January the azimuth of Sirius, the brightest star in the sky, is 222°. A vertical circle drawn from the zenith through Sirius will touch the horizon a little south of southeast.

After you have determined a star's azimuth, you should chart its position upward along the line of the vertical circle. This is the star's altitude above the horizon. Measured from zenith to the horizon, the angle of any vertical circle is 90°. At 9 P.M. in early January, the altitude of Sirius is about 30° above the horizon, meaning it is approximately a third of the way up the sky. Since the stars seem to be moving, both their altitudes and azimuths will change through the night, necessitating different charts for different hours of star study.

CHAPTER 37

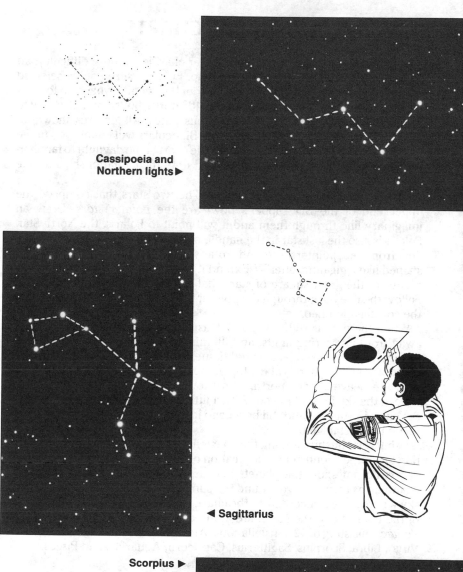

Cassipoeia and Northern lights ▶

◀ Sagittarius

Scorpius ▶

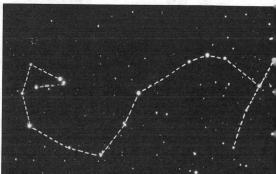

THE NIGHT SKY

USING THE CHARTS

Once you get the hang of it, using a star chart is no more difficult than finding landmarks on a topographic map. First, be sure you've selected the correct chart for the month and hour of the evening you wish to view the sky. Each chart is drawn for latitude 40° north, but should be useful to stargazers anywhere in the 48 contiguous states. All features shown on the charts are visible to the unaided eye. Binoculars will enable you to see celestial objects even better. Look over the chart in the daylight to familiarize yourself with its major features, and note their relationships to one another.

For example, locate the Big Dipper. The two stars that comprise the upper end of the Big Dipper's bowl are the *pointer stars*. Draw an imaginary line through them and it will point to Polaris, the North Star. Polaris is also the last star in the handle of the Little Dipper. Lengthen the line from the pointers through Polaris, and it will enter Cassiopeia, shaped like a gigantic letter W. Extend it further, and the line will touch a corner of the great square of stars that makes up the body of Pegasus. Follow the line back through the pointer stars and beyond, and you'll find the constellation Leo.

When the time is right for a star feast, find an open observation spot away from interfering lights, and illuminate the chart with a flashlight, ideally one with a red lens or red tissue paper covering the end. Notice that north on the chart is at the top of the page. In order to orient the map with the heavens, face north, turn the book upside down, and hold it toward the sky in front of you. With a little practice, you'll be able to hold the chart in your lap and still be able to imagine how the dots on the page relate to the stars above.

Using relationships among the constellations, work from one constellation to another, confirming the location of each on the chart. Note that the charts do not show the planets because their positions are constantly changing as they revolve around the sun. If you see a bright object in the sky where none is recorded on the chart, it is probably a planet. The paths of the planets and the Moon are along a narrow band of sky called the *Zodiac* consisting of 12 constellations: Aries, Taurus, Gemini, Cancer, Leo, Virgo, Libra, Scorpius, Sagittarius, Capricorn, Aquarius, and Pisces.

Star charts on pages 587-98 are courtesy of
D. David Batch, Abrams Planetarium, Michigan State
University, East Lansing, Michigan.

CHAPTER 37

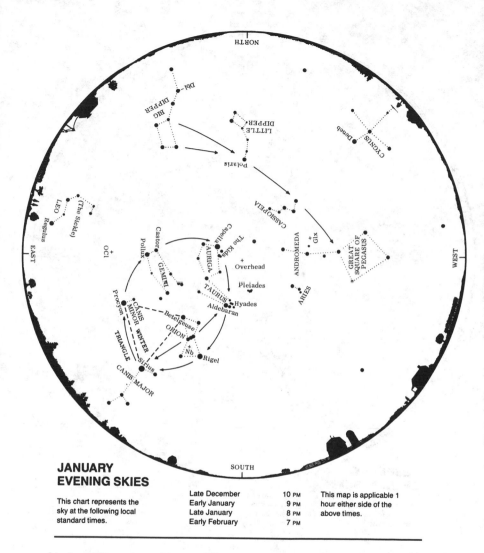

**JANUARY
EVENING SKIES**

This chart represents the
sky at the following local
standard times.

Late December	10 PM	This map is applicable 1
Early January	9 PM	hour either side of the
Late January	8 PM	above times.
Early February	7 PM	

At chart time nine objects of first magnitude or brighter are visible. In order of brightness they are Sirius, Capella, Rigel, Procyon, Betelgeuse, Aldebaran, Pollux, Deneb, and Regulus.

The double star (Dbl) at the bend of the handle of the Big Dipper is easily detected. The famous Orion Nebula, a cloud of gas and dust out of which stars are forming, is marked (Nb) in that constellation. The open or galactic star cluster (OCl) known as the *Beehive* can be located between the Gemini twins and Leo. The position of an external star system, called the *Andromeda Galaxy* after the constellation in which it appears, also is indicated (Glx).

THE NIGHT SKY

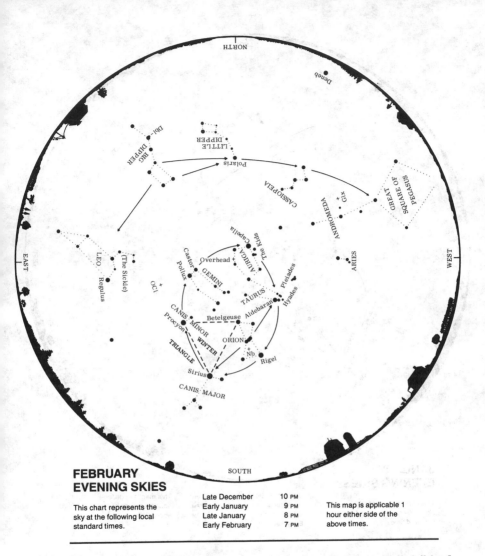

**FEBRUARY
EVENING SKIES**

This chart represents the
sky at the following local
standard times.

Late December	10 PM
Early January	9 PM
Late January	8 PM
Early February	7 PM

This map is applicable 1
hour either side of the
above times.

At chart time nine objects of first magnitude or brighter are visible. In order of brightness they are Sirius, Capella, Rigel, Procyon, Betelgeuse, Aldebaran, Pollux, Deneb, and Regulus.

The double star (Dbl) at the bend of the handle of the Big Dipper is easily detected. The famous Orion Nebula, a cloud of gas and dust out of which stars are forming, is marked (Nb) in that constellation. The open or galactic star cluster (OCl) known as the *Beehive* can be located between the Gemini twins and Leo. The position of an external star system, called the *Andromeda Galaxy* after the constellation in which it appears, also is indicated (Glx).

CHAPTER 37

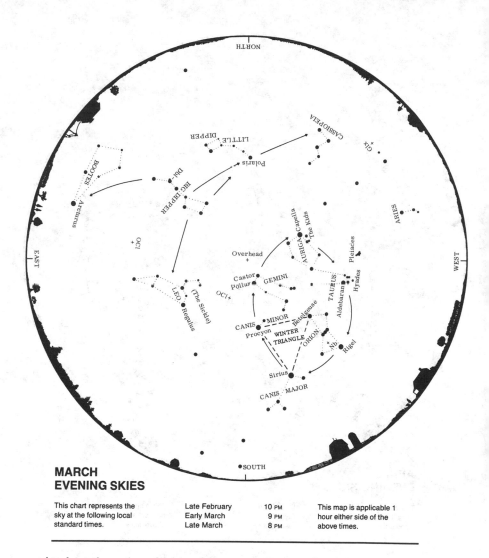

MARCH
EVENING SKIES

This chart represents the sky at the following local standard times.	Late February	10 PM	This map is applicable 1 hour either side of the above times.
	Early March	9 PM	
	Late March	8 PM	

At chart time nine objects of first magnitude or brighter are visible. In order of brightness they are Sirius, Arcturus, Capella, Rigel, Procyon, Betelgeuse, Aldebaran, Pollux, and Regulus.

The double star (Dbl) at the bend of the handle of the Big Dipper is easily detected. The famous Orion Nebula, a cloud of gas and dust out of which stars are forming, is marked (Nb) in that constellation. The open or galactic star cluster (OCl) known as the *Beehive* can be located between the Gemini twins and Leo. Coma Berenices, *the hair of Berenice,* is another open cluster (OCl) between Leo and Bootes.

THE NIGHT SKY

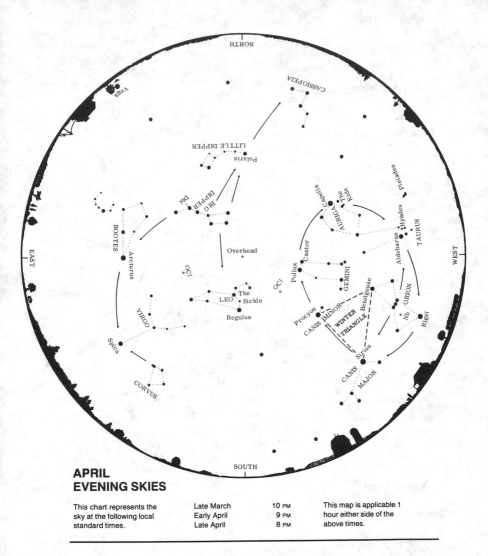

**APRIL
EVENING SKIES**

This chart represents the sky at the following local standard times.	Late March	10 PM	This map is applicable 1 hour either side of the above times.
	Early April	9 PM	
	Late April	8 PM	

At chart time 11 objects of first magnitude or brighter are visible. In order of brightness they are Sirius, Arcturus, Vega, Capella, Rigel, Procyon, Betelgeuse, Aldebaran, Spica, Pollux, and Regulus.

The double star (Dbl) at the bend of the handle of the Big Dipper is easily detected. The famous Orion Nebula, a cloud of gas and dust out of which stars are forming, is marked (Nb) in that constellation. The open or galactic star cluster (OCl) known as the *Beehive* can be located between the Gemini twins and Leo. Coma Berenices, *the hair of Berenice,* is another (OCl) between Leo and Bootes.

CHAPTER 37

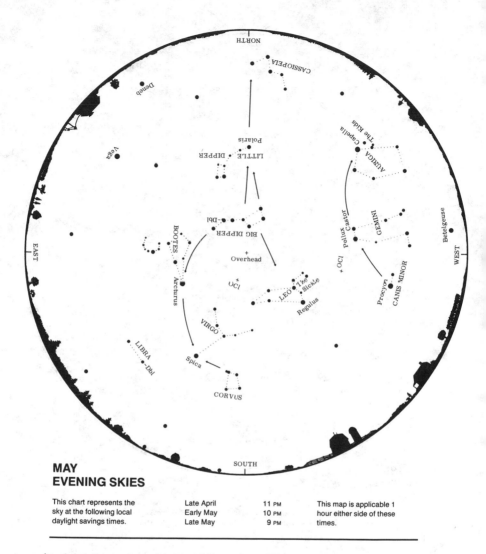

**MAY
EVENING SKIES**

This chart represents the sky at the following local daylight savings times.	Late April	11 PM	This map is applicable 1
	Early May	10 PM	hour either side of these
	Late May	9 PM	times.

At chart time nine objects of first magnitude or brighter are visible. In order of brightness they are Arcturus, Vega, Capella, Procyon, Betelgeuse, Saturn,* Spica, Pollux, Deneb, and Regulus.

The double star (Dbl) at the bend of the handle of the Big Dipper is easily detected. The open or galactic cluster (OCl) known as the *Beehive* can be located between the Gemini twins and Leo. Coma Berenices, *the hair of Berenice,* is another open cluster (OCl) between Leo and Bootes.

*Planets are not shown because their locations change.

THE NIGHT SKY

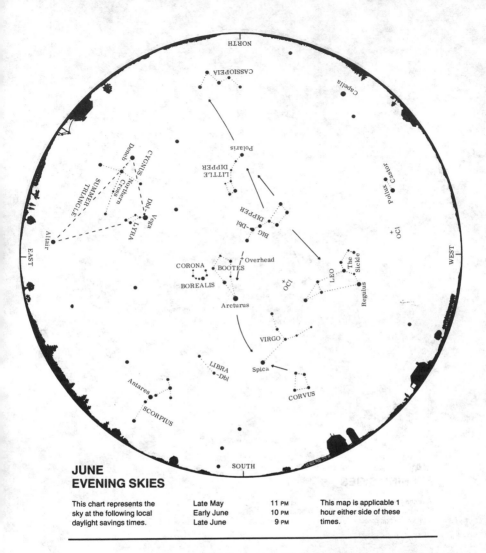

**JUNE
EVENING SKIES**

This chart represents the sky at the following local daylight savings times.	Late May	11 PM	This map is applicable 1 hour either side of these times.
	Early June	10 PM	
	Late June	9 PM	

At chart time nine objects of first magnitude or brighter are visible. In order of brightness they are Arcturus, Vega, Capella, Altair, Antares, Spica, Pollux, Deneb, and Regulus.

The double star (Dbl) at the bend of the handle of the Big Dipper is easily detected. The double star in Libra is more challenging. Much more difficult is the double star near Vega. The open or galactic cluster (OCl) known as the *Beehive* can be located between the Gemini twins (Pollux and Castor) and Leo. Coma Berenices is another open cluster (OCl) between Leo and Bootes.

CHAPTER 37

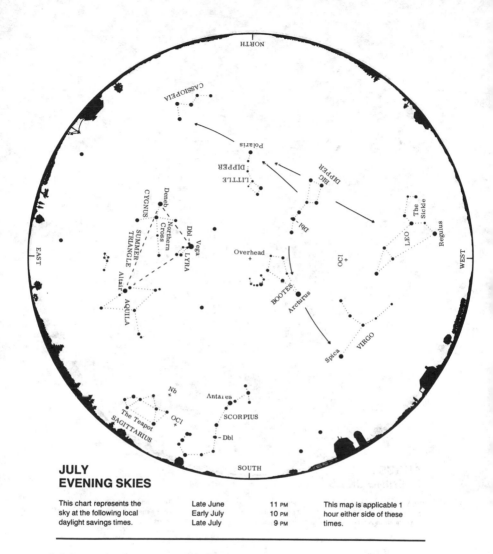

JULY
EVENING SKIES

This chart represents the sky at the following local daylight savings times.	Late June	11 PM	This map is applicable 1 hour either side of these times.
	Early July	10 PM	
	Late July	9 PM	

At chart time seven objects of first magnitude or brighter are visible. In order of brightness they are Arcturus, Vega, Altair, Antares, Spica, Deneb, and Regulus.

The double star (Dbl) at the bend of the handle of the Big Dipper is easily detected. The double in Scorpius is somewhat harder. Much more difficult is the double star near Vega in Lyra. The open or galactic cluster (OCl) Coma Berenices is located between Leo and Bootes. A more compact open cluster is located between Sagittarius and the "tail" of Scorpius. Nearby, marked (Nb) above the "spout" of the "Teapot," is the Lagoon Nebula, a cloud of gas and dust out of which stars are forming.

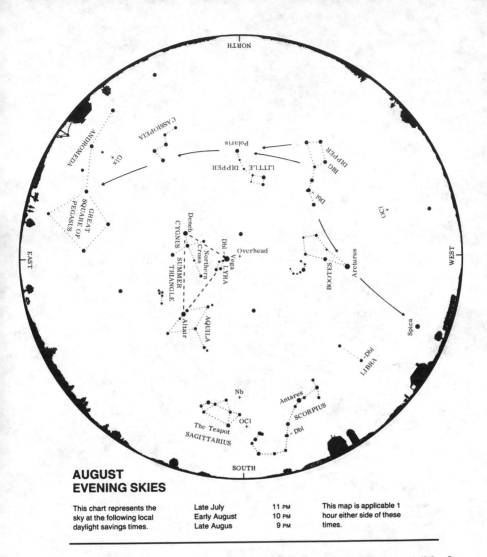

**AUGUST
EVENING SKIES**

This chart represents the sky at the following local daylight savings times.	Late July	11 PM	This map is applicable 1 hour either side of these times.
	Early August	10 PM	
	Late Augus	9 PM	

At chart time seven objects of first magnitude or brighter are visible. In order of brightness they are Arcturus, Vega, Altair, Antares, Spica, and Deneb.

The double star (Dbl) at the bend of the handle of the Big Dipper is easily detected. The double star in Scorpius is somewhat harder. The open or galactic cluster (OCl) Coma Berenices is located between Leo and Bootes. A more compact open cluster is located between Sagittarius and the "tail" of Scorpius. Nearby, marked (Nb) above the "spout" of the "Teapot," is the Lagoon Nebula. The position of an external star system, called the *Andromeda Galaxy,* also is indicated (Glx).

CHAPTER 37

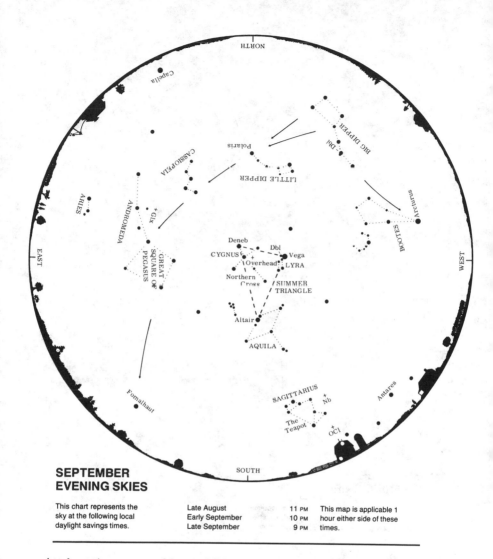

SEPTEMBER EVENING SKIES

This chart represents the sky at the following local daylight savings times.	Late August	11 PM
	Early September	10 PM
	Late September	9 PM

This map is applicable 1 hour either side of these times.

At chart time seven objects of first magnitude or brighter are visible. In order of brightness they are: Arcturus, Vega, Capella, Altair, Antares, Fomalhaut, and Deneb.

An open or galactic cluster (OCl) located below Sagittarius, low in the south-southwest, will challenge the unaided eye. Nearby, marked (Nb) above the "spout" of the "Teapot," is the Lagoon Nebula, a cloud of gas and dust out of which stars are forming. The position of an external star system, called the *Andromeda Galaxy* after the constellation in which it appears, also is indicated (Glx).

THE NIGHT SKY

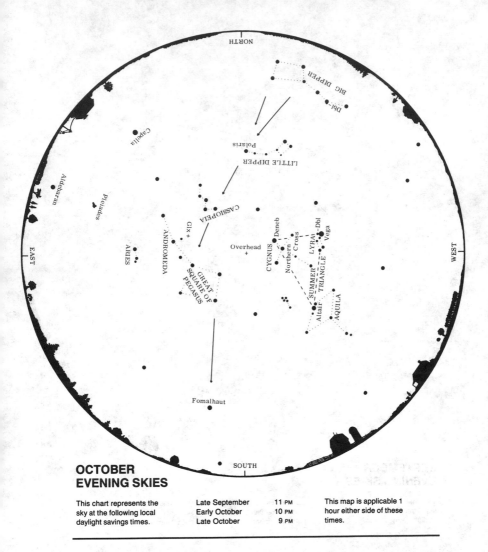

OCTOBER
EVENING SKIES

This chart represents the sky at the following local daylight savings times.	Late September	11 PM	This map is applicable 1 hour either side of these times.
	Early October	10 PM	
	Late October	9 PM	

At chart time six objects of first magnitude or brighter are visible. In order of brightness they are Vega, Capella, Altair, Aldebaran, Fomalhaut, and Deneb.

The double star (Dbl) at the bend of the handle of the Big Dipper is easily detected. Much more difficult is the double star near Vega in Lyra. The position of an external star system, called the *Andromeda Galaxy* after the constellation in which it appears, also is indicated (Glx).

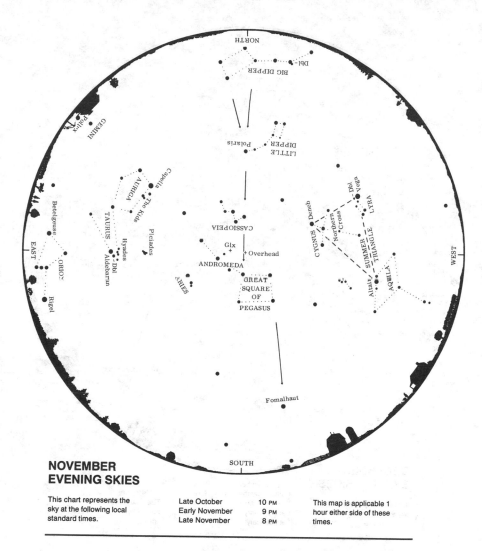

NOVEMBER
EVENING SKIES

This chart represents the sky at the following local standard times.	Late October	10 PM	This map is applicable 1 hour either side of these times.
	Early November	9 PM	
	Late November	8 PM	

At chart time nine objects of first magnitude or brighter are visible. In order of brightness they are Vega, Capella, Rigel, Betelgeuse, Altair, Aldebaran, Pollux, Fomalhaut, and Deneb. Because of the low altitude of several of the bright stars, their relative brilliance will be diminished, accompanied by increased twinkling.

The double star (Dbl) at the bend of the handle of the Big Dipper should be detectable low in the north. Another is close to Aldebaran in the "face" of Taurus. More closely spaced is the double star near Vega in Lyra. The position of an external star system, called the *Andromeda Galaxy* also is indicated (Glx).

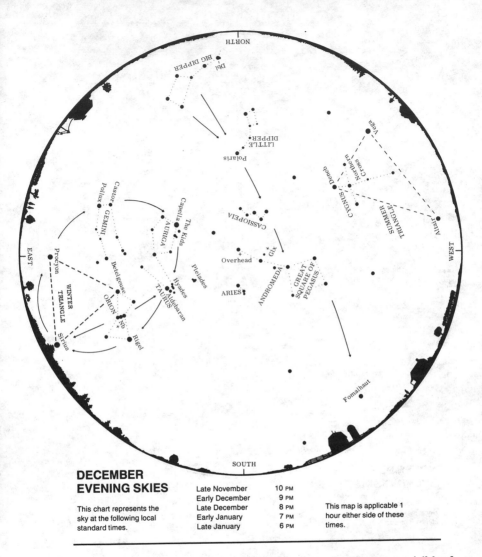

DECEMBER EVENING SKIES

This chart represents the sky at the following local standard times.

Late November	10 PM
Early December	9 PM
Late December	8 PM
Early January	7 PM
Late January	6 PM

This map is applicable 1 hour either side of these times.

At chart time 11 objects of first magnitude or brighter are visible. In order of brightness they are Sirius, Vega, Capella, Rigel, Procyon, Betelgeuse, Altair, Aldebaran, Pollux, Fomalhaut, and Deneb.

The double star (Dbl) at the bend of the handle of the Big Dipper should be detectable above the treetops in the north. The famous Orion Nebula, a cloud of gas and dust out of which stars are forming, is marked (Nb) in that constellation. The position of an external star system, called the *Andromeda Galaxy* after the constellation in which it appears, also is indicated (Glx).

CHAPTER 37

Ursa Major (Big Dipper) over observatory ▶

Mars and Venus ▲ May 28, 1977. Bright objects that you cannot account for are probably planets.

BIOGRAPHICAL SKETCHES FOR PEOPLE QUOTED

Ansel Adams (February 20, 1902–April 22, 1984), photographer and conservationist, served as a director of the Sierra Club from 1934 to 1971. He is renowned for his black and white landscape photographs that have been exhibited extensively. *Ansel Adams Images 1923–1974*, *Photographs of the Southwest*, and *The Portfolios* are among his many published works about photography.

Katherine Lee Bates (August 12, 1859–March 28, 1929), poet, educator, and author, taught at Wellesley College (1885–1925) and wrote children's books as well as poems. Her poem "America the Beautiful" was composed in 1893 while she was on a wagon trip up Pikes Peak.

Daniel Carter Beard (June 21, 1850–June 11, 1941), woodsman, illustrator, and naturalist, merged his own boys' organization, Sons of Daniel Boone, with others to form the Boy Scouts of America. A colorful figure who dressed in buckskins, he was the first national Scout commissioner.

Henry Ward Beecher (June 24, 1813–March 8, 1887), clergyman, was a recognized leader of the anti-slavery movement whose quickness of wit and exuberant good humor made him a moving speaker and Congregationalist preacher.

Sue Browder (1946–) is the author of *American Biking Atlas & Touring Guide*, published in 1974.

John Burroughs (April 3, 1837–March 29, 1921), author and poet, took delight in exploring the fields, woods, and pastoral ranges of the Catskill Mountains and in watching birds. He camped in Yosemite with John Muir and in Yellowstone with President Theodore Roosevelt. Many of his nature essays appeared in the *Atlantic Monthly* and other notable publications.

Richard E. Byrd (October 25, 1888–March 11, 1957), aviator and explorer, explored Antarctica and the South Pole after establishing a base called "Little America" in 1928. Byrd wrote about his many polar experiences in *Little America*, *Alone*, *Discovery*, and *Come North With Me*. An Eagle Scout, Paul Siple was chosen to accompany Byrd on one of his later expeditions to Antarctica.

Samuel Langhorne Clemens (November 30, 1835–April 21, 1910), noted author, wrote of his adventurous boyhood in *Tom Sawyer* and *Huckleberry Finn*. He traveled west where he became known as a frontier humorist and storyteller based upon his experiences as a miner and a journalist, depicted in his book *Roughing It*. Mark Twain was his pen name.

William O. Douglas (October 16, 1898–January 19, 1980), jurist, author, and outdoorsman, served as an Associate Justice on the Supreme Court of the United States from 1939 to 1975, longer than anyone else. He championed many conservation and outdoor causes and wrote many books about his outdoor experiences, including *Of Men and Mountains*.

Rudy Fahl, accountant, health and fitness trainer, is one of the founders of the Pikes Peak Marathon, a 28.3-mile foot race up the Barr trail from the streets of Manitou Springs (6,500 feet elevation) to the summit of the peak (14,110 feet elevation) and back. On many occasions Fahl himself has run the Pikes Peak Marathon, most recently at age 80.

Robert Frost (March 26, 1874–January 29, 1963), famous New England poet, farmer, editor, and schoolteacher, wrote numerous romantic poems about nature and people, including "The Road Not Taken." Frost won Pulitzer Prizes for his poetry in 1924, 1931, 1937, and 1943 and read his poem "The Gift Outright" at the inauguration of President John F. Kennedy in January 1961.

Herbert Hoover (August 10, 1874–October 24, 1964), mining engineer, author, and public administrator, served as the thirty-first President of the United States (1929–1933) and was an avid fisherman and hiker. Hoover was instrumental in organizing food relief programs following both World War I and World War II.

William Temple Hornaday, Ph.D. (December 1, 1854–March 6, 1937), naturalist, taxidermist, author, and conservationist, served as director of the New York Zoological Park and later as director of the New York Zoological Society. Dr. Hornaday was regarded as the foremost benefactor of wildlife of his era and was instrumental in saving the buffalo from extinction. In 1914 he initiated the Hornaday conservation awards program of the Boy Scouts of America.

Capt. J. Lee Humfreville, cavalry officer, employed Jim Bridger (March 17, 1804–June 17, 1881), the famous trapper and explorer, as a scout on a journey through Colorado in 1863–1864. His flair for romantic yarns endeared Humfreville to Bridger. In his book, *Twenty Years Among Our Savage Indians*, Humfreville recounted his experiences.

President Thomas Jefferson (April 13, 1743–July 4, 1826) was a statesman, diplomat, attorney, author, scientist, architect, and apostle of freedom. He authored the "Declaration of Independence" and served as the third President of the United States. After the acquisition of the Louisiana Purchase from Napoleon in 1803, Jefferson wrote instructions to Meriwether Lewis and Benjamin Clark for their mission to explore the 885,000-square-mile region.

Manuel Lisa (September 8, 1772–August 12, 1820), fur trader, established the first trading post on the upper Missouri River at the mouth of the Big Horn River. Between 1807 and his death in 1820 he made a dozen trips on the Missouri River and conducted a profitable furtrading venture.

William G. Long, attorney, jurist, psychologist, and humorist, presided over more than 225,000 cases in Juvenile Court in Seattle and raised burros throughout his lifetime. Civic activities, including the Boy Scouts of America, are among his pursuits. His book, *Asses Versus Jackasses*, published in 1969, is a humorous legal defense of the long-maligned burro.

Wilson MacDonald (1880–1967), poet and lecturer, was a Canadian best known for a collection of verse titled *Out of Wilderness* that was published in 1926.

John Muir (April 21, 1838–December 24, 1914), naturalist and explorer, devoted considerable study to glaciers and forests. His impassioned articles preaching the sacred duty of using the country wisely so that it could be passed on to future generations undiminished in richness and beauty caught the public's attention. On a camping trip in and about Yosemite in the spring of 1903 he strongly influenced President Theodore Roosevelt to set aside national forest reserves and parks.

Sigurd F. Olson (April 4, 1899–January 13, 1982), professor, author, and naturalist, is revered by a generation of canoeists for his perceptive insights in interpreting wilderness. Descriptive works of his encounters with nature include *The Singing Wilderness*, *Listening Point*, *The Lonely Land*, *Ruins of the North*, and *Wilderness Days*. Olson served as president of the National Park Association and was a strong proponent for wilderness preservation.

Dr. Samuel Parker (April 23, 1779–March 21, 1866), congregational clergyman, missionary, and explorer, joined a caravan of the American Fur Company that reached the annual trappers rendezvous on the Green River in Wyoming on August 12, 1835. His book, *Journal of an Exploring Tour Beyond the Rocky Mountains*, published in 1838, describes his experiences.

Waite Phillips (January 19, 1883–January 27, 1964), land, cattle, and oil baron, generously donated 127,000 acres of mountainous terrain now known as Philmont Scout Ranch to the Boy Scouts of America, as well as an office building in Tulsa, Okla. to endow it. Phillips was an accomplished horseman, fishing enthusiast, and outdoorsman who entertained many distinguished guests at his ranch.

Robert Baden-Powell (February 22, 1857–January 8, 1941), English military hero, served in Africa, including the Siege of Mafeking, which he and his men endured for 217 days through sickness and famine. Upon his return to

England, Baden-Powell offered a camp experience for boys on Brownsea Island in 1907 and thereby launched the Scouting movement. He wrote *Scouting for Boys*, which became an instant best seller and attracted thousands of boys to Scouting.

Red Jacket, a Seneca Indian chief, promoted peace between his tribe and early Americans and backed the United States in the War of 1812 with England.

James Whitcomb Riley (October 7 1849–July 22, 1916), who was known as the Hoosier poet for his home state of Indiana, wrote poems depicting rough-and-tumble children with begrimed but laughing faces. *The Complete Works of James Whitcomb Riley* was published in six volumes in 1913.

Israel C. Russell (December 10, 1852–May 1, 1906), geologist, wrote five popular books on geology and was recognized as an authority in the geography of North America. In 1889 he began a series of expeditions to Alaska. Under the joint auspices of the United States Geological Survey and the National Geographic Society, he explored the glaciers and slopes of Mount St. Elias in Alaska and nearly succeeded in reaching the summit.

Edwin L. Sabin (1870-1952), author, poet, and literary critic, wrote many western books for boys. His works included *Old Four Toes*, *With Carson and Fremont*, *Buffalo Bill and the Overland Trail*, *With Sam Houston in Texas*, *Opening of the West with Lewis and Clark*, *Old Jim Bridger on the Moccasin Trail*, and *Wild Men of the West*.

Rufus Sage (March 17, 1817–December 1893), writer and explorer, traveled and explored throughout the Rocky Mountain West including New Mexico, Utah, Idaho, Colorado, Wyoming, and even Canada. *Scenes of the Rocky Mountains*, published in 1864, describes events throughout his journeys.

Carl Sandburg (January 6, 1878–July 22, 1967), poet and writer, won several Pulitzer Prizes. He appreciated the beauty of ordinary people and commonplace things. "The People, Yes" is his famous panoramic depiction of the American spirit expressed in folklore.

Ernest Thompson Seton (August 14, 1860–October 23, 1946), naturalist, artist, and author, was one of the founders of the Boy Scouts of America, which adopted many outdoor skills from his own youth organization, the Woodcraft Indians. Seton became the first Chief Scout in 1910, the birth date of the Boy Scouts of America.

Charles T. Stanton (deceased December 29, 1846) was a brave, courageous, unselfish young man who seemed to be most happy when rendering kindly services to help others in spite of grave danger. He died after bringing dried meat and provisions to the ill-fated

Donner Party. This group of 87 pioneers became stranded in severe cold and deep snow high on a mountain pass in the Sierra Nevada Mountains. Forty-eight of them survived an ordeal of several months.

Henry David Thoreau (July 12, 1817–May 6, 1862), writer and naturalist, composed *Walden's Pond*, an account of two years he spent in a primitive cabin seeking to understand the essentials of his life. Thoreau was an individualist who believed in a moral law superior to statutes and constitutions. His observations of nature were gathered from excursions into the hinterlands of New England.

Stanley Vestal (August 15, 1887–December 1957), educator and author, whose real name was Walter Stanley Campbell, wrote fiction, poetry, and historical studies principally of the Southwestern frontier under his pen name, Stanley Vestal.

Walt Whitman (May 31, 1819–March 26, 1892) was an author and poet whose works were strongly affected after he visited several frontier states. *Leaves of Grass* is a collection of poems for which he is best known.

PHOTO CREDITS

FOREWORD photo spread by John Deeks
Section 1 (pages x1) and section II (pages 25657)
   photo spreads by David Alan Harvey, 1979,
   National Geographic Society
Section III (pages 5045) courtesy of *Texas
   Highways* magazine

Chapter 1
Texas Highways, 2
Dave Bates, 4 (bottom)
Robert Birkby, 7 (top left and bottom right)
BSA file photo, 7 (top right)
Michael Greenbank, 4 (top)
Carol Munch, 7 (bottom left)

Chapter 2
Robert Blrkby, 12
Curtis Boerner, 17, 19
BSA file photos, 11 (top), 18
Gene Daniels, 11 (bottom)
Tim Sweeney, 15
Courtesy *Texas Highways* magazine, 8

Chapter 3
BSA File Photo, 33 (left)
John Page, 32, 33 (right)
Courtesy *Texas Highways* magazine, 20
Jon Wartes, 37

Chapter 4
Dave Bates, 49
Robert Birkby, 47
Curtis Boerner, 44
BSA file photos, 46 (bottom), 50, 52, 54, 56–59, 62
John Page, 59 (compass)
REI (Recreational Equipment, Inc.), 46 (sturdy),
   51, 53, 55, 61

Chapter 5
Dave Bates, 69
Robert Birkby, 64, 76, 86–88, 89 (bottom)
BSA file photo, 89 (top)

Chapter 6
Dave Bates, 90, 101
BSA file photo, 96
Carol Munch, 93

Chapter 7
Dave Bates, 108, 115
Curtis Boerner, 110
John Breitling, 117, 118, 119
BSA file photos, 104, 107 (lower right corner)
REI (Recreational Equipment, Inc.), 106, 107
Robert Maxfield, 11213

Chapter 8
Dave Bates, 130
Robert Birkby, 120, 123, 132
John Breitling, 135
BSA file photos, 127
Robert Maxfield, 133, 134

Chapter 9
Dave Bates, 146
Robert Birkby, 147
Johnny Boehm, 145
Jennifer Dunn, 136
Neil Heilpern, 139

Chapter 10
BSA file photo, 159 (snake)
Bob Cary, 155, 160
Gene Daniels, 148, 150, 162
Steven Kelly, 164
REI (Recreational Equipment, Inc.), 159 (water
   filter)
Doug Wilson, 152

Chapter 11
Robert Birkby, 183
BSA file photo, 166
Bob Cary, 170, 193
Gene Daniels, 169

Chapter 12
BSA file photos, 199, 200 (bottom), 205, 209
Bob Cary, 200 (top)
Gene Daniels, 206
Carol Munch, 194, 197
Lane Stumme, 208

Chapter 13
BSA file photo, 216
Bob Cary, 225
Gene Daniels, 224
Courtesy *Texas Highways* magazine, 210

Chapter 14
Robert Birkby, 266 (top two)
Dave Bates, 226 (center two)
Curtis Boerner, 226 (bottom left)
BSA file photos, 226 (center and bottom right),
   241–43

Chapter 15
Robert Birkby, 249
BSA file photo, 255
BSA file photo, 253
Bob Cary, 244
Gene Daniels, 248, 250
Rob Lesser, 247

Chapter 16
Dave Bates, 258
Robert Birkby, 266
BSA file photos, 261, 268
Gene Daniels, 265

Chapter 17
BSA file photos, 270, 276–79, 283, 287
Bob Cary, 275
Gene Daniels, 282, 284, 286, 288, 289
Dick Pryce, 285

BIBLIOGRAPHY

Chapter 1

Brown, Tom, Jr., and Brandt Morgan. *Tom Brown's Field Guide to Living with the Earth.* Berkley Publishing Group, 1984.
Capone, Lisa, and Cady Goldfield. *The Conservationworks Book: Practical Conservation Tips for the Home and Outdoors.* Appalachian Mountain Club Books, 1992.
Hampton, Bruce, and David Cole. *Soft Paths: How to Enjoy the Wilderness Without Harming It.* Stackpole Books, 1988.
Hart, John. *Walking Softly in the Wilderness.* Sierra Club Books, 1984.
Hodgson, Michael. *Minimizing Impact on the Wilderness: The Basic Essentials.* ICS Books, 1991.
Javna, John. *Fifty Simple Things Kids Can Do to Save the Earth.* Andrews and McMeel, 1990.
Leopold, Aldo. *A Sand Country Almanac.* Oxford University Press, 1989.
Lipkis, Andy. *The Simple Act of Planting a Tree.* Tarcher, 1990.
Soil and Water Conservation merit badge pamphlet. Boy Scouts of America, 1983.

Chapter 2

Elman, Robert. *The Hiker's Bible*, rev. ed. Doubleday, 1982.
Fletcher, Colin. *The Complete Walker III.* Knopf, 1984.
Fuller, Margaret. *Mountains: A Natural History and Hiking Guide.* John Wiley and Sons, 1989.
Hiking merit badge pamphlet. Boy Scouts of America, 1991.
Roberts, Harry. *Movin' Out: Equipment and Technique for Hikers.* Stone Wall Press, 1979.
Wood, Robert. *Dayhiker.* Ten Speed Press, 1991.

Chapter 3

Andreson, Steve. *The Orienteering Book.* Anderson World, 1977.
Blandford, Percy W. *Maps and Compasses*, 2nd ed. TAB Books, 1991.
Carrington, David, and Richard Stephenson, eds. *Map Collections in the United States and Canada*, 4th ed. Special Libraries Association, 1985.
Farrah, Nuruddin. *Maps.* Pantheon, 1987.
Jacobson, Cliff. *Map and Compass: The Basic Essentials.* ICS Books, 1988.
Kals, W. S. *Land Navigation Handbook: The Sierra Club Guide to Map and Compass.* Sierra Club Books, 1983.
Kjellstrom, Bjorn. *Be Expert with Map and Compass.* Scribner, 1976.
Makower, Joel. *The Map Catalog*, rev. ed. Random House, 1990.
McNeill, Carol. *Orienteering: The Skills of the Game.* Crowood, 1991.
McVey, Vicki. *Sierra Club Wayfinding Book.* Little, Brown, 1991.
Morris, M. Thompson. *Maps for America*, 3rd ed. U.S. Geological Survey, 1987.
Orienteering merit badge pamphlet. Boy Scouts of America, 1992.
Randall, Glenn. *The Outward Bound Map and Compass Book.* Lyons and Burford, 1989.
Venture Orienteering. Boy Scouts of America, 1989.
Weiss, Harvey. *Maps: Getting from Here to There.* Houghton Mifflin, 1991.

Chapter 4

Backpacking merit badge pamphlet. Boy Scouts of America, 1983.
Brady, Michael. *Cross-Country Ski Gear*, 2nd ed. Mountaineers, 1987.
Camping merit badge pamphlet. Boy Scouts of America, 1984.
Gerrard, Layne. *Rock Gear.* Ten Speed Press, 1990.

Liebrenz, Noelle, and Penny Hargrove. *Backpackers' Sourcebook*, 3rd ed. Wilderness Press, 1987.
McQuilkin, Robert. *Comfort Below Freezing*. Anderson World, 1980.
Roberts, Harry. *Movin' Out: Equipment & Technique for Hikers*. Stone Wall Press, 1979.

Chapter 5

Hazen, David. *The Stripper's Guide to Canoe-Building*. Tamal Vista, 1982.
Mueller, Betty. *The Packrat Papers*. Signpost, 1977.
Sumner, Louise L. *Sew and Repair Your Own Outdoor Gear*. Mountaineers, 1988.

Chapter 6

Atwood, Margaret. *Wilderness Tips*. Doubleday, 1991.
Bigon, Maria, and Regazzoni, Guido. *Morrow's Guide to Knots*. Morrow, 1982.
Camping merit badge pamphlet. Boy Scouts of America, 1984.
Fleming, June. *Outdoor Idea Book*. Victoria House, 1978.
Hart, John. *Walking Softly in the Wilderness*. Sierra Club Books, 1984.
Jacobson, Cliff. *Camping Secrets*. ICS Books, 1987.
Jacobson, Cliff. *Camping: The Basic Essentials*. ICS Books, 1988.
Jacobson, Cliff. *Knots for the Outdoors: The Basic Essentials*. ICS Books, 1990.
Jarman, Colin. *The Essential Knot Book*. International Marine Publishing, 1987.
Kahn, Hal, and Rick Greenspan. *Camper's Companion*. Foghorn Press, 1991.
Knots and How to Tie Them. Boy Scouts of America, 1978.
Outdoor Skills Instructor's Manual. American Camping Association, 1991.
Petzoldt, Paul. *The New Wilderness Handbook*. Norton, 1984.
Sports Afield Editors. *Sports Afield Outdoor Skills*. Hearst Books, 1991.
Woods Wisdom—Troop Program Features, rev. ed. Boy Scouts of America, 1989.

Chapter 7

Backpacking merit badge pamphlet. Boy Scouts of America, 1983.
Hampton, Bruce, and David Cole. *Soft Paths: How to Enjoy the Wilderness Without Harming It*. Stackpole Books, 1988.
Hart, John. *Walking Softly in the Wilderness*. Sierra Club Books, 1984.
Simer, Peter, and John Sullivan. *National Outdoor Leadership School's Official Wilderness Guide*. Simon and Schuster, 1983.

Chapter 8

Axcell, Claudia, Diane Cook, and Vikki Kinmont. *Simple Foods for the Pack: The Sierra Club Guide to Delicious Natural Foods for the Trail*, rev. ed. Sierra Club Books, 1986.
Bunnelle, Hass, and Shirley Savirs. *Cooking for Camp and Trail*. Sierra Club Books, 1972.
Camp Cookery for Small Groups. Boy Scouts of America, 1983.
Chase, Sarah L. *Cold Weather Cooking*. Workman Publishing, 1990.
Cooking merit badge pamphlet. Boy Scouts of America, 1986.
Fleming, June. *The Well-Fed Backpacker*, rev. ed. Random House, 1986.
Jacobson, Cliff. *Cooking in the Outdoors: The Basic Essentials*. ICS Books, 1989.
Latimer, Carole. *Wilderness Cuisine: How to Prepare and Enjoy Fine Food on the Trail & in Camp*. Wilderness Press, 1990.
Lund, Duane R. *Camp Cooking*. Adventure Publications, 1991.
Marshall, Mel. *The Complete Book of Outdoor Cookery*. Outdoor Life Books, distributed by Reinhold, 1983.

McHugh, Gretchen. *The Hungry Hiker's Book of Good Cooking*. Knopf, 1982.
McMorris, Bill, and Jo McMorris. *Camp Cooking: A Backpacker's Pocket Guide*. Lyons & Burford, 1989.
National Outdoor Leadership School Staff. *The NOLS Cookery*. Stackpole Books, 1991.
Prater, Yvonne, and Ruth Dyar Mendenhall. *Gorp, Glop and Glue Stew*. Mountaineers, 1981.
Ragsdale, John. *Camper's Guide to Outdoor Cooking*. Gulf Publishing, 1989.
Woodruff, Woody. *Cooking the Dutch Oven Way*, 2nd ed. ICS Books, 1989.
Yaffe, Linda F. *High Trail Cookery*. Chicago Review Press, 1989.

Chapter 9

Anderson, Bob. *Stretching*. Shelter Publications, 1980.
Athletics merit badge pamphlet. Boy Scouts of America, 1964.
Cooper, Kenneth H. *Aerobics*. Bantam, 1992.
Cooper, Kenneth H. *Kid Fitness: A Complete Shape-up Program from Birth Through High School*. Bantam, 1991.
Hockey, Robert V. *Physical Fitness, The Pathway to Healthful Living*, 6th ed. Mosby-Year Book, Inc., 1989.
Ilg, Steve. *The Outdoor Athlete's Training Journal*. Cordillera Press, 1992.
Kuntzelman, Charles T. *The Complete Book of Walking*. Pocket Books, 1989.
Personal Fitness merit badge pamphlet. Boy Scouts of America, 1990.
Spring, H., and U. Illi. *Stretching and Strengthening Exercises*. Thieme Medical Publishers, 1990.
Varsity Triathlon. Boy Scouts of America, 1990.
Weaver, Nell. *Stretching Book*. Anderson World, 1982.

Chapter 10

Backpacking merit badge pamphlet. Boy Scouts of America, 1983.
Emergency Preparedness merit badge pamphlet. Boy Scouts of America, 1972.
Klingel, Fitterer. *Outdoor Safety*. Creative Education, 1986.
Safety merit badge pamphlet. Boy Scouts of America, 1986.

Chapter 11

Auerbach, Paul. *Medicine for the Outdoors*, rev. ed. Little, Brown, 1991.
Bowman, Warren. *Outdoor Emergency Care: Comprehensive First Aid for Non-Urban Settings*. National Ski Patrol System, 1988.
Breyfogle, Newell D. *The Common Sense Medical Guide and Outdoor Reference*. McGraw Hill, 1988.
Darvill, Fred T., Jr. *Mountaineering Medicine—A Wilderness Medical Guide*, 13th ed. Wilderness Press, 1992.
Eastman, Peter F. *Advanced First Aid for All Outdoors*. Cornell Maritime, 1976.
First Aid merit badge pamphlet. Boy Scouts of America, 1988.
Forgey, William W. *First Aid for the Outdoors: The Basic Essentials*. ICS Books, 1988.
Forgey, William W. *Hypothermia: The Basic Essentials*. ICS Books, 1991.
Forgey, William W. *Wilderness Medicine*, 3rd ed. ICS Books, 1987.
Goth, Peter. *Outward Bound Wilderness First-Aid Handbook*. Lyons & Burford, 1991.
Hackett, Peter H. *Mountain Sickness: Prevention, Recognition and Treatment*, 5th ed. American Alpine Club, 1980.
Mitchell, Dick. *Mountaineering First Aid: A Guide to Accident Response and First Aid Care*. Mountaineers, 1975.
Schimelpfenig, Todd, and Linda Lindsey. *NOLS Wilderness First Aid*. Stackpole, 1992.
Tilton, Buck, and Frank Hubbell. *Medicine for the Backcountry*. ICS Books, 1990.
Wilkerson, James A. *Medicine for Mountaineering*, 4th ed. Mountaineers, 1992.
Wilkerson, James A., Cameron C. Bangs, and John S. Hayward, eds. *Hypothermia, Frostbite, and Other Cold Injuries*. Mountaineers, 1986.

Chapter 12

American Outdoor Safety League Staff. *Emergency Survival Handbook*. Mountaineers, 1979.

Angier, Bradford. *How to Stay Alive in the Woods*. Smith, 1983.

Brown, Tom, Jr., and Brandt Morgan. *Tom Brown's Guide to Wilderness Survival*. Berkley Publishing Group, 1984.

Canadian Government Staff. *Never Say Die: The Canadian Air Force Survival Manual*. Paladin Press, 1979.

Churchill, James E. *Survival: The Basic Essentials*. ICS Books, 1989.

Craighead, Frank C., Jr., and John J. Craighead. *How to Survive on Land and Sea*, 4th ed. Naval Institute Press, 1984.

Fear, Eugene H. *Surviving the Unexpected Wilderness Emergency*, rev. 6th ed. Survival Education Association, 1979.

Ganci, Dave. *Desert Survival: The Basic Essentials*. ICS Books, 1991.

Jacobson, Cliff. *Trailside Shelters: The Basic Essentials*. ICS Books, 1992.

Lehman, Charles A. *Desert Survival Handbook*. Primer Publishers, 1990.

Meuninck, Jim. *Edible Wild Plants and Useful Herbs: The Basic Essentials*. ICS Books, 1988.

Muston, John. *Survival Training and Technique*. Arms and Armour, 1991.

Olsen, Larry D. *Outdoor Survival Skills*, 5th rev. ed. Chicago Review Press, 1990.

Pioneering merit badge pamphlet. Boy Scouts of America, 1974.

Reader, Dennis J. *Coming Back Alive*. Random House, 1981.

Shanks, Benard. *Wilderness Survival*, rev. ed. Universe, 1987.

Smith, L. *Survival Skills*. EDC Publishing, 1987.

Venture Survival. Boy Scouts of America, 1989.

Wilderness Survival merit badge pamphlet. Boy Scouts of America, 1984.

Wilkinson, Ernest, ed. *Snow Caves for Fun and Survival*. North American Falconry and Hunting Hawks, 1986.

Chapter 13

Ballatore, Ron, and William Miller. *Swimming and Aquatics Today*. West Publishing Company, 1990.

Costill, David L., and Earnest W. Maglischo, and Allen B. Richardson. *Swimming*. Human Kinetics, 1992.

Delzeit, Linda. *Swimming Made Easy and Fun*. Kendall/Hunt, 1991.

Gutman, Bill. *Swimming*. Cavendish, Marshall, 1990.

Katz, Jane, and Nancy P. Bruning. *Swimming for Total Fitness*. Doubleday, 1981.

Lanoue, F. *Drownproofing*. Prentice Hall, 1978.

Lifesaving merit badge pamphlet. Boy Scouts of America, 1980.

Noble, Jim. *Swimming*. Watts, Franklin, 1991.

Orr, C. Rob, and Jane B. Tyler. *Swimming Basics*. Prentice-Hall, 1984.

Swimming merit badge pamphlet. Boy Scouts of America, 1980.

Verrier, John. *Swimming*. Trafalgar Square, 1991.

Vickers, Betty J., and William Vincent. *Swimming*, 5th ed. Brown & Benchmark, 1989.

Chapter 14

Bell, Patricia, ed. *The Paddler's Planner*. Cat's-paw Press, 1989.

Chase, Jim. *Backpacker Magazine's Guide to the Appalachian Trail*. Stackpole Books, 1989.

Cook, Charles. *Essential Guide to Hiking in the United States*. Kesend, 1992.

DeHaan, Vicki. *State Parks of the West: America's Best-Kept Secrets*. Cordillera Press, 1990.

Drotar, David L. *Hiking the U.S.A.: A Sourcebook for Maps, Guidebooks and Inspiration*. Stone Wall Press, 1987.

Foreman, Dave, and Howie Wolke. *The Big Outside: A Descriptive Inventory of the Big Wilderness Areas of the U.S.* Ned Ludd Books, 1989.

Frome, Michael. *National Park Guide*. Prentice-Hall, 1992.

Jones, John O. *U.S. Outdoor Atlas and Recreation Guide*. Houghton Mifflin, 1992.

Schaffer, Jeffrey, Ben Schifrin, Thomas Winnett, and Jenkins Ruby. *The Pacific Crest Trail, Vol. 1: California*, 4th ed. Wilderness Press, 1989.

Schaffer, Jeffrey, and Andy Selters. *The Pacific Crest Trail, Vol. 2: Oregon and Washington*, 5th ed. Wilderness Press, 1990.

Shears, Nick. *Paddle America: A Guide to Trips and Outfitters in All 50 States.* Starfish Press, 1992.
Tours and Expeditions. Boy Scouts of America, 1971.
Wilderness USA. National Geographic Society, 1975.
Williams, Joe. *Philmont: Where Spirits Soar.* Boy Scouts of America, 1989.
Woodall's Tent Camping Guide. Simon & Schuster, 1992.
Wright, Don. *Guide to Free USA Campgrounds,* 6th ed. Cottage Publications, 1990.
Young, Donald. *Sierra Club Book of Our National Parks, Vol. 1.* Little, Brown, 1990.
Ziegler, Ronald. *Wilderness Waterways: A Whole Water Reference for Paddlers.* University of Washington, 1992.

Chapter 15

Backpacking merit badge pamphlet. Boy Scouts of America, 1983.
Curtis, Sam. *Harsh Weather Camping.* Menasha Ridge Press, 1986.
Tours and Expeditions. Boy Scouts of America, 1984.

Chapter 16

Backpacking merit badge pamphlet. Boy Scouts of America, 1983.
Hart, John. *Walking Softly in the Wilderness.* Sierra Club Books, 1984.
Manning, Harvey. *Backpacking: One Step at a Time.* Random House, 1986.
McNeish, Cameron. *The Backpacker's Manual.* Random House, 1984.
Petzoldt, Paul. *The New Wilderness Handbook.* Norton, 1984.
Roberts, Harry. *Backpacking: The Basic Essentials.* ICS Books, 1989.
Simer, Peter, and John Sullivan. *National Outdoor Leadership School's Official Wilderness Guide.* Simon & Schuster, 1983.
Townsend, Chris. *The Backpacker's Handbook.* International Marine Publishing, 1992.
Winnett, Thomas, and Melanie Findling. *Backpacking Basics,* 3rd edition. Wilderness Press, 1988.

Chapter 17

Bell, Patricia, ed. *The Paddler's Planner.* Cat's-paw Press, 1989.
Birkby, Robert. *Learn How to Canoe in One Day.* Stackpole Books, 1990.
Canoeing merit badge pamphlet. Boy Scouts of America, 1989.
Davidson, James West, and John Rugge. *The Complete Wilderness Paddler.* Random House, 1982.
Drabik, Harry. *The Spirit of Canoe Camping.* Nodin Press, 1981.
Gordon, I. Herbert. *Canoeing Made Easy.* Globe Pequot Press, 1992.
Harrison, David. *Sports Illustrated Canoeing.* NAL/Dutton, 1988.
Jacobson, Cliff. *Canoeing and Camping: Beyond the Basics.* ICS Books, 1992.
Jacobson, Cliff. *Canoeing Wild Rivers,* 2nd ed. ICS Books, 1989.
Jacobson, Cliff. *Solo Canoeing: The Basic Essentials.* ICS Books, 1991.
Landry, Paul, and Mattie McNair. *The Outward Bound Canoeing Handbook.* Lyons and Burford, 1992.
McNair, Robert E. *Basic River Canoeing.* American Camping Association, 1987.
Mason, Bill. *Path of the Paddle.* Northword Press, Inc., 1991.
Mead, Robert Douglas. *The Canoer's Bible.* Doubleday, 1989.
Ray, Slim. *The Canoe Handbook.* Stackpole Books, 1992.
Roberts, Harry. *Canoe Paddling: The Basic Essentials.* ICS Books, 1992.
Weber, Anne W., and Janet A. Zeller. *Canoeing and Kayaking for Persons with Physical Disabilities.* American Canoe Association, 1990.

Chapter 18

Bridge, Raymond. *The Complete Guide to Kayaking*. Scribner, 1982.
Ellison, Jib. *Rafting: The Basic Essentials*. ICS Books, 1991.
Hutchinson, Derek C. *Eskimo Rolling*, 2nd ed. International Marine Publishing, 1992.
Kallner, Bill, and Donna Jackson. *Kayaking Whitewater: The Basic Essentials*. ICS Books, 1990.
Kuhne, Cecil. *River Rafting*. Anderson World, 1979.
McGinnis, William. *Whitewater Rafting*. Random House, 1978.
Miskimins, R. W. *Guide to Floating Whitewater Rivers*. Amato Publications, 1987.
Rowe, Ray. *White Water Kayaking*. Stackpole Books, 1989.
Tejada-Flores, Lito. *Wildwater: The Sierra Club Guide to Kayaking and Whitewater Boating*. Sierra Club Books, 1978.
Urban, John T. *White Water Handbook*, 2nd ed. Appalachian Mountain Club Books, 1981.
U'ren, Stephen B. *Performance Kayaking*. Stackpole Books, 1990.
Venture Whitewater. Boy Scouts of America, 1990.
Wyatt, Mike. *Sea Kayaking: The Basic Essentials*. ICS Books, 1990.

Chapter 19

Bonganni, Maurizio. *Simon & Schuster's Guide to Horses & Ponies of the World*. Simon & Schuster, 1988.
Davis, Francis W. *Horse Packing in Pictures*, 2nd ed. Howell Book House, 1991.
Elser, Smoke, and Bill Brown. *Packin' in on Mules and Horses*. Mountain Press, 1980.
Horsemanship merit badge pamphlet. Boy Scouts of America, 1986.
Pervier, Evelyn. *Horsemanship: Basics for Beginners*. Prentice-Hall, 1985.

Chapter 20

Cary, Bob. *Winter Camping*. Viking Penguin, 1979.
Chase, Sarah L. *Cold Weather Cooking*. Workman Publishing, 1990.
Curtis, Sam. *Harsh Weather Camping*. Menasha Ridge Press, 1986.
Gorman, Stephen. *AMC Guide to Winter Camping*. Appalachian Mountain Club Books, 1991.
McQuilkin, Robert. *Comfort Below Freezing*. Anderson World, 1980.
Okpik: Cold-Weather Camping. Boy Scouts of America, 1990.
Randall, Glenn. *Cold Comfort: Keeping Warm in the Outdoors*. Lyons and Burford, 1987.
Venture Snow Camping. Boy Scouts of America, 1989.

Chapter 21

Bein, Vic. *Mountain Skiing*. Mountaineers, 1982.
Brady, Michael. *Waxing and Care of Cross-Country Skis*. Wilderness Press, 1986.
Cliff, Robert. *Ski Mountaineering*. Smith, Peter, 1991.
Daffern, Tony. *Avalanche Safety for Skiers and Climbers*. Cloudcap, 1983.
Gillette, Ned, and John Dostal. *Cross-Country Skiing*, 3rd ed. Mountaineers, 1988.
Moynier, John. *Cross-Country Skiing: The Basic Essentials*. ICS Books, 1990.
Parker, Paul. *Free-Heel Skiing*. Chelsea Green Publishing, 1988.
Skiing merit badge pamphlet. Boy Scouts of America, 1980.
Tejada-Flores, Lito. *Backcountry Skiing*. Sierra Club Books, 1981.
Tejada-Flores, Lito. *Breakthrough on Skis*. Random House, 1986.
Watters, Ron. *Ski Camping*, rev. ed. Great Rift Press, 1989.

Chapter 22

Osgood, William, and Leslie Hurley. *The Snowshoe Book*. Viking Penguin, 1983.
Prater, Gene. *Snowshoeing*, 3rd ed. Mountaineers, 1988.

Chapter 23

Armstrong, Betsy R., and Knox Williams. *The Avalanche Book*, rev. ed. Fulcrum Publishing, 1992.
Graydon, Don, ed. *Mountaineering: The Freedom of the Hills*, 5th ed. Mountaineers, 1992.
Kramer, Stephen. *Avalanche*. Carolrhoda Books, 1991.
LaChapelle, E. R. *The ABC of Avalanche Safety*, 2nd ed. Mountaineers, 1985.
Petzoldt, Paul. *The New Wilderness Handbook*. Norton, 1984.
Riley, Michael J. *Mountain Camping*. Contemporary, 1979.
Sierra Club. *Wilderness Basics: The Complete Handbook for Hikers and Backpackers*, 2nd ed. Mountaineers, 1992.
Simer, Peter, and John Sullivan. *National Outdoor Leadership School's Official Wilderness Guide*. Simon & Schuster, 1983.
Tilton, Buck. *Avalanche Safety: The Basic Essentials*. ICS Books, 1992.

Chapter 24

Ashton, Steve. *Rock Climbing Techniques*. Trafalgar Square, 1991.
Barry, John. *Rock Climbing*. Stackpole Books, 1989.
Barry, John. *Snow and Ice Climbing*. Cloudcap, 1987.
Daffern, Tony. *Avalanche Safety for Skiers and Climbers*. Cloudcap, 1983.
Fawcett, Ron, Jeff Lowe, Jeff, Paul Nunn, and Alan Rouse. *The Climber's Handbook*. Sierra Club Books, 1987.
Graydon, Don, ed. *Mountaineering: The Freedom of the Hills*, 5th ed. Mountaineers, 1992.
Long, John. *Face Climbing*. Chockstone Press, 1991.
Long, John. *How to Rock Climb*. Chockstone Press, 1989.
Loughman, Michael. *Learning to Rock Climb*. Sierra Club Books, 1981.
Moynier, John. *Mountaineering: The Basic Essentials*. ICS Books, 1991.
Riley, Michael J. *Mountain Camping*. Contemporary, 1979.
Robbins, Royal. *Advanced Rockcraft*. La Siesta Press, 1985.
Robbins, Royal. *Basic Rockcraft*. La Siesta Press, 1985.
Strassman, Michael. *Rock Climbing: The Basic Essentials*. ICS Books, 1989.

Chapter 25

Brucker, Robert W., and Richard A. Watson. *The Longest Cave*. Southern Illinois University Press, 1987.
Damon, Paul H., ed. *Caving in America: The Story of the National Speleological Society*. National Speleological Society, 1991.
Halliday, William. *Depths of the Earth: Caves and Cavers of the United States*, rev. ed. Harper and Row, 1976.
Moore, George W., and G. Nicholas Sullivan. *Speleology: The Study of Caves*. Cave Books, 1985.
Padgett, Allen, and Bruce Smith. *On Rope*. National Speleological Society, 1987.
Rea, Tom, ed. *Caving Basics*. National Speleological Society, 1987.
Steele, C. William. *Yochib: The River Cave*. Cave Books, 1985.

Chapter 26

Bechdel, Les, and Slim Ray. *River Rescue*, 2nd ed. Appalachian Mountain Club Books, 1989.

Brown, Tom, Jr., and William J. Watkins. *The Tracker.* Berkley Publishing Group, 1984.
Jones, Anthony S. G. *The Organisation of Mountain Search and Rescue Operations.* Emergency Response Institute, 1988.
Kelley, Dennis. *Mountain Search for the Lost Victim.* Search and Rescue, 1973.
Lavalla, Patrick, Don Cooper, and Robert Stoffel. *Search and Rescue Fundamentals.* Emergency Response Institute, n.d.
Nixon, Robert G., and Candace Brown-Nixon. *Rugged Terrain Search and Rescue,* 2nd ed. EES Publications, n.d.
Rastellini, M. M., ed. *Search and Rescue Survival Training.* (Air Force Regulation Ser.: No. 64-4, V.1). U.S. Government Printing Office, 1985.
Robbins, Roland, and Dennis E. Kelley. *Mantracking.* Search and Rescue, 1977.
Search and Rescue Survival. Gordon Press, 1986.
Setnicka, Tim J. *Wilderness Search and Rescue.* Appalachian Mountain Club, 1980.

Chapter 27

Bashline, Jim. *Trout and Salmon Fisherman's Bible.* Doubleday, 1991.
Cordes, R. A. *Backpacker's Guide to Fly Fishing.* Troutbeck Publishing, 1992.
Fishing merit badge pamphlet. Boy Scouts of America, 1988.
Gartner, Bob. *National Parks Fishing Guide.* Globe Pequot, 1990.
Golad, Frank, ed. *The Sports Afield Fishing Almanac.* Lyons & Burford, 1989.
Kyte, Al. *Fly Fishing: Simple to Sophisticated,* 2nd ed. Leisure Press, 1987.
Lee, David. *Fly Fishing: A Beginner's Guide.* Prentice-Hall, 1982.
Leiser, Eric. *Orvis Guide to Beginning Fly Tying.* Stewart, 1992.
Mojetta, Angelo. *Simon & Schuster's Guide to Saltwater Fish and Fishing.* Simon & Schuster, 1992.
Ovington, Ray. *Basic Bait Fishing.* Stackpole Books, 1984.
Paugh, Tom. *Sports Afield Treasury of Fly Fishing.* Delacorte, 1992.
Rosenbauer, Tom. *The Orvis Fly-Fishing Guide.* Lyons and Burford, 1988.
Rosenthal, Michael. *North America's Freshwater Fishing Book.* Scribners, 1989.
Sosin, Mark, and Lefty Kreh. *Practical Fishing Knots II.* Lyons and Burford, 1991.
Thiffault, Mark, ed. *Illustrated Guide to Better Fishing,* 3rd ed. DBI Books, 1990.
Thiffault, Mark. *Saltwater Fishermen's Digest.* DBI Books, 1989.
Venture Fishing. Boy Scouts of America, 1989.
Walton, Izaak, and Charles Cotton. *The Compleat Angler.* Oxford University Press, 1991.

Chapter 28

Coello, Dennis. The Complete *Mountain Biker.* Lyons and Burford, 1989.
Cycling merit badge pamphlet. Boy Scouts of America, 1984.
Dolan, Edward F., Jr. *Bicycle Touring and Camping.* Simon & Schuster, 1982.
Hodgson, Michael. *Mountain Biking for Mere Mortals.* ICS Books, 1992.
Howard, John. *The Cyclist's Companion.* Viking Penguin, 1984.
Mills, Keith. *Mountain Biking.* Stackpole Books, 1989.
Nealy, William. *Mountain Bike: A Manual of Technique.* Menasha Ridge, 1992.
Nye, Peter. *The Cyclist's Sourcebook.* Putnam, 1991.
Phinney, Davis, and Connie Carpenter. *Training for Cycling: The Ultimate Guide to Improved Performance.* Putnam, 1992.
Sloane, Eugene A. *Sloane's Complete Book of All-Terrain Bicycles.* Simon & Schuster, 1991.
Sloane, Eugene A. *Sloane's New Bicycle Maintenance Manual.* Simon & Schuster, 1991.
Stevenson, John. *Mountain Bikes: Maintenance and Repair.* Bicycle Books, 1992.
Strassman, Michael. *Mountain Biking: The Basic Essentials.* ICS Books, 1989.
Van der Plas, Rob. *Bicycle Technology: Understanding, Selecting, and Maintaining the Modern Bicycle.* Bicycle Books, 1991.
Van der Plas, Rob. *The Bicycle Touring Manual: Using the Bike for Touring and Camping,* rev. ed. Bicycle Books, 1991.
Venture Cycling. Boy Scouts of America, 1989.
Venture Freestyle Biking. Boy Scouts of America, 1990.

Wallack, Roy M. *Traveling Cyclist.* Doubleday, 1991.

Chapter 29

Fitzharris, Jim. *The Audubon Society Guide to Nature Photography.* Little, Brown, 1990.
Grimm, Tom. *The Basic Book of Photography.* Plume, 1985.
Hedgecoe, John. *The Photographer's Handbook,* 2nd ed. Knopf, 1982.
Owens-Knudsen, Vic. *Photography Basics: An Introduction for Young People.* Prentice-Hall, 1983.
Patterson, Freeman. *Photography of Natural Things.* Sierra Club Books, 1989.
Photography merit badge pamphlet. Boy Scouts of America, 1983.
Taylor, Herb, ed. *Photography for Beginners.* Avalon Communications, 1982.
Wyatt, Mike. *Photography Outdoors: The Basic Essentials.* ICS Books, 1991.

Chapter 30

Proudman, Robert D., and William Birchard, Jr. *Trail Design, Construction and Maintenance.* Appalachian Trail Conference, 1981.
Proudman, Robert D., and Reuben Rajala. *Trail Building and Maintenance,* 2nd ed. Appalachian Mountain Club Books, 1981.

Chapter 31

Cornell, Joseph B. *Sharing Nature with Children.* Dawn Publications, 1979.
Environmental Science merit badge pamphlet. Boy Scouts of America, 1983.
Lingelbach, Jenepher R., ed. *Hands-on Nature: Information and Activities for Exploring the Environment with Children.* Vermont Institute of Natural Sciences, 1987.
McVey, Vicki. *The Sierra Club Kid's Guide to Planet Care & Repair.* Sierra Club Books, 1992.
Nature merit badge pamphlet. Boy Scouts of America, 1973.
Oceanography merit badge pamphlet. Boy Scouts of America, 1983.

Chapter 32

Arduini, Paolo, and Giorgio Teruzzi. *Simon & Schuster's Guide to Fossils.* Simon & Schuster, 1987.
Brown, Tom, Jr., and Brandt Morgan. *Tom Brown's Field Guide to Nature Observation and Tracking.* Berkley Publishing Group, 1983.
Brown, Vinson. *Reading the Outdoors at Night.* Stackpole Books, 1982.
Forrest, Louise R. *Field Guide to Tracking Animals in Snow.* Stackpole Books, 1988.
Johnson, Cathy. *The Sierra Club Guide to Sketching in Nature.* Sierra Club Books, 1991.
Mohrhardt, David, and Richard E. Schinkel. *Suburban Nature Guide: How to Discover and Identify the Wildlife in Your Backyard.* Stackpole Books, 1991.
Olaus, Murie J. *A Field Guide to Animal Tracks,* 2nd ed. Houghton Mifflin, 1975.
Suzuki, David. *Looking at the Environment.* Wiley, 1992.

Chapter 33

Cippriani, Curzio, and Alessandro Borelli. *Simon & Schuster's Guide to Gems and Precious Stones.* Simon & Schuster, 1986.
Geology merit badge pamphlet. Boy Scouts of America, 1985.
Kricher, John C. *Peterson First Guide to Dinosaurs.* Houghton Mifflin, 1990.

Mondadori, ed. *Simon & Schuster's Guide to Rocks and Minerals.* Simon & Schuster, 1978.
Pough, Frederick H. *Peterson First Guide to Rocks and Minerals.* Houghton Mifflin, 1991.
Raymo, Chet. *The Crust of Our Earth.* Prentice-Hall, 1986.

Chapter 34

Day, John A., and Vincent Schaefer. *Peterson First Guide to Clouds and Weather.* Houghton Mifflin, 1991.
Hodgson, Michael. *Weather Forecasting: The Basic Essentials.* ICS Books, 1992.
Inwards, Richard. *Weather Lore.* Charles River Books, 1977.
Lee, Albert. *Weather Wisdom: Facts and Folklore of Weather Forecasting,* rev. ed. Congdon and Weed, 1990.
Ludlum, David. *The Audubon Society Field Guide to North American Weather.* Knopf, 1991.
McVey, Vicki. *Sierra Club Book of Weather Wisdom.* Little, Brown, 1991.
Reifsnyder, William E. *Weathering the Wilderness: The Sierra Club Guide to Practical Meteorology.* Sierra Club Books, 1980.
Sanders, Ti. *Weather: A User's Guide to the Atmosphere.* B & L Publishing, 1985.
Schaefer, Vincent, and John A. Day. *Peterson Field Guide to the Atmosphere.* Houghton Mifflin, 1981.
Weather merit badge pamphlet. Boy Scouts of America, 1963.

Chapter 35

Angier, Bradford. *Field Guide to Edible Wild Plants.* Smith, Petger, 1992.
Botany merit badge pamphlet. Boy Scouts of America, 1983.
Brockman, C. Frank. *Trees of North America.* Golden, 1986.
Brown, Lauren. *Grasses: An Identification Guide.* Houghton Mifflin, 1979.
Cobb, Boughton. *A Field Guide to Ferns and Their Related Families.* Houghton Mifflin, 1975.
Forestry merit badge pamphlet. Boy Scouts of America, 1984.
Glimn-Lacy, Janice, and Peter Kaufman. *Botany Illustrated.* Van Norstrand Reinhold, 1984.
Grimm, William C. *The Illustrated Book of Trees.* Stackpole Books, 1983.
Lincoff, Gary, ed. *Simon & Schuster's Guide to Mushrooms.* Simon & Schuster, 1981.
Peterson, Roger T., and Margaret McKenny. *A Field Guide to Wildflowers of Northeastern and North-Central North America.* Houghton Mifflin, 1975.
Phillips, Roger. *Trees of North America and Europe.* Random House, 1978.
Plant Science merit badge pamphlet. Boy Scouts of America, 1983.
Schuler, Stanley, ed. *Simon & Schuster's Guide to Trees.* Simon & Schuster, 1978.
Whitney, Stephen. *Western Forests.* Knopf, 1985.

Chapter 36

Alden, Peter. *Peterson First Guide to Mammals.* Houghton Mifflin, 1987.
Anderson, Sydney, ed. *Simon & Schuster's Guide to Mammals.* Simon & Schuster, 1984.
Bird Study merit badge pamphlet. Boy Scouts of America, 1984.
Bologna, Gianfranco. *Simon & Schuster's Guide to Birds.* Simon & Schuster, 1981.
Burt, William H. *A Field Guide to the Mammals,* 3rd ed. Houghton Mifflin, 1976.
Capula, Massimo. *Simon & Schuster's Guide to Reptiles & Amphibians of the World.* Simon & Schuster, 1990.
Conant, Roger, Joe Collins, and Robert Stebbins. *Peterson First Guide to Reptiles and Amphibians.* Houghton Mifflin, 1992.
Filisky, Michael. *Peterson First Guide to Fishes.* Houghton Mifflin, 1989.
Harrison, George H. *The Backyard Bird-Watcher.* Simon & Schuster, 1988.
Insect Study merit badge pamphlet. Boy Scouts of America, 1985.
Kricher, John C., and Gordon Morrison. *Peterson First Guide to Seashores.* Houghton Mifflin, 1992.
Leahy, Christopher. *Peterson First Guide to Insects.* Houghton Mifflin, 1987.
Leatherwood, Stephen, and Randall R. Reeves. *The Sierra Club Handbook of Whales and Dolphins.* Sierra Club Books, 1983.
Mammal Study merit badge pamphlet. Boy Scouts of America, 1972.

Niering, William A. *Wetlands.* Knopf, 1985.
Reptile Study merit badge pamphlet. Boy Scouts of America, 1972.
Robbins, Chandler S., Bertel Bruun, and Herbert S. Zim. *Birds of North America.* Golden Press, 1983.
Socha, Laura O. *Birding for the Amateur Naturalist.* Globe Pequot, 1989.

Chapter 37

Astronomy merit badge pamphlet. Boy Scouts of America, 1983.
Beyer, Steven L. *The Star Guide.* Little, Brown, 1986.
Chartrand, Mark R. *Audubon Society Field Guide to the Night Sky.* Knopf, 1991.
Dickinson, Terence, and Alan Dyer. *The Backyard Astronomer's Guide,* Firefly Books, 1991.
Pasachoff, Jay M. *Peterson First Guide to Astronomy.* Houghton Mifflin, 1988.
Pasachoff, Jay M. *Peterson First Guide to the Solar System.* Houghton Mifflin, 1990.
Pasachoff, Jay M., and Donald H. Menzel. *A Field Guide to the Stars and Planets.* Houghton Mifflin, 1983.
Sagan, Carl. *Cosmos.* Random House, 1983.

INDEX

619

extinguishing fires, 118
extrusive igneous rock, 536

F

fabric, 42
fallen logs, 385
fanny pack, 57
fasteners, 67
fat, 122, 333
fatigue, 163
faults, geological, 530
fault zone, 529
federal areas, 229
fees, campground, 252
ferns, 554, 556
fiberglass, 357
    canoes, 273
field layer, 558
field operation leader, 436
figure eight follow-through knot, 407
film, 13, 472
filtering devices, 159
filters, 483
fire, 105, 110, 203, 333
firelay, 111
fireplaces, stone, 111
fire starters, 58, 204
fire starting, 117
firewood, 116
first aid, 175
    outdoor, 167
    resources, 167
first aider, 438
first aid kit, 13, 60, 168, 419,
    homemade, 73
fish, 441, 567, 569, 570
Fish and Wildlife Service, 238
fishing,
    conservation, 454
    gear, 63
    license, 63
    lures, 448
    methods, 442
    pole, 443
        reel, 443
        rod, 443
    trips, 454
fish scales, 360
fitness, 137
flammable paste, 106, 108, 204
flares, 206
flash attachment, 485
flash flood paths, 150
flashlight, 13, 59
flat rock firelay, 114
flat tires, 468
flotation
    bags, 295
    devices, 218
floater/diver lures, 450
floating, 217
flooding, 157
Florida National High
    Adventure Sea Base, 242
flowering plants, 554, 555
fluorescent adhesive tape, 463
flutter kick, 212
fly casting, 446
flying pushups, 142
fluid intake, 340
foam, 67
    footwraps, 337
    hat, 76, 338
    insole, 336
    pad, 97
    sleeping bag, 344
    socks, 86
folklore, 550
follow up, 103
food, 13, 124, 164, 208, 253,
    339, 418
    chain, 509, 510
    freeze-dried, 126

food, 124
    preparation time, 124
    prices, 252
    purchasing, 131
    repackaging, 131
    retort, 126
    roughage, 122
    storage, 98
foot,
    mitten, 78
    pegs, 295
    power, 433
    warmer, 341
footwear, 12, 45, 336
    selecting, 46
forecasting resources, 551
forests, 158, 383, 558
forest canopy, 558
forest ecosystem, 575
formation of the earth, 527
forward stroke, 280, 296
foul-weather photography, 481
framing, 477
free wheel, 459
freeze-dried food, 126
friction, 406
fronts, weather, 545
frostbite, 152, 335
frozen, snow-covered lakes, 376
fruit, leather, 14
fruits, 122
    dehydrated, 125
f-stop, 473, 474
fuel, 107, 108, 116
    and water crew, 134
    bottle, 108
full arctic winter camping, 332
full-bench cut, 495
full meals, 130
functional clothing, 12
fungi, 554, 557
funnel, aluminum, 108

G

gait, 325
gaiters, 337
galaxy, 584
garbage bags, 62
gates, 19
gathering winter water, 340
gear, 48
    caving, 417
    fishing, 63
    group, 252
    group cooking, 54
    personal, 252
    planning, 252
    provision, 252
gearing up, 41
gears, bicycle, 459
Gemini, 586
general conditioning, 142
geology, 528
general safety considerations, 150
getting lost, 15
getting up from a skiing
    fall, 367
giardia lamblia, 158, 159
glacier, 532
glass mirror, 206
glide, 361
glissades, 388
gloves, 332, 462
goggles, protective, 494
goose down, 52, 67
gooseneck, 278
Gore-Tex, 67
gneiss, 537
grades of climbing, 401
Grand Canyon, 534
granite, 536
granny gear, 460

grass fires, 158
grassland ecosystem, 574
grasslands, 562
grazers, 574
greenhouse effect, 538
green mountain bearpaws
    snowshoes, 370
green plants, 554
grommets, 67
grotto, 416
ground bed, 97
ground cloth, 51
ground cover, 93
ground-to-air signal, 204
group cooking gear, 54
group gear, 48
Guide and Map to the National
    Parks of the U.S., 229
Guidebook to Council High-
    Adventure Programs, 241
guide hand, 403
guidelines, 439
guides, 63
gymnosperms, 555

H

habitats, 572
    destruction of, 578
habits, of wildlife, 522
half-moons, 360
halter, 310
hand carry, 434
handlebar bags, 466
handlebars, 458, 460
hard hats, 418
hardwoods, 116
hasty search, 430
hats, 338
haul bags, 57
hazards, 250
    of skiing, 376
headgear, 338
headlamp, 59, 418
headstall, 310
health and safety gear, 60
heap clouds, 546
heat escape lessening posture
    (H.E.L.P.), 219
heat exhaustion, 155
heat tabs, 204
heaving lines, 275
heavy hydraulics, 302
helicopter, 434
helmet, 292, 294, 462
help, going for, 208
herbivores, 509
herringbone step, 365
hibernation, 577
hickory, 116
high-adventure bases, 241
high brace, 299
highs, pressure, 543
hike clean, 6
hiker safety, 14
hiking, 9, 379
    difficulty, 400
    stick, 60
hip strap, 57
hobbles, 327
hoisting the pack, 264
holding a fall, 404
homemade items, 68-79
hood, parka, 338
hook and pile closures, 67
hooks, 450
horse latitudes, 543
horse, mounting, 315
hot pot tongs, 54
hot-weather safety, 155
human tripods, 386
hybrids, 48, 50
hydraulics, 302
hypothermia, 15, 151, 152, 182, 335

TRIP LOG

TRIP LOG